RALPH BRENNAN'S
NEW ORLEANS
SEAFOOD COOKBOOK

RALPH BRENNAN'S

NEW ORLEANS
SEAFOOD COOKBOOK

Love To Cook! Live To Eat!
Ralph Br

Ralph Brennan

with Gene Bourg

photographs by Kerri McCaffety

VISSI D'ARTE
BOOKS
NEW ORLEANS

For information about permission to reproduce selections from this book, please contact Permissions, Vissi d'Arte Books, Post Office Box 791054, New Orleans, LA 70119.

Library of Congress Cataloging-in-Publication Data

Brennan, Ralph.
 [New Orleans seafood cookbook]
 Ralph Brennan's New Orleans seafood cookbook / Ralph Brennan with Gene Bourg ; photographs by Kerri McCaffety.
  p. cm.
 Includes index.
 ISBN 978-0-9709336-8-3
 1. Cookery (Seafood) 2. Cookery, American--Louisiana style. I. Bourg, Gene. II. Title. III. Title: New Orleans seafood cookbook.
 TX747.B643 2007
 641.6'92--dc22

                            2007037129

The book is spiced here and there with photos of artistic walls, painted tables and a variety of whimsical sculptures, all to be found in the restaurants owned and operated by Ralph Brennan. Bacco, Red Fish Grill and Ralph's on the Park operate in New Orleans, while Ralph Brennan's Jazz Kitchen is in Anaheim, California. For more information please visit our Web site, www.neworleans-food.com.

Fleur, the baroque crawfish, appears throughout the book to invoke the singular essence of Southeast Louisiana, and her fleur-de-lis shadow reminds the reader of New Orleans' past and future of rebirth.

Book design by Cynthia Reece

Printed in Korea

Vissi d'Arte Books, L.L.C.
P. O. Box 791054
New Orleans, LA 70119

www.vissidartebooks.com

To my parents, John and Claire Brennan.
Had it not been for their many failed attempts to keep me out
of the restaurant industry, I would not be where I am today.

To my family, Susan, Kathryn, Patrick and Kristen,
and to my sisters, brother, aunts, uncle and cousins.
I appreciate your love and your dedication to our family's tradition
of offering great New Orleans food and Southern hospitality.

And to the staffs of Red Fish Grill, Bacco, Ralph Brennan's Jazz Kitchen
and Ralph's on the Park. You are pros, wholeheartedly committed
to making our guests happy. Thank you.

Table of Contents

Preface

My earliest recollections of the restaurant industry go back to my early youth. Frequently, my aunts Adelaide and Ella would snatch me away from my parents for a weekend of adventure in the French Quarter. These adventures included sightseeing, shopping and a movie.

Each adventure culminated with dinner at Brennan's Restaurant* on Royal Street in the French Quarter, which at that time my aunts operated with other members of the Brennan family. Because of business commitments prior to sitting down to dinner, my aunts allowed me to play in the restaurant. I would travel from the kitchen to the wine cellar, and from the dining room to the storeroom. This wonderful historic building and all the workings of the restaurant fascinated me. Often, I would sneak behind the bar to learn famous New Orleans drink recipes. What a theme park for a youngster! I was hooked.

My actual, hands-on restaurant career started as a teenager in the 1960s, again in the kitchen at Brennan's. I was looking for a summer job, and I called my Aunt Ella. My first assignment was in the prep kitchen, Aunt Ella's idea of fun. After a couple of months boning hundreds of chickens and peeling thousands of shrimp, I was promoted to the cooking line, where I learned to poach eggs and make hollandaise and all the other sauces that are essential to New Orleans' classic cuisine.

This was also my first opportunity to experience the great seafood bounty of the Gulf of Mexico. Unfortunately, my father, John, had an allergy to shellfish, and as a result, my mother, Claire, was limited in what she could cook at home. My brother, sisters and I grew up eating lots of meat and potatoes. I distinctly remember tasting my first shrimp Creole and trout amandine prepared by Brennan's Creole chef Jimmy Smith, who would work with me years later at Mr. B's Bistro, a few blocks up Royal Street from Brennan's. Shrimp and trout were soon followed by tastes of crabmeat ravigote and pompano en papillotes. My taste buds were in heaven.

It took a while for me to get around to oysters. I struggled with the texture. One afternoon, I found myself at Bozo's, a great New Orleans neighborhood seafood restaurant. I was with a group who had just finished a round of golf, and they were looking for oysters and beer. The beer I could handle, but the oysters? The peer pressure was intense, so I took my chances with an oyster. I picked the smallest oyster on the bar, put it on a saltine cracker, loaded it up with cocktail sauce and swallowed the entire concoction whole without chewing. Whew! My first oyster was down, and it didn't kill me. It actually tasted good. With the help of cold draft beer, I had several more oysters that day.

Due to an unfortunate business dispute within my extended family, my dream of entering the restaurant industry was delayed until 1981. I graduated in 1975 with an M.B.A. degree from Tulane University and spent about six years working as a certified public accountant. Aunt Ella and I had an agreement that she would call me if she saw an opportunity for me in the restaurant business. Eventually, the call came with an offer to work with her at Commander's Palace. After a short stint at Commander's, I moved to Mr. B's, which was opened in 1979 by my aunts, uncle and father. I quickly became its general manager. My sister Cindy joined me about a year later.

The main culinary feature at Mr. B's was a first for New Orleans, a wood-burning grill fired by hickory and pecan wood. The flavors of fish and the smoky-sweet aroma produced by the wood-burning grill proved to be the perfect combination. Grilled redfish became Mr. B's most popular item, making up over 50 per cent of the entrée sales. Steaks cooked over this hickory and pecan fire were also very popular.

Chef Paul Prudhomme, who created Mr. B's grilled redfish dish, was our chef before moving on to K-Paul's, where he created blackened redfish, another wonderful redfish dish. The national popularity of Cajun and Creole cuisine, and the popularity of blackened redfish, placed intense pressure on the sustainability of redfish in the gulf. As a result, the Louisiana legislature, working with conservation groups and the Louisiana Restaurant Association, passed legislation making redfish a game fish and eliminated its commercial harvesting—along with 50 per cent of our entrée sales!

The scarcity of redfish provided the silver lining for Mr. B's, in the form of an opportunity to introduce new species of finfish into the New Orleans market. I talked with many of our customers who were sport fisherman and learned that they caught many different species and ate them at home. We cautiously introduced other gulf fish such as sheepshead, black drum, tuna and amberjack to our clientele, with favorable results.

In 1990 Cindy and I explored the possibility of creating an Italian restaurant. We believed that visitors to the city needed a dining alternative, something they might want to try after sampling the more mainstream Creole restaurants and those with a contemporary New Orleans spin. Also factoring into our thinking was that during the late 19th and early 20th centuries many immigrants to New Orleans were of Italian descent, principally from Sicily. This fact, coupled with our own love of Italian food, joined the mix of motivations to open Bacco. I'm sure the restaurant's success would have pleased my grandmother, Philomena Vaccaro, whose Italian family prospered in New Orleans'

produce trade, growing bananas in Central America and shipping them to the city. Her Sunday dinners with every type of pasta and meaty red sauce informed and enhanced my childhood

The menu at Bacco is Creole-Italian in style with dishes that rely substantially on regional ingredients, especially the fish and shellfish that fill our nearby waters. We have learned from our customers that, even when looking for an alternative to typical New Orleans cuisine, they still favor seafood from gulf waters.

In December of 1995, in the middle of my term as chairman and president of the National Restaurant Association, I came across a wonderful restaurant site at the gateway to Bourbon Street. In the midst of my struggles to develop a concept, my wife, Susan, and I headed out to dinner one night to celebrate my birthday. Because my NRA travels included many delicious meals in restaurants across the country, I was craving a simple meal of grilled fish. But I couldn't think of a great New Orleans seafood restaurant that didn't serve fried seafood. Thus, the concept Red Fish Grill was born as a high-energy space with a huge raw oyster bar, a funky and festive décor, and a menu loaded with regional seafood featuring such dishes as crab cakes, coconut-crusted shrimp, gumbo and a grilled-fish list that, once again, accounted for half the entrée orders.

Red Fish Grill had been open for about three years when executives from The Walt Disney Company, in town for a convention, stopped in. The restaurant's concept and the food captured their attention, and we soon found ourselves discussing with Disney the prospect of joining in the creation of a New Orleans-style restaurant and jazz club at The Disneyland Resort in Southern California.

Disney gave us an opportunity to showcase New Orleans food and music to millions of guests every year. Ralph Brennan's Jazz Kitchen is a combination of a casual fine-dining restaurant, quick-serve poor boy and beignet shop, and a live music club featuring New Orleans-style jazz.

Shortly after the opening of the Jazz Kitchen, I found myself full of ideas for a new New Orleans restaurant. I envisioned one designed for New Orleanians with a menu infused with imaginative modern dishes with identifiable New Orleans roots. After months of searching, we purchased a historic former tavern with two floors and enough space to serve all our needs. It was in New Orleans' residential Mid-City section, outside the major tourist areas but easily accessible from them. The building's wrap-around, iron-lace balcony and expanse of windows on the ground floor offered panoramic views of a vast grove of ancient, majestic live oaks at the edge of New Orleans' City Park, just across the street.

Ralph's on the Park opened at the end of 2003 with an award-winning menu geared toward locals seeking innovative yet approachable food exemplified by the menu's truffle-infused crab cakes, sesame tuna and redfish blackened in a cast-iron skillet. Unlike our other restaurants with bars that function principally as waiting areas, the bar at Ralph's on the Park has its own neighborhood clientele, leaving little doubt that our customer base in this restaurant is essentially local.

No matter if our customers come from around the corner or around the world, our first objective remains giving them the kind of food and service that has always defined New Orleans as a great restaurant town. For those of us lucky enough to work and play in the city's restaurant industry, our work is more than a job or a career. It's a lifestyle. It's a calling. It's long days working with a team of professionals whose primary motivation is making their customers happy.

New Orleans has a unique culture of food, music and history, plus a joie de vivre not found anywhere else in the United States. New Orleanians view food as more than simple nourishment. Our cuisine generates a passion and a bond shared by just about everybody, whether it's in the eating or the cooking. This was never more evident than after Hurricane Katrina, when those restaurants that opened quickly became gathering places for wayward evacuees returning home. Then and now, restaurateurs remain at the forefront of guarding New Orleans' long-held reputation for great food.

New Orleans is where the cook in a home kitchen and the cook in a neighborhood seafood bar can be just as passionate about the food culture as the high-profile chef in a top fine-dining establishment. Scores of families in the city have seen several generations working in almost every aspect of the restaurant industry, not just in ownership or management, but as cooks, chefs, bartenders, and servers. Many who started out as dishwashers or busboys have become chefs and managers. These long-term employees are the ones who preserve the culture, indoctrinating and initiating new members.

The people who work in any restaurant give the place a personality all its own. Some of it comes from the look of the dining room, but more comes from what isn't so visible. It's the passion found in everybody from the chefs to the cooks, and the managers to the servers. We have hundreds, maybe thousands, of customers who know members of our staff by name. Handshakes are commonplace. This sense of community and continuity makes a positive imprint on a restaurant customer's dining experience.

In New Orleans, cuisine is the great leveler. On a given evening, a family dinner in a Garden District mansion could easily include the same gumbo as the one being served by another family in a shotgun house on the other side of town. And the next day a member of each family could find him or herself in the same waiting line that's snaking through a popular poor boy sandwich shop.

While Red Fish Grill, Bacco, Ralph's on the Park and the Jazz Kitchen each has a strong New Orleans character, they're experiencing the same trends that have been in force nationally for some years. The obvious one is that guests are more adventurous, more willing to experiment than ever before.

This cookbook recognizes those changes with freewheeling recipes that expand the horizons of New Orleans' many-faceted cuisine. At the same time, it celebrates the kinds of dishes that have passed the test of time, the ones that promise to always invigorate the food the city cooks and eats.

Ralph Brennan
New Orleans
January 2008

Brennan's Restaurant on Royal Street in the French Quarter is owned and operated by three of my cousins. Since 1974, there has been no affiliation between Brennan's and the Ralph Brennan Restaurant Group and what is commonly called the Commander's Palace Family of Restaurants.

Acknowledgments

My heartfelt thanks go to our dedicated team of contributors whose time, talent and passion for the four seasons of New Orleans cooking—crawfish, crab, shrimp and oyster—made this book possible.

Special thanks go to Haley Bittermann, Executive Chef of the Ralph Brennan Restaurant Group, and Charlee Williamson, Executive Vice-President of the RBRG, who pulled this book together despite a newborn for Haley, an M.B.A. for Charlee, and the personal and professional havoc wrought on both of them by Hurricane Katrina. It has been exciting to watch the two of them grow over our many years of working together.

Editor and writer extraordinaire Gene Bourg kept us organized and focused on creating a timeless publication. His wisdom, wit, and way with words reflect his talent and passion for New Orleans and her rich culinary traditions.

Publisher and storied photographer Kerri McCaffety was the consummate professional. Her photographs simultaneously convey the bounty of New Orleans seafood and heighten its sensual and visual appeal on the plate, helping to justify the passion New Orleanians feel about their indigenous cuisine. Cynthia Reece labored patiently behind the scenes working her magic to create both a beautiful and reader-friendly publication.

The creativity of Chefs Gregg Collier of Red Fish Grill, Chris Montero of Bacco, Gus Martin of Ralph's on the Park and Darrin Finkel of Ralph Brennan's Jazz Kitchen is forever captured within the pages of this book. Their commitment to sharing their expertise is matched only by their love of cooking and dedication to making people happy.

Recipe tester Paulette Rittenberg painstakingly ensured that professional and "weekend" chefs alike could prepare each and every recipe. With the capable assistance of Sous-Chef Joe Kosarek, Paulette has used an eye for detail and a high level of precision with instructions to ensure that your favorite restaurant recipes really will work at home.

"Source Men" Steve Gauthé, Rich Krumm and Lewis Smith contributed their encyclopedic knowledge of what ingredients to get and where to get them. Richard Shakespeare contributed his knack for the dying art of café brûlot, and Colleen Maley kept the i's dotted and t's crossed in her customary effortless manner.

Introduction

What visitor to New Orleans would leave without having tried a seafood gumbo or a shrimp remoulade or—on the flip side—one of the dozens of innovative seafood dishes turned out every night by the city's growing cadre of creative restaurant chefs?

This cookbook, with a special focus on seafood, contains more than 150 recipes from the chefs at the four restaurants in the New Orleans-based Ralph Brennan Restaurant Group. The book was produced to communicate the authentic flavor and spirit of New Orleans cuisine, whether it comes from a Creole dish from a hundred years ago or one that was thought up yesterday.

While roast-beef poor boy sandwiches and red beans and rice have long been icons of New Orleans cooking, seafood has always been the strongest thread running through the city's signature culinary style. Over many generations, New Orleans cooks relied heavily on fish and shellfish to energize their imaginations. The reason may be that seafood offered them almost limitless options in their seasonings, sauces and methods.

When America's food revolution started some 25 years ago, New Orleans embraced it with new approaches to preparing seafood, without abandoning what had come before. Fish and shrimp from the Gulf of Mexico became prime candidates for grilling as well as the more traditional sautéing. Species never seen before on a New Orleans menu—redfish, tuna, amberjack, sheepshead—joined the familiar trout, pompano and snapper in restaurant kitchens. Lighter sauces for seafood started supplementing the more traditional ones lavished with butter and cream. It was the same open-minded approach taken almost continuously from the time the city was founded in 1718.

Food's texture and color have gained much attention in recent years. But, in New Orleans, the first yardstick will always be flavor. The flavors that identify a good New Orleans dish are typically deep, rich and zestily seasoned. At their best, they deliver not just good taste but an overall sensual satisfaction. The city's most famous native son, Louis Armstrong, is reported to have said, "If you have to ask what jazz is, you'll never know." He could just as well have been talking about the food in his hometown.

Like most places, New Orleans depends heavily on geography for what it eats. The city is situated on the Gulf of Mexico's coastline, where a tropical climate creates a year-round growing season, generating a continual supply of things to stock a pantry with.

It is almost a semi-tropical island, standing just a few feet above sea level at its highest point, and lying between the Mississippi River and brackish Lake Pontchartrain. Just outside the city limits water lies in every direction, covering many thousands of square miles and comprising a web-like network of bayous, bays, canals, marshes and other wetlands teeming with finfish and shellfish in almost limitless variety. A hundred miles to the south is the gulf itself.

The availability of seafood was no doubt vital to the creation of the cuisine that came to be called New Orleans Creole, but just as important were the diverse origins of the people who made it happen.

From the earliest years of la Nouvelle-Orléans, and continuing into the first decades of the 20th century, the city was a major port of entry for the strikingly different cultures that found their way up the Mississippi River. The first were mainly French, African and Caribbean.

The French set the style early on with their love of good food, wine and entertainments. African traditions also took hold early, especially in domestic cooking (gumbo and jambalaya being two of their major contributions). Spanish governors ruled New Orleans from 1762 to 1803. Their lasting legacy was not their food but the French Quarter's colonial architecture. During the entire Spanish period New Orleans' customs and language remained essentially French, as did much of what the population ate. The city became a thriving urban center, blessed with a bustling port and a network of outlying fishing grounds and farms that invigorated the cooking. Good eating became almost a birthright.

From 1790 to 1810 about 10,000 immigrants from the Caribbean came to New Orleans to escape a slave rebellion in what is present-day Haiti. The vast majority were either French- or African-descended, and the imprint of their spicy Caribbean food culture remains to this day on the city's culinary consciousness.

From around 1850 other newcomers started to appear in large numbers—the Germans, who were to operate many of the city's most popular restaurants from the time of the Civil War into the 20th century; the Sicilians, who added their hearty Mediterranean foodways to the Creole mix, and the Croatians, who brought with them from the Adriatic coast the ancient traditions of their fishermen ancestors, and eventually were to open many of New Orleans' first seafood houses.

In the late 1800s, the French Quarter's elegantly appointed French-Creole restaurants started appearing. A good many of their dishes were French classics, some of them "Creolized" with local seasonings and cooking techniques. Sauces with French birth certificates— ravigote, rémoulade, béarnaise—were lavished on fish, shrimp, oysters, soft-shell crabs and crabmeat.

Which takes us to the subject of the words "Creole" and "Cajun." They are often used interchangeably, which is a mistake, since the two groups were separate in both culture and geography.

Today the word "Creole" most often refers to the city's distinctive traditional culture, without regard to specific racial or national origins. However, as the term was used during the 18th and 19th centuries, it denoted people of mixed heritage who were culturally intertwined but maintained largely separate identities. A true Creole was a member of either of two groups—the descendants of the city's French (and to a lesser extent, Spanish) settlers, and others whose descent was both African and either French or Spanish. Most biracial Creoles were not slaves, but rather "free people of color," or more precisely, *gens de couleur libres*.

The first Cajuns were the Acadians, French-descended inhabitants of the colony of Acadia, which occupied much of what is now Nova Scotia. They emigrated to Canada's east coast in the 1620s, and stayed there until England seized control of the territory from France in the early 1700s. In 1755, after the Acadians had repeatedly refused to acknowledge the English Crown, the colony's entire population—numbering some 10,000—was forced out. A great many found their way to Louisiana.

Cajun cooking evolved in an environment that was radically different from that of New Orleans. It was the bayou country, then largely isolated, stretching some 200 miles southwesterly from the city. From the time the Cajuns began arriving in Louisiana in the 1760s, the vast majority lived either on family farms, in small isolated communities, or in fishing camps that dotted the maze of coastal waterways near the Gulf of Mexico.

For most of them, New Orleans was accessible only by boat until the advent of the automobile. So, well into the 20th century the population had to be virtually self-sufficient, relying almost exclusively on their own agriculture, fishing and hunting. Pork was a dietary staple (communal hog butcherings and pig roasts have long been distinctly Cajun food rituals), along with poultry, game and a limitless supply of seafood waiting to be harvested not far from their doorsteps.

The mainstream cuisines of the Cajuns and the Creoles occasionally overlap. Both use roux as a thickener in soups and stews, and each has gumbos and jambalayas.

But the differences between the two are significant. The contrasts show up in all sorts of ways: Delicate Creole cream sauces versus Cajun meat gravies and stews. Butter versus pork lard. Shrimp Creole (with tomatoes, onions and sweet peppers) versus turtle with a sauce piquante. Crème caramel versus cake sweetened with sugar-cane syrup. The bottom line is that traditional Cajun is farmhouse cooking, while the more urban Creole style owes much to western Europe and the Caribbean.

In some of the newer restaurants and cookbooks, the line separating Creole from Cajun is a blur. Some are asking if such changes diminish the essential character of each cuisine. There is strong evidence that, in both cooking styles, the traditional dishes and the innovative ones are thriving side by side.

History has shown that Creole and Cajun cooking have survived for so long because they were able to adapt to change. If past experience is a reliable indicator, the cream will continue to rise to the top.

Gene Bourg

How to Use This Book

The best cookbooks are more than collections of recipes. They are also reference books, offering a wide range of information that may increase a recipe's chances of success. Toward that end, this cookbook offers supplemental information on a variety of subjects.

A Seafood Cook's Manual describes in detail each type of seafood included in the book. This section contains recommendations for determining freshness and storage, and basic instructions for advance preparation of the fish and shellfish used in the recipes.

Tips and Special Instructions are provided to supplement recipes that call for unusual equipment or preparations—making roux, seasoning a cast-iron skillet, fabricating a stove-top smoker, preparing butter sauces on electric-stove burners, and using nonreactive cookware.

A Glossary of Creole and Acadian Food Terms is intended as a handy guide to food terms from the traditional or classic food culture of New Orleans and South Louisiana. Many of the words appear in the book's recipes.

Seafood and Wine offers some general observations on the subject and describes wines that traditionally have been paired with the distinctively spiced and seasoned dishes typical of Creole and Cajun cuisines.

Ingredient Sources lists retailers who sell recipe ingredients that may be hard to find in some parts of the United States, *e.g.,* fresh crawfish and crabs, andouille sausage, and certain spices, condiments and flavorings.

CHAPTER CONTENT AND SEQUENCE

The first five recipe chapters of the book correspond generally to one of the courses of a meal—appetizer, soup, salad, main course and dessert.

The remaining chapters contain recipes that supplement the recipes in the first five chapters—accompaniments, sauces, seasonings, stocks, etc.

The final chapter, "Spirits," is devoted to our favorite cocktails and coffees.

RECIPE CONTENT

The recipes in the book include a substantial amount of information in addition to yield, ingredients and method. The subject matter of each is given below, in the same sequence as they appear in the recipes.

Yield and/or number of servings. Number of servings in a recipe. The yield for each recipe is given directly below the recipe's title. When the yield is expressed in the suggested number of servings, it usually indicates whether the serving size is for a main dish, an appetizer, or in some instances, a dish that is especially suitable for lunch or brunch.

Headnotes. Most of the book's recipes begin with a "headnote," a few paragraphs elaborating on various aspects of the recipe, such as an interesting anecdote, word meanings, historical background, using leftovers, etc.

Recommended alternate fish species. In many of the book's fish recipes, the titles denote species found primarily in the Gulf of Mexico, such as redfish and grouper. For readers outside of the gulf region, a list of species recommended as possible substitutes is provided in the recipes, in the section titled Notes.

Notes. These are often included to alert the reader to a variety of matters, such as a recipe's special requirements, how far in advance a dish can be prepared, or if one tool or appliance is preferred over another.

Advance steps. These are tasks that should be done before beginning the first step of a recipe, such as marinating an ingredient, preparing a supplemental recipe, refrigerating an ingredient overnight, etc.

Special equipment. Under this heading are checklists of cookware and tools recommended for preparing a recipe, but which do not fall into the category of basic kitchen equipment.

Ingredients. Footnotes to the list of ingredients are added when further explanations or recommendations are considered helpful.

Method. The steps in the method section of the recipes are written in substantial detail to eliminate guesswork and insure the recipes' success.

Serving suggestions. These are provided to help with assembling the parts of a dish, using sauces, apportioning the number of servings, etc.

A SEAFOOD COOK'S MANUAL

Finfish

Crabs

Crawfish

Shrimp

Oysters

Alligator, Frog Legs & Turtle

Finfish

CHOOSING A FISH SPECIES FOR A RECIPE

Readers should note that many of this cookbook's recipes designate fish species found primarily in the Gulf of Mexico or other waterways in southern Louisiana. However, most of the recipes also recommend possible alternate species found in other parts of the United States.

FISH SPECIES DESIGNATED IN RECIPE TITLES

Amberjack	Mahi-mahi	Sheepshead
Catfish	Pompano	Speckled trout
Flounder	Redfish	Trout
Grouper	Salmon	Tuna

FISH SPECIES RECOMMENDED AS POSSIBLE ALTERNATES

Cod	Monkfish	Swordfish
Haddock	Red Snapper	Tilapia
Halibut	Sea Bass	Walleye
John Dory	Sole	

DETERMINING FRESHNESS AND QUALITY

Obviously, fish gradually begin losing their freshness once they're out of the water. If you're buying whole raw fish ask the dealer where and when he bought the fish, and whether it was caught locally or shipped in.

Deciding if a fish is fresh means using three senses—smell, sight and touch.

A fresh fish carries a clean, rather astringent smell, with no unpleasant "fishy" odors.

The skin is shiny, and even slippery. The eyes are crystal clear, not cloudy, and the gills are moist and bright red. If the fish has scales, the scales should be firmly attached. Another test of freshness is to press down firmly on the flesh, which should bounce back when it's touched.

Also, be sure to ask if the fish was frozen, since previously frozen fish should not be refrozen.

When buying raw fish fillets look for a bright-red blood line. The color should always be bright and uniform, with no yellow at the edges, and the smell should be free of unpleasant odors.

Finding spoiled fish in a reputable seafood market is rare. Dependable dealers make certain their seafood is checked regularly and stored properly.

STORING FISH

Once store-bought raw fish are at home, store them in the coldest spot in your refrigerator and use a thermometer to keep the temperature set below 40°F. (Keeping them in ice, as restaurants do, is ideal but may not be practical for the home kitchen.)

It is best to use them one or two days, at the latest, after they were bought, since you don't know how long they were in the store or market.

DETERMINING A FISH FILLET'S LEVEL OF "DONENESS"

Before cooking the fillet, estimate its thickness at the thickest part, since this will determine the cooking time.

When you think the fish is approaching the level of doneness you're looking for, briefly insert the tip of a knife into the thickest part of the fillet. Then lay the tip of the blade flat against the inside of your wrist. If the tip feels hot against your skin the fish should be done.

The fillet will continue to cook a bit after it leaves the stove top, oven or grill, so you want it to be slightly underdone when you take it off the heat.

Remember: Overcooking fish robs it of its fresh flavor.

The recommended method for filleting a whole raw fish is on the following page. ☞

FILLETING A WHOLE RAW FISH

Begin by placing a thick layer of newspaper on a cutting board to collect fish fragments and other waste. Once you've cleaned the fish, you can simply fold the newspaper a few times and throw it away.

Clean the outside of the fish under cold running water. If you want to remove the scales from the fish, do it either with a blunt knife edge or a fish scaler.

You'll need at least one knife with a flexible blade that is thin, flat and very sharp, to prevent ripping or tearing the flesh. (A filleting knife is best.) To remove the pin bones, you can use either needle-nose pliers, strong tweezers or a knife.

Safety tips: For demonstration purposes, the seafood handler in the photos below is not using gloves. Gloves are recommended. Always cut away from you. This way, if the knife slips, you're less likely to be cut.

1. Using a thin, flat-bladed and very sharp knife, place the blade point behind the front fin and insert the blade about halfway through the fish. Beginning at the point where the knife blade was inserted, make a cut across the fish below the head until the knife touches the rib cage. The idea is to cut far enough to free the flesh without cutting right through the rib cage.

2. Holding the fish down on its side, insert the knife at the beginning of the fish's backbone. Position the blade neatly between the backbone and the flesh and cut down to the spine from head to tail. While doing so keep the bottom of the blade tight against the bones so that they and the flesh will be neatly separated from the fillet.

3. To separate the flesh from the rib cage, push the knife through and continue cutting, making long, even strokes. When the fillet is almost free, hold it in one hand and finish cutting it from the fish. Then cut the fillet loose at the tail, holding the knife blade tilted downward for this last cut.

4. With one fillet removed from the fish, turn it over and proceed as you did with the first side.

5. To remove the skin from each fillet, hold the tail end within one hand. Place the knife blade between the skin and the flesh and run the knife–again with long, even strokes–down the length of the fillet to remove the skin, cutting in the direction from the tail to the head area. The flatter you keep the knife, the sharper the blade, and the more sweeping your strokes, the neater your fillet will appear, and the better it will keep its shape during cooking.

6. After both fillets have been skinned, remove the red blood line at the middle of them with the knife. You also should remove the needle-like pin bones, which appear in most species of finfish at the middle of the fillet, several inches down from the top edge. They can be removed with tweezers or needle-nosed pliers, or by making a ∨ cut at the top of the fillet with the knife. 🐚

Crabs

Just above the Gulf of Mexico's coastline, Louisiana's hundreds of streams and inlets play host to a creature officially called the Atlantic Blue Crab. Scientifically speaking it's the species *Callinectes sapidus*, which translates as "beautiful, savory swimmer." It's the same crab found along the Atlantic coast, most notably in the Chesapeake Bay near Baltimore.

The most familiar American crab preparation, aside from steaming or boiling, is probably the crab cake. In New Orleans, the number of crab dishes is limited only by the imagination of the cook. Those with hard shells might be boiled in spices and seasonings, or their meat found in a stuffing combined with breadcrumbs, or baked in a cream sauce au gratin, or flavoring any number of gumbos.

The soft-shell kind are usually dusted with flour and sautéed in butter or fried in oil, sometimes to become the filling of a poor boy sandwich.

TYPES OF CRABMEAT AND CRABS

Jumbo lump crabmeat. These especially large nuggets of white meat from boiled hard-shell crabs are the choicest morsels. They have an especially rich, delicious flavor and usually cost about twice as much as other crabmeat. Jumbo lumps are found at the ends of a large crab's two "swimmer fins" when the fins are pulled from the shell. The lumps can be as large as ¾ inch in diameter, and should contain very few, if any, shell pieces.

Lump crabmeat. These pieces of white crab lumps are smaller than the jumbo. They also should be free of shell pieces. The essential difference between the two is the size of the lumps.

Crab claw meat. The attraction of claw meat is its distinctive sweetness. Its somewhat sponge-like texture and partly brown color are what distinguishes it from lump crabmeat. It is often used to flavor stuffings, gumbos and stews.

Crab fingers. Popular as snacks, these are crab claws cracked to expose the darker meat just below the pincers. After cooking, they are often marinated in spicy vinaigrettes or floured and fried, and are eaten with the fingers.

Soft-shell crabs. A crab grows by moulting; that is, by shedding its hard-shell (or exoskeleton) over time and growing a new one. During the moulting process, when the shells are soft and paper-thin, the entire crab, including its shell, is edible once it is properly cleaned (see the instructions for doing this on page 32). In south Louisiana, soft-shell crabs are usually fried, sautéed or broiled. They are known in some parts of the United States as "peelers" or "shedders."

Buster crabs. Fishers will occasionally catch especially small blue crabs that are just ready to moult. The smaller the crab the thinner the shell and the higher the meat content. The smallest ones are called "buster crabs," or "busters," and they are a great delicacy among crab lovers for their high meat content. Like other soft-shells, they are cooked whole (after cleaning), usually by frying, sautéing or broiling.

Gumbo crabs. These are hard-shell crabs that are too scrawny to yield good lump crabmeat and are used to provide crab flavor to gumbos, stocks and other preparations.

DETERMINING FRESHNESS AND QUALITY

Whole hard-shell crabs are sold either live or cooked. Whole soft-shell crabs are usually sold raw and cleaned. The best measure of freshness for store-bought crabs and crabmeat is their smell. The fresh ones carry a clean, rather astringent smell, with no unpleasant "fishy" odors. If crabmeat is sold in a covered container, open it and smell the contents before buying.

Finding spoiled crabs or crabmeat in a reputable seafood market is rare. Dependable dealers make certain their seafood is checked regularly and stored properly.

STORING CRABS

Once store-bought crabs or crabmeat are at home, store them in the coldest spot in your refrigerator and use a thermometer to keep the temperature set below 40°F. (Keeping them in ice, as restaurants do, is ideal but may not be practical for the home kitchen.)

It is best to use them one or two days, at the latest, after they were bought, since you don't know how long they were in the store or market.

Hard-shell Atlantic crabs will stay alive for three to four days if they're kept cold and damp, ideally in a mesh bag in the bottom of the refrigerator covered with a damp cloth. They do need regular checking. (Live crabs should not be iced.) Do not seal live crabs in an airtight container. They will not be able to breathe and will die.

The recommended method for boiling and opening hard-shell crabs is illustrated on the following page. ☞

BOILING HARD-SHELL CRABS

Before the meat is removed from hard-shell crabs, they need to be cooked while live. The following is a recipe for boiling one dozen crabs, or four servings.

Note: Soft-shell crabs should never be boiled.

1. If the live crabs have any dirt or debris on them, rinse them off in a large sink or outside with a water hose.

2. Pour 3 quarts water into an 8-quart stockpot or 8-quart Dutch oven.

3. Add 1 bag Zatarain's Crab Boil seasonings, a half bulb of garlic cut to expose all the cloves and one lemon, quartered.

4. Add ¼ cup kosher salt.

5. Bring the water to a boil.

6. Reduce the heat and simmer, uncovered, for 10 minutes.

7. Add the 12 live crabs one at a time, holding them carefully with tongs to avoid being pinched, and immediately cover the pot.

8. Let the liquid return to a simmer. When the simmer point is reached, turn off the heat and allow the crabs to steep, uncovered, for 10 minutes.

9. Remove the crabs from the pot with a large strainer and allow them to cool for a few minutes.

OPENING HARD-SHELL CRABS AND REMOVING THEIR MEAT

After the boiled crabs are cool enough to handle, they can be opened so their meat can be removed. Among the handy tools for doing this are a small hammer or sturdy knife to crack the claws and nutcrackers, lobster crackers, lobster picks, snail forks, cocktail forks and shellfish picks.

1. Turn the crab to expose its underside. At the center of the bottom shell you'll see a small, tab-like, pointed flap. With your fingernail or a knife point, pull up the pointed tab, which is part of the flat, curved shell known the "apron." Pull the apron back and, with kitchen shears or a knife, cut it off and discard it.

2. Turn the crab over to remove its large top shell. Hold the base of the crab within one hand and, with the thumb of the other hand, pull the upper shell away from the body.

3. With the top shell removed, you'll see two rows of grayish, sponge-like gills at each side of the body. Remove them with a knife or your fingers and discard them. You'll also see little yellow-orange lumps in the cavity at the center of the body. This is the crab fat, which may be discarded or used to flavor a sauce or a crab butter.

4. Twist off the claws and legs. Crack open the claw shells with a nutcracker or by striking them with a heavy knife or a small hammer. Pick out the claw meat with one or more of the tools mentioned in the headnote on the opposite page.

5. With a large knife cut the body in half at the middle and then, if desired, into quarters. Or simply snap the body in half. Pick out the lumps of white meat, again within one or more of the tools mentioned in the headnote on the previous page.

REMOVING SHELL PIECES FROM CRABMEAT

Once the meat is removed from a crab shell, any small remaining shell pieces need to be removed. This is the most efficient way to do it:

1. Pour cool water in a small bowl and place it near where you'll be working.

2. Scatter the crabmeat out on a plate and search for small pieces of shell by gently picking through the meat.

3. After removing a shell piece dip your fingers in the bowl of cool water, which will help remove the shell from your fingers.

PREPARING SOFT-SHELL CRABS FOR COOKING

Cleaning a soft-shell crab is a simple process that can be completed in about a minute. It involves the removal of the underside "apron," the gills and the "face"—the eyes and mouth.

1. Turn the crab to expose its underside. At the center of the bottom shell you'll see a small, tab-like, pointed flap. With your fingernail or a knife point, pull up the pointed tab, which is part of the flat, curved shell known the "apron." Pull the apron back and, with kitchen shears or a knife, cut it off and discard it.

2. Turn the crab over to expose its soft top shell. Without separating the top shell from the crab's body, gently pull up one sharply pointed end of the shell. Beneath it you'll see a row of grayish, spongelike gills. Remove the gills with a knife or shears. Do the same with the gills beneath the other pointed end of the top shell. Discard the gills.

3. With a pair of kitchen shears, remove and discard the crab's "face"—the eyes and mouth at the front edge of the shell. The cut should be about a half-inch behind the eyes and mouth. Directly behind the cut you made there may be a small, water-filled sac. If there is, it needs to be emptied, so squeeze out the contents.

4. This photo of a cleaned soft-shell crab shows the parts that have been removed. Left to right, they are: the face, the gills and the apron. 🐚

Crawfish

"Crayfish" and "crawdad" are words you'll rarely, if ever, hear in south Louisiana. In the bayous, rivers and swampy ponds of the state, the word that denotes this close relative of the lobster is "crawfish," or occasionally "mudbug."

By any name, crawfish resemble lobsters in many ways, but size is not one of them. The average length of a crawfish is only about 4 inches. Like the lobster, the crawfish is composed of a connecting head and thorax, or mid-section, and a segmented abdomen, or "tail." The yellowish substance inside the head is the liver, more often called the "fat."

Of the world's 500-or-so crawfish species, more than half are found in North America, mainly in Louisiana and the Mississippi River basin. Nearly all of them live in fresh water, although a few survive in brackish or salt water, too.

From the bayous and estuaries along the Louisiana coast, crawfish are harvested as early as November and as late as June or July. The season is most bountiful in March, April and May. Farming crawfish has become a major industry in the state, with more than 115,000 acres of ponds devoted to producing them. The crawfish also is one of the state's major export products.

Louisiana cooks make good use of crawfish—in bisques, étouffées, stews, gumbos, stocks and even pies. Still, the crustacean is a relative latecomer to home and restaurant kitchens. New Orleans cookbooks from the late 19th and early 20th centuries contain but a handful of crawfish recipes, with bisque apparently the most familiar dish. It wasn't until the 1960s that crawfish preparations became common in New Orleans homes and restaurants.

Outside of south Louisiana and parts of coastal Texas and Mississippi, this shellfish is especially favored in France (where its essence flavors a traditional *sauce Nantua*), Sweden (where it's steamed whole with dill), and much of Asia.

DETERMINING FRESHNESS AND QUALITY

Finding fresh crawfish outside of coastal Louisiana, and possibly coastal Texas, is admittedly difficult. In south Louisiana, fresh whole crawfish are sold either live (usually in burlap sacks) or boiled. Fresh, cooked crawfish tails are available in some markets as well.

The best measure of freshness for store-bought crawfish and their tail meat is smell. The fresh ones carry a clean, rather astringent smell, with no unpleasant "fishy" odors. If fresh or cooked crawfish tails are sold in a covered container, open it and smell the contents before buying.

Finding spoiled crawfish in a reputable seafood market is rare. Dependable dealers make certain their seafood is checked regularly and stored properly.

STORING CRAWFISH

Once store-bought crawfish or crawfish tails are at home, store them in the coldest spot in your refrigerator and use a thermometer to keep the temperature below 40°F. (Keeping them iced, as restaurants do, is ideal, but may not be practical for the home kitchen.)

It is best to use them one or two days, at the latest, after they were bought, since you don't know how long they were in the store or market.

Live crawfish should remain alive for up to three days if they're kept cold and damp in the bottom of a refrigerator, ideally in a mesh bag covered with a damp cloth. They do need regular checking to be sure they are alive. Live crawfish should not be iced or stored in an airtight container or the crawfish will not be able to breathe and will die.

PURGING LIVE CRAWFISH

Before live crawfish are cooked, they must be purged to remove impurities. These instructions are for purging 4 to 8 pounds of crawfish, using 1 cup of kosher salt. For a full-fledged "crawfish boil," using 20 pounds or more of live crawfish, the amount of crawfish and salt should be multiplied as needed.

1. First, choose the largest, "fattiest" crawfish available, ones that are active, not sluggish.

2. For the purging you'll need a sink, a stockpot or a large bucket deep enough to hold the crawfish with plenty of space to spare, so they can't readily crawl out.

3. Wear heavy work gloves or have a long-handled implement handy, such as a broom handle, to steer them into the sink or other container.

4. To remove any mud or debris from the crawfish, rinse them well with a garden hose or in a deep sink under cool running water. Then transfer them to the sink or other container you're using.

5. Sprinkle the 1 cup of kosher salt evenly over them and fill the sink or bucket with cool water. Stir to dissolve the salt. Let the crawfish sit 20 minutes.

6. Next, rinse them under cool running water until the water runs clear. Drain well.

7. As you rinse the purged crawfish, go through them thoroughly to discard any that appear to be dead or very inactive. Gently coax the inactive ones with the implement or your gloved hands before discarding, to make sure they're actually dead or noticeably inactive.

8. Cook the crawfish immediately, as directed in the recipe that the crawfish will be used with.

BOILING CRAWFISH

Once the crawfish are purged they are ready to boil. A recipe for boiling 4 pounds, or servings, of crawfish, is on the following page. ☞

1.   After the crawfish have been checked to be sure they are all alive, pour 3 quarts of water into an 8-quart stockpot or an 8-quart Dutch oven.

2.   Add 1 bag Zatarain's Crab Boil seasonings and 2 lemons, quartered. Add ¼ cup kosher salt.

3.   Bring the water to a boil.

4.   Reduce the heat and simmer, uncovered, for 10 minutes.

5.   Add the crawfish to the pot and immediately cover it.

6.   Let the liquid return to a boil. When the boiling point is reached, turn off the heat and allow the crawfish to steep, uncovered, for 10 minutes.

7.   Remove the crawfish from the pot with a large strainer and allow them to cool for a few minutes.

SHELLING CRAWFISH

A crawfish shell is much softer than that of a lobster or a crab, which makes removing the crawfish's tail shell much safer and simpler. The process involves pulling the tail from the body, stripping off its shell segments and pulling the tail meat out from the top of the shell while pinching the fan-shaped bottom end of the shell.

1.   Holding the body within one hand, grab the tail and twist it to loosen it from the body.

2.   Pull the tail away from the body.

3. Gently peel away most of the tail shell's armor-like segments, beginning at the top, freeing the shell from the underside and unwrapping the meat.

4. Once all but the last few segments are peeled away, press the fan at the bottom of the tail between your thumb and forefinger. With the other hand, pull the tail meat out of the shell.

Shrimp

Warm-water shrimp are the most popular and plentiful shrimp on the U.S. market. They are primarily harvested in the Gulf of Mexico, along the southeast Atlantic coast and along the east and west coasts of Mexico. Because temperature and salinity changes affect the life stages of each shrimp species in a slightly different way, they occupy many niches in estuaries and open waters.

Most warm-water shrimp are categorized by the color of their shell when raw, either white, brown, pink or "black tiger," referring to the dark stripes around the tail shell. Another warm-water variety known as rock shrimp is found in the Gulf of Mexico, but is most plentiful along the Gulf and Atlantic coasts of Florida.

PRINCIPAL WARM-WATER SHRIMP VARIETIES

White shrimp have grayish-white shells that turn pink when cooked. They're most abundantly harvested in August, September and October, and some adults are harvested year-round. White shrimp are considered the premium large shrimp of Louisiana. They're slightly more tender than other shrimp, and their shells are slightly softer and easier to peel. They may vary in color. Some may be especially pink or have reddish legs. These colors are no indication of quality and do not affect taste.

Brown shrimp have light brown or tan shells that turn coral when cooked. They usually spawn earlier in the year and are most abundantly harvested in May, June and July, although they too are fished throughout the year. In Louisiana's waters, 60 to 65 per cent of brown shrimp are harvested in coastal or bay waters, whereas the majority of white shrimp in Louisiana are harvested in deeper offshore regions.

Rock shrimp, which are deep-water cousins of brown and white shrimp, are fished year round in some areas of the Gulf Coast and Florida's Atlantic coast. Rock shrimp get their name from the toughness of their shells. Because of their high level of perishability they're sold primarily as shelled and frozen tails. The rock shrimp's sweet and somewhat chewy flesh is similar to that of lobster, but lobsters are much larger. Typically, rock shrimp don't grow to a size larger than 21 to 25 per pound.

DETERMINING FRESHNESS AND QUALITY

The best measure of freshness for store-bought shrimp, raw or cooked, is their smell. The fresh ones carry a clean, rather astringent smell, with no unpleasant "fishy" odors. If shrimp are sold in a covered container, open it and smell the contents before buying. When buying raw shrimp, look for those with heads on. Shrimp heads tend to darken as they lose freshness.

Finding spoiled shrimp in a reputable seafood market is rare. Dependable dealers make certain their seafood is checked regularly and stored properly.

STORING SHRIMP

Once raw or cooked store-bought shrimp are at home, store them in the coldest spot in your refrigerator and use a thermometer to keep the temperature set below 40°F. (Keeping them in ice, as restaurants do, is ideal but may not be practical for the home kitchen.)

It is best to use them one or two days, at the latest, after they were bought, since you don't know how long they were in the store or market.

SHRIMP SIZES

Freshness is the first consideration when choosing shrimp for cooking. But selecting the right size has its importance, too. In this cookbook, the recipes that include shrimp specify the best size to use for each dish. The terms range from "miniature" to "colossal." The standard method in determining shrimp sizes is by weight—specifically, the number of shrimp (without heads) per pound. The following table is offered as a guide.

Classification	Shrimp per pound	Classification	Shrimp per pound
Miniature	46 to 100	Extra-large	16 to 20
Small	36 to 45	Jumbo	11 to 15
Medium	31 to 35	Colossal	10 to 12
Large	21 to 30		

BOILING SHRIMP

The following is a recipe for boiling 4 pounds, or servings, of whole raw shrimp.

1. Rinse the 4 pounds of raw, whole shrimp in water to remove any debris or dirt.
2. Pour 3 quarts of water into a stockpot or large saucepan.
3. Add 1 bag of Zatarain's Crab Boil seasonings and one lemon, quartered. Add ¼ cup of kosher salt.
4. Bring the water to a boil.
5. Reduce the heat and simmer, uncovered, for 10 minutes.
6. Add the 4 pounds of shrimp and let the liquid return to a boil.
7. When the boiling point is reached stir the shrimp gently. Turn off the heat and allow them to steep, uncovered, for five minutes or just until cooked through.
8. Remove the shrimp from the pot with a large strainer and allow them to cool for a few minutes.

SHELLING SHRIMP

Shrimp are shelled either raw or boiled. The softness of the shells makes removing them a simple task. The process involves twisting off the head and the legs, separating the shell from the meat and removing the tail end. With shrimp in the "large" to "colossal" category, you may want to remove the "vein" or "sand line" (the dark thread extending down the back of the meat), although this isn't necessary. The heads and shells can be set aside to flavor a seafood or shrimp stock.

1. To remove the head, twist it off. Pull the legs off the body by grasping them between your thumb and forefinger.

2. Peel off the shell, beginning at the thickest part of the shrimp and working your way down to the "fan" at the end of the tail.

3. If you want to remove the end of the tail, pinch the fan and pull it away from the meat.

4. To remove the dark "vein," cut along the back of the shrimp with a paring knife, just deep enough to expose the vein. Remove it by lifting one end and snipping it off. Finally rinse the shrimp. If they're not to be used immediately, keep them refrigerated. 🐚

Oysters

Crassostrea virginica is the species that most American oyster lovers call their own. It thrives all along the Atlantic Coast southward from Canada's Gulf of St. Lawrence to the Caribbean and the coast of the Gulf of Mexico. Along their route, Atlantic oysters vary greatly in size, flavor and appearance, thanks to each region's differences in climate and marine conditions.

Time was, many oyster lovers confined their oyster eating to the "R months," the possible reason being their short shelf life before the advent of refrigerators. During the spawning season in the summer months oysters take on a softer texture and moderately blander taste, but that hasn't seemed to significantly affect the crustacean's year-round popularity.

Other varieties popular in the United States are the Olympias, found along the Pacific coastline from Alaska to the California-Mexico border, and the Pacific variety harvested in Japan. Oyster cultivation has added such varieties as the European Belon and the Japanese Kumamoto.

If you suffer from chronic illness of the liver, stomach or blood, or have any other immune disorder, there may be a health risk associated with consuming raw oysters.

DETERMINING FRESHNESS AND QUALITY

The best measure of a shucked oyster's freshness is its smell. Fresh ones carry a clean, rather astringent smell, with no unpleasant "fishy" odors. If raw oysters are sold in a covered container, open it and smell the contents before buying. During most months, fresh raw oysters contain clear juices. From March to May, the juices may appear a bit cloudy, but this doesn't indicate a lack of freshness.

When buying unshucked oysters, check to see that the top and bottom shells are tightly closed. If they are open, tap the oyster; if it doesn't close immediately, don't buy it. The deeper the cup of the oyster's bottom shell the better it is. For the more elongated Atlantic oysters, look for shells that fan out widely from the hinge, indicating that the oysters have had plenty of room to develop.

Finding a spoiled oyster in a reputable seafood market is rare. Dependable dealers make certain their oysters are checked regularly and stored properly.

STORING OYSTERS

Once containers of fresh shucked oysters are at home, store them in the coldest spot in your refrigerator and use a thermometer to keep the temperature between 35° and 40°F. (Keeping them in ice, as restaurants do, is ideal, but may not be practical for the home kitchen.)

Oysters still in the shell can be stored, bottom shell side down, in a mesh bag or in an open container covered with a damp cloth in the refrigerator (no lower than 40°F). Do not seal live oysters in an airtight container. They will not be able to breathe and will die.

It is best to use them one or two days, at the latest, after they were bought, since you don't know how long they were in the store or market.

OYSTER LIQUOR SUBSTITUTES

Oyster "liquor" is the term for the natural juices usually found in containers of shucked oysters sold by seafood dealers. The oysters' own juices give dishes an especially rich, luxurious flavor.

However, oyster liquor is not always readily available. In such cases the (less desirable) option is to strain as much liquor as possible from the oysters and make up the difference with one of the following:

- chilled chicken stock from the recipe on page 390
- chilled vegetable stock from the recipe on page 397
- chilled clam juice
- chilled water

SHUCKING OYSTERS

In shucking oysters, an oyster knife* is used first to loosen the muscle, or "hinge," that connects the top and bottom shells at the oyster's narrower, back end. Then the two shells are separated by running the knife blade between their edges and gently twisting the blade as it's worked around the seam.

As each oyster is removed from the bottom shell, it should be placed, along with its juices, into a container that can be sealed. The oysters should be refrigerated immediately and removed just before they're to be eaten or cooked.

Most store-bought whole oysters have fairly clean shells. If the shells do need to be cleaned, scrub the beards and dirt from them while holding them under cold running water before opening them.

For demonstration purposes, the seafood handler in the photos opposite is not using gloves. Gloves are recommended for safety. If gloves are not used, while you're holding the oyster in your palm, place a thick towel under it to prevent cuts by the shell.

The recommended shucking method is on the following page. ☞

*Sources of oyster knives include the Web sites www.cooking.com, www.chefknivestogo.com and www.amazon.com.

1. Hold the oyster firmly in the palm of one hand with the deeper cup against your palm. The back end of the oyster (where the hinge is) should rest between your thumb and forefinger. Slip the shucking knife into the slit in the hinge. The knife should be flat side up, with the blade parallel to the shells.

2. With the shucking knife deep enough in the hinge to provide leverage, twist the knife to loosen the hinge until it pops loose.

3. This is the most difficult step. You have to put some muscle into it, but take extra care not to cut or stab yourself. To begin separating the shells, insert the knife blade (still flat side up) near the hinge and between the edges of the shells. Twist the blade a bit as you run it along the seam around the oyster until you get to the other side. Meanwhile, be sure to keep the blade pressed up against the inner surface of the top shell to avoid cutting into the oyster meat, but still severing the muscle at the hinge.

4. Once the top shell is completely off, move the blade under the oyster meat to cut it free from the bottom shell. Take care to retain the juices, the oyster liquor. If the smell is not clean and pleasant, discard the oyster with its shell and sanitize the work surface and anything else—tools, gloves, etc.—that may have been contaminated. 🐚

Alligator, Frog Legs and Turtle

Note: If alligator meat, frog legs or turtle meat are difficult to
find where you live, see Ingredient Sources on page 424.

ALLIGATOR

Alligators are legal game in Louisiana and some other states. They're harvested for their hides as well as their meat.

Dark meat is found in some parts of the alligator, but virtually all of the meat sold at retail sources is from the tail. The mild, subtle flavor of the white tail meat might be compared to that of chicken or veal.

When preparing the meat for cooking, wash it thoroughly and remove all fat from it to be sure it doesn't carry any gamey tastes. Alligator meat is fairly tough, which usually calls for either longer cooking or tenderizing.

FROG LEGS AND TURTLE

Fresh frog legs and turtle meat are much preferred over frozen for cooking, but their availability is very limited outside of the areas where they're harvested. Internet retailers are one possible source of both fresh and frozen. If you live in a large metropolitan area, look for them in Chinese and other Asian markets.

Sea turtles and tortoises are protected under the federal Endangered Species Act, so fresh-water turtles are the only ones lawfully sold for food. Meat from the body and legs is red, while that from the neck is white.

Turtles are caught and processed primarily when demand for their meat exceeds the supply. Processing is labor-intensive, the meat yield is low, and consumer demand is limited—all of which discourage production. The resulting scarcity has prompted some home cooks to rely on such substitutes as oxtail or veal.

STORING ALLIGATOR, FROG LEGS AND TURTLE

Once fresh alligator meat, frog legs or turtle meat are at home, store them in the coldest spot in your refrigerator and use a thermometer to keep the temperature set below 40°F. (Keeping them iced, as restaurants do, is ideal, but may not be practical for the home kitchen.)

It is best to use them one or two days, at the latest, after they were bought, since you don't know how long they were in the store or market.

APPETIZERS

Spicy Boiled Shrimp

Shrimp and Bacon en Brochettes

Coconut-Crusted Shrimp

Crab Cakes

Warm Crab Dip

Crabmeat and Avocado

Fried Green Tomatoes

Crawfish Pie

Crawfish Spring Rolls

Oyster and Artichoke Gratins

Oysters and Bacon en Brochettes

Oyster Patties

Oysters Rockefeller

Baked Oysters Ralph

Charbroiled Garlic Oysters

Red Fish Grill Barbecue Oysters

Sesame-Seared Tuna

Spicy Fried Calamari

Fried Oyster Mushrooms

Chilled Smoked Scallops

Spicy Boiled Shrimp with Cocktail Sauce

For 6 appetizer servings

What we have here are all the makings of an old-fashioned Louisiana shrimp boil, except perhaps for the sheets of newspaper covering the table. The taste of the shrimp is nicely enhanced by the spices in the boiling seasonings and by the horseradish in the cocktail sauce. The shrimp are at their best if served on the same day they're boiled, ideally just after they've had a chance to cool a bit. To wash them down, what could be better than icy-cold beer or lightly chilled white wine?

1	large onion, peeled and coarsely chopped
2	stalks celery, coarsely chopped
½	bulb of garlic, cut to expose all the cloves
2	lemons, halved
3	tablespoons kosher salt
2	tablespoons Zatarain's Liquid Boil seasoning*
½	teaspoon ground cayenne
8	cups water
18	colossal, jumbo or extra-large shrimp, preferred, or 30 large shrimp, peeled and deveined, with tails but not heads
	a double recipe of cocktail sauce, well chilled

*If this ingredient is difficult to find where you live, see "Spices, condiments and seasonings" in Ingredient Sources on page 424.

ADVANCE STEP

Prepare and double the recipe for cocktail sauce on page 366.

SPECIAL EQUIPMENT

- A nonreactive* 5½-quart or similar-size pot
- A large mesh strainer
- A rimmed baking sheet

*See Using Nonreactive Cookware, page 419.

1. In a nonreactive 5½-quart pot, combine the onions, celery, garlic, lemon halves, kosher salt, seafood boil, and cayenne. Add the 8 cups water.

2. Bring the liquid to a boil over high heat. Reduce heat and let simmer, uncovered, for 10 minutes.

3. Add the shrimp and return liquid to a boil. Remove from heat and let sit, uncovered for five minutes.

4. Strain the shrimp and other contents of the pot in a large mesh strainer. Spread the strained shrimp and other ingredients from the strainer on a rimmed baking sheet and refrigerate uncovered until well chilled, at least two hours, before serving. (This can be done early on the day of serving.)

Serving Suggestion: If the shrimp size is extra-large to colossal, allow three shrimp per person. If the size is large, allow five per person.

Spoon the cocktail sauce into small, deep, chilled dishes placed on dinner plates. Either surround the cocktail-sauce dish with the shrimp or arrange them "hooked" around the rim of the dish.

You may have a little sauce left over.

Shrimp and Bacon en Brochettes

For 12 appetizer servings or 6 as a main-dish

This recipe is a spin-off of the more traditional oysters en brochettes, in which oysters and bacon are dusted with flour, skewered together and flash-fried. The method here is to wrap the shrimp in half-slices of bacon before they're skewered and fried. And the results are delectable, especially when served with the lemon-butter sauce on page 363.

48 raw jumbo* shrimp, peeled and deveined but with tails left on
 2 tablespoons minced fresh rosemary leaves
 1 tablespoon minced fresh thyme leaves
 1 tablespoon minced fresh garlic
 2 teaspoons kosher salt
½ teaspoon freshly ground black pepper
 1 cup dark beer
¼ cup fresh lemon juice plus the rinds
24 top-quality, thick-cut bacon strips, applewood-smoked preferred
48 julienned strips of fresh jalapeño pepper, each about 2 inches long and ⅛ inch thick
    about 1 cup seasoned flour, if frying shrimp
    about 4½ cups vegetable oil (preferably canola oil), if frying shrimp
    cooked white long-grain rice, if serving as a main course
    toast points, if serving as an appetizer

*If jumbo shrimp are not available, use the largest you can find.

ADVANCE STEP

Prepare the seasoned flour recipe on page 384.

SPECIAL EQUIPMENT

- A metal rack placed over a rimmed baking sheet
- One additional rimmed baking sheet
- 12 thin wooden or metal skewers, 10 inches long

If frying, you will also need:

- A 12-inch sauté pan 2½ inches deep or a deep 12-inch skillet
- A frying thermometer (preferred, or use the pinch-of-flour method as described in the recipe)
- 2 large slotted spoons

1. In a large mixing bowl, combine the shrimp, rosemary, thyme, garlic, salt, pepper, beer and lemon juice and rinds. Mix well and let sit at room temperature or in the refrigerator for 30 minutes.

2. Preheat the oven to 350°F.

3. Cut the bacon slices crosswise in half and arrange the half-slices in a single layer on a metal rack placed over a rimmed baking sheet.

4. Bake the bacon uncovered until the fatty part no longer looks raw, 18 to 20 minutes. The bacon still needs to be tender enough to wrap around the shrimp and thread a skewer through it.

5. Remove the bacon from the oven and set aside briefly to cool.

6. Once the shrimp have marinated 30 minutes, fill each skewer as follows (each skewer will hold a total of 4 shrimp, 4 julienned strips of jalapeno, and 4 half-slices of bacon):

- First, place a shrimp across 1 slice of bacon with the head end of the shrimp resting on the bacon.

- Arrange a strip of jalapeño lengthwise on top of the shrimp and snugly roll up the bacon.

- Fold the tail of the shrimp under, then thread the shrimp on a skewer, starting at the tail end of the shrimp. If a bacon slice shrank too much during baking to wrap completely around the shrimp, just wrap the slice around the shrimp as much as possible and make sure the skewer passes through both ends of the slice.

7. Prepare three more wrapped shrimp and thread them on the same skewer, with the four wrapped shrimp barely touching each other. Set the prepared skewer aside on a rimmed baking sheet.

8. Repeat this process to prepare the remaining 11 skewers, placing each finished one on the baking sheet.

9. If grilling the shrimp, grill over hot coals just until the shrimp are cooked through and the bacon is crisp, about two minutes on each side.

10. If frying the shrimp, preheat the oven to 200° and place the seasoned flour in a 9-x-13-inch baking dish and set aside.

11. To fry, heat ½ to ¾ inch of oil (about 4½ cups) in a 12-inch sauté pan over medium-high heat to 350° for about seven minutes. If you don't have a thermometer, assess the oil's temperature by adding a pinch of the seasoned flour to the hot oil. If the flour immediately foams up in a lively fashion, the oil is hot enough. If the flour does not foam up, heat the oil a few moments more and retest with more flour.

12. As the oil is approaching the right heat level, lightly dredge three skewers of bacon-wrapped shrimp in the seasoned flour, turning to coat all surfaces well. Shake off any excess.

13. Carefully ease the three skewers into the hot oil.

14. Fry the bacon-wrapped shrimp until the shrimp are cooked through, one to two minutes per side. To turn the skewers while cooking, use two large slotted spoons. Place the skewers (no need to drain them first) on a rimmed baking sheet in the 200° oven to keep warm.

15. Dredge and fry the remaining nine skewers in batches of three at a time, and place them in the warm oven with the other fried skewers.

Serving Suggestions: Serve the brochettes promptly.

If this is an appetizer course, arrange the skewers of shrimp and bacon on top of toast points on a large heated serving platter. Have heated appetizer plates at the table.

If this is a main course, remove the shrimp and bacon from the skewers and serve them over a bed of white rice on heated serving plates.

Coconut-Crusted Shrimp with Hot-Pepper-Jelly Sauce & Mirliton Slaw

For 6 appetizer servings

This appetizer is one of the Red Fish Grill's top-selling dishes, probably because of the winning combination of flavors and textures found in succulent shrimp in a sweet and crunchy coconut coating, the spicy-sweet pepper jelly and a crispy mirliton slaw.

3	cups medium-shred, flaked, sweetened coconut, divided
4	tablespoons cornstarch, divided
4½	teaspoons baking powder, divided
1	teaspoon kosher salt, divided
¾	cup seasoned flour
1	cup milk
1	large egg
30	large peeled shrimp, deveined but with tails left on
1	tablespoon Creole seasoning
1½	cups (approximately) mirliton slaw, for serving
12	tablespoons (¾ cup) hot-pepper-jelly sauce, for serving
3	cups clarified butter, divided

NOTE

The trick to breading the shrimp is to keep one hand dry during the breading process. The dry hand is used strictly to dredge the shrimp in the seasoned flour and the coconut breading, while the other hand is used only to moisten the shrimp in the egg wash. Having two batches of the breading in separate bowls also helps keep it from getting too wet and clumpy.

ADVANCE STEPS

Prepare the recipes for:

- Creole seasoning on page 385
- Seasoned flour on page 384
- Clarified butter on page 355
- Hot-pepper-jelly sauce on page 371 (up to 3 days ahead)
- Mirliton slaw on page 336 (just before reheating the sauce and frying the shrimp for serving, as directed below)

SPECIAL EQUIPMENT

- Three large shallow dishes, such as pie plates
- 2 rimmed baking sheets
- Parchment paper
- A heavy, nonreactive* 1-quart saucepan
- 2 heavy 10-to-12-inch skillets

*See Using Nonreactive Cookware, page 419.

1. In a large shallow dish, thoroughly combine 1½ cups coconut, 2 tablespoons cornstarch, 2¼ teaspoons baking powder, and ½ teaspoon kosher salt. In another large shallow dish, prepare another batch of this coconut breading, using the same amounts used in the first batch.

2. Place the seasoned flour in a third large shallow dish. In a small mixing bowl, lightly whisk together the milk and egg for the egg wash. Line a rimmed baking sheet with parchment paper.

3. Place the shrimp in a large mixing bowl. Sprinkle the Creole seasoning over the shrimp, mixing with your hands to coat all surfaces evenly. Next, using one hand and without breading the tails, dredge a batch of the shrimp in the seasoned flour, shaking off the excess. Then, using the other hand, moisten the floured shrimp all over with the egg wash, letting the excess drip off.

4. With the hand you used in the seasoned flour, dredge the shrimp in one of the dishes of coconut breading, shaking off the excess. Repeat to bread all the shrimp. As each shrimp is finished being breaded, place it on the prepared baking sheet. Once all the shrimp are breaded, refrigerate for one hour.

5. Preheat the oven to 200°F.

6. Line a second rimmed baking sheet with several layers of paper towels.

7. Prepare the mirliton slaw. Chill the slaw for 15 minutes while reheating the sauce and pan-frying the shrimp.

8. Place the hot-pepper-jelly sauce in a heavy 1-quart saucepan over very low heat to gently reheat it.

9. For the shrimp, place 1½ cups clarified butter in each of 2 heavy 10-to-12-inch skillets. Heat both skillets of clarified butter over medium-high heat until hot, about four minutes. Pan-fry the shrimp in small batches (roughly 8 shrimp per batch per skillet), easing one shrimp at a time into the skillets, until golden brown and cooked through, about two minutes on each side. As the shrimp finish cooking, gently transfer them with metal tongs to drain on the pre-pared baking sheet, being careful not to knock off the delicate crust. Place the baking sheet in the oven to keep the finished shrimp warm while frying the remaining shrimp. Serve piping hot.

Serving Suggestion: For each serving, drizzle 2 tablespoons of hot-pepper-jelly sauce around the edge of a heated dinner plate. Arrange five shrimp on top of the sauce, and mound 2 heaping tablespoons mirliton slaw in the center of the plate. 🐚

Crab Cakes with Ravigote Sauce

For 8 cakes or 4 servings

In the hearts and minds of diehard seafood lovers, few dishes command the affection held for crab cakes. While Maryland's crab cakes hold sway along the eastern seaboard, Louisiana's spicier versions don't lack for fans. This recipe produces especially delicate pan-fried crab cakes enlivened with Creole seasonings and a hint of pepper sauce. A small amount of freshly made, soft breadcrumbs makes them light in texture, so much so that they must be prepared gently so they don't fall apart. But it's the crabmeat that's the star of the show.

1	pound jumbo lump crabmeat,* picked over
2	tablespoons finely chopped red sweet peppers
2	tablespoons finely chopped green sweet peppers
1	tablespoon minced green onions, green parts only
1	teaspoon Creole seasoning
1	teaspoon Louisiana pepper sauce
1	teaspoon worcestershire sauce
½	teaspoon table salt
½	teaspoon freshly ground black pepper
⅓	cup mayonnaise
2	large eggs, divided
3	cups fresh soft breadcrumbs, divided
1	cup whole milk
2	cups all-purpose flour, seasoned with 1 teaspoon table salt and ½ teaspoon freshly ground black pepper
⅓	cup clarified butter
½	recipe ravigote sauce with crabmeat
1	tablespoon minced chives or Italian (flat-leaf) parsley leaves, for garnish

*If this ingredient is difficult to find where you live, see Ingredient Sources on page 424.

ADVANCE STEPS

Prepare the recipes for:

- Creole seasoning on page 385
- Fresh soft breadcrumbs on page 382
- Clarified butter on page 355
- Ravigote sauce with crabmeat on page 372

SPECIAL EQUIPMENT

- A cookie sheet or shallow pan
- Parchment paper
- 3 rimmed baking sheets (1 to hold breaded crab cakes and 1 on which they will bake)
- A heavy 12-inch sauté pan or a heavy 12-inch skillet

1. In a large mixing bowl combine the crabmeat, red and green sweet peppers, green onions, Creole seasoning, pepper sauce, worcestershire sauce, table salt and pepper. Lightly but thoroughly mix with a fork, being careful to keep the lumps of crabmeat intact.

2. Gently blend in the mayonnaise and one lightly beaten egg, then 2 tablespoons of the breadcrumbs. Taste the mixture and adjust seasonings to your liking. Cover and refrigerate for one hour.

3. Line a cookie sheet or shallow pan with parchment paper. Shape the chilled crabmeat mixture into eight equal-size balls, using a rounded ¼-cup measure for each ball. Place them on the parchment-lined sheet or pan.

4. Refrigerate the crab balls for about three hours, until they are firm enough to hold together well. Keep them refrigerated until you are ready to continue with the recipe.

5. Preheat the oven to 350°F.

6. In a small mixing bowl, lightly whisk together 1 egg and the milk to make egg wash.

7. Place the seasoned flour in a pie pan, and the remaining scant 3 cups of breadcrumbs in a separate pie pan in a separate pie pan. Line a rimmed baking sheet with parchment paper. One at a time, gently and lightly dust the chilled crabmeat balls in the flour, then quickly moisten all over with the egg wash, letting excess liquid drain off. (Do not leave the crabmeat balls sitting in the egg wash or they will fall apart.)

8. Gently roll the crabmeat balls in the breadcrumbs and place them on the prepared baking sheet.

9. Heat the clarified butter in a heavy 12-inch sauté pan or heavy skillet over medium heat for about three minutes, being careful not to burn the butter.

10. Meanwhile, line another rimmed baking sheet with parchment paper. The baking sheet should be large enough to hold all the crabmeat balls, each separated by about an inch. Form the crabmeat balls into cakes about ¾-inch thick, pressing them gently together to make them fairly solid, and place them on the prepared baking sheet.

11. Pan-fry four of the cakes in the heated butter, placing them in the sauté pan at least a half-inch to an inch apart, for about three minutes or until the undersides are nicely browned.

12. With a spatula, gently turn the cakes over and brown the other sides, about two minutes more. As the cakes brown, transfer them to a third parchment-lined baking sheet.

13. Repeat Steps 11 and 12 to brown the remaining four crab cakes.

14. Bake the cakes uncovered just until they are cooked through and lightly plumped, five to seven minutes.

    Serving Suggestion: Top each crab cake with a dollop of ravigote sauce and a sprinkle of chives or parsley.

    Serve warm, allowing two cakes per serving. ❦

For 6 to 8 hors d'oeuvres or appetizer servings

The addition of crabmeat makes this warm cheese dip extra special for cocktail parties and other gatherings.

ADVANCE STEP

Prepare the crab stock recipe on page 391.

SPECIAL EQUIPMENT

- A 6-cup gratin dish, or 6 one-cup ramekins, or eight ¾-cup ramekins
- 2 rimmed baking sheets
- A heavy 10-inch skillet

	non-stick vegetable spray
24	diagonal slices, ¼-inch thick, of ciabatta or similar good-quality bread (from a 12-to-16-ounce loaf)
1	pound fresh crab claw meat, picked through
2	tablespoons Dijon mustard
1	tablespoon Crystal pepper sauce or other relatively mild Louisiana pepper sauce
3	tablespoons minced fresh Italian (flat-leaf) parsley leaves
2	teaspoons dried tarragon leaves
¼	teaspoon freshly ground nutmeg
½	teaspoon kosher salt, or to taste
½	teaspoon freshly ground black pepper, or to taste
1	tablespoon extra-virgin olive oil
2	tablespoons unsalted butter, divided
1¾	cups finely julienned Vidalia or other sweet onions, ⅛ inch wide and about 2 inches long
1¾	cups finely julienned red onions, ⅛ inch wide and about 2 inches long
½	cup finely julienned shallots ⅛ inch wide and about 2 inches long
2	tablespoons minced fresh garlic
1	tablespoon all-purpose flour
⅓	cup good quality dry sherry
⅔	cup heavy cream
7	ounces Fontina cheese, cut into ¼-inch cubes
7	ounces Asiago cheese, cut into ¼-inch cubes
1	ounce Gorgonzola cheese, crumbled
6 to 8	tablespoons freshly and finely grated Parmigiano-Reggiano cheese

1. Preheat oven to 375°F.

2. Using the non-stick vegetable spray, spray the gratin dish or individual ramekins and set them aside.

3. On a rimmed baking sheet arrange the bread slices in a single layer and set aside.

4. In a large mixing bowl combine the crab with the mustard, pepper sauce, parsley, tarragon, nutmeg and ½ teaspoon each kosher salt and pepper or to taste. Mix well and set aside.

5. In a heavy 10-inch skillet over medium-high heat, heat the olive oil with 1 tablespoon butter until the butter melts. Add the Vidalia and red onions, shallots and garlic. Sauté until the onions are lightly browned, 15 to 20 minutes, stirring occasionally. Transfer the onion mixture from the skillet to a bowl and set aside.

6. In the same skillet, melt 1 tablespoon butter over medium-high heat. Whisk in the flour until smooth, and cook until the flour very lightly browns, about 1½ minutes, whisking constantly. Add the sherry and cook 30 seconds.

7. Whisk in the cream, turn heat to high and cook until the sauce comes to a boil and becomes noticeably thicker, three to five minutes, whisking constantly.

8. Reduce heat to medium-low and stir in the Fontina, Asiago and Gorgonzola cheeses. Continue cooking just until all the cheese cubes are melted, stirring constantly.

9. Remove from heat. Stir the cheese mixture and onions into the reserved crab mixture, mixing thoroughly. Spoon the dip into the prepared gratin dish or ramekins. Sprinkle the top(s) with Parmigiano-Reggiano cheese and place on a rimmed baking sheet.

10. Bake the dip, uncovered, for 10 minutes. Once the dip has baked for 10 minutes, add the baking sheet of bread slices to the oven, and continue baking until the top is golden brown and the bread is lightly toasted, about 10 minutes.

    Serving Suggestion: Serve immediately, with the toasted bread in a serving bowl or a basket alongside the dip. 🐚

Crabmeat and Avocado with Spicy Vinaigrette

For 12 appetizers or 6 main-dish servings for lunch or brunch

The rich but subtle flavor of avocado is a marvelous foil for the taste of fresh shellfish, especially on a warm summer's day when coolness and freshness are so welcome in a lunch dish. This recipe, along with the separate one for the spicy vinaigrette, more than fills the bill.

3 perfectly ripe, medium-to-large Creole* tomatoes
3 avocados, 7 to 8 ounces each, preferably the Hass variety
   kosher salt
   freshly ground black pepper
2 cups spicy vinaigrette
1 pound jumbo lump crabmeat,** picked through
6 sprigs of fresh Italian (flat-leaf) parsley (if for a main-dish) or 12 sprigs (if for
      an appetizer), for garnish

*South Louisiana's Creole tomatoes are preferred for this recipe, although other good, peak-of-season regional varieties can be used.
**If this ingredient is difficult to find where you live, see Ingredient Sources on page 424.

ADVANCE STEP

Prepare the recipe for spicy vinaigrette on page 378.

FOR A MAIN DISH

1. Trim the ends from the tomatoes and cut each tomato into three slices, each about ¾-inch thick. Cut each slice in half crosswise.

2. Cut each avocado in half lengthwise, peel the halves, and cut each of them lengthwise into three slices.

3. On each of six chilled dinner plates, alternate three tomato half-slices (placed on their sides) with three avocado slices (also on their sides) on one half of the plate. Season each portion with a total of ¼ teaspoon kosher salt and ¼ teaspoon pepper.

4. In a large mixing bowl, vigorously whisk 1 cup vinaigrette to blend ingredients well, then promptly add the crabmeat to the bowl, mixing very gently with a spoon to keep the lumps intact.

5. Divide the crabmeat among the six plates, mounding it on the opposite side of the plate from the sliced tomatoes and avocados. Vigorously whisk 1 cup vinaigrette and drizzle a portion (about 2½ tablespoons) over each serving of sliced tomatoes and avocados, and garnish with a parsley sprig.

1. Trim ends of each tomato and cut each into four slices, each about a half-inch thick.

2. Cut each avocado in half lengthwise, peel the halves, and cut each half lengthwise into four slices.

3. In the center of each of 12 chilled salad plates, arrange one tomato slice. Fan two avocado slices over each tomato slice and season lightly with kosher salt and pepper.

4. In a large mixing bowl, vigorously whisk 1 cup vinaigrette to blend all ingredients, then promptly add the crabmeat to the bowl, mixing very gently with a spoon to keep the lumps intact.

5. Vigorously whisk 1 cup vinaigrette and drizzle about 1 tablespoon over each serving of tomato and avocado. Spoon a portion of the crabmeat over the edge of the tomato and avocado, allowing most of it to fall onto the bare plate, and decorate with a parsley sprig. Serve immediately.

Fried Green Tomatoes with Ravigote Sauce & Hot Butter Sauce

For 6 appetizer servings

Fried green tomatoes are most often identified with the traditional home cooking of the rural South. But *The Picayune Creole Cook Book*, first published in New Orleans in 1901, contains a recipe for fried tomatoes, although it calls for "firm," rather than green, ones. So, if you have very firm tomatoes that are just past the green stage, they should do quite well for this recipe. The two sauces and the crabmeat, of course, take this dish far beyond its simple, homey origins. The hot butter sauce, a delicious component of this dish, is a pretty salmon color.

¾	cup ravigote sauce without crabmeat, for serving
1	cup hot butter sauce (see recipe below), for serving
4	(about 1½ to 1¾ pounds) firm medium-size green tomatoes*
¼	cup Crystal brand pepper sauce, or other relatively mild pepper sauce
2	teaspoons kosher salt, divided
2	cups all-purpose flour
1	cup corn flour
½	cup yellow cornmeal
1	tablespoon dried oregano leaves
1	tablespoon dried thyme leaves
2	teaspoons sweet paprika
1	teaspoon chili powder
1	teaspoon freshly ground black pepper
1	large egg
1	cup whole milk
½	cup clarified butter, divided
1	cup lump crabmeat, preferably jumbo, picked through
	a mix of young, small salad greens or fresh, minced Italian (flat-leaf) parsley or chives, for garnish

*South Louisiana's Creole tomatoes are preferred for this recipe, although other good, peak-of-season regional varieties can be used also.

ADVANCE STEPS

Prepare the following recipes:

- Ravigote sauce (without crabmeat) on page 372
- Clarified butter on page 355

SPECIAL EQUIPMENT

- A 9-by-13-inch glass baking dish
- A heavy, nonreactive* 12-inch skillet or 12-inch sauté pan
- 2 rimmed baking sheets
- Parchment paper or wax paper
- 6 rimmed appetizer plates

*See Using Nonreactive Cookware, page 419.

1. Make the ravigote sauce, omitting the crabmeat.

2. At the last moment possible, make the hot butter sauce (see the recipe below this one). Keep it warm as directed in the recipe while frying the tomatoes.

3. Trim both ends of the tomatoes as minimally as possible. Cut each tomato into ½-inch-thick slices. You will need a total of 12 slices. Arrange the tomato slices in a single layer in a 9-by-13-inch glass baking dish. Drizzle the Crystal pepper sauce evenly over the tomatoes and lightly sprinkle the tops with ½ teaspoon

salt. Turn the slices several times to evenly coat both sides with the hot-sauce marinade, and let them sit at room temperature for 20 minutes.

4. Preheat the oven to 400°F. While the oven is heating, in a large mixing bowl thoroughly combine the flour, corn flour, cornmeal, oregano, thyme, paprika, chili powder, black pepper and 1½ teaspoons of kosher salt.

5. In a medium-size mixing bowl, whisk the egg until smooth, then whisk in the milk to make an egg wash.

6. Prepare half the tomato slices for pan-frying as follows: Have at hand a baking sheet lined with parchment or waxed paper. One at a time, dredge a slice in the flour mixture, coating evenly and shaking off any excess. Next, submerge the slice in the egg wash, then dredge it again in the flour mixture, shaking off the excess. Place the slices on the prepared baking sheet as breaded.

7. In a heavy, nonreactive, 12-inch skillet, heat ¼ cup butter over medium-high heat until hot, about three minutes. The butter is hot enough when a pinch of flour dropped into the pan floats and sizzles.

8. Arrange the breaded tomato slices in a single layer in the skillet and fry them until they are golden brown on both sides and crisp and tender, two to three minutes per side. Drain them on paper towels.

9. Drain any butter remaining in the skillet into a heat-proof container, and wipe the skillet clean with paper towels. Add the remaining ¼ cup of butter to the skillet and let it heat while you bread the second batch of tomato slices. Fry and drain the second batch as you did the first batch. Now arrange the tomato slices in a single layer on a rimmed baking sheet lined with at least two thicknesses of paper towels. Bake uncovered until tomatoes are fork tender, no longer than three minutes. Remove from oven promptly.

Serving Suggestions: Serve the tomatoes immediately.

For each serving, overlap two slices on a rimmed appetizer plate and drizzle 2 tablespoons hot butter sauce over and around them. Next, place 1 tablespoon ravigote sauce on top of each tomato slice, and mound 1 tablespoon crabmeat on each slice. Garnish with the salad greens or a sprinkle of parsley or chives.

FOR THE HOT BUTTER SAUCE

- ¼ cup Crystal brand pepper sauce, or other relatively mild Louisiana pepper sauce
- ¼ cup heavy cream
- ½ pound (2 sticks) cold unsalted butter, cut into 10 pats
- ¼ teaspoon kosher salt
- 1 pinch freshly ground black pepper

1. Place the pepper sauce in a heavy, nonreactive 2-quart saucepan.

NOTES

The sauce must be used within an hour of being made to insure its ingredients don't separate. If it is not used promptly after it is made, keep it warm in the uncovered top of a double boiler over hot—not simmering—water.

Since you need only 1 cup of sauce for the fried green tomatoes

2. Cook over medium heat until it is reduced by half (about 2 tablespoons), two to three minutes, whisking constantly with a metal whisk.

3. Whisk the cream into the pepper sauce and bring the liquid to a boil.

4. Reduce the heat to low and add the butter, 2 pats at a time, whisking constantly, until all the butter is added and incorporated into the sauce. Each addition of butter should be almost completely melted in before adding more. This will take five to 10 minutes total. Remove from heat.

5. Whisk in the kosher salt and pepper.

Serving Suggestion: Use the sauce immediately, or keep it warm in the uncovered top of a double boiler over warm (not simmering) water for no more than one hour before using. 🐚

recipe, you may want to serve the leftover ¼ cup of sauce at the same meal you're serving the tomatoes. It would be excellent, for example, served over sautéed or fried fish, used as a dip for shrimp or other seafood, or tossed with just-cooked chicken wings.

If you are using an electric stove top to prepare this recipe, please see the recommendations on page 418.

page 418.

SPECIAL EQUIPMENT

*   A heavy, nonreactive 2-quart saucepan
*   A metal whisk
*   A double boiler, if preparing ahead

Crawfish Pie

For one 9-inch double-crusted savory pie or 6 to 8 servings

The bounty of Louisiana's lakes, streams and wetlands inspires New Orleans cooks to create a huge variety of savory shellfish dishes, even seafood fritters, cheesecakes and sausages. This savory pie, with a crawfish filling, should draw raves on special occasions or just any old time. The filling is taken from this book's recipe for crawfish bread.

FOR THE PIE CRUST

- 2 cups all-purpose flour, plus flour to roll out dough
- ¾ teaspoon kosher salt
- 5 tablespoons very cold unsalted butter, cut into ¼-inch cubes
- 3 tablespoons very cold solid vegetable shortening, cut into small bits
  about 5 to 6½ tablespoons ice water, divided

1. Into a large mixing bowl, sift together 2 cups flour and the kosher salt. Add the butter and shortening, and quickly work them into the flour with a pastry blender or your fingertips until the mixture looks like coarse meal with just a few pea-size lumps of butter and shortening in it.

2. Gradually add the ice water to the dough, 1 tablespoon at a time, until you've added 5 tablespoons water, tossing lightly with your hand or a fork until blended in.

3. Gently gather the mixture together to form a ball. If it doesn't hold together, add another ½ tablespoon of water at a time, adding only the minimum amount of water needed so the mixture is sufficiently damp to hold together.

4. Transfer the dough to a piece of plastic wrap and shape the dough ball into a smooth 6-inch disk. Wrap the disc snugly with a double layer of plastic wrap. Refrigerate for at least one hour or overnight before rolling out.

FOR FINISHING THE PIE

- 1 cup milk
- 1 egg, any size
- 1 recipe crawfish bread stuffing (see Advance Steps, above right)

1. If the pie dough was refrigerated for more than an hour, let it sit at room temperature until flexible enough to roll out, 15 to 20 minutes. Cut the dough into two pieces, one piece slightly larger than the other. Wrap the smaller piece of dough in plastic wrap and set it aside at room temperature.

ADVANCE STEPS

As close as possible to cooking the pie, prepare the crawfish stuffing from the recipe for crawfish bread (Steps 1 through 7) on page 328.

Keep the stuffing in a covered container in the refrigerator while preparing the dough for the pie crust.

SPECIAL EQUIPMENT

- A pastry blender (or your fingertips)
- A 9-inch glass pie pan
- A pie shield or a 2-inch-wide ring of aluminum foil, to prevent the edge of the pie from burning
- A metal rack

2. Preheat the oven to 350°F.

3. Meanwhile, in a small mixing bowl, lightly whisk together the milk and egg for the egg wash.

4. For the bottom crust, form the larger piece of dough into a disc. With a floured rolling pin, roll out the dough on a lightly floured surface into a circle about 11½ inches in diameter and ⅛ inch thick. Very lightly flour the dough, fold it in half, and carefully transfer it to a 9-inch glass pie pan. Unfold the dough and gently fit it into the pan.

5. Fill this pie shell with the crawfish stuffing and smooth the top.

6. Next, form the smaller piece of dough into a disc and roll it out as you did the first piece of dough.

7. Moisten the rim of the filled pie shell with cold water.

8. Very lightly flour the dough for the top crust and fold it in half. Unfold the dough over the crawfish stuffing, and use a knife to trim the dough for the top crust so there is about a ½-inch overhang. Fold the overhanging dough under the edge of the dough for the bottom crust, then crimp the pie's edge. Cut slits in the top to vent the pie. Brush the top but not the edge with egg wash.

9. Bake the pie on the middle shelf of the oven until the crust is golden on the bottom and edge, and the juices from the stuffing are bubbling out of the slits, about 1 hour and 10 minutes. Once the edge of the pie has browned, about 30 minutes, cover the edge with a pie shield or use a 2-inch ring of aluminum foil to prevent the edge from burning.

10. Near the end of the baking time, lift the pie to examine the bottom of the crust to see if it has browned nicely. Remove the pie from the oven and lift off the shield or foil from edge.

11. Transfer the pie to a metal rack to cool for at least 15 minutes before serving.

    Serving Suggestion: Cut the pie into wedges and serve hot on heated dinner plates. Refrigerate leftovers. To re-warm the pie, briefly heat it in a 250° oven. ❁

Crawfish Spring Rolls with Roasted Corn Relish & Chile-Garlic Sauce

For 6 servings

The inspiration for these bracingly flavored spring rolls came from Southeast Asia, but there are more than a few traces of Southeast Louisiana in the taste, too. They could be a luncheon main course or a generous appetizer for dinner. The sauce is sweet and spicy but not over-the-top hot.

FOR THE ROASTED-CORN RELISH

- 3 ears corn in the husk, each 7 to 9 inches long
  water for soaking corn
- 1 large fresh jalapeno pepper, stemmed
- ½ cup finely chopped red sweet peppers
- ¼ cup finely chopped red onions
- ¼ cup finely sliced green onions (green and white parts)
- 3 tablespoons chopped fresh Italian (flat-leaf) parsley leaves
- 1 tablespoon minced garlic
- 2 tablespoons extra-virgin olive oil
- 1 tablespoon mild-flavored honey, such as clover honey
- 1 tablespoon fresh lemon juice
- 1 tablespoon apple cider vinegar
- ½ teaspoon kosher salt, or to taste
- ¼ teaspoon freshly ground black pepper, or to taste

1. Preheat the oven to 350°F.

2. Soak the ears of corn in the husks in a large pan of water for 30 minutes. Drain. Bake on a rimmed baking sheet for 35 minutes. Let corn cool, then strip off the husks and silk, and cut the kernels from the ears. You should have about 2 cups kernels. While the corn bakes, prepare the jalapeno pepper.

3. Preheat the broiler. Broil the jalapeño, about 5 inches from the heat source, until the flesh is tender but still plump, and the skin blisters and turns very dark brown to black all over, about nine minutes. Turn occasionally with tongs. If in doubt, under-roast so the flesh is not overcooked.

4. Place the jalapeño in a small heat-proof bowl and cover bowl with plastic to let the jalapeño steam while it cools for 10 minutes. Peel the jalapeño and mince enough to have 1½ tablespoons minced flesh.

5. In a large mixing bowl, combine the jalapeño and roasted corn kernels with the remaining corn relish ingredients, mixing well. Cover and refrigerate at

The corn relish and chile-garlic sauce may be prepared a day ahead.

If making the spring rolls for freezing, once the rolls are formed freeze them in a single layer on a small cookie sheet until firm, transfer them to a self-sealing plastic freezer bag and keep frozen until ready to fry. Do not thaw before frying.

The spring rolls will keep frozen for up to one month.

SPECIAL EQUIPMENT

- A rimmed baking sheet
- A pair of heat-proof tongs
- A small heat-proof bowl
- A heavy 10-inch skillet
- A cookie sheet large enough to hold 12 spring rolls with a little room to spare
- Parchment paper
- A pastry brush
- A deep fryer or a deep 5-quart Dutch oven

least two hours or overnight before serving. The relish should be served chilled.

FOR THE CHILE-GARLIC SAUCE

½   cup plus 3 tablespoons rice vinegar

¼   cup mild-flavored honey, such as clover honey

1   tablespoon plus 1½ teaspoons minced garlic

1   tablespoon plus 1½ teaspoons soy sauce

1   tablespoon plus 1½ teaspoons vegetable oil

2   teaspoons thinly sliced green onions, green parts only

½   teaspoon crushed red pepper

1. Thoroughly combine all the chile-garlic sauce ingredients in a small mixing bowl. (The sauce will have a thin consistency.)

2. Cover and refrigerate until the flavors marry, at least three hours or overnight. Serve chilled.

FOR THE SPRING ROLLS

      1   teaspoon vegetable oil
      1   cup finely chopped onions
      8   ounces by weight peeled crawfish tails*
      1   teaspoon minced garlic
      1   tablespoon soy sauce
     ¼   teaspoon kosher salt, plus to taste
     ¼   teaspoon freshly ground black pepper, plus to taste
      3   cups finely shredded Napa cabbage
      1   cup peeled and coarsely shredded carrots
   1½   tablespoons minced fresh cilantro leaves
      1   white from any size egg
     12   egg-roll wrappers, 6¾ inches square
          oil for deep-frying
      6   ounces by weight (24 very loosely packed cups) mixed baby-lettuce greens,
             for serving

      *If this ingredient is difficult to find where you live, see Ingredient Sources on page 424.

1. For the filling, in a heavy 10-inch skillet, heat 1 teaspoon oil over medium heat until hot, 30 to 40 seconds. Add the onions and cook until soft, about four minutes, stirring occasionally. Add the crawfish and garlic and cook for three minutes, stirring occasionally.

2. Stir in the soy sauce, ¼ teaspoon kosher salt and ¼ teaspoon pepper, and continue cooking about one minute more. Remove from heat.

3. Transfer the mixture to a shallow bowl or plate and refrigerate until cool, about 10 minutes.

4. Add to the cooled mixture the cabbage, carrots and cilantro, mixing well. Season with more kosher salt and pepper if needed.

5. Line a small cookie sheet with parchment paper. The cookie sheet should be large enough to hold 12 spring rolls with a little room to spare. Beat the egg white in a small bowl until frothy.

6. Place one of the egg-roll wrappers on a work surface. Using a pastry brush, brush the side of the wrapper farthest from you with a 1-inch swath of egg

white. Likewise, brush a swath of egg white on the right and left sides of the wrapper.

7. Place 3 tablespoons filling in a log shape along the wrapper's edge closest to you, keeping the filling within the border formed by the egg white.

8. Fold the side nearest you over the filling and tuck the edge under the filling. Then fold over the left and right sides of the wrapper, using the edge of the filling as the crease point for the fold.

9. Brush more egg white on the right and left sides of the wrapper that are folded over, and finish snugly rolling up the spring roll. Gently press all the seams to make sure the filling is completely sealed inside the wrapper. You should end with a spring roll that is about 5 inches long and 1¼ inches in diameter. Place the finished spring roll, seam up, on the prepared cookie sheet.

10. Repeat this procedure to form 11 more spring rolls.

11. Heat the oil in a deep fryer to 350°F, or heat 2½ inches of oil in a deep 5-quart Dutch oven to 350°. While the oil is heating, mound lettuce greens in the center of each of six chilled dinner plates. Set aside the plates momentarily.

12. Deep-fry the spring rolls in small batches in the hot oil until golden brown on both sides, about three minutes total, turning at least once.

13. Drain briefly on absorbent paper and serve immediately. (If necessary, keep the finished rolls in a 200° oven while frying the remaining ones.)

    Serving Suggestions: For each serving, cut two spring rolls in half on the bias. Arrange the four halves on top of the mound of lettuce greens so the cut ends of the halves face each other to form an X. Spoon 2 tablespoons of the chilled chile-garlic sauce around the lettuce (you will have a little sauce left over), and scatter a portion (about ⅓ cup) of the corn relish over all, with most of the corn mounded in the very center of the plate. Serve hot. 🐚

Oyster and Artichoke Gratins

For 6 generous appetizers or 6 small main dishes

Pairing the flavors of oyster and artichoke is a recurring theme in New Orleans cooking. For example, oyster and artichoke soup or bisque has acquired the status of a classic in the city's catalog of home-grown dishes. This recipe uses the two ingredients in a different way—baked in individual dishes with garlic and seasonings, and then gratinéed with breadcrumbs, olive oil and Parmigiano-Reggiano cheese to produce a crisp and golden crust. It is one of this cookbook's quickest and easiest dishes to prepare, and would perform nicely alongside a salad or a cooked green vegetable such as creamed spinach.

3   cups unseasoned fine, dry breadcrumbs, preferably made from New Orleans-style French bread*

3   cups finely chopped fresh, blanched artichoke hearts,** preferred

¾   cup plus 6 tablespoons finely grated Parmigiano-Reggiano cheese, divided

¼   cup plus 2 tablespoons minced fresh garlic

1   tablespoon plus 1 teaspoon minced fresh Italian (flat-leaf) parsley leaves, divided

1   tablespoon Creole seasoning

1   tablespoon freshly ground black pepper

1½ teaspoons kosher salt

16 tablespoons extra-virgin olive oil, divided

36 large shucked oysters

*If this bread is not available, one possible substitute is a sugarless, natural-yeast white bread with a low gluten content and a thin crust.
**If fresh artichoke hearts are not available, frozen or canned ones may be used.

ADVANCE STEPS

If using fresh blanched artichoke hearts, prepare the recipe for:

• Blanched artichokes on page 320

Prepare the recipe for:

• Creole seasoning on page 385

SPECIAL EQUIPMENT

• A very large mixing bowl

• A heavy 12-inch sauté pan or heavy 12-inch skillet

• A pair of tongs

• Six shallow 12-ounce baking dishes, such as au gratin or shirred-egg dishes, measuring about 6½ inches in diameter and about 1⅛ inch deep

• As many rimmed baking sheets as needed to hold the baking dishes.

1. Preheat the oven to 425°F.

2. In a very large mixing bowl, combine the breadcrumbs with the artichokes, ¾ cup Parmigiano-Reggiano cheese, garlic, 1 tablespoon parsley, Creole seasoning, pepper, kosher salt and 10 tablespoons olive oil. Thoroughly mix by hand until the mixture resembles graham-cracker crumbs, breaking up the artichoke pieces into smaller bits as you mix. Set aside momentarily.

3. Heat a heavy 12-inch sauté pan over high heat for one minute, then quickly drain the liquor from the oysters (they should still be very wet) and add the oysters in a single layer to the pan. Cook just until the edges curl, about one minute. Do not overcook.

4. Using tongs, transfer 6 oysters, drained a few seconds, to each baking dish in a single layer. If there is more than just a teaspoon or so of the oyster liquor in the dish, drain off the liquid.

5. Gradually add an equal amount of the artichoke mixture to each of the six baking dishes, patting the mixture into the dish fairly firmly so all of it will fit.

6. Place the filled dishes on 1 or more rimmed baking sheets and bake them, uncovered, until the tops are browned with a few tiny spots of charred crispness, five to 10 minutes. Remove the baking sheets from the oven momentarily, leaving the oven set at 425°.

7. Over the top of each gratin evenly sprinkle 1 tablespoon Parmigiano-Reggiano cheese, then drizzle 1 tablespoon olive oil over the top, making sure the edges get a few more drops of oil than the rest of the surface (since the edges dry out more than the center). It is not necessary to moisten all the dry cheese you have just added.

8. Return the baking sheet(s) to the oven and continue baking the gratins until they bubble around the edges, three to five minutes more. Remove them from the oven.

Serving Suggestions: Let the gratins sit in their baking dishes for five minutes to allow them to cool a bit. Garnish the tops with a light sprinkle of the remaining parsley. When they're ready to eat, place each gratin in its baking dish on a dinner plate and serve. 🐚

Oysters and Bacon en Brochettes with Meunière Sauce

For 2 servings as an appetizer or 6 servings as a main dish

We don't know who first thought of combining seafood and pork, but this pairing of oysters and bacon in a fryer or sauté pan has won over hundreds of thousands of gourmands—Creole and otherwise—over the past century and half. That the dish is rich is undeniable.

21 top-quality, thick-cut bacon strips, applewood-smoked preferred
2 cups seasoned flour
72 large raw oysters,* drained (about 2 pounds, 2 ounces in weight)
9 cups vegetable oil, preferably canola oil, or enough to change frying oil midway, divided
toast points, if serving as an appetizer
cooked white long-grain rice, if serving as a main course
⅔ cup warm meunière sauce
about 2 tablespoons minced Italian (flat-leaf) parsley leaves, for garnish
lemon wedges for the table

*Louisiana oysters are ideal for this dish, but if you're near coastal waters with beds of fresh native oysters, by all means use them.

NOTES

It is essential to change the frying oil midway through the oyster-cooking process.

ADVANCE STEPS

Prepare the recipes for:
• Seasoned flour on page 384
• Meunière sauce on page 370

SPECIAL EQUIPMENT
• A metal rack placed over a rimmed baking sheet
• A large shallow baking dish such as a pie plate
• 12 thin wooden skewers, 10 inches long
• One or two additional rimmed baking sheets
• A 12-inch sauté pan or heavy skillet 2½ inches deep
• A frying thermometer, preferred, or use the pinch-of-flour method described in the recipe
• Two large slotted spoons
• A heat-proof container for disposing of hot oil

1. Preheat the oven to 350°F.

2. Cut the bacon slices in quarters and arrange the quarter-slices in a single layer on a metal rack placed over a rimmed baking sheet.

3. Bake the bacon uncovered for 18 to 20 minutes or until the fatty part no longer looks raw. The bacon still needs to be tender enough to thread a skewer through it.

4. Remove the bacon from the oven and set aside briefly to cool.

5. Reduce the oven setting to 200°F.

6. Place the seasoned flour in a large, shallow baking dish and set aside.

7. Fill each skewer as follows (each skewer will hold a total of 6 oysters and 7 quarter-slices of bacon):

   • First, thread 1 of the quarter-slices of bacon onto the skewer, moving it to the bottom end of the skewer.

   • Next, insert a skewer into the center of an oyster, moving it to barely touch the already-skewered bacon.

- Now thread 1 more quarter-slice of bacon on the skewer as you did with the first one, and then another oyster, taking care not to crowd the food too much. Continue in this fashion until you have alternately skewered 6 oysters and 7 quarter-slices of bacon, beginning and ending with bacon.

8. Set the prepared skewer aside on a clean, rimmed baking sheet.

9. Repeat this process to prepare the remaining 11 skewers, placing each finished one on the baking sheet.

10. Heat ½ to ¾ inch of oil (about 4½ cups) into a 12-inch sauté pan over medium-high heat to about 350°, about seven minutes. If you don't have a thermometer, assess the oil's temperature by adding a pinch of the seasoned flour to the hot oil. If the flour immediately foams up in a lively fashion, the oil is hot enough. If the flour does not foam up, heat it a few moments more and retest with more flour.

11. As the oil is approaching the right heat level, dredge three skewers of oysters and bacon in the seasoned flour, turning to coat all surfaces well. Shake off any excess.

12. Carefully ease the three skewers into the hot oil.

13. Fry the oysters and bacon for about two minutes per side, or until the oysters are golden brown on both sides and the bacon is crisp all the way to the skewer. To turn the skewers while cooking, use two large slotted spoons.

14. Drain the skewers on paper towels and place them on a baking sheet in the 200° oven to keep warm.

15. Dredge and fry three more skewers of oysters and bacon as you did the first three, and place them in the warm oven with the other fried skewers.

16. Remove the saucepan from the heat and carefully pour the hot oil into a heatproof container.

17. Carefully wipe the hot saucepan clean with several thicknesses of paper towels, and pour another ½ to ¾ inch of clean oil into the pan. Heat the oil to 350° and repeat the process of dredging and frying the remaining six prepared skewers, three at a time, keeping the fried food on the skewers warm in the oven while finishing the last batch.

Serving Suggestions: Serve the brochettes promptly.

If this is an appetizer course, serve the oysters and bacon still on the skewers, arranged on top of toast points on a large serving platter. Have heated appetizer plates at the table.

If it is a main course, remove the oysters and bacon from the skewers and serve them over a bed of white rice on heated serving plates.

Either way, just before serving, drizzle with a scant tablespoon of meunière sauce and sprinkle lightly with parsley. Serve with lemon wedges.

Oyster Patties

For 6 appetizers or 3 main-dish servings

"Patties" is something of a misnomer for this old-fashioned New Orleans dish, made by filling round pastry shells with oyster bits in a rich and herbal cream sauce. In bygone days they could be found in miniature size on many a cocktail-party tray. But the only source of the tiny pastry cups was a local bakery chain that is no longer in business. This version calls for ready-to-bake pastry shells that are about twice the size of the miniatures. The classic oyster patties recipe often contains fresh thyme. This one uses sage instead.

<table>
<tr><td>6</td><td>ready-to-bake puff pastry shells, about 3 inches round and ¼-inch thick</td></tr>
<tr><td>6</td><td>ounces top-quality bacon strips (not applewood-smoked), chopped in ½-inch by ¼-inch rectangles</td></tr>
<tr><td></td><td>butter, if needed to add to the rendered bacon fat to make ¼ cup</td></tr>
<tr><td>1</td><td>pint medium-sized fresh raw oysters,* whole, halved or coarsely chopped</td></tr>
<tr><td>1</td><td>cup strained oyster liquor**</td></tr>
<tr><td>1</td><td>cup finely chopped onions</td></tr>
<tr><td>2</td><td>tablespoons minced fresh garlic</td></tr>
<tr><td>3</td><td>tablespoons all-purpose flour</td></tr>
<tr><td>1</td><td>cup heavy cream</td></tr>
<tr><td>2</td><td>tablespoons minced fresh Italian (flat-leaf) parsley leaves</td></tr>
<tr><td>1½</td><td>tablespoons very finely chopped fresh sage leaves</td></tr>
<tr><td>½</td><td>teaspoon ground cayenne***</td></tr>
<tr><td>¼</td><td>teaspoon freshly ground black pepper</td></tr>
<tr><td></td><td>kosher salt, to taste</td></tr>
<tr><td>1</td><td>tablespoon very finely sliced green onions (green parts only) or 6 attractive sage leaves, for garnish</td></tr>
</table>

*Louisiana oysters are ideal for this dish, but if you are near coastal waters with beds of fresh native oysters, by all means use them.
**If sufficient oyster liquor is not available, add cold water to make 1 cup.
***For a milder pepper level, reduce the amount of ground cayenne by half.

SPECIAL EQUIPMENT
• A heavy 10-inch skillet
• A heat-proof measuring cup

1. Bake the puff pastry shells according to package directions until golden brown and puffed, 20 to 25 minutes. Remove from the oven and immediately use the tip of a small kitchen knife to lift off the lids, discarding lids. If the inside of the pastry is still a little raw, lightly scrape out the uncooked pastry with the tines of a table fork. Set the shells aside at room temperature.

2. In a heavy 10-inch skillet fry the bacon over medium heat until crisp, about 15 minutes, stirring occasionally; drain on paper towels. Transfer the bacon fat from the skillet to a heat-proof measuring cup. If you don't have ¼ cup fat, make up the balance with butter.

3. If not already done, drain the oysters through a fine-mesh strainer placed over a bowl to catch the oyster liquor. Measure out 1 cup liquor. If necessary, add cold water to make up the balance. Set aside momentarily.

4. In the same skillet used for frying the bacon, heat the ¼ cup bacon fat over medium-high heat until hot, about one minute. Add the onions and garlic, and sauté until the onions are soft and barely browned, about three minutes, stirring frequently.

5. Add the flour, whisking to blend thoroughly. Continue cooking until the flour turns very light brown, about 1½ minutes, whisking constantly and thoroughly.

6. Whisk in the oyster liquor and cream, mixing well. Bring the mixture to a boil over high heat, about 1½ minutes, whisking constantly and being sure to scrape the bottom and side of skillet clean as you whisk.

7. Add the drained oysters, parsley, sage, cayenne and black peppers, and the reserved bacon. Reduce the heat to low and cook just until the edges of the oysters curl, about two minutes, stirring constantly with a spoon. Do not overcook the oysters.

8. Remove from heat and add kosher salt to taste. Serve immediately.

Serving Suggestions: If this is an appetizer course, place a puff pastry shell in the bottom of each of six heated individual pasta bowls. Fill the shells with the oyster mixture, and once all the shells are filled, spoon the remaining oyster mixture around the shells. Garnish each serving with a pinch of green onions or a sage leaf.

If this is a main course, allow two oyster patties per serving in three heated individual pasta bowls. 🐚

Oysters Rockefeller

For 6 appetizer servings or 24 hors d'oeuvres

Certainly the king of baked-oyster dishes, oysters Rockefeller was so named for the richness of its sauce, which in this version contains generous amounts of butter and cream. Maybe it's just coincidental that the sauce is also the color of greenbacks.

Not all of the many different recipes for oysters Rockefeller call for spinach. Some use watercress, parsley and other greens. But spinach is the one found most often, so spinach is the choice here.

In the classic version of the dish, the oysters are baked on the half-shell. This recipe offers the additional options of cooking and serving them in individual baking dishes or a deep-dish glass pie plate. It also allows the cook the option of shucking the oysters just before cooking for optimum freshness. Another twist is the additional topping of breadcrumbs and Grana Padano cheese.

The sauce produced with this recipe is creamy, pale green, dotted with flecks of darker green spinach. There probably will be a surplus of the sauce, which may be transformed into an excellent cream soup by thinning with oyster liquor, milk or seafood stock.

FOR THE ROCKEFELLER SAUCE

- 3 tablespoons unsalted butter
- 1 tablespoon minced fresh garlic
- 1 cup minced yellow onions
- ⅓ cup minced celery
- 3 tablespoons all-purpose flour
- 1 cup strained oyster liquor, or a combination of strained oyster liquor and cold water or chilled vegetable or chicken stock
- 1 cup heavy cream
- 2 tablespoons plus about 2 teaspoons anisette liquor such as Herbsaint,* preferred, or Pernod, divided
- ¾ teaspoon kosher salt, plus to taste
- 7 ounces rinsed and dried fresh spinach, stems trimmed and leaves cut into strips 1/16 inch wide by ½ inch long

*If this ingredient is difficult to find where you live, see Ingredient Sources on page 424.

1. Melt the butter in a heavy, nonreactive 2-quart saucepan over medium-high heat. Add the garlic and cook just until it starts to brown, about 20 seconds, stirring constantly.

2. Add the onions and celery, stirring well. Cook until the onions are translucent, about two minutes, stirring frequently.

NOTES

The Rockefeller sauce should be prepared a day ahead to let the flavors develop.

See Special Instructions for Baking or Broiling Oysters on the Half-Shell on page 83.

ADVANCE STEP

Prepare the recipe for fresh soft breadcrumbs on page 382

SPECIAL EQUIPMENT

- A heavy, nonreactive* 2-quart saucepan
- A nonreactive* container

*See Using Nonreactive Cookware, page 419.

3. Stir in the flour and let it cook for 90 seconds, stirring and scraping the pan bottom constantly to prevent scorching. The flour will lightly brown during this process.

4. Slowly add the oyster liquor, stirring constantly until smooth. Gradually add the heavy cream, blending well.

5. Bring to a simmer, then reduce the heat and continue simmering for 10 minutes, stirring and scraping the pan bottom frequently.

6. Stir in 2 tablespoons of anisette liqueur and ¾ teaspoon kosher salt, then stir in the spinach, a handful at the time, until all has been added. Continue simmering and stirring until the sauce is noticeably thicker, about 15 minutes more. Remove the sauce from heat and let cool for 15 minutes.

7. Taste the sauce for salt and anisette liqueur flavors. If needed, add more salt and up to about 2 teaspoons anisette liqueur, adding only enough to lend a subtle taste of anisette to the sauce. Let the sauce finish cooling, then refrigerate overnight in a covered nonreactive container before using.

FOR THE GRANA PADANO BREADCRUMB TOPPING AND FINISHING THE DISH

1	cup fresh soft breadcrumbs
2½	tablespoons minced Italian (flat-leaf) parsley leaves
2	tablespoons finely grated Grana Padano, preferred, or Parmigiano-Reggiano cheese
1	teaspoon kosher salt
⅛	teaspoon freshly ground black pepper
2	tablespoons melted unsalted butter
24	medium-to-large oysters,* undrained

IF BAKING THE OYSTERS ON THE HALF-SHELL

	about 10 pounds rock salt,** divided
24	scrubbed and dried bottom-shells

*Louisiana oysters are ideal for this dish, but if you're near coastal waters with beds of fresh native oysters, by all means use them.
**Baking oysters on the half-shell on a bed of rock salt helps them stay level and cook evenly. This also keeps them from sliding on the plate and helps them stay hot.

1. Preheat the oven to 350°F.

2. To prepare the breadcrumb topping, in a medium-size mixing bowl mix together the breadcrumbs, parsley, cheese, kosher salt and pepper. Add the butter, mixing thoroughly. Set aside at room temperature.

SPECIAL EQUIPMENT

If you are using individual baking dishes or a deep-dish pie plate:

- For appetizers: Six individual oval baking dishes with a 7-ounce capacity, measuring about 7 inches long, 4 inches wide, and 1 inch deep
- For hors d'oeuvres: A deep-dish, glass pie plate, 9 inches in diameter and 1¾ inches deep

If you are using oyster bottom shells:

- One or more rimmed baking sheets large enough to hold 24 oysters on the half-shell in a single layer
- Oyster forks for serving

3. Remove the chilled sauce from the refrigerator and let sit at room temperature for 10 minutes before using.

IF BAKING THE OYSTERS IN INDIVIDUAL BAKING DISHES FOR APPETIZERS

1. Place 4 very well drained oysters in each oval baking dish. Spoon about 1½ tablespoons of the sauce over each oyster to cover it. Sprinkle the topping evenly over the oysters, using it all.

2. Bake uncovered on the middle shelf of the oven until the topping turns light golden brown and liquid is bubbling around the edges of the dishes, about 25 minutes.

IF BAKING THE OYSTERS IN A DEEP-DISH, GLASS PIE PLATE FOR HORS D'OEUVRES

1. Place the 24 very well drained oysters in the pie plate in a single layer. Spoon the sauce evenly over the oysters, using it all. Sprinkle the topping over the sauce, using it all.

2. Bake uncovered on the middle shelf of the oven until the topping turns light golden brown and liquid is bubbling around the edges of the dish, about 30 minutes.

IF BAKING THE OYSTERS ON THE HALF-SHELL

1. Place a thick, even layer (roughly 4 pounds) of rock salt over the bottom of a rimmed baking sheet that will hold 24 oysters on the half-shell in a single layer. Place one undrained oyster in each bottom shell. Arrange the oysters on the half-shell on the baking sheet, upright and level, nestling them into the rock salt.

2. Spoon enough of the sauce (about 1 to 1½ tablespoons) evenly over each oyster to cover the oyster but not overflow onto the shell.

3. Sprinkle the reserved topping evenly over the oysters, using it all. If the oysters are a first course, mound about 1¼ to 1½ cups rock salt in the middle of each heated, standard-sized, rimmed dinner plate. If the oysters are for hors d'oeuvres, line serving trays or platters with rock salt.

4. Bake the oysters, uncovered, on the middle shelf of the oven until they're just plump and the topping turns golden brown, about 20 minutes. Serve the oysters piping hot with oyster forks.

   Serving Suggestions: If serving as hors d'oeuvres cooked in a pie plate, serve from a buffet table.

   If serving as hors d'oeuvres on the half-shell, place the oysters on the prepared rock-salt-lined trays or platters to pass to your guests, or place them on a buffet table.

If serving as appetizers in individual baking dishes, place the baking dishes on dinner plates.

If serving as appetizers on the half-shell, for each serving allow four oysters, nestling each on top of the rock-salt bed on a prepared dinner plate, facing the pointed ends of the shells toward the center of the plate.

SPECIAL INSTRUCTIONS FOR BAKING OR BROILING OYSTERS ON THE HALF-SHELL

This recipe and the two to follow include the option of cooking and serving the oysters on the half-shell. If you choose that option, these are some suggestions.

- You will need bottom oyster shells for cooking and serving. The ideal shell size is about 4½ to 5 inches long.

- If you are using pre-shucked oysters, scrub the inside of the bottom shells, dry them and leave them at room temperature until called for in the recipe. (If you do not have the shells, fresh seafood dealers should be able to provide them.)

- If you are shucking the oysters, do so at the last possible moment. After opening each oyster, detach the flesh from the bottom shell, but leave the oyster in place and do not drain off the liquid. Pick out any bits of shell that may have remained with the oysters.

- If you are baking or broiling and serving the oysters in individual baking dishes or a deep-dish pie plate, drain the oysters well just before called for in the recipe so the finished dish isn't too watery.

- Be sure to keep the oysters refrigerated in their juices until needed.

Baked Oysters Ralph

For 8 or 9 appetizer servings, or 5 lunch or brunch main-course dishes

The variations on the theme of sauced and baked oysters is almost endless. This one is a kind of upside-down oysters Rockefeller: The oyster tops the spinach rather than vice versa. Spooned onto the oyster itself is a roux-based sauce enriched with butter, cream and egg yolk and energized with bacon, jalapeño, tomatoes and sweet pepper.

While the definitive version of oysters Ralph calls for baking them on the half-shell, you have the option of doing it in individual baking dishes.

FOR THE SAUCE

5	tablespoons unsalted butter
⅓	cup plus 1 tablespoon all-purpose flour, divided
3	ounces (about 4 strips) finely chopped, top-quality, thick-cut bacon strips, applewood-smoked preferred
⅓	cup minced red onions
⅓	cup finely chopped sweet green peppers
⅓	cup finely chopped fresh jalapeño peppers, leaving a few seeds to add a little heat
2	whole bay leaves
1	teaspoon kosher salt, plus to taste
1	teaspoon freshly ground black pepper, plus to taste
1	teaspoon dry thyme leaves
½	teaspoon crushed red pepper
2	cups whole milk
2	cups heavy cream
3	yolks from large eggs
⅓	cup peeled, seeded and chopped ripe tomatoes (or canned chopped Roma tomatoes), well drained
¼	cup freshly grated Romano cheese

NOTES

See Special Instructions for Baking or Broiling Oysters on the Half-Shell on page 83.

The color of the roux in this recipe is keyed to the color chart on page 415.

The sauce may be prepared a day ahead.

SPECIAL EQUIPMENT

- An oyster knife, if you are shucking the oysters
- A heavy 8-inch skillet or heavy 2-quart saucepan
- A long-handled metal whisk
- A heavy, nonreactive* 5-quart saucepan
- A long-handled mixing spoon
- A large, heat-proof mixing bowl

*See Using Nonreactive Cookware, page 419.

1. For the roux, in a heavy 8-inch skillet melt the butter over medium heat. Very slowly (so you don't burn yourself) add ⅓ cup flour, whisking constantly with a long-handled metal whisk until all the flour has been added and the mixture is smooth.

2. Reduce the heat to medium-low and continue cooking the roux, whisking constantly so it doesn't scorch, until the roux turns "blond" (pale golden), two to three minutes. Set the roux aside.

3. In a heavy, nonreactive 5-quart saucepan, cook the bacon over medium-low heat until most of the fat is rendered from the bacon and the bacon is slightly crisp, about 12 minutes.

4. Leaving the bacon in the pan, pour off all but 1½ tablespoons of the rendered fat. If less than 1½ tablespoons of fat was rendered from the bacon, do not add more fat to the pan.

5. Add to the saucepan the onions, sweet peppers and jalapeños. Cook over medium-low heat until the vegetables are cooked through, about two minutes, frequently stirring and scraping the pan bottom clean with a long-handled mixing spoon.

6. Reduce the heat to very low and whisk in 1 tablespoon flour, mixing until well blended. Cook for one minute, stirring constantly. Add ¼ cup of the reserved roux, stirring until it's blended into the mixture. Whisk in the bay leaves, 1 teaspoon kosher salt, 1 teaspoon black pepper, and the thyme and crushed red pepper. Gradually add the milk, whisking constantly.

7. Bring to a boil over medium heat, whisking constantly so the mixture doesn't scorch. Reduce heat to medium-low and cook until the sauce is fairly thick, about four minutes, whisking frequently.

8. Gradually add the cream, whisking constantly, and heat mixture until it is just short of reaching a simmer, whisking frequently. Meanwhile, place the remaining scant ¼ cup roux in a medium-size mixing bowl. Once the sauce is close to simmering, gradually add ½ cup of the sauce to the roux, whisking until smooth.

9. Reduce the heat under the saucepan to very low, and add the sauce-roux mixture to the rest of the sauce in the pan, whisking thoroughly. Cook until the sauce is very thick, about 10 minutes, whisking as often as needed to keep the mixture from sticking to the pan bottom.

10. Meanwhile, in a small mixing bowl, whisk together the egg yolks. Once the sauce is very thick, stir about 2 tablespoons of it into the yolks, then very gradually drizzle the yolk mixture into the pan of sauce, whisking constantly and thoroughly.

11. Drain the tomatoes again and add them and the Romano cheese to the pan, whisking until well blended. Season lightly with kosher salt. (You may want to under-salt the sauce since you will be adding a salty cheese topping to the dish before it's baked.)

12. Continue cooking and whisking for one minute more. By now the sauce should be the consistency of very thick cream, leaving a distinct track on the back of a spoon when you draw a finger through it. If not, cook a little longer.

13. Promptly transfer the sauce to a large, heat-proof mixing bowl and continue whisking one to two minutes more.

14. Refrigerate the sauce, uncovered, to cool it quickly, about 20 minutes, stirring it frequently. Once the sauce is cool, discard the bay leaves. Cover and chill until it's the consistency of a thick pudding, at least one hour or overnight.

FOR FINISHING THE DISH

SPECIAL EQUIPMENT

- A heavy 12-inch skillet or heavy 12-inch saucepan
- A pair of tongs
- A platter
- A mesh strainer

If you are using individual baking dishes:

- For appetizers: eight or nine individual oval baking dishes with a 7-ounce capacity, measuring about 7 inches long, 4 inches wide, and 1 inch deep
- For entrées: five shallow 12-ounce shallow, round baking dishes, such as au gratin or shirred-egg dishes, measuring about 6½ inches in diameter and about 1⅛ inches deep
- One or more rimmed baking sheets large enough to hold the baking dishes or 35 oysters on the half-shell in a single layer
- Oyster forks for serving

1	tablespoon unsalted butter
1	pound baby spinach leaves with stems, washed and drained (drying not necessary)
	kosher salt, to taste
	freshly ground black pepper, to taste
⅓	cup very fine, dry breadcrumbs
⅓	cup freshly grated Romano cheese
35	medium-to-large oysters,* undrained
	about 10 pounds rock salt,** if baking the oysters on the half-shell
35	scrubbed and dried oyster bottom shells, if baking the oysters on the half-shell

*Louisiana oysters are ideal for this dish, but if you're near coastal waters with beds of fresh native oysters, by all means use them.
**Baking the oysters and their shells on a bed of rock salt helps them stay level and cook evenly. This also keeps them from sliding on the plate and helps them stay hot.

1. In a heavy 12-inch skillet, melt the butter over medium-high heat. Add the spinach and turn with tongs to coat all the leaves with butter. Season with a little kosher salt and pepper and cook until just barely wilted, about 30 to 45 seconds. When done, the leaves should still be separate rather than stuck together.

2. Immediately spread the spinach out on a platter so it won't continue cooking by residual heat. Once the spinach is cool, drain in a mesh strainer, lightly pressing to extract as much liquid as possible. Place in a bowl and set aside.

3. For the topping, combine the breadcrumbs and Romano cheese.

4. Preheat the oven to 475°F. If cooking all the oysters on the same baking sheet, place an oven rack in the middle of the oven before preheating it, for safety reasons. If cooking them on two different oven racks, position the two racks in the middle third of the oven before preheating it.

IF BAKING THE OYSTERS IN INDIVIDUAL OVAL BAKING DISHES FOR APPETIZERS

1. For each oyster being served, mound 1 heaping tablespoon of the reserved spinach in each of the 8 or 9 oval baking dishes; you should have either 3 or 4 separate mounds of spinach in each dish.

2. Next, arrange a very well drained oyster on top of each mound of spinach. Sprinkle ½ teaspoon of the breadcrumb topping over each oyster. Evenly spread a rounded 1 tablespoon of sauce over each oyster and sprinkle another

½ teaspoon of breadcrumb topping over the sauce. Place the dishes on a rimmed baking sheet.

3.   Bake uncovered on the middle shelf of the oven until the topping is light golden brown and liquid is bubbling around the edges of the dishes, about 12 minutes.

IF BAKING THE OYSTERS IN INDIVIDUAL ROUND BAKING DISHES FOR ENTRÉES

1.   Place 7 separate, heaping tablespoons of the reserved spinach in each of 5 round baking dishes. Arrange a very well drained oyster on top of each mound of spinach.

2.   Sprinkle ½ teaspoon of the breadcrumb topping over each oyster. Evenly spread a rounded 1 tablespoon of sauce over each oyster and sprinkle another ½ teaspoon of breadcrumb topping over the sauce. Place the dishes on a rimmed baking sheet.

3.   Bake uncovered on the middle shelf of the oven until the topping is light golden brown and liquid is bubbling around the edges of the dishes, about 12 minutes.

IF BAKING THE OYSTERS ON THE HALF-SHELL

1.   Sprinkle a layer of rock salt, ¼ inch or thicker, over the bottom of a rimmed baking sheet that will hold 35 oysters on the half-shell in a single layer.

2.   Remove the chilled sauce from the refrigerator. Place one undrained oyster in each bottom shell.

3.   To assemble the oysters for baking, mound 1 rounded tablespoon of the spinach under each oyster. Next, sprinkle ½ teaspoon of the breadcrumb topping over the oyster. Spread a rounded tablespoon of sauce completely over the oyster to coat it with a ¼-inch-thick layer of sauce, sealing the oyster between the sauce and the shell.

4.   Now, sprinkle ½ teaspoon additional breadcrumb topping over the sauce. As the oysters are assembled, arrange them level and upright on the baking sheet, nestling them into the salt.

5.   If baking all the oysters at once on one rack of the oven, bake uncovered until the tops are just browned and the sauce melts slightly, about six minutes. If baking all the oysters at once on two racks of the oven, bake them for three minutes, then rotate and switch the pans to be on the other rack, and continue baking three minutes more.

6.   While the oysters are baking, mound about 1½ cups rock salt in the middle of each heated standard-size, rimmed dinner plate.

Serving Suggestions: Serve the oysters while piping hot.

If serving the oysters in individual baking dishes, place the dishes on dinner plates.

If serving them on the half-shell, allow three or four oysters for each appetizer serving, or seven as a main course, nestling each on top of the rock-salt bed on a prepared dinner plate, facing the pointed ends of the shells toward the center of the plate. 🐚

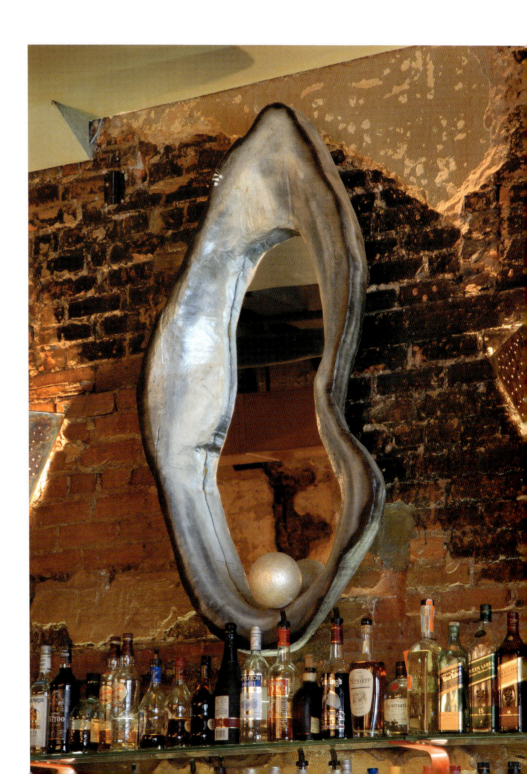

Charbroiled Garlic Oysters with Grana Padano Breadcrumb Topping

For 6 appetizer servings or 3 or 4 main-course servings

No charcoal is called for in this recipe. But the oysters are broiled to the point where a slight char appears at their edges. This cooking method adds character and flavor to the dish, as do the garlic butter and the breadcrumb topping that's enriched with either Grana Padano or Parmigiano-Reggiano cheese. The breadcrumb topping adds a pleasant crispness to the oysters, as well as great flavor.

FOR THE GRANA PADANO BREADCRUMB TOPPING

- ½ cup very fine dry breadcrumbs
- 2 tablespoons coarsely grated Grana Padano, preferred, or Parmigiano-Reggiano cheese
- 1 tablespoon minced fresh Italian (flat-leaf) parsley leaves
- 1 rounded teaspoon minced fresh garlic
- ½ teaspoon kosher salt
- ¼ teaspoon freshly ground black pepper
- 4 teaspoons vegetable oil
- 2 teaspoons olive oil

In a large mixing bowl, thoroughly combine all the topping ingredients, mixing with your hands. When you're done, all the breadcrumbs should be so well moistened with oil that the topping will momentarily clump when you squeeze a handful together. Set aside at room temperature.

FOR THE GARLIC BUTTER

- ½ cup clarified butter
- 2 tablespoons packed, very thinly sliced fresh garlic

In a heavy 8-inch skillet, combine the clarified butter and garlic. Cook over medium heat until the garlic is just short of browning but still pungent, about 1½ minutes, stirring occasionally. Remove from heat and set aside at room temperature.

FOR FINISHING THE DISH

- 24 medium-to-large fresh oysters,* undrained
- ½ teaspoon kosher salt
  about 10 pounds rock salt,** divided (if broiling the oysters on the half-shell)
- 24 scrubbed and dried oyster bottom shells (if broiling the oysters on the half-shell)
  lemon wedges, for serving

NOTES

See Special Instructions for Baking or Broiling Oysters on the Half-Shell on page 83.

NOTES

You will have garlic butter left over, which may be refrigerated and used later to make garlic bread.

You will have some of the breadcrumb topping left over. You may want to use it for other purposes, such as sprinkling it over a vegetable dish before baking.

ADVANCE STEP

Prepare the clarified butter recipe on page 355.

SPECIAL EQUIPMENT

- A heavy 8-inch skillet

NOTES

Cook the oysters in batches if the broiler is not large enough to hold a broiler pan with 6 individual appetizer baking dishes, 3 individual entrée baking dishes, or 24 oysters on the half-shell in a single layer.

*Louisiana oysters are ideal for this dish, but if you're near coastal waters with beds of fresh native oysters, by all means use them.

**Broiling the oysters on a bed of rock salt helps them stay level and cook evenly. This also keeps them from sliding on the plate and helps them stay hot.

Preheat the broiler.

IF BROILING THE OYSTERS IN INDIVIDUAL OVAL OR ROUND BAKING DISHES

1. For appetizers, place 4 very well drained oysters in each oval baking dish.

2. For entrées, place 8 very well drained oysters in each round baking dish.

3. Lightly salt the tops of the oysters, using a total of ½ teaspoon kosher salt.

4. Drizzle ½ teaspoon of the reserved garlic butter over each oyster, being sure each gets some of the garlic slices on it.

5. Sprinkle 1 teaspoon of the reserved topping evenly over each oyster.

6. Arrange the baking dishes in a broiler pan without the rack.

7. Broil the oysters about 2 inches from the heat source until the topping starts to develop a few tiny dark brown areas, two minutes.

8. Next, move the pan to about 4 inches from the heat source and continue broiling until the oysters are just plump and the topping turns golden brown with several tiny dark areas that appear charred, about two or three minutes more. Check often so the crumbs don't actually burn. If in doubt, carefully taste a tiny bit of charred area. The darkest areas should not taste burned, but rather will add a wonderful crispiness to the finished dish.

IF BROILING THE OYSTERS IN ALUMINUM PIE PLATES

1. Place 12 very well drained oysters in each pie plate.

2. Lightly salt, drizzle with garlic butter and sprinkle on the topping as described immediately above in Steps 3, 4 and 5.

3. Place the pie plates in a broiler pan without the rack.

4. Broil the oysters about 4 inches from the heat source, as described in Step 8 above.

IF BROILING THE OYSTERS ON THE HALF-SHELL

1. While the broiler is heating, mound about 1½ cups rock salt in the middle of each standard-sized rimmed dinner plate. For appetizers, use six dinner plates. For entrées, use three dinner plates. For hors d'oeuvres, place beds of rock salt on trays or platters and set aside.

If broiling the oysters on the half-shell, See Special Instructions for Baking or Broiling Oysters on the Half-Shell on page 83.

ADVANCE STEP

If you are broiling the oysters in individual baking dishes or aluminum pie plates, drain the oysters well just before called for in the recipe so the finished dish isn't too watery.

SPECIAL EQUIPMENT

• Heavy-duty aluminum foil

If using individual baking dishes or aluminum pie plates:

• For appetizers, six individual oval baking dishes with a 7-ounce capacity, measuring about 7 inches long, 4 inches wide, and 1 inch deep

• For entrées, three shallow, round, 12-ounce baking dishes, such as au gratin or shirred-egg dishes, measuring about 6½ inches in diameter and about 1⅛ inches deep

• For hors d'oeuvres, two 9-inch aluminum pie plates

• If broiling the oysters on the half-shell, a broiler pan (without the rack) large enough to hold 24 oysters on the half-shell in a single layer

• Oyster forks for serving

2. Cover a broiler pan (without a rack) with heavy-duty aluminum foil.

3. Place a thick, even layer (roughly 4 pounds) of rock salt in the bottom of the broiler pan.

4. Arrange the oysters on the half-shell in the broiler pan in a single layer, nestling them into the salt and making sure they're level so you don't lose any of the garlic butter or topping as they are prepared and cooked.

5. Lightly salt the tops of the oysters, using a total of ½ teaspoon kosher salt.

6. Drizzle ½ teaspoon of the reserved garlic butter over each oyster, being sure each gets some of the garlic slices on it.

7. Sprinkle 1 teaspoon of the reserved topping evenly over each oyster.

8. Broil the oysters about two inches from the heat source until the topping starts to develop a few tiny dark brown areas, one to two minutes.

9. Next, move the pan to about 4 inches from the heat source and continue broiling until the oysters are just plump and the topping turns golden brown with several tiny dark areas that appear charred, about two to three minutes more. Check often so the crumbs don't actually burn. If in doubt, carefully taste a tiny bit of charred area. The darkest areas shouldn't taste burned, but rather will add a wonderful crispiness to the finished dish. Rotate the pan two or three times during this final stage of cooking.

Serving Suggestions: Serve the oysters while piping hot, with oyster forks.

If serving in individual baking dishes as appetizers or entrées, place the baking dishes on heated dinner plates.

If serving in aluminum pie plates as hors d'oeuvres, transfer the oysters to a serving platter or place the pie plates on a platter and serve from a buffet table.

If serving on the half-shell as appetizers or entrées, for each appetizer allow four oysters. For each entrée allow eight oysters. Nestle each oyster on top of the rock-salt bed on a prepared dinner plate, facing the pointed ends of the shells toward the center of the plate.

If serving on the half-shell as hors d'oeuvres, place the oysters on the prepared rock-salt-lined trays or platters to pass to your guests or to serve from a buffet table.

Serve with lemon wedges.

Red Fish Grill Barbecue Oysters with Blue-Cheese Dipping Sauce

For 6 appetizer servings or 3 or 4 main-course servings

No barbecue pits are needed for either the barbecue shrimp recipe in this cookbook or for this one, which features fried oysters. There is a barbecue sauce, though, and it takes on a golden hue from honey, clarified butter and pepper sauce. The barbecue sauce may diminish the oysters' crispness somewhat, but it adds to their succulence. The bonus is a blue-cheese dipping sauce that pitches in to add interest to the dish.

FOR THE BARBECUE SAUCE

- ¼ cup plus 2 tablespoons mild-flavored Louisiana pepper sauce, such as Crystal brand
- 1 tablespoon clover honey
- 6 tablespoons clarified butter

1. Combine the hot sauce and honey in a blender. Set aside. In a very small saucepan, heat the clarified butter to 140°F over medium heat, using a frying thermometer to access temperature.

2. You may also heat the butter in a microwave oven in a small microwaveable bowl. (If you just prepared the clarified butter and it's still over 140°, you don't need to cool it to 140°.)

3. Promptly turn the blender to low speed and slowly pour the 140° butter in a thin steady stream through the hole in the blender's lid. Pour this barbecue sauce in a large, nonreactive mixing bowl and set aside.

FOR THE OYSTERS

-     canola oil, for deep frying
- 2 cups seasoned flour
- 36 medium-to-large oysters,* drained
- 1 cup blue-cheese dipping sauce or salad dressing

    *Louisiana oysters are ideal for this dish, but if you are near coastal waters with beds of fresh native oysters, by all means use them.

1. Heat the oil in a deep fryer to 350°F, or heat 1½ to 2 inches of oil in a 5-quart Dutch oven over medium-high heat to 350°.

2. Place the seasoned flour in a large mixing bowl.

NOTES

Keep the oysters refrigerated in their juices until needed.

ADVANCE STEPS

Prepare the recipes for:

- Clarified butter on page 355
- Seasoned flour on page 384
- Blue-cheese dipping sauce or dressing on page 354

SPECIAL EQUIPMENT

- A very small saucepan
- A frying thermometer
- A large, nonreactive* mixing bowl

*See Using Nonreactive Cookware, page 419.

⌇ FOR THE OYSTERS ⌇

SPECIAL EQUIPMENT

- A deep fryer or 5-quart Dutch oven
- Oyster forks for serving, optional

3. Once the oil has almost reached 350°, drain any excess oyster liquor from a batch of the oysters and dredge them in the seasoned flour.

4. Carefully slide the oysters into the oil. (As the cold oysters come in contact with the hot oil, it may momentarily bubble up in the pan.) Fry the oysters just until golden brown and crispy, about two minutes. Remove the finished oysters from the oil with a slotted spoon and drain on paper towels. Repeat to dredge and fry the remaining oysters.

5. As soon as all the oysters have been fried and drained, add small batches of them to the bowl of barbecue sauce and toss to coat well. Serve while still warm.

Serving Suggestions: Allow six oysters for each appetizer serving or nine to 12 as a main course. The dipping sauce may be passed at the table or served on the plates with the oysters.

Provide oyster forks at the table if you have them. 🦪

Sesame-Seared Tuna with Avocado-Horseradish Sauce

For 6 appetizer servings

When a lunch or dinner calls for a cool and bracing first course, this one could be just the right thing. Slices of seared and chilled tuna, edged with black sesame seeds, join a creamy sauce with avocado and horseradish.

FOR THE AVOCADO-HORSERADISH SAUCE

1	large (about 10 ounces) very ripe avocado, preferably Hass
⅓	cup water
1	tablespoon plus 1 teaspoon rice-wine vinegar
1	tablespoon prepared horseradish
2	teaspoons fresh lemon juice
2	teaspoons dairy sour cream
	kosher salt, to taste
	freshly ground black pepper, to taste

1. In the bowl of a blender, combine all ingredients and process to a smooth sauce.

2. Transfer the mixture to a nonreactive storage bowl, and cover with plastic wrap so the plastic touches the entire surface of the sauce to keep it from turning brown. Chill at least one hour before serving.

FOR THE TUNA

3	tuna steaks, 6 to 7 ounces each, 1 inch thick
	kosher salt, to taste
	freshly ground black pepper, to taste
3	tablespoons plus 1 teaspoon black sesame seeds
1	tablespoon extra-virgin olive oil

1. Generously season each tuna steak with kosher salt and pepper to taste. Sprinkle each steak on all sides with black sesame seeds, using a total of 3 tablespoons plus 1 teaspoon black sesame seeds distributed among the 3 steaks.

2. Heat an empty, heavy non-stick 12-inch skillet over high heat just until short of smoking, about two minutes. Add the olive oil to the hot skillet and heat for 30 seconds. Arrange the tuna steaks in the skillet without crowding them (sauté in batches if needed), and sauté on the four sides (think of the four sides of a shoe box), but not the ends, for just 15 seconds per side, to sear the outside while keeping the inside rare.

NOTES

The sauce may be prepared one day ahead.

About 3 tablespoons of the sauce are needed to garnish the dish. Leftover sauce would make a good dip for cold boiled seafood or tortilla chips, or it can be used as a salad dressing.

The tuna steaks are cooked rare for this dish. Cooking them longer will make them more difficult to slice.

SPECIAL EQUIPMENT

- An electric blender or food processor
- A nonreactive* storage bowl

*See Using Nonreactive Cookware, page 419.

⊰ FOR THE TUNA ⊱

SPECIAL EQUIPMENT

- A heavy, non-stick 12-inch skillet

3.   Remove the skillet from heat and transfer the steaks to a plate. Cool briefly, cover and refrigerate at least two hours or up to eight hours.

FOR SERVING

    2   large ripe avocados, preferably Hass, about 10 ounces each
2½ to 3   ounces fresh sprouts (such as radish sprouts or pea shoots or other
           sprouts with a bite), or 1½ ounces baby arugula leaves
    1   tablespoon black sesame seeds, for garnish

1.   Peel and halve the avocados and remove the pits. Cut two of the avocado halves lengthwise into four slices each. Cut the other two halves lengthwise into five slices each.

2.   Slice each of the 3 chilled tuna steaks crosswise into six equal slices, to produce a total of 18 slices.

3.   Mound a portion of the sprouts in the center of each chilled salad plate, then arrange three avocado slices and three tuna slices alternately around the sprouts, like spokes on a wheel.

4.   Spoon ½ teaspoon of the avocado sauce at the foot of each tuna slice.

5.   Season to taste with kosher salt and pepper and garnish with a sprinkle of black sesame seeds. Serve immediately. 🐚

Spicy Fried Calamari with Lemon Aioli

For 3 to 4 appetizer servings

In this recipe the calamari are spicy hot from being seasoned liberally with cayenne pepper, while the delicious lemon flavor and creamy texture of the lemon aioli soothes the palate from the cayenne's heat.

1¼ to 1½	pounds calamari, fresh (preferred) or thawed frozen
	vegetable oil (preferably canola oil), for deep frying
1½	cups seasoned flour
¾	cup fine-ground cornmeal or durum wheat flour*
1½	tablespoons cornstarch
1	tablespoon ground cayenne, or to taste
¾	teaspoon table salt, or to taste
¾	cup lemon aioli (approximately)

*For information on ordering durum flour, see Ingredient Sources on page 424.

NOTE

For the calamari to be served as hot and crisp as possible, all of them need to be fried at the same time, which requires using two broad-based pans. In this way the pieces can fry in a single layer, or almost so, allowing the maximum degree of even frying and producing a crisp crust on each piece.

ADVANCE STEPS

Prepare the recipes for:

- Seasoned flour on page 384
- Lemon aioli on page 353

SPECIAL EQUIPMENT

- Two broad-based, heavy 12-to-14-inch sauté pans, sauce pans or Dutch ovens
- A frying thermometer
- A pair of tongs

1. Rinse the calamari under cool running water. Trim off the tentacles just below the eyes and reserve tentacles. Pull the heads away from the bodies and discard them. From each body, pull out and discard all soft matter and the long transparent, plastic-like quill. Peel off and discard the very thin, spotted outer membrane and the fins. Rinse tentacles and bodies well, and recheck that all matter from inside bodies has been removed. Cut the bodies crosswise into ¼-inch rings. Drain in a colander for 15 minutes.

2. In each of two broad-based, heavy 12-to-14-inch sauté pans, heat 1 inch of oil until a frying thermometer registers 350°F. While the oil is heating, prepare the breading and bread the calamari as follows:

    In a large mixing bowl, thoroughly combine the seasoned flour, cornmeal or durum flour and cornstarch. Add the calamari to this breading, tossing well so all pieces are coated on all surfaces, shaking off any excess. Separate the tentacles from one another.

3. Carefully ease each piece of calamari separately into the hot oil in the two pans. (This will help keep the hot oil from bubbling up and possibly overflowing the pans.) Deep-fry the calamari until golden, two to three minutes. (The rings will not come out as golden as the tentacles.) As they fry, turn the pieces with tongs to separate and help them brown evenly. Do not overcook or the calamari's texture will become rubbery.

4. Transfer the calamari with a slotted spoon to drain briefly on paper towels. While draining, evenly sprinkle the calamari with 1 tablespoon cayenne and ¾ teaspoon table salt or to taste. Serve while piping hot.

Serving Suggestion: Serve each portion of calamari on a heated dinner plate with a very small bowl holding about 2 tablespoons of lemon aioli placed in the center of the plate. 🐚

Florettes of Fried Oyster Mushrooms with Rosemary Mayonnaise

For 6 appetizer servings and 1½ cups mayonnaise

The oyster mushroom, which is found most commonly during the last half of autumn, lives up to its name. Its cap resembles an oyster and its taste is not unlike that of one, too. Hairless and smoky gray in color, the cap can reach almost 8 inches in diameter, but the best size for this recipe is 3 to 4 ounces in weight.

When fried in a coating of egg wash and seasoned flour, the deliciously meaty and crispy mushrooms take on a lovely floral aspect. And the rosemary mayonnaise's acidity and smoothness on the palate contrast nicely with the mushrooms' crusty texture.

FOR THE ROSEMARY MAYONNAISE

1 tablespoon water	1 cup vegetable oil
1 yolk from a large egg	¼ cup olive oil
1 tablespoon minced fresh rosemary leaves	¼ cup good-quality red-wine vinegar
1 teaspoon minced fresh garlic	1 teaspoon kosher salt
1 teaspoon Dijon mustard	⅛ teaspoon freshly ground black pepper

1. In a large stainless-steel mixing bowl, combine the water, egg yolk, rosemary, garlic and mustard, using a metal whisk to blend them well.

2. Combine the vegetable and olive oils and very gradually add to the egg yolk mixture in a thin, steady stream, whisking constantly until all is incorporated and the mayonnaise is thick.

3. Gradually add the red-wine vinegar, whisking to blend well.

4. Whisk in the kosher salt and pepper.

5. Before using, refrigerate at least one hour or overnight in a covered container to let the flavors develop, then season with more salt and pepper if desired. Keep refrigerated and use within four days.

FOR THE FRIED OYSTER MUSHROOMS

6 fresh oyster mushrooms, each 3 to 4 ounces	2 large eggs
4 cups all-purpose flour	oil for deep frying
4 cups seasoned flour	kosher salt
2 cups whole milk	6 ounces mixed salad greens, for serving

NOTE

The mayonnaise can be paired with other fried vegetables or fish and seafood and, of course, be used as a salad or sandwich dressing.

ADVANCE STEP

Prepare the recipe for seasoned flour on page 384.

SPECIAL EQUIPMENT

- A large stainless-steel mixing bowl
- A metal whisk

1. If the mushrooms are clean, you don't need to wash or wipe them. If not clean, wash them quickly under cool water, drain well, and gently pat dry with a clean kitchen towel.

2. Place the all-purpose flour in a large mixing bowl and the seasoned flour in another large mixing bowl. For the egg wash, in a third large mixing bowl whisk together the milk and eggs until well blended.

3. Preheat the oil in a deep fryer to 350°F or preheat 2 inches of oil in a 5-to-6-quart saucepan to 350°. Also, preheat the oven to 200°.

4. While the oil is heating, divide the salad greens between six chilled serving plates to function as beds for the mushrooms. Refrigerate the plates while frying the mushrooms.

5. Line a cookie sheet with paper towels and set aside.

6. As you dredge each oyster mushroom, if you prefer a lighter crust, don't focus on getting the breading into every crevice of the mushroom's overlapping rows. For a thicker crust, however, dredge very thoroughly so that more of the all-purpose flour and seasoned flour stick onto all surfaces possible.

7. Now, dredge each mushroom in the all-purpose flour, shaking off the excess. Dip the mushroom in the egg wash, moistening it completely, then dredge it in the seasoned flour, shaking off the excess. As the mushrooms are prepared, place them on a rimmed baking sheet.

8. Once the oil has reached the proper temperature, fry each mushroom individually or in small batches (do not crowd) until light golden brown and crispy, about four minutes. While the mushrooms are frying, turn occasionally with a slotted spoon. Return the oil to 350° between frying each batch.

9. With the slotted spoon, transfer the fried mushroom(s) to the pan lined with paper towels to drain briefly, then place on an unlined rimmed baking sheet and keep warm in the oven while frying the remaining batches. Add the remaining batches to the baking sheet as fried and drained.

10. Once all the mushrooms have been fried, lightly salt all with kosher salt.

    Serving Suggestion: Serve while hot on the plates of salad greens. Pass the mayonnaise at the table, or spoon 1 to 2 tablespoons mayonnaise on each plate and pass the rest in a bowl. 🐚

For 6 appetizer servings

This dish is a feast for the palate and the nose. As the first bite reaches your lips, you get the enticing aroma of the smoky scallops and the sweet acidity of the marmalade.

The recipe calls for large scallops, but smaller ones would be delicious in a green salad.

In the absence of a commercial stove-top smoker, we suggest making a temporary one at home. (See the note in the sidebar on the next page.) You can smoke shrimp or chicken breasts this way as well.

FOR THE TOMATO-AND-ONION MARMALADE

- 1 cup red wine vinegar
- 1 cup light brown sugar, packed
- 1 tablespoon olive oil, not extra-virgin
- 2 cups finely julienned Vidalia onions or other sweet onions, about ⅛ inch by 1½ inches
- ½ teaspoon tomato paste
- 2 cups peeled and chopped Creole tomatoes or other vine-ripened tomatoes*

*Use the best tomatoes available since their taste is a dominant one in this dish.

1. In a heavy, nonreactive 3-quart saucepan, heat together the vinegar and brown sugar over medium heat until the sugar dissolves and the liquid reduces to 1 cup, about 10 minutes, stirring occasionally.

2. Transfer the vinegar reduction to a small heat-proof bowl and set aside. Clean the saucepan.

3. In the cleaned saucepan, heat the olive oil over medium heat until hot, one to two minutes. Add the onions, reduce heat to low, and cook until the onions are soft but not yet browning, about five minutes, stirring frequently.

4. Add the tomato paste, stirring to evenly blend it into the onions. Cook for three minutes, stirring constantly.

5. Add the tomatoes, stirring well. Cook for five minutes, stirring occasionally.

6. Stir in the reserved vinegar reduction and cook until the marmalade is thick enough to leave a distinct track on the back of a spoon when you draw a finger through it, about 35 minutes, stirring occasionally. Remove from heat.

NOTE

The marmalade may be prepared a day ahead and kept refrigerated.

ADVANCE STEPS

The ingredients list includes 1½ cups of hickory chips. Before smoking the scallops, soak the chips in water for at least four hours or according to package directions. Drain them just before using, leaving them dripping wet.

SPECIAL EQUIPMENT

- A heavy, nonreactive* 3-quart saucepan
- A small heat-proof bowl

*See Using Nonreactive Cookware, page 419.

After allowing the marmalade to cool, refrigerate it in a covered glass or ceramic container until well chilled, about three hours or until ready to serve. The marmalade will thicken more as it chills but it will still be fairly thin.

FOR FINISHING THE DISH

1½	cups fine hickory chips
18	(2¼ to 2½ pounds) jumbo sea scallops, well rinsed, with the small, tough muscle on the side of each removed
¼	cup plus 2 tablespoons extra-virgin olive oil
½	teaspoon kosher salt
¼	teaspoon freshly ground black pepper
	non-stick vegetable spray, if using a homemade smoker
	radish sprouts or baby salad greens, for garnish

1. To begin, soak the hickory chips in water according to the directions in Advance Steps, opposite.

2. Place the scallops in a large mixing bowl. Add the olive oil, kosher salt and pepper. Mix with your hands or a spoon to coat all surfaces of the scallops well with the seasoned oil. Cover and refrigerate until well chilled, at least one and a half hours, so the centers of the scallops are cold when put into the smoker.

3. Place the smoker on the stove top. Scatter the wet hickory chips evenly over the bottom of the space designed to hold the chips, but don't turn the burner on yet.

4. If using a store-bought smoker, follow the manufacturer's directions and smoke the scallops until they are barely done, about 13 minutes over medium heat. Then proceed to Step 8 below.

5. If using a temporary homemade smoker, spray the perforated or cooling rack with non-stick vegetable spray and return the rack to the smoker.

6. Transfer the chilled scallops from the refrigerator to the rack in the smoker. Be sure the food is at the opposite end of the smoker from the hickory chips.

7. Next, completely seal the scallops inside the roasting pan with heavy-duty aluminum foil, and smoke the scallops over high heat on the stove top for 11 minutes.

8. After the prescribed smoking time has been reached, leave the smoker over high heat while you remove the lid or foil high enough to remove a scallop. (This must be done very carefully to prevent being burned by the steam.)

ADVANCE STEP

Step 2 of this section can be done early on the day of smoking.

SPECIAL EQUIPMENT

• A stove-top smoker*

*See below.

A NOTE ABOUT STOVE-TOP SMOKERS

If you don't have a commercial stove-top smoker, it's easy to make a temporary one at home with materials you probably already have on hand—namely, a roasting pan, heavy-duty aluminum foil and a perforated rack or cooling rack to fit in the roasting pan to hold the food.

In our experience, a homemade smoker performs better than a store-bought one, because it lends the scallops an attractive "golden-smoked" hue. Instructions for making one are on page 416.

9. Promptly re-seal the smoker, then place the scallop on a cutting surface. Cut the scallop in half to assess its doneness at the center. If the scallop isn't quite done, return it to the smoker and smoke until the scallops are barely cooked through. (You may also place the underdone scallop in a moderate oven, un-covered, to finish cooking.)

10. Remove the smoker and scallops from heat. Very carefully remove the smoker lid or foil.

11. Let the scallops cool briefly, then cover and refrigerate them until they're well chilled, at least one and a half hours, before serving. They should be served the same day as they're smoked.

Serving Suggestions: Serve the chilled scallops either home-style on a large, chilled serving platter or on individual chilled dinner plates.

If a large serving platter is used, arrange the scallops around the edge of it and mound the marmalade in the center.

If individual plates are used, arrange three scallops in the center of each plate. Add a heaping tablespoon of marmalade to one side of the plate and a green gar-nish, such as radish sprouts or baby lettuce leaves, on the opposite side. 🐚

GUMBOS, SOUPS
AND
BISQUES

Gumbo Filé

Seafood and Okra Gumbo

Seafood and Okra Gumbo with Alligator Sausage

Golden Crab and Oyster-Mushroom Gumbo

Shrimp Bisque

Crab Bisque

Crab and Corn Soup

Crawfish-Boil Gazpacho

Crawfish Bisque

Oyster and Artichoke Bisque

Turtle Soup

Gumbo Filé

For 16 appetizer servings or 8 main-dish servings

Traditionally, three general categories of gumbo could be found in Creole and Cajun cooking. *Gombo maigre* is meatless. *Gombo févi* contains okra. And *gombo filé* is thickened, not with a roux, but with filé—that is, sassafras leaves, dried and ground to a powder.

Filé is a contribution of the Native American tribes who settled the region around New Orleans. (The word *fil* is French for "string," and filé means "stringy," a reference to the threads the sassafras powder can form.)

It is best to buy filé in very small quantities and use it as soon as possible. Also, it is important to use very fresh filé, and to add it at the end of the cooking process, since it becomes unstable; that is, it breaks down if it is returned to high heat after being incorporated into the liquid.

This is a simple gumbo made with an unusual variety of meats and seafood—chicken, bacon or ham, oysters or other shellfish. As gumbos go, it is relatively quick to prepare, and has the distinctively earthy flavors that make it an archetypal Louisiana dish.

Gumbo usually is served over white, long-grain rice and can be offered as an appetizer or a complete meal with nothing more than saltine crackers and perhaps pepper sauce.

¼	cup vegetable oil
1	chicken, 2½ to 3 pounds, boned, skinned and meat diced into ¾-inch pieces
5	ounces lean thick-slab bacon, such as applewood-smoked bacon, cut into ¼-inch squares
3	cups chopped yellow onions
2	teaspoons kosher salt, plus to taste
1½	teaspoons freshly ground black pepper, plus to taste
1	teaspoon dried thyme leaves
½	teaspoon crushed red pepper
2	tablespoons all-purpose flour
1	quart oyster liquor*
2	quarts seafood stock**
2	cups chopped mustard green leaves
	water for blanching mustard greens
1	pint shucked oysters, chopped coarse
2½	tablespoons fresh filé powder***
	cooked long-grain white rice, optional, for serving
	hot or mild pepper sauce, for the table
	saltine crackers or crusty French bread, for the table

*If a sufficient amount of oyster liquor is not available, see Notes, right.
**A high-quality, low-sodium store-bought seafood stock may be used, although freshly made stock is preferred.
***If this ingredient is difficult to find where you live, see Ingredient Sources on page 424.

NOTES

If 1 quart of oyster liquor is not available, use the liquor drained from the oysters used in this recipe (which should amount to about ¾ cup liquid), and make up the difference with additional seafood stock. If using seafood stock for most of the 1 quart of oyster liquor, increase the amount of chopped oysters used in the recipe by 1 to 2 cups.

The gumbo can be prepared a day or two ahead, but the filé should be added after the gumbo has been reheated for serving.

ADVANCE STEP

Prepare the recipe for seafood stock on page 394.

SPECIAL EQUIPMENT

- A heavy 8-quart stockpot or Dutch oven
- A long-handled metal whisk
- A wooden spoon

1. In a heavy 8-quart stockpot, heat the oil over high heat until just short of smoking, about two minutes. Add the chicken and cook until lightly browned, about one minute, whisking or stirring constantly with a wooden spoon. Add the bacon and cook just until some of the fat is rendered out, about one minute, stirring and scraping the bottom of the pan with the wooden spoon.

2. Add the onions, kosher salt, black pepper, thyme and crushed red pepper to the pan, stirring well. Sprinkle the flour over the mixture. Cook two minutes, stirring and scraping the pan bottom often to prevent scorching. The flour will lightly brown during this process.

3. Stir in the 1 quart oyster liquor and cook one minute. Add the 2 quarts seafood stock and bring to a boil. Reduce heat and simmer 15 minutes, stirring occasionally.

4. While the gumbo is simmering, blanch the mustard greens in boiling water for five minutes; drain and squeeze dry. Once the gumbo has simmered 15 minutes, add the mustard greens to the pan and cook 15 minutes.

5. Add the oysters and continue cooking five minutes more. Season to taste with more kosher salt and pepper. Remove from heat.

    Serving Suggestions: If you're serving the gumbo immediately, whisk in the filé or offer it in a small bowl at the table for people to add it, pinch by pinch, to their taste.

    If you're making the gumbo ahead, do not add the filé to the gumbo at this time. Instead, let the gumbo cool, then refrigerate it in a covered container. Just before serving, reheat it until all ingredients are just hot so the oysters don't overcook. At the last moment, whisk in the filé or pass it at the table.

    Serve the gumbo in heated cups or soup bowls. If rice is to be eaten with it, either add it to the bowls or pass the rice at the table along with pepper sauce and saltine crackers or French bread. 🐚

Seafood and Okra Gumbo

For 24 appetizer servings or 12 main-dish servings

The chances of two Louisiana cooks coming up with gumbos that are exactly alike are about the same as the New Orleans Saints football team winning two Super Bowls in succession. Gumbo, which can be light as broth or thick as stew, is the quintessential dish of both Creole and Cajun cooking. It dates back more than 200 years, from the time Africans first began to appear in New Orleans and Southwest Louisiana's Cajun country. The word itself comes from *quingombó*, a west-African word for okra.

But okra is just the beginning of a very long list of possible ingredient combinations in a single gumbo. Almost any meat or seafood could conceivably be found, although the ones most often used are shrimp, crab, oysters, crawfish, chicken, turkey, pork sausages and ham, alone or in various combinations. During the days when meat was not eaten during the period of Lent, as Easter Sunday approached, New Orleans Roman Catholics came up with *gombo aux herbes* ("gumbo z' herbes" in the old Creole dialect), made with little more than a variety of torn greens and seasonings.

Traditionally, gumbos were thickened with either *roux* (flour browned in lard or oil) or *filé* (ground sassafras leaves). This one takes a different path and uses both. The main ingredients, however, are the classic combination of oysters, shrimp and crab.

2	pounds yellow onions, chopped
2	pounds green sweet peppers, chopped
1	pound red sweet peppers, chopped
3	celery stalks, chopped
¾	pound fresh okra, sliced in half-inch rounds
1	cup fresh plum tomatoes, chopped
2	tablespoons minced garlic
1	cup vegetable oil
1	cup all-purpose flour
6	quarts seafood stock, divided
3	tablespoons dried thyme leaves
2	tablespoons dried basil leaves
2	tablespoons dried oregano leaves
1	tablespoon chili powder
2	teaspoons kosher salt
2	teaspoons sweet paprika
1½	teaspoons freshly ground black pepper
1	teaspoon crushed red pepper
4	whole small bay leaves
3	cups coarsely chopped fresh oysters
1½	cups crab claw meat
1	cup peeled and chopped medium shrimp
3	tablespoons fresh filé powder*

NOTES

The color of the roux in this recipe is keyed to the color chart on page 415.

It's best to buy filé in very small quantities and use it as soon as possible. Also, it is important to use very fresh filé, and to add it at the end of the cooking process.

The gumbo can be prepared a day or two ahead, but the filé should be added after the gumbo has been reheated for serving. Filé becomes unstable; that is, it breaks down when it's returned to high heat if it has already been incorporated into the liquid.

ADVANCE STEP

Prepare the recipe for seafood stock on page 394.

cooked long-grain white rice, for serving
hot or mild pepper sauce, for the table
saltine crackers or crusty French bread, for the table

*If this ingredient is difficult to find where you live, see Ingredient Sources on page 424.

SPECIAL EQUIPMENT
• A heavy 19-quart stockpot or Dutch oven
• A long-handled metal whisk
• A wooden spoon

1. In a large mixing bowl, combine the onions, green and red sweet peppers, celery, okra, tomatoes and garlic. Set aside.

2. In a heavy 12-quart stockpot, heat the oil over medium-high heat until hot, about four minutes. Very slowly (so you won't burn yourself) add the flour, whisking constantly and thoroughly with a long-handled metal whisk until all the flour has been added and the mixture is smooth.

3. Reduce the heat to medium-low. Continue cooking the roux, whisking constantly so it doesn't scorch, until it turns a dark chocolate brown, about four minutes.

4. With a wooden spoon promptly stir in the reserved vegetable mixture—the onions, peppers, celery, etc.—and cook until the vegetables are soft, about 15 minutes, stirring almost constantly.

5. Add 1 quart of stock to the roux mixture, whisking thoroughly until all the roux dissolves and blends into the liquid. Remove from heat momentarily.

6. In a small mixing bowl, thoroughly combine the thyme, basil, oregano, chili powder, kosher salt, paprika, black pepper, crushed red pepper and bay leaves.

7. Stir this seasoning mixture into the roux mixture containing the 1 quart of stock. Gradually add the remaining 5 quarts of stock, stirring constantly.

8. Bring the gumbo to a boil, then reduce the heat and simmer for one and a half hours, stirring occasionally and skimming any fat that rises to the surface. By the end of the cooking time the gumbo should have thickened to the consistency of cream.

9. Taste and adjust the seasonings to your liking.

   If you're making the gumbo ahead, let it cool at this point, then cover and refrigerate it until it is time to reheat and proceed with the recipe.

10. Next, thoroughly stir in the oysters, crabmeat and shrimp. Cook the shellfish until they are just done, about 10 minutes, stirring occasionally. Remove from heat and serve.

    Serving Suggestions: Immediately before serving the gumbo, whisk in the filé. Ladle the gumbo into heated cups or soup bowls over rice, or pass the rice at the table, along with pepper sauce and saltine crackers or French bread. 🐚

Seafood and Okra Gumbo with Alligator Sausage

For 14 appetizer servings or 7 main-dish servings

In the world of gumbos, there are few diehard rules. The only inviolable one is that the gumbo taste good. While this one does bow to tradition with okra as an ingredient, it also strays from the traditional path in calling for alligator sausage (although smoked pork sausages can be substituted).

Alligators, which are legal game in Louisiana, are harvested for their hides as well as their meat. The tail is the edible part, and its subtle flavor might be compared to white meat of chicken or white veal.

1	cup vegetable oil
1	cup all-purpose flour
¼	pound (1 stick) unsalted butter
4	tablespoons minced fresh garlic
4	cups chopped onions
2	cups chopped green sweet peppers
1½	cups sliced celery
3	whole bay leaves
2	cups chopped fresh ripe tomatoes
1	pound alligator sausage, cut in half-inch slices*
3	tablespoons Creole seasoning
1	rounded tablespoon minced fresh thyme leaves
10	cups crab stock, preferred, or seafood stock**
1	tablespoon minced fresh Italian (flat-leaf) parsley leaves
2	cups trimmed and sliced okra, fresh (preferred) or frozen
¼	cup worcestershire sauce, optional
1½	tablespoons Crystal brand pepper sauce, or other relatively mild pepper sauce
1	tablespoon kosher salt, plus to taste
½	teaspoon freshly ground black pepper, plus to taste
1	pound medium shrimp, peeled with tails removed
½	pound crab claw meat, picked through
¾	pound shucked oysters, not drained
	thinly sliced green onions (green parts only), for garnish
	cooked long-grain white rice, for serving
	hot or mild pepper sauce, for the table
	saltine crackers or crusty French bread, for the table

*If this ingredient is difficult to find where you live, see Ingredient Sources on page 424. Also, andouille or other smoked pork sausage may be substituted for the alligator sausage. Also see Ingredient Sources for andouille.
**A high-quality, low-sodium, store-bought seafood stock may be used, although freshly made stock is preferred.

NOTE

This gumbo is especially good when made a day ahead to allow the flavors to marry.

The color of the roux in this recipe is keyed to the color chart on page 415.

ADVANCE STEPS

Prepare the following recipes:

- Creole seasoning on page 385
- Crab stock (preferred) on page 391 or seafood stock on page 394

SPECIAL EQUIPMENT

- A heavy 10-inch skillet
- A long-handled metal whisk or wooden spoon
- A heavy 8-quart saucepan or Dutch oven

1. For the roux, in a heavy 10-inch skillet combine the oil and flour. Place the skillet over medium-high heat and cook for three minutes, mixing constantly and thoroughly with a long-handled metal whisk or a wooden spoon until smooth.

2. Reduce heat to medium, and continue cooking the roux, whisking or stirring constantly so it doesn't scorch, until it turns a peanut-butter brown, about nine minutes. Remove from heat and continue whisking constantly until the roux stops getting darker, about three minutes. Set aside.

3. In a heavy 8-quart saucepan, melt the butter over medium heat. Add the garlic and cook until it just starts to turn golden brown (the color of a pumpkin-pie filling), about one minute, stirring constantly. Stir in the onions, sweet peppers, celery, and bay leaves and cook and stir for one minute.

4. Add the tomatoes, sausage, Creole seasoning, and thyme to the pan, stirring well. Cook until all the vegetables are tender, about five minutes, occasionally stirring and scraping the pan bottom clean.

5. Stir in the stock and parsley, mixing well, and bring to a boil over high heat. Reduce the heat and simmer for 15 minutes.

6. Gradually add the reserved roux, stirring constantly until all the roux is thoroughly blended in.

7. Stir in the okra, worcestershire, the 1½ tablespoons mildly hot pepper sauce, 1 tablespoon kosher salt, and ½ teaspoon pepper. Simmer for 25 minutes, stirring occasionally.

   If you're making the gumbo ahead, which is preferable, let it cool at this point, then cover and refrigerate it until it is time to reheat and proceed with the recipe.

8. Next, stir in the shrimp and crabmeat and let the shrimp cook about half way, about two minutes. Do not overcook the shrimp.

9. Add the oysters and bring to a boil, skimming any foam. Continue cooking just until the oysters are plump and their edges curl, one to two minutes more. Remove from heat. Season the gumbo with more kosher salt and pepper if needed.

   Serving Suggestions: If prepared ahead, which is preferable, do not add more salt and pepper at this time. Instead, let the gumbo cool down and refrigerate in a covered container. Just before serving, reheat until all the ingredients are just hot so the seafood doesn't overcook, then season with more kosher salt and pepper if needed.

   If serving immediately, season the gumbo with more kosher salt and pepper to taste before dishing out.

   Serve the gumbo, garnished with a light sprinkle of green onions, in heated cups or bowls over rice, or pass the rice at the table, along with hot or mildly hot pepper sauce and saltine crackers or crusty French bread. 🐚

Golden Crab and Oyster-Mushroom Gumbo
with Shrimp-Potato Salad

For 16 appetizer servings or 8 main-dish servings

This gumbo is anything but traditional.

One difference is the inclusion of oyster mushrooms, which lend a slight oyster flavor to the gumbo. Another new wrinkle is found in the color of the roux, which is golden, rather than the more familiar deep brown.

The recipe's foundation is the crab stock, which acquires much of its sweetish seafood flavor from roasted gumbo crabs and crab claw meat.

The biggest difference of all is the shrimp-potato salad that pinch-hits for the much more traditional rice, although no law will be violated if you opt for either cooked long-grain white rice or our green-onion rice on page 344.

¾	cup vegetable oil
¼	cup olive oil
1¾	cups all-purpose flour
3	cups chopped onions
2	cups chopped celery
2	cups chopped green sweet peppers
1	tablespoon plus ½ teaspoon finely chopped fresh garlic
3	medium-size bay leaves
1	teaspoon dried thyme leaves
4	quarts crab stock
2	cups canned, drained Roma tomatoes
4	cups (8 ounces) coarsely chopped oyster mushrooms
2	tablespoons kosher salt, plus to taste
1	tablespoon fresh filé* powder
1	teaspoon freshly ground black pepper
1	pound fresh crab claw meat, picked through**

*If this ingredient is difficult to find where you live, see Ingredient Sources on page 424.
**If serving the gumbo as a main-dish, stir in an additional 1 pound of fresh crabmeat (preferably jumbo lump) to the gumbo just before serving.

1. To make the roux, heat together the vegetable and olive oils in a heavy 5-quart saucepan over medium-high heat until just short of smoking, 10 to 15 minutes. (The time will depend on the gauge of the pan used.)

2. Very slowly, so you don't burn yourself, add the flour, whisking or stirring constantly and thoroughly with a whisk or wooden spoon until all the flour has been added and the mixture is smooth.

NOTES

For a more traditional gumbo, use rice rather than shrimp-potato salad.

The color of the roux in this recipe is keyed to the color chart on page 415.

It is important to use very fresh filé and to add it near the end of the cooking process. The gumbo may be prepared a day ahead, but the filé should be added after the gumbo has been reheated for serving. Filé becomes unstable and breaks down when it's returned to high heat if it has already been incorporated into the liquid.

ADVANCE STEPS

Prepare the recipes for:
• Crab stock on page 391
If using shrimp-potato salad:
• Creole seasoning on page 385
• Basic mayonnaise on page 369
If using green-onion rice:
• the recipe on page 344

3. Reduce heat to medium-low and continue cooking the roux, whisking constantly so it doesn't scorch, until the roux turns golden, 15 to 30 minutes depending on the pan gauge. Remove pan from heat and continue whisking constantly until the roux stops getting darker, about five minutes.

4. Once the roux has cooled enough for some of the oil to collect on the surface, five to 10 minutes, tilt the pan and carefully spoon 3 tablespoons of this hot oil into a heavy 8-quart saucepan. Heat the oil over high heat if not already very hot. Stir in the onions, celery, sweet peppers, garlic, bay leaves, and thyme, blending well. Cook over high heat until vegetables start to get tender, about four minutes.

5. Gradually add the reserved roux to the onion mixture, stirring constantly with a wooden spoon until it's thoroughly blended in. Gradually add the crab stock, stirring until the roux completely dissolves in the stock. Bring to a boil over high heat, whisking frequently.

6. Add the tomatoes and oyster mushrooms and cook five minutes, skimming the foam from the surface as the mixture returns to a boil. Add 2 tablespoons kosher salt and pepper. Reduce heat to medium.

    If the gumbo is to be served a few minutes after it's prepared, now whisk in the filé powder.

    If preparing the gumbo a day ahead, do not add the filé to the gumbo at this time. (The filé will be whisked in just before serving the gumbo.)

7. Cook the gumbo over medium heat for five minutes, continuing to stir the gumbo and skim any foam.

8. Stir in the crab claw meat and reduce heat, if needed, to maintain a slow simmer. Continue cooking 15 minutes more. Remove from heat.

    Serving Suggestions: If the gumbo is to be served a few minutes after it's prepared, season it, if needed, with more kosher salt.

    If the gumbo is prepared a day ahead, let it cool, then cover and refrigerate.

    Just before serving, reheat until all ingredients are just hot so the crab doesn't overcook. At the last moment, whisk in the filé and season with more salt, if needed.

    (See additional serving suggestions at the end of the shrimp-potato salad recipe on the next page.)

SPECIAL EQUIPMENT
- A heavy 5-quart saucepan or Dutch oven
- A long-handled metal whisk or wooden spoon
- A heavy 8-quart saucepan or Dutch oven

FOR THE SHRIMP-POTATO SALAD

1	large (about 1 pound) Idaho potato, peeled and cut in ¼-inch cubes
	water for blanching potatoes
4	tablespoons unsalted butter
8	ounces medium shrimp, peeled and coarsely chopped (or use whole small or miniature shrimp)
1	tablespoon Creole seasoning
½	cup finely chopped red onions
½	cup finely chopped celery
2	tablespoons finely chopped fresh Italian (flat-leaf) parsley leaves
¼	cup Creole mustard*
¼	cup mayonnaise, preferably homemade
2 to 3	tablespoons finely chopped green onions, for garnish

*If this ingredient is difficult to find where you live, see Ingredient Sources on page 424.

1. In a large pan of boiling water, blanch the potato cubes until just tender, about five minutes. Drain and spread on a cookie sheet or platter. Refrigerate, uncovered, until no longer steaming hot, about 15 minutes.

2. In a heavy 10-inch skillet, melt the butter over medium-high heat. Add the shrimp and sprinkle over it the Creole seasoning. Cook until the shrimp are just cooked through, about two minutes, stirring frequently.

3. Stir in the red onions and celery and continue cooking about 30 seconds more. Remove from heat.

4. Transfer the potato cubes to a large mixing bowl, and add the cooked shrimp, parsley, Creole mustard, and mayonnaise, mixing well. Serve immediately.

Serving Suggestions: For each appetizer serving, allow 1 cup of gumbo in a heated soup bowl. Mold 3 to 4 tablespoons of shrimp-potato salad or rice in a ¼-cup measuring cup and turn out in the center of the gumbo.

For each main-dish serving, allow twice the amount of both the gumbo and potato salad or rice in a large heated soup bowl.

Garnish with a small sprinkle of chopped green onions. 🐚

Shrimp Bisque

For 8 appetizer servings or 5 main-dish servings

This hearty New Orleans-style bisque differs from the classic French ones in using rice and much less cream. What the two versions have in common is a concentrated flavor stemming from the use of a rich stock—in this case a strained crab stock. The stock recipe is one of the many in this cookbook book that uses crushed seafood shells to get as much of their flavor as possible into the finished dish, always a priority of both Creole and Cajun cooks.

2	pounds large shrimp with heads and tails still on
¼	pound (1 stick) unsalted butter
2	tablespoons minced fresh garlic
5	cups chopped onions
1½	cups sliced celery
1	cup chopped Creole* tomatoes
2	tablespoons tomato paste
1	tablespoon minced fresh thyme leaves
4	small bay leaves
⅓	cup all-purpose flour
8	cups crab stock**
2	teaspoons kosher salt
2	tablespoons heavy cream
½	cup good-quality brandy, optional but preferred
2	tablespoons Dry Sack or other good-quality, medium-dry sherry, optional but preferred
	cooked long-grain white rice, optional
	very finely sliced chives or green onions, green parts only, for garnish
	warm French bread, for the table

*South Louisiana's Creole tomatoes are preferred for this recipe, although other good, peak-of-season regional varieties can be used also.
**Crab stock is preferred, but fish fumet or vegetable stock also may be used.

ADVANCE STEP

Prepare the crab stock on page 391.

SPECIAL EQUIPMENT

- A heavy, nonreactive* 5½-quart Dutch oven or saucepan
- A wooden spoon
- A very fine mesh strainer (the finer the better) or a strainer lined with several layers of cheesecloth
- A sturdy mixing spoon

*See Using Nonreactive Cookware, page 419.

1. Peel and devein the shrimp and remove the heads. Set aside the shells and heads at room temperature. Cover and refrigerate the shrimp.

2. In a heavy, nonreactive 5½-quart Dutch oven, melt the butter over medium-high heat. Add the garlic and cook until it barely starts to brown, about one minute, scraping the pan bottom constantly with a wooden spoon.

3. Add the onions and celery and cook until the vegetables just start to get soft, about three minutes, stirring occasionally.

4. Add the reserved shrimp shells and heads, stirring well. Cook until the heads turn red and the mixture gets juicy, about six minutes. During this cooking

time, spend about one minute crushing the shells and heads with the side of the wooden spoon to release more shrimp flavor into the mixture.

5. Add the tomatoes, tomato paste and thyme, blending well. Add the bay leaves and cook for three minutes, stirring occasionally.

6. Sprinkle the flour over the mixture, stirring until well blended. Cook for three minutes, scraping the pan bottom and the side of the pan almost constantly to keep the mixture from scorching.

7. Gradually add the crab stock, stirring constantly to blend well. Bring the mixture to a simmer over high heat. Reduce the heat and slowly simmer for 45 minutes, stirring occasionally and skimming any foam as it develops. Remove from heat.

8. Strain the mixture through a very fine mesh strainer or through several layers of cheesecloth, using the back of a sturdy spoon to force as much liquid through as possible.

9. Wash the pan used for the bisque and return the strained bisque to the pan. Bring to a boil over high heat.

10. Stir in the reserved shrimp. Return the bisque to a boil, then reduce the heat and simmer just until the shrimp are cooked through, about three minutes, skimming any foam from the surface. Remove from heat.

11. Stir in the kosher salt and cream and, if using, the brandy and sherry. Serve immediately.

    Serving Suggestions: If using as a main course, ladle 1½ cups bisque into each heated serving bowl.

    If using as an appetizer, use 1 cup of bisque.

    If using rice, mound about 2 teaspoons cooked rice in the center of the bowl as a main course, and 1 teaspoon as an appetizer.

    Either way, garnish with chives or green onions. Pass the bread at the table. 🐚

Crab Bisque with Cauliflower and Brie

For 12 appetizer servings or 6 main-dish servings

If this bisque were prepared in the classic French style, all of the crabmeat would be puréed and blended with the cream. However, the use of whole crabmeat lumps from the backfin as a garnish in this recipe bolsters the crab flavor, while the pieces of claw meat lend their own sweetish taste to the soup. The bisque has a consistency much like a thick potato cream soup and all the ingredients come together synergistically to create an outstanding dish.

4	tablespoons unsalted butter
1½	teaspoons minced garlic
2½	cups coarsely chopped yellow onions
½	cup coarsely sliced celery
4½	cups (4 ounces) 1¼-inch cubes of French bread with crust on
5½	cups crab stock, divided
1	head cauliflower (about 2¼ pounds), cored and cut into florets about 2 inches long and 2 inches wide at the fullest part
1	tablespoon kosher salt
⅛	teaspoon freshly ground black pepper
½	cup heavy cream
2¼	teaspoons minced fresh thyme leaves
1½	teaspoons packed chopped parsley
4	ounces Brie, rim trimmed, cheese cut into ½-inch cubes
8	ounces crab claw meat, picked through
1	pound jumbo lump crabmeat, for garnish
2	tablespoons finely sliced chives, for garnish

NOTES

The bisque should not be made more than one day ahead to make sure the crabmeat is at its best.

If the bisque is made ahead, re-heat it for serving by bringing it to a strong boil over medium heat, stirring frequently to keep it from scorching.

The texture comes out better if you purée the soup in a blender, not a food processor.

ADVANCE STEP

Prepare the crab stock recipe on page 391.

SPECIAL EQUIPMENT

- A heavy 6-quart saucepan
- A blender (preferred) or a food processor

1. In a heavy 6-quart saucepan, melt the butter over medium-high heat. Add the garlic and cook just until it starts to color, about one minute, stirring constantly. Add the onions and celery and cook until the vegetables are very soft and just starting to brown, about seven minutes, stirring occasionally.

2. Add the bread to the pan and cook for one minute. Stir in 1 cup crab stock and cook until the bread cubes are pasty and pick up all the flavors in the pan, about one minute, stirring constantly. Gradually add 4½ cups more of crab stock, stirring well. Stir in the cauliflower, kosher salt and pepper.

3. Bring the soup to a rolling boil, then reduce heat and slowly simmer until cauliflower is tender and bread is mushy, about 15 minutes, stirring occasionally and skimming as you would a stock. Remove from heat, and while still hot, process the soup in a blender (in batches if necessary) to a smooth purée. Blend in the cream, then the thyme and parsley.

4. Return the soup to the same saucepan, and bring to a simmer over high heat. Stir in the cheese. Reduce the heat and slowly simmer until all the cheese cubes melt, six to seven minutes, stirring and scraping the pan bottom almost constantly so the soup doesn't scorch. Add the crab claw meat, stirring well. Continue slowly simmering about two minutes more, scraping pan bottom as needed. Remove from heat and serve immediately.

Serving Suggestions: If this is a main course, allow 1½ cups of soup in each heated soup bowl. Garnish the center of each serving with a portion (about ½ cup loosely packed) of jumbo lump crabmeat and 1 teaspoon of chives. If this is an appetizer, serve half the amount in heated cups. 🐚

Crab and Corn Soup

For 12 to 16 appetizer servings or 6 to 8 main-dish servings

Over the years, crab and corn soup has come to join the list of classic Creole dishes. The reasons are evident in the grand flavor combination of sweet corn and crabmeat, not to mention the silky richness of the cream and butter.

This recipe calls for the crab's claw meat, which has its own sweet taste.

The soup would be an excellent appetizer for a special-occasion dinner, although it can be enjoyed more simply alongside a sandwich.

3	ears fresh sweet corn, still in the husks
1	crab stock recipe*
1¼	cups finely chopped celery
1	cup finely chopped yellow onions
1	cup finely chopped leeks (white part only)
¾	cup finely chopped red sweet peppers
¾	cup finely chopped green sweet peppers
½	pound (2 sticks) unsalted butter
2	cups all-purpose flour
1½	tablespoons kosher salt
2	teaspoons freshly ground black pepper
½	teaspoon dried thyme leaves
¼	teaspoon onion powder
¼	teaspoon garlic powder
1	bay leaf
2	cups heavy cream
1	tablespoon mild-flavored Louisiana pepper sauce, such as Crystal brand
8	ounces crab claw meat, picked through
	green onions (green parts only), chopped very fine, for garnish.

*If the crab stock recipe yields less than 4 quarts, make up the difference with water.

NOTES

The color of the roux in this recipe is keyed to the color chart on page 415.

This soup is especially good when made a day ahead to allow the flavors to marry.

ADVANCE STEP

Prepare the crab stock recipe on page 391.

SPECIAL EQUIPMENT

- A heavy 6-quart saucepan or Dutch oven
- A heavy 3-quart saucepan
- A long-handled metal whisk

1. Preheat the oven to 325°F.

2. Soak the ears of corn, in their husks, in cool water for 30 minutes. Drain briefly.

3. Roast the ears, still in their husks, in the hot oven, uncovered, for 20 minutes.

4. Remove the corn from the oven and let sit at room temperature. When the ears are cool enough to work with, strip off the husks and silk from the ears, discarding husks and silk.

5. Cut the corn kernels from the cobs.

6. Refrigerate the kernels and place the cobs in a heavy 6-quart saucepan with the stock. Bring the stock to a simmer, then slowly simmer for one hour, skimming any foam from the surface as it develops.

7. Meanwhile, in a medium-size mixing bowl, combine the celery, onions, leeks, and the red and green sweet peppers, and set aside.

8. For the roux, in a heavy 3-quart saucepan melt the butter over medium heat. Gradually add the flour to the butter, whisking constantly with a long-handled metal whisk until all the flour has been added and the mixture is smooth. Whisking constantly to prevent scorching, continue cooking the roux until it turns "blond" (pale golden), three to four minutes.

9. Promptly add the reserved chopped celery, onions, leeks and sweet peppers to the roux, whisking or stirring with a large spoon until the vegetables and the roux are thoroughly mixed.

10. Reduce the heat to medium-low and, stirring constantly, continue cooking the roux for 5 minutes. Remove the saucepan from the heat and let the roux cool for 10 minutes, stirring occasionally.

11. Once the stock has simmered for one hour, remove and discard the corn cobs. With the hot stock still simmering, add the roux to the stock, one spoonful at a time, stirring until the roux completely dissolves into the stock before adding more.

12. Bring the soup to a boil, then reduce the heat to maintain a slow simmer. Stir in the reserved corn kernels and the salt, pepper, thyme, onion powder, garlic powder and bay leaf. Slowly simmer for one hour, stirring and scraping the pan bottom as needed so the soup doesn't scorch.

13. When the simmer is complete, gradually add the cream, stirring until well blended. Add the pepper sauce and crabmeat.

14. If the soup is too thick, thin it with crab stock or water. Taste and adjust seasonings as desired.

    Serving Suggestion: Serve in warm cups or bowls, garnished with a sprinkle of chopped green onions. If made ahead, reheat gently. 🐚

(PICTURED ON THE FOLLOWING PAGE)

Crawfish-Boil Gazpacho with Corn-Chive Cream

For 5 main-dish servings or 10 appetizer servings

The term "crawfish boil" has a double meaning in South Louisiana. In one connotation, it refers to a gathering of crawfish lovers to cook and eat boiled crawfish, as New Englanders do at clambakes.

The word also connotes the combination of spices and seasonings used in boiling crawfish (or crabs or shrimp), such as those in the list of ingredients below to season the gazpacho. In this gazpacho recipe the mixture of crawfish-boil spices is toasted to intensify the chilled soup's flavors.

Topped with a dollop of chilled corn-chive cream, it can be a soothing tonic on a hot summer's day.

FOR THE GAZPACHO

1	teaspoon unsalted butter
1	pound cooked and peeled crawfish tails,* rinsed and drained
2½	teaspoons kosher salt, divided
2	teaspoons freshly ground black pepper, divided
2	cups peeled and chopped Yukon Gold potatoes, preferred, or round red boiling potatoes
2	cups water, for cooking potatoes
1½	teaspoons ground allspice, divided
1½	teaspoons ground coriander, divided
1½	teaspoons dry mustard, divided
¼	teaspoon ground cayenne pepper
4	cups top-quality canned tomato juice
1¼	cups finely chopped red onions
1	cup finely chopped celery
1	cup finely chopped red sweet peppers
1	cup finely chopped yellow sweet peppers
1½	cups seeded and chopped Creole** tomatoes
1	teaspoon minced fresh garlic
¼	cup good-quality sherry vinegar
2	tablespoons finely sliced fresh basil leaves
1	tablespoon finely sliced fresh Italian (flat-leaf) parsley leaves

*If this ingredient is difficult to find where you live, see Ingredient Sources on page 424.
**South Louisiana's Creole tomatoes are preferred for this recipe, although other good, peak-of-season regional varieties can be used.

NOTE

This soup tastes best on the same day it is made, or no more than one day later. The corn-chive cream also may be prepared a day in advance.

SPECIAL EQUIPMENT

- A heavy 10-inch skillet
- A heavy 7-inch skillet
- A large, nonreactive* mixing bowl

*See Using Nonreactive Cookware, page 419.

1. Melt the butter in a heavy 10-inch skillet over high heat. Add the crawfish tails and ½ teaspoon each of kosher salt and black pepper. Sauté until heated through, two to three minutes.

2. Remove the skillet from heat and spread the crawfish on a heat-proof plate. Refrigerate until cool, about 25 minutes.

3. In a small saucepan, combine the potatoes and water. Add 1 teaspoon each of kosher salt, allspice, coriander and dry mustard, ½ teaspoon black pepper and the cayenne pepper. Bring the mixture to a boil over high heat, then reduce the heat and simmer until the potatoes are just cooked through, about four minutes. Remove from heat and drain but do not rinse. Spread the potatoes on a plate and refrigerate until cool, about 15 minutes.

4. Place ½ teaspoon each of allspice, coriander and dry mustard in a dry, heavy 7-inch skillet and toast the spices over high heat until they just begin to smoke, about one minute, stirring occasionally. Remove from heat and promptly transfer to a small heat-proof bowl to cool at room temperature.

5. In a blender, combine the tomato juice with 2 tablespoons each of the onions, celery, red sweet peppers and yellow sweet peppers. Add the tomatoes, garlic, the cooled toasted spices, and 1 teaspoon each kosher salt and black pepper. Purée the mixture until smooth.

6. Transfer the purée to a large, nonreactive mixing bowl and add the remaining onions, celery, red and yellow sweet peppers, then the vinegar, crawfish, potatoes, basil and parsley. Cover and refrigerate until well chilled, at least two hours, before serving.

7. While the gazpacho is chilling, prepare the corn-chive cream.

FOR THE CORN-CHIVE CREAM AND TO SERVE

- ½ cup crème fraîche or sour cream
- ¼ cup cooked corn kernels, preferably fresh
- 1 tablespoon very finely sliced fresh chives
- ¼ teaspoon kosher salt
- ¼ teaspoon freshly ground white pepper
    optional garnishes: pickled okra, green beans, asparagus spears, raw cucumber spears

In a small mixing bowl, thoroughly mix together the crème fraîche, corn, chives, kosher salt and white pepper. Cover and refrigerate until ready to serve the soup.

Serving Suggestion: Serve the gazpacho in chilled cups or bowls with a portion of the corn-chive cream spooned in the center of each serving. If desired, add one or more of the optional garnishes (pickled okra, green beans, asparagus spears and raw cucumber spears). 🐚

Crawfish Bisque

For 12 main-dish servings

A Creole purist might protest the presence of cream in this otherwise traditional New Orleans crawfish bisque. But she might change her mind after a taste of its luxurious flavor and richness.

Tradition is certainly served in other aspects of this bisque recipe. It delivers the natural essence of crawfish. The seasonings are definitely robust. Adding to its attractions is the addition of stuffed body shells (the round shells between the head and the tail), which are filled with a spicy breadcrumb stuffing loaded with chopped tail meat.

This is a labor-intensive and time-consuming recipe. But the cook is rewarded with a dish that delivers just the balance of elegance and earthiness that's a hallmark of classic New Orleans cuisine.

Before beginning the recipe, you must purge some of the crawfish. (Instructions for the purging process are on page 35). This master recipe is divided into four parts. To complete all of them you'll need to purge and boil 7 pounds of live crawfish. Three pounds will be required in "For the spicy boiled crawfish," below. Four pounds are needed to make the crawfish stock in the section, "To finish the bisque and serve" on page 131.

Crawfish must be alive when placed in the boiling pot. Once they're purged, they're not likely to remain alive for more than a few minutes. This means the first batch of 3 pounds of live crawfish must be purged separately from the batch of 4 pounds.

FOR THE SPICY BOILED CRAWFISH

1	large onion, peeled and coarsely chopped
2	stalks celery, coarsely chopped
½	bulb fresh garlic
2	lemons, halved
¼	cup kosher salt
1	tablespoon Creole seasoning
1	teaspoon whole black peppercorns
½	teaspoon ground cayenne
2	tablespoons Zatarain's Liquid Boil seasoning*
10	cups water
50	large (about 3 pounds) purged live crawfish*

*If this ingredient is difficult to find where you live, see Ingredient Sources on page 424.

NOTES

To prepare the bisque, you'll need a little more than 2 pounds of store-bought boiled and peeled crawfish tails.

The recipe calls for stuffing and baking the crawfish's body shells. If you're using frozen shells, soak them in cool water for 30 minutes before stuffing to make them more pliable.

The boiling, preparation of the stuffing and final preparation of the bisque can be done a day or two ahead (its flavors actually will improve), but stuffing and baking the shells should not be done until just before serving.

ADVANCE STEPS

Prepare the recipes for:
• Creole seasoning on page 385
• Crab stock on page 391
• Clarified butter on page 355

❧ FOR THE SPICY BOILED CRAWFISH ☙

ADVANCE STEP

Just before preparing this recipe, purge the 50 (about 3 pounds) live crawfish. (See remarks, above left.)

1. In an 8-quart stockpot, combine the onions, celery, garlic, lemon halves, kosher salt, Creole seasoning, peppercorns, cayenne, crab-boil seasoning and water. Bring the liquid to a boil over high heat.

2. Reduce the heat and simmer, uncovered, for 10 minutes.

3. Add the 50 purged crawfish to the pot and immediately cover it. Return the liquid to a boil. Remove the stockpot from heat, uncover it, and let it sit for 10 minutes.

4. Strain the crawfish and other ingredients through a large strainer. Spread the strained mixture on a rimmed baking sheet. Refrigerate, uncovered, at least one hour or overnight. After an hour of chilling, loosely cover the baking sheet or transfer the crawfish and the rest of the strained mixture to a covered container. Return it to the refrigerator.

5. While the crawfish are chilling, prepare the stuffing.

FOR THE STUFFING

4	tablespoons unsalted butter
1	tablespoon minced fresh garlic
1	cup finely chopped onions
½	cup finely chopped celery
½	cup finely chopped green sweet peppers
1	tablespoon Creole seasoning
1	teaspoon finely chopped fresh thyme leaves
1	pound boiled and peeled crawfish tails,* coarsely chopped
1	cup crab stock
½	cup finely sliced green onions, mostly green parts
1	cup very fine, dry breadcrumbs
1	teaspoon kosher salt
¼	teaspoon ground black pepper

*If this ingredient is difficult to find where you live, see Ingredient Sources on page 424.

1. Melt the butter in a heavy 4-quart saucepan over medium-high heat. Add the garlic and sauté until it barely starts to brown, about one minute, stirring frequently.

2. Add the onions, celery and sweet peppers. Sauté the mixture until the onions are translucent, one to two minutes, stirring occasionally.

3. Add the Creole seasoning and thyme and cook for one minute. Add the peeled crawfish tails, stirring well, then stir in the crab stock and green onions.

4. Add the breadcrumbs, thoroughly mixing them in. Add the kosher salt and pepper and continue cooking for one minute more. Remove from heat.

5. Spread out the stuffing on a rimmed baking sheet and refrigerate uncovered for at least one hour. If the stuffing is made ahead, after an hour of chilling cover the baking sheet or transfer it to a covered container and return it to the refrigerator.

FOR THE STUFFED SHELLS

NOTES

For instructions on shelling craw-fish, see page 36.

1. First, separate the large round thorax shell (which forms the crawfish's main body cavity) of each spicy boiled crawfish from its tail by gently twisting off the tail and pulling it away from the thorax shell. Set the shells aside.

The recipe calls for stuffing 36 shells, for 12 servings. After stuffing those, you will probably have some stuffing and body shells left over. This provides the option of making and serving a few more than the 36 indicated in the recipe.

2. Peel the tails as follows: While holding the small end of each crawfish tail with one hand, use your other hand to peel away the ring of shell at the thicker end. Continue peeling away the rings of shell until you are close to the end of the tail, then squeeze the base of the shell, which should allow you to pull out the tail meat in one piece. Save any yellow-orange "fat" (which is actually the liver) that may be attached to the thick end of the tail. Refrigerate the tails and fat together in a covered container. (They will be added to the bisque itself in For finishing the bisque and serving, below.)

3. Next, prepare the shells for stuffing. Gently pull the section beneath each crawfish's round thorax shell (where the legs are attached to the thorax) away from the top part of the thorax shell. Discard the leg sections, but leave the head (with the eyes and antennae) attached to the thorax shell. Scoop out any yellow-orange fat you see in the thoracic cavity at the head end and add this to the tails and fat in the refrigerator. Now the shells are ready to be stuffed. (If preparing the bisque ahead, cover the shells loosely and refrigerate until ready to proceed with Step 4.)

4. Fill the shells with the chilled stuffing, packing them firmly. Cover and refrigerate the stuffed shells until time to bake for serving.

FOR FINISHING THE BISQUE AND SERVING

NOTE

Brandy is added to the bisque and flamed while it is cooking. For safety's sake, be sure to use a ladle to pour the brandy into the bisque as directed in the recipe. (Do not pour the brandy directly from the bottle, which can cause the bottle to explode.)

5	tablespoons clarified butter
4	pounds purged live crawfish
16	cups crab stock*, divided
¼	pound (1 stick) unsalted butter, plus butter to grease the roasting pan
1	tablespoon minced fresh garlic
2	cups finely chopped onions
1	cup finely chopped green sweet peppers
½	cup finely chopped celery
1	cup chopped fresh tomatoes
2	tablespoons tomato paste
1	cup good-quality brandy
1	tablespoon Creole seasoning

ADVANCE STEP

Just before preparing this recipe, purge the 4 pounds of live craw-fish needed to finish the bisque.

1½ cups all-purpose flour

    the reserved peeled crawfish tails from the stuffed-shells recipe above

1 pound boiled and peeled crawfish tails

1 tablespoon kosher salt

1 teaspoon finely chopped fresh thyme leaves

½ teaspoon freshly ground black pepper

2 cups heavy cream

½ cup good-quality dry sherry

    about 3 tablespoons good-quality white wine

    reserved stuffed crawfish shells, for serving (see Step 12, below)

*If necessary, add water to make 16 cups.

1. Begin making the crawfish stock by heating the 5 tablespoons clarified butter in a heavy 8-quart saucepan with a lid, over very high heat until very hot, two to three minutes. Slide the 4 pounds purged live crawfish carefully into the saucepan and quickly cover. Reduce heat to high and cook three minutes, then uncover.

2. Add 2 cups of the crab stock and cook for about 15 minutes. During this cooking time, and using a heavy-duty kitchen mallet or sturdy mixing spoon, firmly press the utensil down on each crawfish to crush its shell into the smallest bits you can. This will take roughly eight minutes to do and should produce a good, earthy crawfish aroma and a liquid that has a pleasant crawfish flavor, which is essential to ending up with a stock that tastes of crawfish essence. As you are crushing the crawfish, be careful not to slosh the hot liquid in the pan on you. Transfer the boiled and crushed crawfish to a heat-proof container and set aside.

3. Before proceeding with finishing the bisque, check to make sure nothing is near the stove that can catch fire while you're flaming the brandy in Step 5 below.

4. In a clean, heavy 8-quart saucepan, melt the ¼ pound butter over medium-high heat. Add the garlic and cook until it barely starts to color, about 30 seconds. Thoroughly stir in the onions, sweet peppers and celery. Cook one minute.

5. Add the tomatoes and tomato paste, stirring well. Bring the mixture to a bubbling hot stage, then place the brandy in a ladle, and pour the brandy from the ladle over the food. (Do not pour the brandy from the bottle.) Keep your face away from the saucepan as you carefully ignite the brandy with a long kitchen match or a butane gas lighter with a long neck. Cook a few seconds until the flame goes out.

6. Add the reserved 4 pounds boiled and crushed crawfish to the saucepan, stirring well. Cook and stir about seven minutes.

7. Add the Creole seasoning and cook and stir about 30 seconds. Sprinkle the flour over the mixture and cook two minutes, stirring thoroughly and constantly with a wooden spoon so the flour doesn't stick to the bottom of the saucepan.

8. Gradually add the remaining 14 cups crab stock, stirring constantly until all the stock is blended in. Bring to a boil, stirring occasionally. Reduce the heat and simmer, uncovered, for 45 minutes more, stirring occasionally. Remove from heat.

9. Let the mixture cool about five minutes, then in batches strain the liquid from the mixture through a coarse-mesh strainer or colander placed over a pan, pressing on the shells and vegetables with the back of a sturdy ladle to extract all liquid possible. Discard the shells and vegetables in the strainer after straining each batch.

10. Now strain the mixture again through a fine-mesh strainer (the finer the better) or through several layers of cheesecloth. Strain again if needed to make sure the bisque is completely free of tiny particles of shells.

11. In a clean, heavy 8-quart saucepan, heat the strained liquid over medium-high heat until hot, stirring as needed. Add the reserved crawfish tails and fat from preparing the shells for stuffing. Also add the additional 1 pound of boiled and peeled crawfish tails, the kosher salt, thyme and pepper, as well as the cream and sherry. Bring to a simmer and serve immediately or, preferably, make a day ahead and reheat gently for serving.

12. Just before serving time, preheat the oven to 350°F and bake the stuffed shells in a buttered roasting pan in a single layer until well browned, about 10 minutes. Drizzle with white wine and serve immediately.

    Serving Suggestion: Spoon 1 cup crawfish bisque in each heated soup bowl, and garnish each serving with three stuffed shells. 🐚

Oyster and Artichoke Bisque

For 16 appetizer servings or 8 main-dish servings

The flavor marriage of oysters and artichokes is one of the great traditions of New Orleans cookery. And rarely do those two flavors combine so deliciously as they do in this bisque. Unlike most Creole bisques, this one calls for a cup of heavy cream, strengthening its ties to classic French cooking. The presence of cream amounts to one more reason to enjoy this rich and luxurious dish to the fullest.

¼ pound (1 stick) plus 2 tablespoons unsalted butter
2 tablespoons minced fresh garlic
4½ cups finely chopped onions
2 cups finely chopped celery
¾ cup all-purpose flour
8 cups oyster liquor*
4 bay leaves
6 medium-to-large artichokes, blanched, hearts and flesh from stems only, chopped fine
6 ounces fresh spinach, washed, with stems removed and sliced fine
1 cup heavy cream
6 sprigs thyme, chopped
6 sprigs Italian (flat-leaf) parsley, washed and chopped fine
2 teaspoons kosher salt
½ teaspoon freshly ground black pepper
2 cups fresh raw oysters**
  ground cayenne, optional
  Louisiana-style pepper sauce, optional
  Herbsaint*** or Pernod anisette liqueur, optional but preferred

*If 8 cups of oyster liquor is not available, see Notes, right, for substitutes.
**Louisiana oysters are ideal for this dish, but if you are near coastal waters with beds of fresh native oysters, by all means use them.
***If this ingredient is difficult to find where you live, see Ingredient Sources on page 424.

1. Melt the butter in a heavy, nonreactive 6-quart saucepan over medium-high heat.

2. Add the garlic and cook until it turns light brown, about one minute.

3. Add the onions and celery and cook until they are translucent, about eight minutes.

4. Stir in the flour and cook about two minutes, constantly stirring the mixture and scraping the pan bottom clean to keep the flour from burning.

NOTES

Making the bisque a day or two ahead and refrigerating it intensifies the combined flavor of the oysters and artichokes.

If the 8 cups of oyster liquor called for in the recipe are not available, strain as much oyster liquor as possible from the oysters and make up the difference with the liquid (chilled) used to blanch the artichokes, or with chilled bottled clam juice or vegetable or chicken stock.

ADVANCE STEPS

If using a stock to substitute for some of the oyster liquor, prepare one of the following:

- Vegetable stock on page 397
- Chicken stock on page 390

SPECIAL EQUIPMENT

- A heavy, nonreactive* 6-quart saucepan

*See Using Nonreactive Cookware on page 419.

5. Slowly add the oyster liquor, stirring constantly to prevent lumps from forming. Increase heat to bring the bisque to a simmer.

6. Add the bay leaves, lower the heat and simmer the bisque for 20 minutes.

7. Add the artichokes, spinach, cream, thyme, parsley, kosher salt, black pepper and oysters.

8. Increase the heat to bring the bisque to a boil, then reduce the heat and simmer just until the oysters are plump and their edges curl, about two minutes.

9. Let the bisque cool slightly and refrigerate it overnight or for up to two days before serving. When ready to serve, reheat the bisque gently and taste for salt.

Serving Suggestion: Serve warm in heated bowls. If you wish, add a pinch of cayenne or a dash of pepper sauce or anisette liqueur.

Turtle Soup

For 16 appetizer servings or 8 main-dish servings

The closest encounter some have had with turtle soup was to watch French actress Stéphane Audran ladle it out as *potage à la tortue* in the 1988 movie "Babette's Feast."

While this delicious soup may be hard to get in most parts of the world, in New Orleans it remains a familiar dish on the tables of many restaurants and family dining rooms. Thanks to the abundant supply of the amphibian from South Louisiana's vast system of natural waterways, New Orleans Creoles have been enjoying their spicy *soupe à la tortue* for centuries, and variations on the basic recipe are as numerous as the cooks who prepare the dish.

Making the soup at home from scratch is best left to cooks capable of confronting the task of dressing a live snapping turtle. The rest of us can settle for buying fresh or frozen turtle meat (soft-shell and snapping turtles being the most common species) either from specialty markets or by mail order from seafood dealers in and around New Orleans.

The recipe below adheres to tradition, except perhaps for the addition of spinach. The leaf vegetable lends the soup touches of both color and interesting flavor.

This rich soup can be offered either as a first or main course, with crusty French bread or toast points.

4	tablespoons unsalted butter
1½	pounds turtle meat,* trimmed of all sinew and cut into ¼-inch cubes
8	cloves garlic, minced
2	medium-size onions, chopped fine
4	stalks celery, chopped fine
2	medium-size green sweet peppers, chopped fine
1½	tablespoons kosher salt, plus to taste
1	teaspoon freshly ground black pepper
2	medium-size Creole** tomatoes, seeded and chopped fine
¾	cup all-purpose flour
3	quarts beef stock
1	cup worcestershire sauce
2	tablespoons Crystal brand pepper sauce, or other relatively mild pepper sauce
2	tablespoons finely chopped Italian (flat-leaf) parsley leaves
2	tablespoons finely chopped fresh thyme leaves
5	large eggs, hard-boiled, chopped fine
6	ounces fresh spinach, washed, stemmed and leaves sliced fine
	zest from 3 lemons, chopped fine
⅓	cup fresh lemon juice
½	cup good-quality pale sherry

NOTE

If the soup is made ahead, check the level of lemon juice and sherry before serving.

ADVANCE STEP

Prepare the recipe for beef stock on page 389.

SPECIAL EQUIPMENT

• A heavy 7-quart saucepan or Dutch oven

*If this ingredient is difficult to find where you live, see Ingredient Sources on page 124.

**South Louisiana's Creole tomatoes are preferred for this recipe, although other good, peak-of-season regional varieties can be used.

1. Over medium-high heat, melt the butter in a heavy 7-quart saucepan.

2. Add the turtle meat and garlic. Cook until the meat is no longer pink, about five minutes, stirring occasionally.

3. Stir in the onions, celery, sweet peppers, kosher salt, and pepper. Cook until the vegetables start to become translucent, about 10 minutes.

4. Add the tomatoes and cook about five minutes, stirring often so the bottom of the pan does not scorch. Reduce the heat to medium.

5. Dust the vegetables with the flour and cook five minutes, stirring constantly and scraping the pan bottom clean so the flour does not burn.

6. Slowly add the stock, stirring and scraping the pan bottom constantly to prevent dough balls from forming in the soup.

7. Stir in the worcestershire, pepper sauce, parsley and thyme. Simmer 30 minutes.

8. Add the eggs, spinach, lemon zest, lemon juice and sherry. Continue simmering 10 minutes more.

    Serving Suggestion: Taste for salt and serve warm in heated cups or bowls. 🐚

SALADS

Fried-Oyster Salad with Garlic Mayonnaise

For 6 servings

Crisp and succulent fried oysters, crunchy spinach and endive, and a piquant garlic mayonnaise come together deliciously in a salad that could serve as a first course for dinner or an entrée for a light lunch.

FOR THE GARLIC MAYONNAISE

1	large egg yolk
1½	teaspoons minced fresh garlic
1½	teaspoons red wine vinegar
1½	teaspoons water
½	teaspoon dry mustard
¾	cup vegetable oil
1	tablespoon freshly grated Pecorino-Romano cheese
2¼	teaspoons very finely sliced chives
1½	teaspoons fresh lemon juice
¼	teaspoon kosher salt, plus to taste
⅛	teaspoon freshly ground black pepper, plus to taste

ADVANCE STEPS

Prepare the recipes for:
• Seasoned flour on page 384
• Creole seasoning on page 385

1. In a large mixing bowl, combine the egg yolk, garlic, vinegar, water and dry mustard, whisking about 30 seconds until the mustard is thoroughly blended in.

2. Very gradually add the oil in a thin, steady stream, whisking constantly until all is incorporated and the mayonnaise is thick.

3. Whisk in the cheese, chives, lemon juice, ¼ teaspoon kosher salt and ⅛ teaspoon pepper.

4. Before using, refrigerate in a covered container for at least one hour or overnight to let the flavors develop, then season with more salt and pepper if desired. Keep refrigerated and use within four days.

FOR THE GREENS

2	heads Belgian endive, rinsed and well drained
12	ounces baby spinach leaves with stems, washed, drained well and patted dry with paper towels

1. Separate the endive leaves and set aside 18 of the most attractive outer leaves to use as garnish. Trim the core end of the remaining leaves and cut them crosswise into ¹⁄₁₆-inch wide slices.

2. In a large mixing bowl, mix together the sliced endive with the baby spinach. Set aside the mixture and the 18 endive leaves separately at room temperature.

FOR FRYING THE OYSTERS AND SERVING

30 medium-sized fresh raw oysters*
3 cups seasoned flour
2 tablespoons Creole seasoning
  vegetable oil, for frying
3 ounces Parmigiano-Reggiano cheese, shaved into thin strips about 2 inches long and ½ inch wide

*Louisiana oysters are ideal for this dish, but if you're near coastal waters with beds of fresh native oysters, by all means use them.

SPECIAL EQUIPMENT
- A heavy, deep 12-inch skillet or 12-inch sauté pan
- A frying thermometer

1. Drain the oysters for 15 minutes in a colander or coarse-mesh strainer. In a large mixing bowl combine the seasoned flour with the Creole seasoning.

2. In a heavy, deep 12-inch skillet, heat ½ inch of oil over medium-high heat until it reaches 375°F, about three minutes.

3. Once the oil is just short of reaching 375°, dredge half of the oysters in the seasoned-flour mixture, tossing them to coat all surfaces. Shake off any excess.

4. Carefully slide the dredged oysters into the hot oil. (As the cold oysters come in contact with the hot oil, the oil may momentarily bubble up.)

5. Fry the oysters until just golden brown and crispy, about two minutes. Remove them from the skillet with a slotted spoon and drain on paper towels while dredging and frying the second batch. Drain the second batch briefly on paper towels, then serve promptly.

Serving Suggestions: Toss the greens with the garlic mayonnaise, mixing well. Divide the greens among six chilled dinner plates. Arrange three endive leaves around each mound of greens, with the pointed ends facing outward. Place five fried oysters around the edge of the greens. Garnish with the shaved Parmigiano-Reggiano.

Blackened-Redfish "Seasar" Salad with Firecracker Cornbread

For 4 generous lunch or brunch main dishes or 8 generous appetizer servings

The combination of salad greens and seafood seems to gain in popularity every year. This one should draw applause for its grand combination of flavors—spicy blackened redfish, subtle-tasting greens, crunchy capers and an invigorating dressing.

FOR THE SALAD DRESSING

1 packed teaspoon rinsed and minced brined anchovies, preferably Hungarian	2 teaspoons Dijon mustard
2 yolks from large eggs	¾ cup vegetable oil
1½ tablespoons minced fresh garlic	¼ cup olive oil
2 teaspoons fresh lemon juice	½ teaspoon kosher salt
	⅛ teaspoon freshly ground black pepper

1. In a medium-size mixing bowl, combine the anchovies, egg yolks, garlic, lemon juice and mustard.

2. Combine the vegetable oil and olive oil and very gradually add to the bowl in a thin, steady stream, whisking constantly until all is incorporated and the dressing is thick. Whisk in the kosher salt and pepper.

3. Before using the dressing, cover and refrigerate it at least two hours, preferably overnight, to let the flavors develop. If desired, season with more salt just before using. Keep the dressing refrigerated in a covered container and use within four days.

FOR THE FRIED CAPERS GARNISH

canola oil, for frying
¼ cup nonpareil capers, drained for several minutes in a strainer and blotted completely dry (see Notes, right)

1. Heat 1 inch of oil in a deep 2-quart saucepan to 275°F over high heat, three to four minutes. It's important to use a frying thermometer.

2. Carefully ease the capers into the hot oil. Reduce heat to very low (to reduce the temperature to between 250° and 275° as quickly as possible) and fry until all the water is released by the capers and they become browned and crispy, about five to nine minutes, depending on the capers. By the end of frying time the oil should be barely fizzing.

3. Transfer the capers with a slotted spoon to absorbent paper to drain. Set aside at room temperature while blackening the fish and assembling the salads.

NOTES

Prepare the salad dressing and the fried capers before cooking the redfish.

It's important to have the capers in this recipe thoroughly dry to prevent the hot oil from popping when they are added to the oil. Be sure to use a deep pan for frying the capers, because the hot oil will boil up momentarily when the capers are added to it, and if the oil is in too shallow a pan, the hot oil may boil over.

ADVANCE STEP

Prepare the recipe for firecracker cornbread on page 323.

SPECIAL EQUIPMENT

- A deep 2-quart saucepan
- A frying thermometer
- A salad spinner
- A very large mixing bowl

ADVANCE STEP

Just before finishing the salad, prepare the recipe for blackened redfish on page 183.

FOR FINISHING THE DISH

1	recipe firecracker cornbread
3	hearts of romaine, about 1 pound 10 ounces total
½	teaspoon kosher salt
¼	teaspoon freshly ground black pepper

4	tablespoons coarsely grated Parmigiano-Reggiano cheese, or to taste
4	blackened redfish fillets, 8 ounces each
	a pepper mill, for the table

1. If the cornbread is made ahead, warm it as directed in the recipe.

2. Meanwhile, slice each head of romaine lengthwise in quarters and trim the edges if needed. Rinse under cool running water and drain well, cut side down, on paper towels.

3. With a sharp knife cut the leaves crosswise (or tear the leaves) into half-inch slices and place them in a very large mixing bowl. Add the salad dressing, kosher salt and pepper, mixing by hand until all the pieces of romaine are well coated with dressing.

Serving Suggestions: For each main-dish serving, mound one-fourth of the dressed romaine on each of four chilled dinner plates. On each plate, sprinkle the romaine with 1 tablespoon Parmigiano-Reggiano cheese or to taste, then arrange a whole blackened-redfish fillet on top and sprinkle with some of the fried capers.

For each appetizer serving, use half the amounts (mentioned above) of cheese, romaine, redfish and capers on eight chilled salad plates.

Pass the cornbread and a pepper mill at the table. ❦

Red Fish Grill House Salad with Apple-Rosemary Vinaigrette

For 6 main-dish servings or 12 appetizer servings

Tomatoes, red onions and blue cheese add their exceptional flavors to this salad, which functions as the house salad at Red Fish Grill.

The recipe's ingredients list contains hearts of romaine, which are the inner leaves of the lettuce's head. These tend to be sweeter and have more crunch. Any lettuce or lettuce mix also may be used.

FOR THE APPLE-ROSEMARY VINAIGRETTE

½	cup apple-cider vinegar
¼	cup apple juice
½	Granny Smith or other green apple, peeled and finely chopped (¾ cup chopped)
1¼	teaspoons minced fresh rosemary leaves
1	teaspoon Dijon mustard
½	cup plus 2 tablespoons olive oil (not extra-virgin)
2	tablespoons vegetable oil
¼	teaspoon kosher salt, or to taste
¼	teaspoon freshly ground black pepper, or to taste

SPECIAL EQUIPMENT

• A heavy, nonreactive* 1-quart saucepan

*See Using Nonreactive Cookware, page 419.

1. In a heavy, nonreactive 1-quart saucepan, combine the vinegar, apple juice, apples and rosemary. Bring to a simmer over medium-high heat. Reduce heat and continue simmering until the apples are mushy, about five minutes (they do not need stirring). Remove from heat.

2. Transfer the apple mixture to the bowl of a blender and add the mustard. Blend on low speed as you very gradually add the olive and vegetable oils through the blender's lid in a slow, steady stream. Season with ¼ teaspoon kosher salt and ¼ teaspoon pepper or to taste.

3. Before using, cover and refrigerate at least two hours, preferably overnight, to let the flavors develop. Keep refrigerated and use within one month.

FOR FINISHING THE SALAD

3	hearts (about 1 pound 10 ounces total) romaine lettuce
1½	cups pecan pieces
2	tablespoons minced shallots
1¼	teaspoons minced fresh rosemary leaves
2	tablespoons extra-virgin olive oil
½	teaspoon kosher salt, or to taste, divided
½	teaspoon freshly ground black pepper, or to taste, divided

SPECIAL EQUIPMENT

• A 9-inch pie pan or rimmed cookie sheet

3½   cups finely chopped Creole tomatoes*
½   medium-size red onion, peeled and shaved thin
¾   pound good-quality blue cheese, preferably Stilton, crumbled

*South Louisiana's Creole tomatoes are preferred for this recipe, although other good, peak-of-season regional varieties can be used.

1.   Preheat the oven to 350°F.

2.   Slice each head of romaine lengthwise in half and trim the edges if needed. Rinse under cool running water and drain well, cut-side-down, on paper towels. Trim away the stem base, keeping each half intact.

3.   In a medium-size mixing bowl, combine the pecans, shallots, rosemary, olive oil, ¼ teaspoon kosher salt, and ¼ teaspoon pepper, tossing with a spoon to evenly season all the pecan pieces.

4.   Spread out the mixture in the bottom of a 9-inch pie pan (not greased). Bake uncovered until golden brown, about 15 minutes, thoroughly stirring occasionally. Set aside to cool.

5.   If the salad is a main course (with six servings), the romaine halves need not be divided further. If the salad is an appetizer (with 12 servings), cut each romaine half lengthwise. In either case, be careful to keep the individual wedges intact. Serve immediately.

Serving Suggestions: Arrange the romaine wedges cut-side-up on a very large serving platter.

Scatter the tomatoes over the wedges and season all lightly with ¼ teaspoon kosher salt and ¼ teaspoon pepper or to taste.

Evenly drizzle the apple-rosemary vinaigrette over the romaine wedges and tomatoes, using all the vinaigrette. Sprinkle the reserved seasoned pecan pieces, the red onions and the blue cheese over the salad.

Transfer the salad to chilled dinner plates at the table. 🐚

Roasted-Shrimp and Penne Pasta Salad with Feta Cheese Dressing

For 6 main-dish lunch or brunch servings

If green salads with pasta have become a standby dish with home cooks, the reasons are no mystery. Pasta adds substance to a green salad. It gives dressings and sauces more surface to cling to. And pasta salads can be served warm or chilled.

This one features little tubes of penne pasta swathed in a vinaigrette with onions and sweet peppers. Two more popular salad ingredients also appear. One is feta cheese, used in a simple dressing. The other is shrimp, gently roasted with olive oil, garlic and peppers.

The result is an ideal main-course salad for lunch or brunch.

FOR THE FETA CHEESE DRESSING

- ¾ cup crumbled feta cheese
- ¼ cup hot water
- 2 tablespoons plus 2 teaspoons rice vinegar
- ⅓ cup extra-virgin olive oil

SPECIAL EQUIPMENT
- An electric blender

1. In an electric blender, combine the feta cheese, hot water and vinegar. Pulse about three times to blend well.

2. With the blender still running, very gradually add the oil in a thin, steady stream and purée a few more seconds until the dressing is smooth.

   Use immediately, or refrigerate in a covered container until ready to use. Keep refrigerated and use within four days.

FOR THE ROASTED-SHRIMP AND PENNE SALAD

-    sufficient salted water for cooking pasta
- 1 pound penne pasta
- 30 extra-large shrimp, peeled and deveined, with tails left on
- 1 tablespoon minced fresh garlic
- 8 tablespoons extra-virgin olive oil, divided
- ¾ teaspoon plus ⅛ teaspoon kosher salt, divided
- ¾ teaspoon plus ⅛ teaspoon freshly ground black pepper, divided
- ½ teaspoon crushed red pepper
- 1 cup thinly sliced green onions, green parts only
- ¾ cup finely chopped red sweet peppers
- ¾ cup finely chopped green sweet peppers
- ¾ cup crumbled feta cheese
- ½ cup rice vinegar
- 6 ounces (8 cups, not packed) mixed salad greens

SPECIAL EQUIPMENT
- 3 large mixing bowls
- A rimmed baking sheet
- Parchment paper

¾ cup feta cheese dressing

1 cup very finely julienned red onions, about 1/16 inch wide and 2 inches long, for garnish

1. Preheat the oven to 350°F.

2. Heat the salted water and cook the pasta according to package directions to the al dente stage. While the pasta is cooking, roast the shrimp.

3. Drain the pasta well in a colander and set aside.

4. In a large mixing bowl, combine the shrimp with the garlic, 1 tablespoon olive oil, ½ teaspoon kosher salt, ½ teaspoon black pepper and the crushed red pepper, tossing until well blended.

5. Line a rimmed baking sheet with parchment paper, and arrange the shrimp on the sheet in a single layer. Bake uncovered until the shrimp are just cooked through, about six minutes. Remove from the oven and set aside.

6. In a large, clean mixing bowl, thoroughly combine the drained pasta with the green onions, red and green sweet peppers, feta cheese, rice vinegar, 4 tablespoons olive oil, ¼ teaspoon kosher salt, and ¼ teaspoon black pepper.

7. In another large mixing bowl, toss the salad greens with 3 tablespoons olive oil, ⅛ teaspoon kosher salt and ⅛ teaspoon black pepper, mixing well. Serve immediately.

Serving Suggestions: For each serving, arrange a portion of the salad greens on one half of a dinner plate. On the plate's other half spoon a portion of the pasta mixture. Arrange five shrimp in a row on top of the greens. Drizzle on 2 tablespoons of the feta cheese dressing, and sprinkle about 2½ tablespoons red onions on top. 🐚

Jazz Kitchen French Quarter Salad
with Candied Pecans & Cane-Sugar Vinaigrette

For 6 generous servings

This one is for salad lovers who enjoy a bit of sweetness with their greens. The pecans aren't over-sugared, allowing the natural flavor of pecans to come through, and the bacon adds a nice salty crunchiness.

FOR THE CANE-SYRUP VINAIGRETTE

- 3 tablespoons plus 1 teaspoon apple juice
- 1 tablespoon Steen's cane syrup*
- 1 tablespoon, packed, light brown sugar
- 1½ teaspoons Dijon mustard
- 1 teaspoon very finely chopped shallots
- ½ cup plus 2 tablespoons canola oil
- ¼ teaspoon kosher salt, or to taste
- ¼ teaspoon freshly ground black pepper, or to taste

    *If this ingredient is difficult to find where you live, see Ingredient Sources on page 424.

1. In a medium-size mixing bowl, combine the apple juice, cane syrup, brown sugar, mustard, and shallots, whisking with a metal whisk until blended.

2. Very gradually add the oil in a thin, steady stream, whisking constantly until all is incorporated. Season with ¼ teaspoon kosher salt and ¼ teaspoon pepper or to taste. Cover and refrigerate if not using within an hour.

FOR THE CANDIED PECANS

- 1 cup chopped pecans or pecan pieces
- 1 tablespoon, packed, light brown sugar
- 1 teaspoon lightly beaten egg white (from any size egg)
- ¼ teaspoon vanilla extract
    a very light sprinkle of table salt, optional

1. Preheat the oven to 300°F.

2. Line a rimmed baking sheet with parchment paper and set aside.

3. In a small mixing bowl, combine the pecans with the brown sugar, egg white and vanilla, mixing thoroughly with your hands until all the pecans are moistened with egg white and vanilla and feel grainy with sugar.

NOTE

Both the vinaigrette and the candied pecans may be prepared up to two days ahead.

SPECIAL EQUIPMENT

- A medium-size, nonreactive* mixing bowl
- A metal whisk

*See Using Nonreactive Cookware, page 419.

SPECIAL EQUIPMENT

- A rimmed baking sheet
- Parchment paper

4. Scatter the pecans on the lined baking sheet, separating the pieces so they aren't clumped together. Bake uncovered on the middle shelf of the oven for five minutes.

5. Remove from the oven, stir the pecans well and continue baking until the sugar on the pecans feels dry to the touch, about six minutes more.

6. Remove from the oven, stir the pecans again and, if desired, lightly sprinkle with table salt. Let the pecans cool completely on the baking sheet. If made ahead, transfer the cooled pecans to an airtight container and store at room temperature.

FOR FINISHING THE SALAD

SPECIAL EQUIPMENT
• A very large mixing bowl

    6   top-quality, thick-cut bacon strips, applewood-smoked preferred
   12   ounces mixed salad greens
   18   cherry tomatoes or 30 grape tomatoes, halved

1. Just before serving time, fry the bacon strips until crisp. Drain on paper towels and while still warm cut the strips crosswise into thin slices. Set aside at room temperature.

2. Place the greens in a very large mixing bowl. Pour the vinaigrette over the greens, tossing until all greens are coated evenly with vinaigrette.

   Serving Suggestion: Divide the greens equally among six chilled salad plates. Arrange a portion of the tomato halves on each salad and sprinkle each with a portion of the bacon strips and candied pecans. Serve immediately. 🐚

Bacco Insalata Mista

For 6 servings

This salad was inspired by the salads of mixed greens and other vegetables served in Italian homes and restaurants. It gets its own character from sun-dried tomatoes, goat cheese and pine nuts.

¼ cup firmly packed sun-dried tomatoes, drained if packed in oil, coarsely chopped or julienned
1 cup boiling hot water
¼ cup rice vinegar
1 tablespoon finely chopped shallots
1 teaspoon minced fresh garlic
1 pinch chopped fresh or dried rosemary leaves
  kosher salt, to taste
  freshly ground black pepper, to taste
¼ cup vegetable oil
12 ounces mixed baby-lettuce greens
3 ounces crumbled goat cheese, for garnish
⅓ cup lightly colored dry-roasted pine nuts, for garnish

NOTE

The vinaigrette may be prepared up to four days ahead.

SPECIAL EQUIPMENT

• A rubber spatula

1. Soak the sun-dried tomatoes in the boiled hot water until soft, about 10 minutes. Drain the tomatoes through a mesh strainer placed over a bowl to catch the liquid. Place 2 tablespoons of the drained liquid in the bowl of a blender. Discard remaining liquid.

2. Add to the blender the drained tomatoes, vinegar, shallots, garlic, rosemary, kosher salt and pepper, pulsing in about three-second bursts until all the ingredients are chopped into fairly small bits. With the blender running very slowly add the oil, then stop the blender and scrape down the sides of the bowl with a rubber spatula. Continue running the blender until the vinaigrette is emulsified and thick, about 30 seconds more. Refrigerate in a covered container if made ahead.

3. Place the greens in a large mixing bowl and toss with the vinaigrette.

    Serving Suggestion: Divide the salad between six chilled salad plates and serve immediately. Garnish each salad with a sprinkle of goat cheese, and then pine nuts.

Crab and Shrimp Cobb Salad with Remoulade Sauce

For 6 generous lunch or brunch servings

The Cobb salad is said to date back to the 1920s, when Bob Cobb, the manager of the Brown Derby nightclub in Hollywood, decided to diversify his diet with an entirely new dish. He chopped up an avocado, along with lettuce, tomato, bacon, chicken breast, eggs and some Roquefort, and finally added a few herbs and a dressing.

The salad quickly found its way to the Brown Derby's list of food offerings, and later gained a following around the United States.

Cobb's creation is the inspiration for this salad. It's a no-chicken, no-cheese version, with bits of shrimp and crab and a corn relish. The dressing is a classic New Orleans remoulade sauce.

Besides having a bounty of appealing tastes, this pretty salad is easy to put together because you can prepare and refrigerate the components in advance.

FOR THE BOILED SHRIMP

10	cups water
⅓	cup kosher salt
1	tablespoon liquid seafood boil*
¼	teaspoon Creole seasoning
2	lemons
36	large raw shrimp, peeled and deveined, with heads removed and tails remaining

*If this ingredient is difficult to find where you live, see Ingredient Sources on page 424.

1. In a heavy 5-quart, nonreactive saucepan, combine the water, kosher salt, crab boil and Creole seasoning. Halve the lemons, squeeze the juice into the water, and also add the lemon rinds to the water.

2. Bring to a boil over high heat. Reduce the heat and simmer for five minutes.

3. Ease the shrimp into the simmering water and return to a boil, stirring once or twice. Remove from heat.

4. Let the shrimp sit in the hot water, uncovered, for three minutes, then promptly drain them and spread them out on a platter. Let the shrimp cool slightly, then refrigerate them until they start to feel chilled. If they were boiled more than one hour ahead, cover them and return them to the refrigerator until it's time to assemble the salads.

NOTE

To prepare the salad in advance:

- Three days ahead, wash the romaine lettuce, thoroughly dry it and refrigerate it in an airtight container.

- Two days ahead, prepare the remoulade sauce and refrigerate it in a covered container.

- One day ahead, prepare the boiled shrimp, corn relish, bacon and hard-boiled eggs and refrigerate them in covered containers.

ADVANCE STEPS

Prepare the recipes for:
- Creole seasoning on page 385
- Remoulade sauce on page 373

SPECIAL EQUIPMENT

- A heavy, 5-quart nonreactive* saucepan

*See Using Nonreactive Cookware, page 419.

FOR THE ROASTED CORN RELISH

4   ears sweet corn in the husk, each 7 to 9 inches long
    water, for soaking corn
1   cup cubed (¼ inch cubes) Creole tomatoes,* plus juice
3   tablespoons fresh lemon juice
1   rounded tablespoon minced fresh jalapeño peppers (remove seeds if desired
        to decrease heat of peppers)
1½ teaspoons kosher salt
¼   teaspoon freshly ground black pepper

*South Louisiana's Creole tomatoes are preferred for this recipe, although other good, peak-of-season regional varieties can be used.

1. Preheat oven to 350°F.

2. Soak the ears of corn in their husks in a pan of water for 30 minutes, then drain them.

3. Bake the ears on a rimmed baking sheet until they are just cooked, about 35 minutes.

4. Once the corn is cool enough to handle, strip off the husks and silk, and cut the kernels from the ears. You should have about 2¼ to 2½ cups kernels.

5. In a large mixing bowl, thoroughly combine the corn kernels with the tomatoes, lemon juice, jalapeños, kosher salt and pepper. Refrigerate in a covered container until time to assemble the salads.

FOR THE AVOCADO RELISH

½   medium-to-large cucumber
3   semi-firm, medium-size avocados (7 to 8 ounces each), preferably the Hass
        variety
2   tablespoons fresh lime juice
1   tablespoon minced fresh Italian (flat-leaf) parsley leaves
1½ teaspoons kosher salt
⅛   teaspoon freshly ground black pepper

1. Peel the cucumber lengthwise, leaving narrow strips of peeling intermittently so the cucumber is striped. Cut in half lengthwise and scoop out the seeds. Cut each half lengthwise again in half, and finely chop the relish. Set aside at room temperature.

2. Slice each avocado in half lengthwise, remove the pit, and scoop out the flesh. Cut the flesh into ½-inch cubes.

SPECIAL EQUIPMENT
• A rimmed baking sheet

SPECIAL EQUIPMENT
• A medium-size, nonreactive* mixing bowl

*See Using Nonreactive Cookware, page 419.

3. In a medium-size, nonreactive mixing bowl, thoroughly combine the avocado cubes and reserved cucumbers with the lime juice, parsley, kosher salt and pepper.

4. Refrigerate the relish until it is time to assemble the salads. Cover it with plastic wrap and press the wrap to touch the entire surface of the relish so the avocados don't turn brown.

FOR FINISHING THE SALAD

SPECIAL EQUIPMENT
• A very large mixing bowl

2	heads romaine lettuce, washed and dried thoroughly
	kosher salt, to taste
	freshly ground black pepper, to taste
1¾	cups remoulade sauce, divided
18	ounces fresh jumbo lump crabmeat, picked through
2	large eggs, hard-boiled, cooled and chopped fine
6	slices (about 6 ounces) applewood-smoked, center-cut bacon, preferred, or other thick-sliced bacon, chopped fine and then fried crisp

1. Trim the heads of romaine and discard the outer leaves. Trim each head lengthwise in quarters, and cut quarters crosswise into ¼-inch strips.

2. Place the romaine in a very large mixing bowl and lightly season with kosher salt and pepper. Toss the romaine to evenly distribute the various green shades of the lettuce. Toss with 1½ cups remoulade sauce, mixing well.

    Serving Suggestions: To serve the salad, mound about 3 cups of the romaine in the center of each chilled dinner plate.

    Lightly season the crabmeat with kosher salt and pepper and arrange a portion of the crab and reserved boiled shrimp on top of the lettuce. Arrange portions of the relishes, the hard-boiled eggs and the bacon around the crab and shrimp, and drizzle a line of remoulade sauce on top of the shrimp, using about 2 teaspoons of the sauce for each serving of shrimp.

    Once all the salads are prepared, serve promptly. 🐚

Ralph's City Park Salad

For 8 lunch or brunch main-dish servings

The views of New Orleans' City Park and its majestic old oaks make for a relaxing setting at Ralph's on the Park. To compliment this leafy panorama, the restaurant's menu contains a green salad that's appealing and rich without being heavy.

The ideal oil to use in the vinaigrette is a blend of 80 percent olive oil and 20 percent vegetable oil. The vegetable oil tempers the dressing's flavor, letting the salad's other flavors come through. In tossing the greens, it's best to coat them with the vinaigrette without any excess pooling on the plate.

Served simply with warm crusty French bread, this salad makes an excellent entrée for brunch or lunch. The versatile vinaigrette can be used with a variety of salads and other chilled savory dishes.

FOR THE VINAIGRETTE

- 1 tablespoon minced shallots
- ½ teaspoon very finely chopped fresh basil leaves
- ½ teaspoon very finely chopped fresh oregano leaves
- ½ teaspoon very finely chopped fresh Italian (flat-leaf) parsley leaves
- ½ teaspoon very finely chopped fresh thyme leaves
- ¼ teaspoon minced fresh garlic
- 2 tablespoons top-quality red-wine vinegar
- ½ teaspoon Dijon mustard
- ¾ cup blended salad oil, preferably about 80 per cent olive oil and 20 per cent vegetable oil
- ¼ teaspoon kosher salt, plus to taste
- ⅛ teaspoon freshly ground black pepper, plus to taste

1. In a medium-size, nonreactive mixing bowl, combine the shallots, basil, oregano, parsley, thyme, garlic and vinegar, mixing with a metal whisk to blend well.

2. Whisk in the mustard, then add the oil all at once and whisk. Season with ¼ teaspoon kosher salt and ⅛ teaspoon black pepper.

3. Let the vinaigrette sit for one hour at room temperature, then taste and add more salt and pepper, if needed.

   Serving Suggestion: Use immediately or store in a sealed glass jar in the refrigerator for up to one month.

NOTE

The vinaigrette, which makes a generous ¾ cup, may be prepared in a mixing bowl with a metal whisk (as described below) or in a glass jar with a tight-fitting lid.

ADVANCE STEP

Prepare the vinaigrette an hour before using and let it sit at room temperature to develop its flavors.

SPECIAL EQUIPMENT

- A medium-size, nonreactive* mixing bowl
- A metal whisk or a glass jar with a tight-fitting lid
- A heavy 10-inch skillet
- A very large mixing bowl

*See Using Nonreactive Cookware, page 419.

FOR FINISHING THE SALAD

- 12 ounces applewood-smoked bacon (preferably lean and in ¼-inch-thick slices) cut into ½-inch squares*
- 4 yolks from large eggs
- 4 ounces Roquefort cheese, at room temperature
- 1⅓ cups peeled and finely chopped Granny Smith or other green apples
- 6½ quarts unpacked, torn romaine lettuce leaves from hearts of romaine, from about 1½ pounds of trimmed leaves, rinsed and spun dry

*Applewood-smoked bacon gives this salad an extra special taste. If it is not available, substitute a good-quality bacon, preferably sliced ¼-inch thick.

1. In a heavy 10-inch skillet over medium-low heat, cook the bacon squares just until the fat is rendered and the meat is somewhat crispy, about 15 minutes, stirring often toward the end of the cooking time (which will vary according to the thickness of the bacon used).

2. Pour off all except about 1 tablespoon of the rendered fat from the skillet. If your bacon didn't render 1 tablespoon fat, reserve whatever fat it did. Set the skillet aside in a warm place. (If prepared earlier in the day, warm the bacon and fat again just before using so they will melt the Roquefort into the salad.)

3. In a very large mixing bowl, whisk the egg yolks until smooth. Stir the reserved vinaigrette well and add all except 3 tablespoons of it to the mixing bowl, along with the reserved warm bacon and rendered fat. Set aside the 3 tablespoons vinaigrette.

4. Add the Roquefort and whisk until it is almost dissolved. Add the apples and mix lightly to coat all the apple bits.

5. Add the romaine and toss with a large spoon to coat all the lettuce leaves with the vinaigrette, adding the reserved 3 tablespoons vinaigrette near the end of the mixing process if needed.

Serving Suggestion: Divide the salad among eight chilled dinner plates and serve immediately. Pass a peppermill at the table. 🐚

MAIN COURSES

For 6 servings

A stuffing of oysters and artichokes, seasoned with garlic, onions and herbs, forms the crust of this baked-fish dish. The fillets rest on a colorful bed of stewed tomatoes.

FOR THE STUFFING

¼	pound (1 stick) unsalted butter
1	tablespoon minced fresh garlic
1	cup finely chopped onions
1	cup finely chopped green sweet peppers
¾	cup finely chopped blanched artichoke hearts from 2 to 3 medium-sized artichokes, preferred, or frozen or canned artichoke hearts, drained and finely chopped
½	cup finely chopped celery
1	tablespoon minced fresh Italian (flat-leaf) parsley leaves
1½	teaspoons minced fresh thyme leaves
1	cup oyster liquor
2	tablespoons Herbsaint* or Pernod anisette liqueur, optional but preferred
1	teaspoon kosher salt
¼	teaspoon freshly ground black pepper
1	pound fresh raw oysters,** drained and chopped into pieces 1 to 1½ inches (saving the drained oyster liquor)
2½ to 3½	cups fresh breadcrumbs, preferably from brioche

*If this ingredient is difficult to find where you live, see Ingredient Sources on page 424.
**Louisiana oysters are ideal for this dish, but if you're near coastal waters with beds of fresh native oysters, by all means use them.

1. In a heavy 12-inch skillet, melt the butter over medium heat. Add the garlic and cook until it starts to brown, about one minute, stirring constantly. Add the onions, sweet peppers, artichokes, celery, parsley and thyme, mixing well. Cook until the vegetables are soft but not yet browning, about three minutes, stirring occasionally.

2. Stir in the oyster liquor, anisette liqueur if using, and the kosher salt and pepper. Cook for two minutes, stirring occasionally. Add the chopped oysters and bring to a boil.

3. Add 2½ cups breadcrumbs, stirring well. If the mixture is wetter than the consistency of soft scrambled eggs, add more breadcrumbs to bring to scrambled-egg consistency. Continue cooking and stirring the stuffing for two minutes more. Remove from heat.

NOTES

Recommended alternate species: halibut, redfish, sea bass, tilapia

Vegetable or chicken stock may be substituted for the oyster liquor listed in ingredients.

Only small batches of the fillets are cooked at a time to allow sufficient space in the pan for even cooking.

ADVANCE STEPS

Prepare the recipes for:

- Blanched artichoke hearts on page 320

If using stock in place of oyster liquor, either of the following:

  - Vegetable stock on page 397
  - Chicken stock on page 390
- Fresh breadcrumbs (preferably using brioche) on page 382
- Stewed Creole tomatoes on page 349
- Seasoned flour on page 384
- Clarified butter on page 355

SPECIAL EQUIPMENT

- A heavy 12-inch skillet or 12-inch sauté pan

Refrigerate the stuffing, uncovered, for at least one hour before using. It may be prepared early on the day of serving. After one hour of chilling uncovered, cover the stuffing and return to the refrigerator.

FOR FINISHING THE DISH

- 1 recipe stewed Creole tomatoes
  kosher salt to taste for the stuffing, plus 1½ teaspoons kosher salt to season the fish
  freshly ground black pepper to taste for the stuffing, plus ½ teaspoon freshly ground black pepper to season the fish
- 6 redfish fillets, each 6 to 8 ounces
- 2 tablespoons plus ½ cup seasoned flour, divided
- 4 tablespoons unsalted butter
- 1 cup good-quality dry white wine
- ½ cup clarified butter, melted and divided
- 12 attractive chive stems, for garnish

1. Prepare the stewed tomatoes, if not already done. Set them aside at room temperature.

2. Once the stuffing has chilled for at least an hour, season to taste with more kosher salt and pepper. Separate the stuffing into six equal portions and form the portions into balls.

3. Arrange the fillets in a single layer on a work surface. Salt and pepper each fillet on both sides, using a total of 1½ teaspoons kosher salt and ½ teaspoon pepper distributed among the six fillets.

4. Spread a stuffing ball evenly over the entire top of each fillet, patting it firmly into place to help it adhere to the fish and make the layer of stuffing uniformly thick.

5. Using a small fine-mesh strainer, sift seasoned flour evenly over the top of the stuffing, using 2 tablespoons seasoned flour distributed among the six fillets.

6. Evenly spread ½ cup seasoned flour in a large, shallow dish, such as a pie plate. Place a fish fillet in the dish, stuffing side up, and let it sit in the flour for about five seconds to give the bottom surface of the fish a light coating of flour.

   Transfer the fillet to a work surface covered with parchment paper, still with stuffing side up.

7. Repeat this procedure to flour the bottom surfaces of the remaining fillets.

8. Preheat the oven to 350°F.

9. Line a rimmed baking sheet (large enough to hold all six fish fillets) with heavy-duty aluminum foil. Generously grease the foil evenly with the 4 table-spoons regular (not clarified) butter and add the wine to the pan. Set aside.

10. In a heavy 12-inch sauté pan, heat ¼ cup clarified butter over medium-high heat until hot, about three minutes. Using 2 broad, large and sturdy spatulas, gently slide two of the fillets, stuffing side down, into the hot butter. Be careful not to slosh the hot butter to avoid burning yourself. Cook the fillets until the stuffing is dark golden, about two minutes.

11. Gently turn the fillets over with the two spatulas. Cook one minute more to start building a crust.

12. Transfer the fish to the reserved baking sheet, stuffing side up.

13. Add 2 tablespoons (⅛ cup) more clarified butter to the butter already in the sauté pan, and heat for about 30 seconds.

14. Repeat the procedure of browning the remaining four fillets, two fillets at a time, first browning the stuffed sides, then turning the fillets over to briefly brown the second side.

15. Transfer the two fillets to the baking sheet with the other browned fish. Add 2 tablespoons (⅛ cup) more clarified butter to the pan and brown the last two fillets, adding them to the baking sheet.

16. Now bake the fillets, uncovered, in the oven until all are just cooked through, about nine minutes. (The cooking time will depend on the thickness of the fish. Be careful not to overcook.)

17. While the fish are baking, reheat the stewed tomatoes over medium-low heat.

18. To test the fish for doneness, insert the tip of a thin-bladed knife into the thickest part of the fillet for approximately 10 seconds. Remove the knife and lay the tip of the blade flat against the inside of your wrist. If the tip feels hot against your skin, the fish is done.

19. Once the fish are done, serve immediately.

    Serving Suggestion: Divide the stewed tomatoes equally among six heated dinner plates. Arrange the fish, stuffing side up, over the tomatoes.

    Garnish each portion with two chive stems laid one across the other. ❦

Baked Catfish
with Sweet Potato "Scales" & Andouille Sauce

For 6 servings

Because of the catfish's boniness, it did not emerge as a popular food fish until fairly recently, when catfish farms developed ways to process it efficiently. Catfish fillets are now a seafood staple in many homes, thanks to their mild, pleasant flavor.

In this recipe the fillets are enveloped in sweet potatoes, first as a creamy purée and then in thinly sliced rounds to resemble fish scales.

The sauce is flavored with andouille, the lean, rather spicy pork sausage that has become a favorite of cooks in South Louisiana.

FOR THE ANDOUILLE SAUCE

2 tablespoons unsalted butter	2 tablespoons minced fresh thyme leaves
2 teaspoons minced fresh garlic	
¾ cup (3½ ounces) finely chopped andouille* sausage	2 cups chicken stock
	1½ cups heavy cream
1 cup finely chopped onions	½ teaspoon kosher salt
2 tablespoons all-purpose flour	½ teaspoon freshly ground black pepper

*If this ingredient is difficult to find where you live, see Ingredient Sources on page 424.

1. Heat a heavy 2-quart saucepan for 1 minute over high heat. Add the butter to the pan and let it melt, then reduce the heat to medium-high. Add the garlic and cook until it barely starts to brown, about 2 minutes, stirring frequently.

2. Add the andouille and onions and cook until the onions are translucent, about 2 minutes, stirring occasionally.

3. Sprinkle the flour over the andouille mixture and add the thyme to the pan. Cook for 2 minutes, stirring constantly to prevent the mixture from scorching.

4. Gradually add the stock, whisking constantly with a metal whisk. Next, gradually add the cream, whisking constantly until the mixture reaches a low boil.

5. Reduce the heat and add the kosher salt and pepper. Simmer the sauce until it reduces to the consistency of a fairly thin cream soup, 10 to 12 minutes. Remove from heat. Let cool, cover and refrigerate until time to reheat for serving.

NOTES

Recommended alternate species: Cod, grouper, haddock, mahi-mahi, red snapper, tilapia

The sauce may be prepared a day in advance.

ADVANCE STEP

Prepare the chicken stock recipe on page 390.

SPECIAL EQUIPMENT

- A heavy 2-quart saucepan
- A metal whisk

FOR THE CATFISH

2	pounds small sweet potatoes of uniform size, skins scrubbed, divided
	about 4 to 5 tablespoons vegetable oil, preferably canola, divided
2	tablespoons heavy cream
1½	teaspoons plus 1 tablespoon Creole seasoning, divided
½	teaspoon kosher salt
	pinch of freshly ground black pepper
	rounded ½ tablespoon plus 2 teaspoons minced fresh Italian (flat-leaf)
	parsley leaves, divided
6	catfish fillets, each weighing 6½ to 8 ounces
¼	cup good-quality dry white wine

SPECIAL EQUIPMENT

- A mandoline slicer or a food processor with a very fine slicing disk

1. Preheat the oven to 425°F.

2. Pierce 1 pound of the sweet potatoes with fork tines to prevent them from bursting while baking.

3. Bake the potatoes on a rimmed baking sheet until very tender, about 45 minutes. Remove them from the oven and set aside to cool.

4. Reduce the oven setting to 350°F.

5. Peel the remaining 1 pound of sweet potatoes. Using a mandoline slicer or food processor with a very fine slicing disk (2 millimeters or less), slice the sweet potatoes crosswise into very thin rounds, about the thickness of potato chips. Oil the bottom of one or more rimmed baking sheets with vegetable oil. Arrange the rounds in a single layer on the baking sheet(s) and oil the top sides of the rounds.

6. Bake the sweet potato rounds, uncovered, until "al dente," about 7 minutes. Remove rounds from oven, leaving the oven set at 350°. Set aside.

7. Peel the cooled, whole baked sweet potatoes and place in the bowl of a food processor fitted with a metal blade. Add the cream, 1½ teaspoons Creole seasoning, kosher salt, pepper and a rounded ½ tablespoon minced parsley. Process the mixture to a smooth purée.

8. Season the fish fillets on both sides with a total of 1 tablespoon Creole seasoning. Grease a baking sheet large enough to hold all six fish fillets with 2 tablespoons vegetable oil. Arrange the fillets on the baking sheet with the boned sides up (skinned sides down). Coat the top of each fillet with ¼ cup of the sweet potato purée, spreading it evenly with a rubber spatula. Next, cover the entire top of each fillet with a layer of overlapping sweet potato rounds (to approximate the fish's scales), using roughly 16 "scales" (about 2 ounces) per fillet. Pour the wine around the edges of the fillets.

9. Bake the fish, uncovered, in the 350° oven until just cooked through, about 20 minutes. (The cooking time will depend on the thickness of the fillets.) To test for doneness, lift up a fillet with a broad, large and sturdy spatula and use a fork to open it from the bottom to check if the middle is cooked.

10. While the fish are baking, reheat the andouille sauce. Once the fish are done, serve immediately.

Serving Suggestion: Transfer each fillet, scales side up, to a heated dinner plate. Surround the fillet with 3 tablespoons of the andouille sauce and garnish with ½ teaspoon minced parsley. Pass the remaining sauce at the table. 🐚

Crispy Baked Flounder
with Salmon-Roe Butter Sauce & Seafood-Vegetable Rice

For 4 to 6 servings

The flounder's delicate texture and deliciously mild flavor make it especially suited to baking. In this version, the flounder is lightly breaded before cooking to add succulence to it. The fish is served with a butter sauce tinged with the flavor of salmon roe, which is added at the last minute.

A lavishly seasoned seafood-vegetable rice is the suggested accompaniment.

FOR THE SALMON-ROE BUTTER SAUCE

¼ cup shrimp stock, crab stock or bottled clam juice
2 tablespoons good-quality, moderately dry white wine
½ teaspoon lemon zest
2 tablespoons heavy cream
6 tablespoons cold unsalted butter, preferably Plugra or other European-style butter, cut into 6 pats
6 tablespoons (3 ounces) cold crab butter, cut into 6 pats

1. You will need to prepare everything as close to serving time as possible. Here is a suggested sequence of steps to help do that:

   • Set out all the measured ingredients for the rice, flounder and sauce.

   • Cook the basmati rice for the rice dish.

   • Prepare the butter sauce and keep it warm over a double boiler while you finish the rice dish.

   • Bake the flounder.

2. In a heavy 2-quart saucepan, combine the stock, wine and lemon zest. Cook over medium-high heat until the liquid reduces to 1 to 2 tablespoons, two to three minutes.

3. Blend in the cream with a metal whisk and cook until the liquid in the pan reduces to 1 tablespoon, about two minutes.

4. Reduce the heat to medium-low and cook as you add 1 pat of each type of butter at a time, whisking constantly, until both butters are added and incorporated into the sauce. Each addition of the butters should be almost completely melted in before adding more. This should take 5 to 10 minutes total.

5. Remove from heat and set aside in a warm place while preparing the flounder. If not serving the sauce within 15 minutes, transfer it to the top of a

NOTES

Recommended alternate species: drum, John Dory, sea bass, sheepshead, tilapia, walleye

If you are using an electric stove to prepare this recipe, please see the recommendations on page 418.

ADVANCE STEPS

Prepare the following recipes:

If using homemade stock for the sauce, prepare either:

   • Shrimp stock on page 396 or

   • Crab stock on page 391

• Crab butter on page 356

• Soft breadcrumbs on page 382

• If serving the seafood-vegetable rice with the flounder, the recipe on page 345. Prepare it as close to serving time as possible, and no more than 30 minutes ahead.

SPECIAL EQUIPMENT

• A heavy 2-quart saucepan

• A metal whisk

• A double boiler, if preparing ahead

double boiler and serve as soon as possible and definitely within one hour, keeping the uncovered sauce warm over hot (not simmering) water. (Just before serving the sauce, you will add the butternut squash and salmon roe, as instructed below.)

FOR FINISHING AND SERVING THE DISH

2 cups fresh soft breadcrumbs

3 tablespoons very finely sliced chives, plus 4 to 6 teaspoons for garnish

¼ pound (1 stick) unsalted butter, melted and cooled

4 to 6 flounder fillets, each weighing about 6 ounces

kosher salt

freshly ground black pepper

2½ tablespoons peeled, blanched and cubed (⅛-inch cubes) butternut squash*

2 teaspoons salmon roe, preferred, or other fish roe

1 recipe seafood-vegetable rice, optional

*You may blanch the cubes as follows: In a small saucepan over high heat, bring 1 cup water and ¼ teaspoon kosher salt to a boil. Add the squash cubes and blanch them for one minute. Drain, rinse with cold tap water to shock, and drain again.

1. Preheat the oven to 450°F.

2. Thoroughly mix together the breadcrumbs and 3 tablespoons of chives in a large, shallow dish such as a pie plate. Place the melted butter in a separate large, shallow dish.

3. Season the flounder fillets lightly on both sides with kosher salt and pepper. Dip each fillet in the butter, gently shaking off any excess, then lightly coat each with breadcrumbs on both sides. As prepared, place the fillets on a rimmed baking sheet large enough to hold all the fillets.

4. Once all the fillets are breaded, bake them until just cooked through, about eight minutes. While the fish is baking, add the 2½ tablespoons butternut squash cubes and the salmon roe to the warm sauce. When the fish is finished cooking, serve immediately.

Serving Suggestion: If you are serving the seafood-vegetable rice with the flounder, mound ½ cup of the seafood-vegetable rice to one side of each heated serving plate. Use a broad, large and sturdy spatula to transfer a fillet to each plate opposite the rice. Drizzle 2 to 3 tablespoons of sauce over each serving of fish and rice and garnish with 1 teaspoon chives. 🐚

SPECIAL EQUIPMENT

- Two large, shallow dishes such as pie plates
- A rimmed baking sheet large enough to hold the fillets
- A broad, large and sturdy spatula

Seafood-Stuffed Flounder with Garlic Butter Sauce

For 6 servings

Because flounder is a flatfish, many a New Orleans cook thinks the only way to deal with it is to stuff it with shellfish and bake it. This recipe respects that tradition with crabmeat, shrimp and crawfish in a breadcrumb stuffing lavished with garlic, leeks and lemon, among other aromatics.

If you have a smoker, you may want to smoke the shrimp lightly, instead of sautéing them, and fold them into the stuffing. (For instructions on making a stove-top smoker, see page 416.)

The recipe calls for "hinge-cutting" the fish, which can be done by your fish dealer. In a hinge cut, the head is removed and the fish is completely boned with the top and bottom still attached at the tail. Once the fillets are hinge-cut, the brown (top) side should be slit in two lengthwise so that some of the stuffing will show down the center of each fillet. After being hinge-cut, the fillets will weigh about 10 ounces each.

FOR THE GARLIC BUTTER SAUCE

1	cup whole peeled cloves of garlic
¾	cup vegetable oil
¼	cup olive oil
1	cup good-quality dry white wine
⅓	cup rice-wine vinegar
3	bay leaves
3	tablespoons chopped shallots
8	black peppercorns
¼	cup heavy cream
1	pound cold unsalted butter, cut into about 16 pats
1	teaspoon kosher salt or to taste

1. To brown the garlic cloves, heat them in the vegetable and olive oils in a deep, heavy 1-quart saucepan over very low heat, uncovered, for 1 hour. If the cloves start darkening to more than medium golden-brown, remove the pan from heat and let the cloves steep in the hot oil for 30 minutes to 1 hour.

2. Drain the garlic in a coarse-mesh strainer placed over a small heat-proof bowl to catch the oil. Thoroughly mash the cloves with the back of a table fork. You should end up with ⅓ cup mashed cloves. Set aside the garlic cloves and garlic oil separately for up to an hour at room temperature, then cover and refrigerate until they are ready to use.

3. In a heavy 3-quart saucepan, combine the wine, vinegar, mashed garlic, bay leaves, shallots, and peppercorns. Cook over high heat until the liquid comes to a boil, about two minutes.

NOTES

Steps 1 and 2 of the garlic butter sauce recipe should be prepared first because the ingredients for the seafood stuffing include ½ cup of garlic oil.

If you are using an electric stove to prepare this recipe, please see the recommendations on page 418.

ADVANCE STEPS

Prepare the recipes for:

- Creole seasoning on page 385
- Fresh soft breadcrumbs on page 382
- Prepare the first six steps of the garlic butter sauce recipe.

SPECIAL EQUIPMENT

- A deep, heavy 1-quart saucepan
- A coarse-mesh strainer
- A heavy 3-quart saucepan
- A metal whisk
- A fine-mesh strainer
- A double boiler, if preparing ahead

4. Reduce the heat to medium-high and cook the mixture until thick enough to start coating a spoon, about eight minutes, stirring occasionally.

5. Next, reduce the heat to low and cook until the mixture is noticeably thicker, about six minutes, stirring occasionally.

6. Whisk in the cream. (The sauce may be prepared to this point up to 45 minutes ahead and left at room temperature. Reheat the cream mixture briefly over medium heat, whisking constantly, before proceeding to Step 7.)

7. Increase the heat to medium and cook as you add 2 pats of butter at a time, whisking constantly, until all the butter is added and incorporated into the sauce. Each addition of butter should be almost completely melted in before adding more. This will take 10 to 15 minutes total. Remove from heat and whisk in the kosher salt.

8. Strain the sauce through a fine-mesh strainer, pressing all liquid possible through the strainer with the back of a ladle.

    If you are not serving the strained sauce promptly, place it in the top of a double boiler and serve as soon as possible, and definitely within one hour, keeping it warm, uncovered, over hot (not simmering) water.

FOR THE SEAFOOD STUFFING

- ½ cup garlic oil, from browning the garlic for the butter sauce
- 2 scant cups julienned small fresh shiitake mushrooms
- 1 cup sliced leeks, white parts only (¼-inch slices cut in half)
- 1 teaspoon Creole seasoning
- 1 teaspoon kosher salt
- ½ teaspoon cracked black pepper
- 8 ounces medium-size shrimp, peeled
- 8 ounces crabmeat,* preferably jumbo lump, or crab claw meat, picked through
- 8 ounces peeled fresh crawfish* tails plus any of the crawfish's "fat"
- 2 tablespoons very finely grated lemon zest
- 1⅔ cups fresh soft breadcrumbs
- 2 tablespoons minced fresh Italian (flat-leaf) parsley leaves
- 2 tablespoons minced fresh thyme leaves

    *If this ingredient is difficult to find where you live, see Ingredient Sources on page 424.

SPECIAL EQUIPMENT

- A heavy 10-inch sauté pan
- A rimmed baking sheet
- A broad, large and sturdy spatula

1. In a heavy 10-inch sauté pan, heat the garlic oil over medium-high heat until hot, two to three minutes. Add the mushrooms, leeks, Creole seasoning, kosher salt, and cracked pepper. Cook until the vegetables start to wilt, about one minute, stirring occasionally.

2. Stir in the shrimp and continue cooking until the shrimp are cooked about half-way through, about one minute more. Remove from heat.

3. In a large mixing bowl, combine the crabmeat, crawfish tails and any fat, and lemon zest, tossing lightly to keep the crabmeat lumps intact.

4. Add the shrimp mixture to the crabmeat mixture and about two-thirds of the breadcrumbs, mixing lightly. Add the remaining breadcrumbs and mix thoroughly to distribute all ingredients and make sure they are all moistened. At this point, the stuffing will not be very moist.

5. Mix in the parsley and thyme. Set the stuffing aside momentarily.

FOR STUFFING THE FLOUNDERS AND FINISHING THE DISH

  6   whole flounders, each about 1½ pounds, hinge-cut*
      about 1½ teaspoons kosher salt
      about 1½ teaspoons cracked black pepper
  2   tablespoons unsalted butter, cut in 12 bits
  ¾   cup water
  1   tablespoon finely chopped green onions, green parts only, for garnish

      *See the headnote on page 168.

1. Neatly trim the tip end of the tails and sides of the fish fillets, and check to make sure no bones remain in the sides of the fish.

2. Fold back the tops of the fillets and sprinkle a scant ¼ teaspoon kosher salt and a scant ¼ teaspoon cracked pepper over the inside of each fillet.

3. Using a rounded 1 cup (about 5 ounces in weight) of seafood stuffing per fillet, spread the reserved stuffing over the inside of each fillet and close the fillet again so the stuffing can only be seen through the lengthwise split. (The recipe may be prepared up to this point a day ahead; keep well-covered in the refrigerator.) Twenty minutes before baking, set out the stuffed fillets at room temperature.

4. Finish preparing the garlic butter sauce (see Steps 7 and 8 of the sauce recipe on the previous page) and keep it warm in the top of a double boiler until time to serve, as described at the end of the sauce recipe.

5. To bake the flounder, preheat the oven to 350°F.

6. While the oven is heating, arrange the stuffed fillets on an ungreased, rimmed baking sheet. Scatter the bits of butter around the edges of the fillets. Add the water around but not on the fillets.

7. Bake the fillets uncovered until just cooked through, 12 to 25 minutes. The cooking time will vary according to the thickness of the fish. To test for doneness, lift up the top half of one or more of the fillets to make sure the flesh of the fish looks cooked all the way through. Serve immediately.

Serving Suggestion: Use a broad, large and sturdy spatula to transfer a fillet to each heated dinner plate. Spoon 4 tablespoons of the sauce around the fillet and garnish the exposed stuffing with a light sprinkle of green onions.

Pass the remaining sauce at the table to spoon onto the stuffing once it is more exposed as the fish is eaten. 🐚

Horseradish-Crusted Grouper with Creole-Mustard Aioli & Three-Pepper Coleslaw

For 6 servings

Baked fish takes on a whole new identity in this recipe. The fillets are topped with a thick crust of sweet onions, horseradish and breadcrumbs that's enriched with wine and cream.

¼ pound (1 stick) unsalted butter (for melting), plus 5 tablespoons additional butter at room temperature, divided

6 cups finely chopped Vidalia or Walla Walla sweet onions

2 tablespoons minced fresh thyme leaves

1½ cups good-quality dry white wine, divided

½ cup heavy cream

1¾ cups fresh breadcrumbs, divided

⅔ cup loosely packed, freshly grated horseradish, preferred, or ½ cup prepared horseradish

3 tablespoons mild-flavored Louisiana pepper sauce, such as Crystal brand

4 teaspoons kosher salt, divided

1½ teaspoons freshly ground black pepper, divided

6 fillets (6 to 8 ounces) of grouper or alternate species

1 tablespoon finely chopped fresh Italian (flat-leaf) parsley leaves

1 tablespoon minced garlic

1 recipe Creole-mustard aioli, for serving

1 recipe three-pepper coleslaw, for serving

NOTES

Recommended alternate species: catfish, grouper, redfish, salmon, sea bass

ADVANCE STEPS

Prepare the following recipes:

• Fresh breadcrumbs, preferably using French bread on page 382

• Creole-mustard aioli on page 353

• Three-pepper coleslaw on page 322

SPECIAL EQUIPMENT

• A heavy 12-inch skillet or 12-inch sauté pan

• A rimmed baking sheet large enough to hold six fish fillets

• Heavy-duty aluminum foil

• A broad, large and sturdy spatula

1. Preheat the oven to 350°F.

2. In a heavy 12-inch skillet, melt ¼ pound butter over medium heat. Add the onions and sauté until they start to get translucent, about six minutes, stirring occasionally.

3. Add the thyme and cook until the onions are lightly browned, about eight minutes, stirring occasionally.

4. Add ½ cup wine and continue cooking until most of the liquid has evaporated and the mixture is starting to stick, about 12 minutes more.

5. Stir in the cream and continue cooking for seven minutes more. Remove from heat.

6. Transfer the onion mixture to a large mixing bowl. Add 1½ cup breadcrumbs, the horseradish and pepper sauce, 2 teaspoons kosher salt, and ¼ teaspoon pepper, mixing thoroughly. Separate this "stuffing" into six equal portions.

7. Arrange the fillets on a work surface and season each fillet on both sides with kosher salt and pepper, using a total of 1½ teaspoons salt and 1 teaspoon pepper distributed among the six fillets.

8. Cover a rimmed baking sheet large enough to hold all 6 fish fillets with heavy-duty aluminum foil. Grease the foil evenly with 3 tablespoons butter and add 1 cup wine to the pan.

9. Arrange the fillets in a single layer on the foil, with the skinned side down. Spread a portion of the horseradish stuffing evenly over the entire top of each fillet, lightly pressing it into place to help the stuffing adhere to the fish and to make the layer of stuffing uniformly thick.

10. In a small mixing bowl, thoroughly combine ¼ cup breadcrumbs with the parsley, garlic, ½ teaspoon kosher salt, and ¼ teaspoon pepper. Evenly sprinkle an equal portion (about 1½ tablespoons) of the mixture over the top of each fillet, patting it in lightly.

11. Cut 2 tablespoons butter into very small bits and dot each fillet with a portion of the bits.

12. Bake the fillets, uncovered, until they are just cooked through, about 15 minutes.

13. The cooking time will depend on the thickness of the fish. Be careful not to overcook it. To test for doneness, transfer one piece of the fish to a plate and insert the tip of a thin-bladed knife into the thickest part of the fillet for approximately 10 seconds. Remove the knife and lay the tip of the blade flat against the inside of your wrist. If the tip feels hot against your skin, the fish is done. Serve immediately.

Serving Suggestion: Using a broad, large and sturdy spatula, transfer each fillet to a heated dinner plate, stuffing side up. Top each fillet with a dollop of the aioli and serve the coleslaw on the side. Pass any remaining aioli at the table. 🐚

Mahi-Mahi
with an Andouille Crust & Creole-Mustard Aioli

For 6 servings

This recipe calls for a couple of ingredients that are unusual for fish dishes. One is andouille, the lean and spicy smoked sausage found in many parts of South Louisiana.

The other is panko crumbs, which are made from a very dry wheat bread, and are coarser, flakier and lighter than other breadcrumbs. When cooked they take on a lovely golden brown color and also stay crisp longer. They're available in specialty food stores, Asian markets and on-line grocers.

½	cup whole milk
1	large egg
2	cups panko crumbs
4½	ounces andouille sausage,* casing removed and sausage minced in a food processor
1½	teaspoons Creole seasoning
6	mahi-mahi fillets (8 ounces each), about 1 inch thick at the thickest part
1½	teaspoons kosher salt
¼	teaspoon freshly ground black pepper
1	cup clarified butter, divided
1	recipe Creole-mustard aioli, for serving

*If this ingredient is difficult to find where you live, see Ingredient Sources on page 424.

1. In a large mixing bowl, lightly whisk together the milk and egg for the egg wash. In a separate large bowl, combine the panko crumbs, andouille and Creole seasoning, mixing well.

2. Evenly season the fillets on both sides with the kosher salt and pepper. One at a time, dip the fillets into the egg wash, shaking off any excess, then coat them with the panko mixture.

3. Heat ½ cup clarified butter in each of two heavy 10-inch skillets over medium-high heat until hot, about three minutes. Reduce the heat under each skillet to medium, and add three fillets to each skillet.

4. Cook the fillets until golden brown on both sides and just cooked through, about eight to 12 minutes total. The cooking time will vary according to the thickness of the fillets. To test for doneness, transfer one piece of the fish to a plate and insert the tip of a thin-bladed knife into the thickest part of the

NOTES

Recommended alternate species: catfish, cod, grouper, haddock, sea bass, tilapia

Two small batches of the fillets are cooked simultaneously in separate skillets to allow sufficient space for even cooking. Each batch is cooked in fresh clarified butter to achieve the best flavor and color of the finished dish.

ADVANCE STEPS

Prepare the recipes for:
- Creole seasoning on page 385
- Clarified butter on page 355
- Creole mustard aioli on page 353

SPECIAL EQUIPMENT

- 2 large mixing bowls
- 2 heavy 10-inch skillets or heavy 10-inch sauté pans
- A broad, large and sturdy spatula

fillet for approximately 10 seconds. Remove the knife and lay the tip of the blade flat against the inside of your wrist. If the tip feels hot against your skin, the fish is done.

5. Serve immediately.

Serving Suggestion: Use a broad, large and sturdy spatula to transfer a fillet to each heated dinner plate and top each fillet with about 1 tablespoon Creole-mustard aioli. Pass the remaining aioli at the table. ◍

Pompano en Papillotes with Crab Butter Sauce

For 4 main-dish servings

To the well heeled French-Creoles of New Orleans in the early 1900s, restaurant dining meant much more than having food cooked in a kitchen and brought to table. Romance and spectacle could be an important aspect of a grand dinner as well. The evidence appears in such time-honored New Orleans dishes as pompano *en papillotes*.

In this classic concoction, fillets of the fish from the Gulf of Mexico known as pompano are baked with a sauce inside a sealed packet of parchment paper, called a papillote (and pronounced pah-pea-YAWT). As the fish bakes, steam collects in the packet and it puffs into a balloon. The air-filled papillotes are then brought from the oven to the table to be cut open, revealing the ready-to-eat sauced fish.

Legend says the original pompano en papillotes was created to honor the French Brazilian hot-air balloonist Alberto Santos-Dumont, who designed the first practical balloons during the early 1900s.

The pompano species apparently was chosen not only for its delicate but distinct flavor, but because its firm flesh did not break up in the cooking process and its uniform thickness made for even cooking. Unlike the traditional dish, this one calls for pieces of roasted tomato.

4	skinless pompano* fillets, 7 to 8 ounces each (See Notes, right)
¼	cup extra-virgin olive oil
1	medium-size clove garlic, peeled and cut crosswise in thin slices
1	fennel bulb (about 7 ounces) julienned ¼ inch thick by 1 inch long (about 1½ cups of julienne)
1	red onion (about 7 ounces) julienned ¼ inch thick by 1 inch long (about 1¾ cups of julienne)
1	recipe crab butter sauce
1¼	teaspoons kosher salt, divided
1	teaspoon freshly ground black pepper, divided
4	tablespoons unsalted butter, divided
1	recipe slow-roasted Roma tomatoes with fresh tarragon
4	small fresh sprigs of tarragon
6	ounces crab butter, sliced into 8 equal-sized rounds
	non-stick vegetable spray or vegetable oil, to oil the tops of the papillotes

1. Use a knife to neatly cut away the bloodlines extending down the center of each pompano fillet, creating two fillet strips for each serving. Cover the fillets and refrigerate them.

NOTES

To keep the pompano from tasting oily, completely remove the blood line at the middle of the fillet.

If pompano is not available, other white, firm-fleshed fish may be substituted, such as mahi-mahi, swordfish, drum, wahoo, sheepshead or redfish.

ADVANCE STEPS

Prepare the recipes for:

- Slow-roasted Roma tomatoes with fresh tarragon on page 348
- Crab butter on page 356 (The crab butter is an ingredient of both the pompano en papillotes recipe and the crab butter sauce recipe on page 362.)

2. While the fillets are chilling, create the parchment-paper papillotes. (See the instructions at the end of this recipe.)

3. Preheat the oven to 450°F.

4. Heat an empty, heavy, nonreactive 12-inch skillet over high heat for 1 minute. Add the olive oil and garlic and cook for 30 seconds, stirring constantly.

5. Add the fennel and red onions, and reduce the heat to low-to-very-low. Cook until the vegetables are soft but not mushy, about 25 minutes, stirring occasionally and thoroughly to coat all the vegetable pieces with oil. (During the cooking process, the oil will bubble slightly.)

6. Meanwhile, prepare the crab butter sauce. (The crabmeat will not be added to the sauce until serving time.)

7. Once the fennel and red onion mixture is cooked, stir in ½ teaspoon kosher salt and ½ teaspoon pepper. Remove the vegetables from heat and drain them for 5 to 10 minutes in a colander placed over a bowl to get rid of any excess oil. Set the vegetables aside. (Reserve the oil for another use, since it has a pleasant flavoring of fennel and onions.)

FILLING THE PAPILLOTES

8. Working within one heart-shaped paper sheet at a time, place the sheet on a large work surface. Unfold it and lay it sideways, with the middle crease at a horizontal position. The point should be to your right. Rub 1 tablespoon of unsalted butter to lightly coat the parchment, which will be the inside surface of the papillote.

9. On the top half of each paper sheet, mound 3 level tablespoons of the drained fennel and onion mixture. Next, arrange two pompano fillets over the mound of vegetables and sprinkle the fillets with salt and pepper. For the entire 8 fillets, use a total of ¾ teaspoon kosher salt and ½ teaspoon pepper.

10. Arrange four tomato halves, cut side up, across the top of each serving of fillets. Scatter 3 tablespoons more of the fennel and onion mixture over each group of tomatoes. Arrange a sprig of fresh tarragon and 2 rounds of crab butter on each serving of fish.

11. Close and seal the parchment packets. (See instructions, opposite.)

BAKING THE PAPILLOTES

12. Place the filled packets on an ungreased rimmed baking sheet and spray the tops with non-stick vegetable spray, or lightly brush with vegetable oil. Bake the packets on the baking sheet in the middle of the oven for 10 minutes. They should inflate as steam builds up inside.

13. Meanwhile, when the packets are almost finished baking, add the crabmeat to the crab butter sauce and transfer it to a warm sauce bowl.

    Serving Suggestions: Promptly transfer the baked papillotes from the oven to well heated dinner plates and serve at once.

    At the table, use a serrated knife to make a slit at the side of each papillote and cut near (but not on) the edge to open the packet most of the way, being careful that the escaping steam doesn't burn you.

    Roll the paper back with a fork. The food is eaten from the opened packet. Pass the sauce at the table. ✾

SPECIAL EQUIPMENT

- A heavy, stainless steel or other nonreactive* 12-inch skillet
- 4 sheets of parchment paper, each 24 by 15½ inches
- A rimmed baking sheet

*See Using Nonreactive Cookware, page 419.

INSTRUCTIONS FOR MAKING THE PARCHMENT-PAPER PAPILLOTES

1. Cut four sheets of parchment paper to create four rectangles 24 by 15½ inches.

2. Fold the long side of each sheet in half so the folded sheet measures 12 inches by 15½ inches. Press the fold to crease it.

3. Along the folded edge of each sheet, measure 3 inches from the top of the sheet. Mark the 3-inch point on the paper.

4. Begin cutting the folded sheet at the 3-inch point to form the rounded top of a half-heart. Then cut out the remainder of the half-heart, ending at the bottom point and making the half-heart as large as the paper permits.

5. Unfolded, each of the four finished hearts should measure roughly:

    –12 inches long at the fold

    –16 inches long when measured diagonally from the bottom point of the heart to the widest part of the top curve

    –11 inches wide at the widest part of the heart at the top.

CLOSING AND SEALING THE PAPILLOTES. After the fish and vegetables have been placed on the top half of each heart-shaped paper sheet, the paper's curved edges need to be closed and sealed as tightly as possible, so that the resulting paper container will balloon as steam collects while the fish bakes.

1. With the pointed end of the paper at the right, bring the curved bottom edge of the paper up to about ¼ inch below the edge of the top half. The parchment is now ready to be sealed.

2. Starting at the end of the curve at the bottom-left of the half-heart, fold the top half's edge over the bottom half's edge. Continue making overlapping folds of about 1½ inches along the curved edges of the paper. Each fold should be doubled, to create as tight a seal as possible.

3. After completing the folds all the way to the pointed end at the right, twist the point and fold it under to completely seal the fish inside the paper container.

 Redfish Court-Bouillon

For 4 to 6 servings

This Louisiana classic is derived from the traditional court-bouillon (pronounced koo-bee-YAWN) that has been known to generations of cooks throughout France as a flavored stock for poaching seafood or meat.

To the Creole cooks of New Orleans, who took their cues from African and Caribbean traditions, a court-bouillon was a whole, firm-fleshed fish baked in a thickened stock bursting with herbal and spicy flavors. In some parts of South Louisiana, cooks also have used catfish, shrimp and turtle for this old standby.

Our court-bouillon recipe calls for stove-top cooking, with pieces of fish simmered just long enough to cook them through, producing especially light and fresh flavors. It is healthful and easy to prepare, with very little butter and lots of vegetables and herbs.

Serve it with rice or pasta and slices of crusty French bread.

1	tablespoon unsalted butter
8	medium-sized garlic cloves garlic, minced
1	large onion, cored and chopped fine
2	celery stalks, chopped fine
2	medium-size green sweet peppers, chopped fine
6	medium-sized Creole tomatoes,* chopped fine
2½	cups fish fumet
	leaves from 5 sprigs of Italian (flat-leaf) parsley, chopped fine
	leaves from 4 sprigs of thyme, chopped fine
1	tablespoon plus ½ teaspoon kosher salt, divided
½	teaspoon plus ¼ teaspoon fresh-ground black pepper, divided
2	pounds redfish fillets, cut into 4-ounce pieces

*South Louisiana's Creole tomatoes are preferred for this recipe, although other good, peak-of-season regional varieties can be used also.

NOTE

Recommended alternate species: cod, monkfish, sea bass, grouper, catfish, red snapper

ADVANCE STEP

Prepare the recipe for fish fumet on page 388.

SPECIAL EQUIPMENT

• A heavy, nonreactive,* 4-quart saucepan

*See Using Nonreactive Cookware, page 419.

1. Place a heavy, nonreactive 4-quart saucepan over medium-high heat. Add the butter and garlic and cook just until the garlic starts to brown, about seven minutes, stirring almost constantly.

2. Stir in the chopped onions, celery, and sweet pepper. Cook until the onions are clear, about five minutes, stirring occasionally.

3. Add the tomatoes, fumet, parsley, thyme, 1 tablespoon of kosher salt and ½ teaspoon of pepper. Simmer 20 minutes.

4. Season the redfish pieces lightly, using a total of ½ teaspoon of salt and ¼ teaspoon of pepper.

5. After the vegetables have simmered 20 minutes, add the fish to the liquid. Let the court-bouillon return to a simmer, and continue simmering about seven minutes more, until the fish pieces are just cooked through.

6. To test for doneness, transfer one piece of the fish to a plate and insert the tip of a thin-bladed knife into the thickest part of the fillet for approximately ten seconds. Remove the knife and lay the tip of the blade flat against the inside of your wrist. If the tip feels hot against your skin, the fish is done.

Serving Suggestion: Serve the court-bouillon warm, alongside boiled rice or pasta, in heated, shallow soup bowls, with bread for sopping up the sauce. 🐚

Blackened Redfish with Maître d'Hôtel Butter (recipe opposite)

Blackened Redfish with Maître d'Hôtel Butter

For 4 generous servings

Blackening fish is an easy method of cooking them in a seasoned skillet to produce a dark-brown exterior and a wonderfully moist interior. Although the blackened fish may look slightly burned, if cooked properly it will taste heavenly.

While the use of a cast-iron skillet is preferred, a sauté pan also can be used with good results.

½ cup good-quality dry white wine
2 tablespoons unsalted butter, melted
4 8-ounce redfish fillets
2 tablespoons Creole seasoning, divided
1 recipe maître d'hôtel butter

1. Preheat the oven to 350°F.

2. Combine the wine and melted butter. Place the mixture in the rimmed baking sheet and set it aside.

3. Place an empty seasoned cast-iron skillet over medium-high heat.

4. Meanwhile, evenly distribute the 2 tablespoons of Creole seasoning mix on both sides of the four fillets, rubbing ½ tablespoon onto each fillet.

5. After the skillet has been on the burner for three or four minutes, it should be hot and just starting to smoke. Place two of the fillets in the skillet and cook until each is dark golden on both sides but slightly undercooked, about 1½ minutes per side. (The cooking time will depend on the thickness of the fish.)

6. Transfer the cooked fillets to the rimmed baking sheet with a broad, large and sturdy spatula and set them aside. Cook the remaining two fillets as you did the first two, and transfer them to the baking sheet as well.

7. Place the pan with the four fillets, uncovered, in the oven and bake until they are just cooked through, about five minutes. To test for doneness, insert the tip of a thin-bladed knife into the thickest part of the fillet for approximately 10 seconds. Remove the knife and lay the tip of the blade flat against the inside of your wrist. If the tip feels hot against your skin, the fish is done.

Serving Suggestion: Serve the fish immediately, topped with rounds of maître d'hôtel butter, using 1 to 2 tablespoons of butter for each serving.

NOTES

Recommended alternate species: Catfish, cod, grouper, halibut, salmon, tilapia, tuna fish

Only two fillets are cooked at once to allow sufficient space for even cooking.

ADVANCE STEPS

Prepare the recipes for:
• Creole seasoning on page 385
• Maître d'hôtel butter on page 360

SPECIAL EQUIPMENT

• A rimmed baking sheet
• A seasoned 12-inch cast-iron skillet*
• A broad, large and sturdy spatula

*A heavy-gauge, 12-inch sauté pan which does not require seasoning can be substituted for the cast-iron skillet with good results. If the cast-iron skillet is new, it must be seasoned to keep the fish from sticking to the pan during cooking. For suggestions on doing this, see page 418.

Blackened-Redfish Burgers with Pan-Fried Eggplant & Avery Island Aioli

For 6 burgers

The blackening method has been used for all sorts of fish and meats. In this recipe, a new blackening trail is blazed with zestily seasoned patties of ground redfish subbing for ground beef in a hamburger. The olive oil provides flavor and helps hold the burger together, much as fat in ground meat or sausage holds the meat together.

This burger is usually served "dressed," which in New Orleans means "with the works." In this case the "works" are lettuce leaves, tomato slices, red onion and an aioli mayonnaise with a Louisiana kick to it. Rounds of pan-fried eggplant are the side dish.

6   redfish fillets, 8 ounces each, thoroughly chilled
¼   cup plus 2 tablespoons vegetable oil, preferably canola, plus oil to grease
       skillet
2   tablespoons olive oil
½   cup finely sliced green onions, green and white parts
2   tablespoons Creole seasoning
1   recipe pan-fried eggplant
       kosher salt, to taste
       freshly ground black pepper, to taste
       lettuce leaves
       sliced tomatoes
       thinly slivered red onions
6   toasted and buttered hamburger buns, preferably topped with sesame-seed
1   recipe Avery Island aioli
       optional garnishes: 12 slices of dill pickle or 12 whole pickled okra

1.   If using a meat grinder, chill all the non-electric parts of the grinder, including the plate with ³⁄₁₆-inch holes, in the freezer until very cold, about five minutes. Likewise, chill a large mixing bowl until cold.

2.   Once the grinder parts are well chilled, grind the fish. If the ground fish still feels cold to the touch, you don't need to re-chill the fish before proceeding to Step 4 below.

3.   If hand-chopping the fish, chop it very finely and refrigerate it again for 35 to 45 minutes until it's well chilled.

4.   In the chilled large mixing bowl, use your hands to mix together the cold fish with the vegetable and olive oils, green onions and Creole seasoning. Lightly blend the mixture until all the fish is coated with oil and the seasonings are evenly distributed.

NOTES

Recommended alternate species: amberjack, cod, mahi-mahi, sea bass, tilapia, tuna

The fish fillets should be thoroughly chilled for at least one hour before they are ground or chopped, so the patties will hold together while being cooked.

Because the pan-fried eggplant rounds need to be finished as close to serving time as possible, prepare the eggplant recipe just before blackening the burgers.

If a meat grinder is not available, the fish may be chopped fine instead, with excellent results.

ADVANCE STEPS

Prepare the recipes for:
- Creole seasoning on page 385
- Pan-fried eggplant on page 333 (See Notes above.)
- Avery Island aioli on page 353

SPECIAL EQUIPMENT

- An electric or hand-operated meat grinder with a plate that has ³⁄₁₆-inch holes, optional
- A 13-inch or similar size cast-iron skillet
- A broad, large and sturdy spatula

5. Form a very small "sample" patty using 1 to 2 teaspoons of the ground or chopped fish. This sample patty will be cooked after all of them have been chilled (as directed in Step 8 below), in order to assess if the large patties need to be salted and peppered.

6. Next, form the remaining fish into six equal-size patties about ¾ inch thick and 4¼ inches in diameter. Cover and refrigerate the sample patty and six large patties for at least one hour or up to three hours.

7. Just before cooking the fish patties, cook the pan-fried eggplant as described in the eggplant recipe. Keep the eggplant slices warm on a rimmed baking sheet lined with paper towels in a 200°F oven. They will stay as good as new for 15 to 20 minutes, which allows sufficient time for blackening the burgers.

8. To blacken the burgers, grease a 13-inch or similar-size cast-iron skillet with vegetable oil. Heat the skillet over high heat until hot, about two minutes. When the skillet is fairly hot, cook the sample patty to taste. Taste the sample, and if needed, sprinkle kosher salt and pepper to taste on the six large patties.

9. Add three of the patties to the hot skillet. Cook the patties on both sides until they are very dark brown, about four minutes on each side, turning with a broad, large and sturdy spatula. To test for doneness, transfer one patty to a plate and insert the tip of a thin-bladed knife into the thickest part of the patty for approximately 10 seconds. Remove the knife and lay the tip of the blade flat against the inside of your wrist. If the tip feels hot against your skin, the fish is done.

10. Transfer the cooked fish patties to a platter and blacken the second batch of patties as you did the first. Serve immediately.

    Serving Suggestions: To serve the fish burgers open-faced, place lettuce, tomato slices and onion slivers on the bottom half of a toasted and buttered bun and the fish patty on the top half. Mound ¾ teaspoon aioli in the center of each patty, and arrange three eggplant slices at the side of the plate. If garnishing the plate, use two dill pickle slices or two whole pickled okra.

    Offer a very small bowl of the remaining aioli on the side of each plate as a dip for the eggplant, or pass the aioli in a larger bowl at the table.   🐚

Grilled Redfish and Crabmeat with Lemon-Butter Sauce

For 8 servings

Fish laden with crabmeat and sauced with lemon and butter—it's a classic New Orleans dish that tastes every bit as good as it sounds.

The combination is especially elegant and luxurious if the crab atop the fish is in jumbo lumps. These may be hard to find, as well as expensive—they cost twice to three times more than other crabmeat—but their sumptuous flavor can be worth the time and money.

The fish's very flattering sauce is a beurre blanc zapped with lemon. Hickory chips are suggested here for their sweetness, although mesquite and other woods suitable for grilling can be substituted. Soaking the hickory will increase the fish's smoky flavor.

Speckled trout and red snapper are especially good pinch-hitters for redfish.

1   recipe lemon butter sauce
     salad oil (not olive oil) for brushing on the grill rack and fish fillets
¼   cup good-quality dry white wine, divided, plus a few tablespoons of the wine
       if grilling the fillets in batches
6   skinless redfish fillets, 6 to 8 ounces each, neatly trimmed, with the "belly"
       removed if it is still attached
2   tablespoons Creole seasoning
4   tablespoons unsalted butter
1   pound jumbo lump crabmeat,* picked through
1   teaspoon kosher salt
⅛   teaspoon freshly ground black pepper
     warm French bread, for the table

*If this ingredient is difficult to find where you live, see Ingredient Sources on page 424.

NOTES

Recommended alternate species: speckled trout, red snapper, grouper, mahi-mahi, sea bass, swordfish, tilapia

You will have some of the sauce left over. It won't keep for another meal and is delicious as a dip for bread pieces.

ADVANCE STEPS

Prepare the recipes for:

• Creole seasoning on page 385

Just before grilling the fish:

• Lemon butter sauce on page 363

SPECIAL EQUIPMENT

• An outdoor grill
• Hickory (or your favorite) wood chips
• A broad, large and sturdy spatula
• A heat-proof platter, if grilling the fillets in batches

1. Clean the grill rack with a wire brush and preheat it until it is hot. Then add wet or dry hickory or other wood chips. Brush the rack with a thick wad of paper towels saturated in salad oil, holding the paper towels with long-handled tongs so you don't burn yourself.

2. While the grill is preheating, prepare the lemon butter sauce if this is not already done, and keep it warm as directed in the sauce recipe.

3. Place the fillets on a work surface. Brush both sides with salad oil, and season each fillet evenly on both sides with Creole seasoning, using ½ teaspoon of the seasoning on each side of each fillet.

4.   Once the grill is ready, place the fillets directly on it and cook until they are done, about 2½ to 4 minutes per side. The cooking time will vary according to the heat of the grill and the thickness of the fillets. (Watch closely so the fish does not overcook.) Use a broad, large and sturdy spatula to turn over the fillets at least once while cooking.

5.   When you think the fish is approaching the level of doneness you're looking for, briefly insert the tip of a knife into the thickest part of the fillet. Then lay the tip of the blade flat against the inside of your wrist. If the tip feels hot against your skin the fish should be done.

6.   If cooking the fillets in batches, transfer them to a heat-proof platter placed in a warm spot, and drizzle the fillets with white wine to keep them moist while grilling the remaining fish.

7.   While the fillets are grilling, sauté the crabmeat.

8.   In a heavy 12-inch sauté pan, melt butter over medium-high heat until hot, about three minutes. Add ¼ cup wine and heat for 30 seconds. Add the crabmeat and season with 1 teaspoon kosher salt and ⅛ teaspoon pepper.

9.   Cook until the crabmeat is just warmed through, about two minutes, lightly tossing so the lumps of crabmeat stay intact. Serve immediately.

Serving Suggestion: Arrange a fish fillet on each heated dinner plate. Top each with a portion of the crabmeat, and spoon 3 tablespoons of the sauce over it.

Grilled Redfish "on the Half-Shell" with Maître d'Hôtel Butter

For 6 servings

The title of this recipe comes from the cooking method, which calls for grilling only on one side, with the scales and skin side down. The benefits are increasing succulence and flavor.

Baking or broiling does not achieve the same results, since the heat source must come from the bottom.

Hickory chips will impart sweetness, although mesquite and other woods suitable for grilling can be substituted. Soaking the hickory will increase the smoky flavor.

salad oil (not olive oil) for brushing onto the grill rack and fish fillets

6   redfish fillets with skin and scales still attached on one side, each 6 to 8
      ounces, neatly trimmed, including removing the "belly" if still attached

1   tablespoon Creole seasoning
     a few tablespoons of dry white wine, if grilling in batches

1   recipe maître d'hôtel butter

1. Clean the grill rack with a wire brush and preheat it until it is hot. Then add wet or dry hickory or other wood chips. Brush the rack with a thick wad of paper towels saturated in salad oil, holding the paper towels with long-handled tongs so you don't burn yourself.

2. Place the fillets skin down on a work surface. Make sure the skinless sides are free of any loose scales. Brush the skinless sides with salad oil, and season each fillet evenly on the skinless side with ½ teaspoon Creole seasoning.

3. Once the grill is ready, place the fillets directly on it, skin side down, and cook until they are done, about five to eight minutes. The cooking time will vary according to the heat of the grill and the thickness of the fillets. (Watch closely so the fish does not overcook.) Do not turn over the fillets. Use a broad, large and sturdy spatula to lift each fillet from the grill at least once while cooking so it doesn't stick excessively. To test for doneness, insert the tip of a knife into the thickest part of a fillet to separate the flesh a little to assess if it's cooked all the way through.

4. If cooking the fillets in batches, transfer the cooked fillets, skin side down, to a heat-proof platter placed in a warm spot, and drizzle the fillets with white wine to keep them moist while grilling the remaining fish.

Serving Suggestion: Once all the fillets are cooked, serve immediately, skin side down on heated dinner plates. Top the fillets with rounds of maître d'hôtel butter, using a total of 1 to 1½ tablespoons of butter for each serving.

NOTES

Recommended alternate species: pompano, salmon, sea bass

If you'd like the fish to have a smokier flavor, soak the wood chips for at least four hours, or according to package directions, before grilling. Drain the chips just before using, but leave them dripping wet and add them after the fire is hot.

ADVANCE STEP

Prepare the recipes for:

• Creole seasoning on page 385

• Maître d'hôtel butter on page 360

SPECIAL EQUIPMENT

• An outdoor grill

• Hickory (or your favorite) wood chips

• A broad, large and sturdy spatula

• A heat-proof platter, if grilling the fillets in batches

Bronzed Salmon and Crabmeat with Honey-Lemon Butter Sauce

For 6 servings

In New Orleans' culinary language, *bronzing* means cooking a fish in a very hot skillet, but not going so far as to blacken it. Bronzing is a notch or two below blackening, or just enough to lend the fish a golden-brown color. The technique creates an especially crisp crust on the fish, which in this case is salmon. The crispness contrasts nicely with the softness of the butter sauce and lump crabmeat.

FOR THE HONEY-LEMON BUTTER SAUCE

¾   cup plus 3 tablespoons good-quality dry white wine
1   tablespoon fresh lemon juice
1   teaspoon finely grated lemon zest
2   tablespoons minced shallots
2   tablespoons heavy cream
⅜   pound cold unsalted butter, cut into 12 pats
¼   teaspoon kosher salt
1   tablespoon clover honey

1. In a heavy, nonreactive 2-quart saucepan, combine the wine, lemon juice and zest, and shallots. Cook over medium-high heat until the liquid in the mixture reduces to 1 to 2 tablespoons, about seven minutes.

2. Add the cream and cook until the liquid in the pan reduces to 1 to 2 tablespoons, about four minutes. (The sauce may be prepared to this point up to 45 minutes ahead and left at room temperature. Reheat the cream mixture briefly over medium heat, whisking constantly, before proceeding to Step 3.)

3. Reduce heat to medium-low and cook as you add 1 pat of butter at a time, whisking constantly, until all the butter is added and incorporated into the sauce. Each addition of butter should be almost completely melted in before adding more. This will take roughly 10 minutes total.

4. Remove from heat and whisk in the kosher salt.

5. If serving the sauce immediately, strain through a fine-mesh strainer into a small saucepan. If serving later, strain the sauce into the top of a double boiler and serve as soon as possible and definitely within one hour, keeping it warm, uncovered, over hot (not simmering) water.

6. Either way, whisk in the honey immediately after straining the sauce.

NOTES

Just before cooking the salmon, prepare the lemon and honey butter sauce.

If you are using an electric stove top to prepare this recipe, please see the recommendations on page 418.

SPECIAL EQUIPMENT

• A heavy, nonreactive,* 2-quart saucepan
• A fine-mesh strainer
• A double boiler, if preparing ahead

*See Using Nonreactive Cookware, page 419.

FOR THE BRONZED SALMON AND CRABMEAT

- 1 cup clarified butter, melted
- 1 tablespoon kosher salt
- 1½ teaspoons freshly ground black pepper
- 6 salmon fillets, each 5 to 6 ounces and about 1½ inches thick at the thickest part
- 2 teaspoons extra-virgin olive oil
- 1 pound fresh jumbo lump crabmeat, picked through
- 1 tablespoon minced fresh Italian (flat-leaf) parsley leaves

1. Pour the melted clarified butter into a large, shallow dish such as a pie plate. Set aside.

2. Salt and pepper each fillet evenly on both sides, using a total of 1 tablespoon kosher salt and 1½ teaspoons pepper divided among the 6 fillets. Pat the seasonings in with your fingertips.

NOTES

It's important to use a heavy skillet or heavy sauté pan for this bronzing technique. If you don't have a heavy skillet or sauté pan large enough to hold all the fillets at once, use two smaller heavy pans and cook the fillets in two batches simultaneously so all the fillets can be served quickly once done.

While bronzing the salmon, be sure to have your stove vent on and ventilate your kitchen well so the smoke created from cooking doesn't set off your smoke alarm.

3. Heat an empty heavy 12-inch skillet over high heat until it just starts to smoke, about two minutes.

4. Once the skillet is hot, submerge the fillets in the clarified butter one at a time and add the fillet and any butter drippings to the skillet.

5. Promptly reduce the heat to medium, and cook the fillets until the undersides are a bronze color and they have turned white up the sides about ¼ inch, about two and a half minutes.

6. Turn the fillets over with a broad, large and sturdy spatula, and continue cooking until the undersides have turned bronze and the fish is rare to medium rare at the thickest part, about one and a half minutes more. (If you like salmon cooked to medium doneness, cook about three and a half minutes on the first side and two minutes on the second side.) To test for doneness, use a thin-bladed knife to make a slit in the thickest part of the fillet and look inside for the desired level of doneness.

7. While the fillets are cooking, prepare the crab garnish. Once each fillet is finished cooking, promptly transfer it to the center of a heated dinner plate.

8. In a heavy 10-inch skillet over medium-high heat, heat the olive oil just until hot, about 45 seconds. Add the crabmeat and parsley and reduce heat to low. Cook, lightly tossing so the lumps of crabmeat stay intact, just until the crabmeat is warmed through, about three minutes. Serve immediately.

Serving Suggestion: Mound a portion of the crabmeat on top of each salmon fillet. Spoon 1 tablespoon of the honey-lemon butter sauce over the fillet, and drizzle another 1 tablespoon of the sauce on the plate around the fillet. 🦪

ADVANCE STEP

Prepare the recipe for clarified butter on page 355.

SPECIAL EQUIPMENT
- A large, shallow dish such as a pie plate
- A heavy 12-inch skillet or a heavy 12-inch sauté pan
- A broad, large and sturdy spatula
- A heavy 10-inch skillet

Sautéed Sheepshead with Potato "Scales" & Hollandaise Sauce

For 6 generous servings

This succulent, garlicky fish with its lemony rich hollandaise goes exceptionally well with wilted spinach or other green-vegetable side dishes.

The presentation, with very thin slices of potato representing the fish's scales, is worth the trouble, especially if you're serving it on a special occasion. Hollandaise sauce proves an ideal partner.

Be sure to save the oil from the roasted garlic to flavor vinaigrettes or drizzle over rice, potatoes, pastas, vegetables, meats or warm bread.

100	medium-to-large (2½ cups peeled) garlic cloves, peeled and trimmed
2¼	cups vegetable oil (approximately)
¾	cup olive oil (approximately)
1	large (about 1 pound) Idaho potato
2	cups plus 2 tablespoons clarified butter, divided
½	cup good-quality dry white wine
6	sheepshead fillets, each 6 to 8 ounces
1	tablespoon minced fresh thyme leaves
¾	teaspoon kosher salt or to taste
½	teaspoon freshly ground black pepper or to taste
1	recipe hollandaise sauce
12	chive stems or 6 sprigs of Italian (flat leaf) parsley, for garnish

1. Preheat the oven to 350°F.

2. Place the garlic cloves in a 1½-quart casserole and pour enough of the vegetable and olive oils over the cloves to submerge them. Cover the casserole and bake the cloves in the oven until tender and pale golden, about one hour. Remove from the oven and let the garlic and oil cool uncovered for 30 minutes.

3. Drain the garlic cloves in a mesh strainer placed over a bowl to catch the garlic-flavored oil, draining well. Once the garlic oil is cool, cover and refrigerate to use within a few days in another dish. The roasted garlic may be prepared several hours ahead. Store it in a covered container in the refrigerator until ready to use.

4. In a food processor or blender, purée the roasted garlic until smooth. Set aside at room temperature.

5. Peel the potato. Using a mandoline or sharp, thin-bladed knife, slice the potato crosswise into ¹⁄₁₆-inch-thick slices. Cover snugly with plastic wrap to keep the slices from discoloring. Set aside.

NOTES

Recommended alternate species: Red snapper, speckled trout, snapper

Only small batches of the fillets are cooked at once to allow sufficient space for even cooking. Each batch is cooked in fresh clarified butter to achieve the best flavor and color of the finished dish.

ADVANCE STEPS

Prepare the clarified-butter recipe on page 355.

Just before seasoning the fish (Step 7 below), and no more than 30 minutes before serving, prepare the hollandaise sauce recipe on page 367.

SPECIAL EQUIPMENT

- A 1½-quart casserole with a lid
- An electric food processor or blender
- A mandoline slicer or a sharp thin-bladed knife
- Heavy-duty aluminum foil
- A rimmed baking sheet large enough to hold all six fish fillets
- A rubber spatula
- 2 heavy 12-to-14-inch skillets
- 2 large, broad and sturdy spatulas

6.   Using heavy-duty aluminum foil, cover a rimmed baking sheet large enough to hold six fish fillets in a single layer. Grease the foil evenly with 2 tablespoons clarified butter, and add the wine to the pan. Set aside.

7.   Arrange the fillets in a single layer on a work surface. Season on both sides with thyme, salt and pepper, using a total of 1 tablespoon thyme, ¾ teaspoon kosher salt and ½ teaspoon pepper (or salt and pepper to taste) distributed among the six fillets.

8.   With the fillets skinned-side down, use a rubber spatula to evenly spread a portion (about 3 tablespoons) of the reserved roasted garlic purée over the entire top surface of each fillet. Next, cover the fillets lengthwise with one row of the reserved potato slices, overlapping the slices slightly to resemble fish scales. If the fillets are considerably wider than the potato scales, add another row of scales or half-scales to cover the entire surface.

9.   Preheat the oven to 350° degrees once more. Place 1 cup clarified butter in each of two heavy 12-to-14-inch skillets. Heat the butter over medium-high heat until bubbly hot, about two and a half minutes.

10. Once the butter is bubbling, use two broad, large and sturdy spatulas to carefully transfer two fillets, one at a time, to each skillet with the potato side down. (To do this, lift a fillet from the work surface with one spatula and use the other spatula to help support the fish and hold the potatoes in place as you gently flip the fish over, easing it into the skillet and being careful not to splash yourself with hot butter.) Cook the fillets until the potatoes are light golden brown, one to two minutes.

11. Now, without browning the other sides of the fillets, transfer the fillets from the skillets to the prepared baking sheet, carefully turning each over so the potato side is up. Realign the potato "scales" if they've slipped out of place. Wipe the spatulas clean after transferring each fillet to the baking sheet.

12. Set the baking sheet aside while you cook the remaining two fillets, one in each of the two skillets, as you did the first four fillets.

13. Transfer the last two fillets to the baking sheet with the other fillets and realign the potato scales if needed.

14. Bake the fillets, uncovered, until they are just cooked through, about 10 minutes. (The cooking time will depend on the thickness of the fish. Be careful not to overcook.) To test for doneness, insert the tip of a thin-bladed knife into the thickest part of the fillet for approximately 10 seconds. Remove the knife and lay the tip of the blade flat against the inside of your wrist. If the tip feels hot against your skin, the fish is done. Serve immediately.

Serving Suggestion: Using a clean broad, large and sturdy spatula, transfer the fillets to heated dinner plates, potato sides up. Spoon 4 tablespoons of the hollandaise across and around each fillet. Garnish each serving with 2 chive stems laid across one another or a sprig of parsley. 🐚

Trout Amandine

For 6 servings

In French cooking, the word *amandine* can be tagged onto any preparation that is flavored with almonds, especially pastry.

In New Orleans' French-Creole cuisine, amandine always refers to a method of cooking trout—or, to be more specific, to add butter-toasted almond slivers onto trout meunière, which is trout fillets that have been dusted with flour, sautéed in butter, moistened with a bit of lemon and garnished with parsley.

Trout amandine has been a menu staple in New Orleans restaurants for a hundred years or more. Taste it and you'll understand why.

6	skinless trout fillets, each weighing 5 to 6 ounces
2½	teaspoons kosher salt, divided
¾	teaspoon freshly ground black pepper
1½	cups clarified butter, divided
1	cup seasoned flour
⅔	rounded cup blanched sliced almonds
3	tablespoons fresh lemon juice
1	teaspoon minced fresh Italian (flat-leaf) parsley leaves

1. Preheat oven to 350°F.

2. Line a rimmed baking sheet large enough to hold all six fish fillets with heavy-duty aluminum foil. Set aside.

3. Arrange the fillets in a single layer on a work surface.

4. Sprinkle kosher salt and pepper on each fillet on both sides, using a total of 1½ teaspoons kosher salt and the pepper.

5. In each of two heavy 12-inch sauté pans, heat ½ cup clarified butter over medium-high heat until hot, about three minutes.

6. While the butter is heating, place the seasoned flour in a large, shallow dish such as a pie plate. Dredge each fillet in the seasoned flour, pressing the flour in lightly so it adheres to the fish, then shaking off any excess.

7. Once the butter in the two skillets is hot, reduce the heat under each skillet to medium, and carefully slide three fillets, skinned side up, into each skillet of butter. Cook until light golden brown on the underside, two to three minutes.

8. Gently turn the fillets over with a broad, large and sturdy spatula. Continue cooking for one minute more. With the spatula, lift each fillet from the skillet and blot some of the butter with paper towels as you transfer it to the baking sheet.

NOTES

Recommended alternate species: flounder, red snapper, sea bass, walleye

Two small batches of the fillets are cooked at once in separate skillets to allow sufficient space for even cooking.

Each batch is cooked in fresh clarified butter to achieve the best flavor and color in the finished dish.

ADVANCE STEP

Prepare the recipes for:

- Clarified butter on page 355
- Seasoned flour on page 384

SPECIAL EQUIPMENT

- A rimmed baking sheet large enough to hold all six fish fillets
- Heavy-duty aluminum foil
- 2 heavy 12-inch sauté pans or heavy 12-inch skillets
- A large, shallow dish, such as a pie plate
- A large, broad and sturdy spatula
- A heavy 9-inch skillet

9. Now, bake the fillets, uncovered, until all are just cooked through, about two minutes. To test the fish for doneness, insert the tip of a thin-bladed knife into the thickest part of the fillet for approximately 10 seconds. Remove the knife and lay the tip of the blade flat against the inside of your wrist. If the tip feels hot against your skin, the fish is done.

10. While the fillets are baking, in a heavy 9-inch skillet heat ½ cup clarified butter over high heat until hot, about three minutes. Add the almonds and cook about 30 seconds. Add the lemon juice, remove from heat and swirl the pan a few seconds. Add 1 teaspoon kosher salt and the parsley and return pan to high heat for about 30 seconds more until the almonds are golden, stirring or swirling pan as they brown. Remove from heat and serve immediately.

Serving Suggestion: Arrange a fish fillet on each heated dinner plate and top each with a portion of the almonds and butter in which they were browned. 🐚

Trout Meunière

For 4 servings

The light flour coating on the fish inspired the French to name this dish *truite à la meunière*, or "trout in the style of the miller's wife." In France, à la meunière has always meant simply lightly coating the fish in flour, cooking it in butter and serving it with a splash of lemon juice, chopped parsley and a tablespoon or two of the browned butter (*beurre noisette*).

The French-Creole cooks of New Orleans added their own fillip—an actual sauce using the original flour, butter, lemon and parsley, but adding worcestershire and vinegar.

Trout is the species that usually gets the miller's-wife treatment, but the other species, such as those listed above, with soft textures and delicate flavors can be cooked this way, too. So can scallops, frog legs and some meats.

about 1 cup vegetable oil, preferably canola oil*
1½ to 2 cups seasoned flour
   6 skinless trout fillets, each weighing 7 to 8 ounces
      kosher salt to taste
      fresh-ground black pepper to taste
   1 recipe meunière sauce, for serving

*Clarified butter may be substituted for the oil for more flavor, but whole butter is not recommended. Oils with a distinct flavor, such as olive oil, should not be used. (A recipe for clarified butter appears on page 355.)

NOTE

Recommended alternate species: Flounder, sole, red snapper, sea bass, walleye

ADVANCE STEP

Prepare the recipes for:

- Seasoned flour on page 384
- Meunière sauce on page 370

SPECIAL EQUIPMENT

- A heavy 12-inch skillet or a heavy 12-inch sauté pan
- A large, shallow baking dish such as a pie plate
- A broad, large and sturdy spatula
- A rimmed baking sheet large enough to hold all six fish fillets

1. Preheat the oven to 425°F.

2. Pour enough of the oil into a heavy 12-inch skillet to produce a ⅛-inch layer on the bottom.

3. Heat the oil over medium heat for about three minutes, or until it reaches a temperature of about 350°F. Since the oil will be too shallow to measure the precise temperature, a good way to determine if it's hot enough is to dip the tip end of a trout fillet in the hot oil. If the oil immediately sizzles, it's ready to use. If it doesn't sizzle immediately, let the oil continue heating, checking each minute, until it is ready.

4. While the oil is heating, place the seasoned flour in a large, shallow baking dish. Season both sides of each trout fillet with kosher salt and pepper, and dredge two of the fillets in the flour.

5. Shake off any excess flour and carefully slide them into the hot oil. Cook them until golden brown, about two minutes on each side. Gently turn the fillets over by carefully sliding a broad, large and sturdy spatula under each,

tilting the pan away from you so the oil pools in that side of pan. Be careful not to slosh the hot oil to avoid burning yourself.

6. Transfer the browned fish to a rimmed baking sheet large enough to hold all six fillets.

7. Repeat this procedure to season, dredge and brown the remaining fish, adjusting the heat if the fillets are browning too quickly or too slowly.

8. Heat the fillets in the oven for two to three minutes, or until they are just cooked through. Be careful not to overcook them.

9. While the fish are in the oven, reheat the sauce over medium-low heat. Stir in the parsley reserved from the meunière sauce recipe.

10. To test the fish for doneness, insert the tip of a thin-bladed knife into the thickest part of the fillet for approximately 10 seconds. Remove the knife and lay the tip of the blade flat against the inside of your wrist. If the tip feels hot against your skin, the fish is done. Serve immediately.

Serving Suggestion: Use the spatula to transfer each fish fillet to a heated dinner plate. Stir the sauce well and top each fillet with about 2 tablespoons of the sauce.

Sautéed Speckled Trout with Lemon-Thyme Tartar Sauce

For 6 servings

While speckled trout is used in this recipe, almost any food fish could be substituted for it. And a simple squeeze of lemon juice might be the only garnish, although the tartar sauce certainly flatters the fish's flavor.

Each batch is sautéed in fresh clarified butter, which lends its color and sumptuous taste to the dish.

butter or non-stick vegetable spray, for baking sheet
6   speckled trout fillets, 6 to 7 ounces each
1½   teaspoons kosher salt
1   teaspoon freshly ground black pepper
1   cup clarified butter, divided
1   cup seasoned flour
1   cup whole milk
1   large egg
1   recipe lemon-thyme tartar sauce

NOTES

Recommended alternate species: flounder, red snapper, sea bass, walleye

Only small batches of the fillets are cooked at once to allow sufficient space for even cooking.

ADVANCE STEPS

Prepare the recipes for:

• Clarified butter on page 355
• Seasoned flour on page 384
• Lemon-thyme tartar sauce on page 377

SPECIAL EQUIPMENT

• A rimmed baking sheet large enough to hold all six fish fillets
• Heavy-duty aluminum foil
• A heavy 12-inch sauté pan or a heavy 12-inch skillet
• Two large, shallow dishes such as pie plates
• A large, broad and sturdy spatula

1. Preheat the oven to 350°F.

2. Line a rimmed baking sheet large enough to hold all six fish fillets with heavy-duty aluminum foil. Lightly butter the foil or spray it with non-stick vegetable spray. Set aside.

3. Arrange the fillets in a single layer on a work surface.

4. Salt and pepper each fillet on both sides, using a total of 1½ teaspoons kosher salt and 1 teaspoon pepper.

5. In a heavy 12-inch sauté pan, heat ⅓ cup clarified butter over medium-high heat until hot, about three minutes.

6. While the butter is heating, place the seasoned flour in a large, shallow dish, such as a pie plate. In another large, shallow dish, lightly whisk together the milk and egg for the egg wash.

7. Moisten two of the fillets all over with the egg wash, letting the excess drip off. Next, dredge in the seasoned flour, pressing the flour in lightly so it adheres to the fish, then shaking off any excess.

8. Once the butter is hot, carefully slide the two fillets, skinned side up, into the butter. Cook until golden brown on the underside, about two minutes.

9. Gently turn the fillets over with a broad, large and sturdy spatula. Continue cooking until the second side is golden brown and the fillets are just cooked through, about two minutes more. Transfer the fish to the reserved baking sheet.

10. Pour off the clarified butter left in the pan and wipe out the pan. Add ⅓ cup fresh clarified butter to the pan and heat the butter while you moisten two more fillets with egg wash and dredge them in the flour.

11. Cook the two fillets as you did the first two, and transfer them to the baking sheet with the other cooked fillets.

12. Again, pour off the butter left in the pan and wipe the pan clean. Heat another ⅓ cup fresh butter while you moisten the last two fillets with egg wash and dredge in flour. Sauté the fillets as you did the others and add to the baking sheet.

13. Now, bake the fillets, uncovered, until all are just heated through, about three minutes. To test the fish for doneness, insert the tip of a thin-bladed knife into the thickest part of the fillet for approximately 10 seconds. Remove the knife and lay the tip of the blade flat against the inside of your wrist. If the tip feels hot against your skin, the fish is done. Serve immediately.

Serving Suggestion: Arrange a fish fillet on each heated dinner plate and top each with 2 tablespoons of the tartar sauce. Pass the remaining tartar sauce at the table. 🐚

Pecan-Crusted Speckled Trout with Rum-Butter Sauce

For 4 servings

Coating fish in flour or a similar dry ingredient can add a pleasant crispness to it. In this recipe, fish fillets are first dredged in pecan flour, then lightly sautéed in butter. The fillet joins sweet-potato cubes and wilted spinach before it's swathed in a creamy sauce with rum and white balsamic vinegar.

1	pound sweet potatoes, peeled and cut into ½-inch cubes
2	tablespoons packed light-brown sugar
4	teaspoons vegetable oil
	about 1½ teaspoons kosher salt, divided
	about 1½ teaspoons freshly ground black pepper, divided
½	pound (2 sticks) unsalted butter, cold
5	tablespoons unsalted butter at room temperature
¼	cup good-quality dark rum
¼	cup white balsamic vinegar
2	tablespoons thinly sliced shallots, ½ to 1 inch long and ⅛ inch wide
1	tablespoon heavy cream
¾	pound baby spinach leaves with stems, washed and drained (drying not necessary)
4	speckled trout fillets, each weighing 5 to 6 ounces
1	cup or more pecan flour
2	tablespoons dry-roasted pecan pieces, optional garnish for fish

1. Preheat the oven to 350°F.

2. In a large mixing bowl, toss the sweet potato cubes with the brown sugar, vegetable oil, ¼ teaspoon kosher salt and ¼ teaspoon pepper, tossing with your hands to coat all the cubes evenly.

3. Line a rimmed baking sheet with parchment paper and spread out the potato cubes in a single layer.

4. Bake the potato cubes just until tender, about 20 minutes.

5. Remove the potatoes from the oven and set aside at room temperature. While the potatoes are baking, make the rum butter sauce.

6. For the sauce, cut the ½ pound of the cold butter into 12 pats and set aside.

7. In a heavy 2-quart saucepan, combine the rum, balsamic vinegar and shallots. Cook over medium-high heat until the liquid in the mixture reduces to 1 to 2 tablespoons, about five minutes.

NOTES

Recommended alternate species: catfish, redfish, trout, walleye

ADVANCE STEP

Prepare the recipe for pecan flour on page 383.

SPECIAL EQUIPMENT

- A rimmed baking sheet
- Parchment paper
- A heavy 2-quart saucepan
- A fine-mesh strainer
- A double boiler
- A heavy 5½-quart Dutch oven
- A pair of tongs
- A large, shallow dish such as a pie plate
- A heavy 14-inch skillet

8.   Add the cream and cook for one minute, stirring constantly.

9.   Reduce the heat to medium-low and cook as you add 2 of the reserved pats of butter at a time, whisking constantly, until all the butter is added and incorporated into the sauce. Each addition of butter should be almost completely melted in before adding more. This will take five to 10 minutes total. Remove from heat.

10. Season the sauce with ¼ teaspoon kosher salt and ¼ teaspoon pepper or to taste. Strain the sauce through a fine-mesh strainer into the top of a double boiler. Serve within one hour, keeping the sauce warm, uncovered, over hot (not simmering) water while finishing the dish.

11. In a heavy 5½-quart saucepan, melt 1 tablespoon of butter at room temperature over medium-high heat. Add half the spinach and cook just until it wilts enough to make room for the remaining spinach, about one minute, tossing constantly with tongs. Add the remaining spinach and continue cooking just until all the spinach is wilted, one to two minutes more.

12. Stir the reserved sweet potatoes into the spinach, blending well. Remove from heat and set aside in a warm place while sautéing the fish.

13. Arrange the fillets in a single layer on a work surface. Very lightly salt and pepper each side of each fillet with ⅛ teaspoon or less kosher salt and ⅛ teaspoon or less pepper.

14. Place the pecan flour in a large, shallow dish such as a pie plate. Dredge each fillet in the pecan flour, pressing the flour in lightly so it adheres to the fish, then shaking off any excess. Add more pecan flour to the dish if needed.

15. In a heavy 14-inch skillet, melt the remaining 4 tablespoons of butter over medium-high heat. Add the fish to the skillet in a single layer, skinned side up.

16. Cook the fish until golden brown on both sides and cooked through, about three minutes per side. Do not overcook. The cooking time will vary according to the thickness of the fish.

17. To test for doneness, transfer one piece of the fish to a plate and insert the tip of a thin-bladed knife into the thickest part of the fillet for approximately 10 seconds. Remove the knife and lay the tip of the blade flat against the inside of your wrist. If the tip feels hot against your skin, the fish is done.

Serving Suggestion: Place a portion of the spinach and sweet potato mixture in the center of each heated dinner plate. Arrange a fish fillet on top of the mixture, and drizzle 2 to 3 tablespoons of the sauce over the fish and onto the plate. If using the dry-roasted pecan pieces, garnish the plate with ½ tablespoon of them. 🐚

For 6 servings

This pretty and colorful dish can amount to a full meal on the plate. An ideal accompaniment would be Pugliese or French bread.

FOR THE SEARED TUNA WITH SHRIMP AND CAPERS

1	large eggplant, about 1 pound and about 7 inches long
1	large onion, peeled and sliced into ⅛-inch rings
8	tablespoons extra-virgin olive oil, divided
	about 2 teaspoons kosher salt, divided
	about 2 teaspoons freshly ground black pepper, divided
8	ounces fresh green beans
	water and ice water to blanch and cool blanched beans
1	tablespoon unsalted butter
1	recipe balsamic-vinegar brown butter sauce (see below)
2	tablespoons minced fresh garlic
1½	pounds raw medium shrimp, peeled with tails removed
6	fresh tuna steaks, each 5 to 6 ounces and 1 inch thick
2¼	cups unpeeled, seeded and finely chopped Creole tomatoes*
2	cups nonpareil** capers, drained and rinsed

*South Louisiana's Creole tomatoes are preferred for this recipe, although other good, peak-of-season regional varieties can be used.
**This tiny variety is considered the best.

1. Preheat the oven to 350°F.

2. Line a rimmed baking sheet with parchment paper and set aside.

3. Slice the ends off the unpeeled eggplant and, cutting crosswise, slice six rounds from the eggplant, each about 1 inch thick. (Use any leftover eggplant in another dish.)

4. Place the rounds on the prepared baking sheet in a single layer. Spread the onion rings on the same baking sheet in as thin a layer as possible, keeping them separated from the eggplant.

5. With a pastry brush, brush the eggplant rounds on both sides with 2 tablespoons olive oil and brush the tops of the onion rings with 2 tablespoons more olive oil. Sprinkle salt and pepper over the tops of the eggplant rounds and onion rings, using a total of a rounded ¼ teaspoon kosher salt and a rounded ¼ teaspoon pepper.

NOTES

You may bake the eggplant rounds and prepare the onion-ring and green-bean mélange a day ahead; keep refrigerated.

Prepare the balsamic-vinegar brown-butter sauce just before cooking the shrimp (See Step 8 on page 208) so the sauce doesn't sit too long before being served.

SPECIAL EQUIPMENT
- A rimmed baking sheet
- Parchment paper
- A pastry brush
- A heavy 12-inch skillet
- A heavy, nonreactive* 10-to-12-inch skillet
- A heavy 11-to-12-inch sauté pan

*See Using Nonreactive Cookware, page 419.

6. Bake uncovered until the eggplant rounds are cooked through and the onions are somewhat soft and starting to brown, about 20 minutes. Meanwhile, blanch the green beans in a pan of boiling unsalted water until crisp but tender, about two minutes. Remove from the heat, drain and shock in ice water. Drain again.

7. Once the eggplant and onion rings are finished baking, melt the butter in a heavy 12-inch skillet over medium heat. Add the green beans, onion rings, ⅛ teaspoon kosher salt, and ⅛ teaspoon pepper, stirring well. Cook just until green beans are reheated, about two minutes, stirring occasionally. Cover and set aside in a warm place. (If the eggplant, onions and green beans were cooked earlier in the day, let cool slightly, then cover and refrigerate until ready to reheat for serving. Reheat in a 250°F oven while cooking the shrimp and tuna.)

8. Prepare the balsamic-vinegar brown-butter sauce (recipe on the next page) and set aside.

9. In a heavy, nonreactive 10-to-12-inch skillet, heat 2 tablespoons olive oil over high heat until hot, about 1½ minutes. Add the garlic and sauté until lightly browned, about 20 seconds. Add the shrimp and season with ½ teaspoon kosher salt and ½ teaspoon pepper. Cook until the shrimp are almost cooked through, about three minutes, stirring occasionally.

10. Meanwhile, season the tuna steaks on both sides with salt and pepper, using 1 teaspoon kosher salt and 1 teaspoon pepper distributed among the six steaks. Also now, in a heavy 11-to-12-inch sauté pan, heat 2 tablespoons olive oil over high heat until just short of smoking, about two minutes.

11. While the sauté pan is heating, and once the shrimp are almost cooked, add the tomatoes and capers to the skillet, stirring well. Continue cooking just until the tomatoes are noticeably bright, about one minute. Remove from heat and set the skillet aside, uncovered, while you cook the tuna.

12. Add the six tuna steaks in a single layer to the hot oil in the sauté pan. Cook until medium-rare and golden brown, about a minute and a half per side, turning only once. To test for doneness, use a thin-bladed knife to make a slit in the thickest part of the fillet and look inside for the desired level of doneness. Remove from heat and serve immediately.

FOR THE BALSAMIC-VINEGAR BROWN-BUTTER SAUCE

⅜ pound (1½ sticks) unsalted butter
 1 tablespoon good-quality balsamic vinegar
⅛ teaspoon kosher salt
⅛ teaspoon freshly ground black pepper

1. In a heavy 1-quart saucepan heat the butter over medium heat until it melts, the foam settles and the solids sink to the bottom of the pan, about three minutes.

2. Reduce the heat to medium-low and continue cooking just until bits of milk solids in the bottom of the pan and around the edge of the surface turn a dark honey-brown, about 10 minutes, stirring occasionally. If in doubt, remove the sauce from the heat a few seconds early, because the solids can burn in a matter of seconds. Immediately transfer the butter to a medium-size, heat-proof mixing bowl and whisk constantly until it stops darkening.

3. Let the butter cool for 15 minutes, then add the balsamic vinegar, kosher salt and pepper, whisking vigorously until the sauce is temporarily emulsified and the salt dissolves.

Serving Suggestions: For each serving, arrange a bed of green beans and onions in the center of a heated dinner plate. Arrange an eggplant round on top of the green beans and onions, and place a tuna steak on top of the eggplant. Spoon a portion of the shrimp, tomatoes and capers over and around the tuna.

If the butter in the sauce has started to solidify, gently reheat the sauce briefly. Vigorously whisk the sauce until it momentarily emulsifies, and drizzle 2 tablespoons of the sauce over all. ❧

NOTE

Make the sauce as close to serving time as possible, since the butter in it will start to solidify if it sits too long. If this happens, just before serving gently reheat the sauce in a small saucepan over low heat to liquefy the butter.

SPECIAL EQUIPMENT

• A heavy 1-quart saucepan
• A medium-size, heat-proof mixing bowl

Shrimp and Crawfish Vol-au-Vents with Crawfish Cardinale Sauce

For 4 main-dish servings

When crawfish are cooked, their shells quickly turn bright red, a phenomenon that inspired the creators of crawfish cardinale to name the dish for the color of the vestments worn by Roman Catholic cardinals. The more traditional version of this classic Creole-French dish is an appetizer served on toast points. In this version, however, crawfish tails and jumbo shrimp are elegantly presented in the puff-pastry shells the French call *vol-au-vents*, which translates as "flies with the wind," a tribute to the pastry's airy lightness.

Like many sauces with French pedigrees, this one is quite rich. You will have 1 to 1½ cups of the sumptuous cardinale sauce left over for later use. An excellent way to use it is to gently reheat it for serving over fish or seafood.

FOR THE VOL-AU-VENTS

1 package puff pastry sheets (17.3-ounces with two sheets 9¼ by 9¾ inches), thawed according to package instructions
1 small egg, lightly beaten

1. Spread a sheet of parchment paper on a work surface. Using a 3¾-inch cookie cutter, cut out eight rounds of puff pastry on top of the parchment paper. With a pastry brush, moisten the top sides of four of the pastry rounds with beaten egg, brushing up to ⅛ inch from the edges. Don't get any egg on the edges or the pastry won't rise.

2. Arrange the remaining four pastry rounds directly on top of the four moistened rounds with the edges even. Brush the four tops with more beaten egg as you did the first four rounds. (You will have some of the egg left over.)

3. Using a 2½-inch cookie cutter, score an evenly spaced circle on each of the four double-layered pastries, cutting through the top pastry round but not into the second. With the tip of a small kitchen knife, cut a shallow cross-hatch design in the 2½-inch circle of each pastry. Place the vol-au-vents about 1 inch apart on a rimmed baking sheet 9½ by 13 inches or larger. Lay a piece of parchment paper over the pastry and refrigerate for 30 minutes before baking.

4. Preheat the oven to 425°F.

5. Once the vol-au-vents have chilled for 30 minutes, remove them from the refrigerator and place another baking sheet underneath the sheet holding them. Bake on the middle shelf of the 425° oven until the pastry is puffed and evenly browned to a light-to-medium golden color. This will take about 18 minutes total; but after 15 minutes, check to make sure the vol-au-vents are not too brown on top. If they are, lay a piece of parchment paper over them and continue to Step 6.

6. Now, reduce the oven setting to 200°, prop open the oven door 1 inch with metal tongs, and continue baking the vol-au-vents 25 minutes more to dry out the interiors.

7. Remove the vol-au-vents from the oven and let them cool on a wire rack. Set aside at room temperature until ready to finish the dish.

FOR THE CARDINALE SAUCE

1½ quarts water
2 teaspoons kosher salt, divided
1 pound live, purged Louisiana crawfish* (select the largest possible active crawfish)
1½ cups coarsely chopped onions

NOTE

The vol-au-vents taste best when used within three hours after baking.

ADVANCE STEP

In preparing the cardinale sauce, you will need 1 pound of live, purged crawfish. For instructions on purging crawfish see page 35, and use only ⅓ cup of kosher salt instead of a full cup.

SPECIAL EQUIPMENT

- Parchment paper
- A 3¾-inch cookie cutter and a 2½-inch cookie cutter, scallop-edged or plain
- A pastry brush
- Two rimmed baking sheets, each 9½ by 13 inches or larger
- A pair of metal tongs
- A wire cooling rack

1	cup coarsely chopped celery
⅔	cup coarsely chopped fennel bulb
½	cup peeled and coarsely chopped carrots
2	medium-size whole bay leaves
2	thyme sprigs
12	black peppercorns
½	teaspoon sweet paprika
½	teaspoon freshly ground black pepper
5	tablespoons unsalted butter, preferably Plugra or other European-style butter
¼	cup all-purpose flour
1	cup canned Italian Roma tomatoes, whole or chopped, in their juice
½	cup good-quality, dry white wine
¼	cup heavy cream

*If this ingredient is difficult to find where you live, see Ingredient Sources on page 424.

SPECIAL EQUIPMENT
• A heavy 6-quart saucepan
• A colander placed over a heat-proof bowl
• A heavy, nonreactive* 5-quart saucepan
• A heavy-duty kitchen mallet
• A heavy-duty potato masher or similar sturdy utensil
• A fine mesh strainer and a very fine mesh strainer (or use a strainer lined with cheesecloth)
• A heavy 4-quart saucepan
• A heavy 10-inch skillet

*See Using Nonreactive Cookware, page 419.

1. Combine the water and 1 teaspoon kosher salt in a heavy 6-quart saucepan. Bring the water to a boil over high heat, then add the live crawfish and cook uncovered for two minutes without stirring. Remove the pan from heat and drain the crawfish in a colander placed over a heatproof bowl to catch the cooking liquid. Measure out 4 cups of the cooking liquid and set it and the crawfish aside separately. Discard the leftover cooking liquid.

2. In a medium-size mixing bowl, combine the onions, celery, fennel, carrots, bay leaves, thyme sprigs, peppercorns, 1 teaspoon salt, and the paprika and pepper. In a heavy, nonreactive 5-quart saucepan, melt the butter over high heat. Add the onion mixture, stirring well. Cook until the vegetables are soft, about eight minutes, stirring occasionally.

3. Add the reserved crawfish and cook for five minutes. During this cooking time, stir occasionally and use a heavy-duty kitchen mallet or other sturdy utensil to crush the crawfish shells into bits as thoroughly as possible. (Crushing the crawfish shells well is key to giving the finished sauce its crawfish flavor.)

4. Reduce the heat to medium low and sprinkle the flour over the crawfish, stirring and scraping the pan bottom well until the flour is thoroughly blended in. Add the tomatoes and their juice, crushing the tomatoes with your fingers as you add them. Stir in the white wine and cook until the mixture is no longer runny but still moist, two to three minutes.

5. Add the 4 cups reserved crawfish cooking liquid to the pan, stirring well. Bring to a simmer over high heat, stirring occasionally. Reduce heat and very slowly cook, just under a simmer, for 25 minutes. (This very slow cooking process helps to release the flavor from the crawfish and vegetables.) Remove the pan from the heat.

6. Strain the mixture through a fine mesh strainer, using the back of a sturdy spoon to extract as much liquid from the solids as possible.

7. Place the strained sauce in a heavy 4-quart saucepan and slowly bring to a boil over medium heat. Reduce the heat and simmer until the sauce reduces to between 2½ and 3 cups, about 15 minutes. Whisk in the cream and continue cooking two to three minutes more, whisking occasionally. Remove the pan from the heat and strain the sauce through a very fine strainer or a strainer lined with cheesecloth. Return the sauce to a clean 4-quart saucepan and set it aside briefly in a warm spot on the stove top or at room temperature.

FOR FINISHING THE DISH

- 12 jumbo shrimp, peeled and deveined
- ½ cup good-quality, dry white wine
- ¼ teaspoon kosher salt, plus to taste
- ⅛ teaspoon freshly ground black pepper, plus to taste
- 12 ounces peeled fresh Louisiana crawfish tails*
- ¼ cup mascarpone cheese
- 4 tablespoons unsalted butter, preferably Plugra or other European-style butter, cut in ½-inch cubes
    paper-thin slices of sautéed asparagus, or small sprigs of Italian (flat-leaf) parsley, for optional garnish

*If this ingredient is difficult to find where you live, see Ingredient Sources on page 424.

1. Use the tip of a small kitchen knife to make a shallow cut around the small scored circle on the top of each reserved vol-au-vent and lift off this "lid." If the inside of the pastry is still a little raw, lightly scrape out the uncooked pastry with the tines of a table fork.

2. Place a vol-au-vent on each heated serving plate. Set aside the lids separately.

3. In a heavy 10-inch skillet, combine the shrimp and wine, and sprinkle ¼ teaspoon kosher salt and ⅛ teaspoon pepper over the shrimp. Cook over high heat until the shrimp are half cooked, about two minutes, turning them at least once.

4. Add 1½ cups of the reserved cardinale sauce and the crawfish tails to the skillet and cook just until the shrimp are barely cooked, about one minute. (Save the leftover cardinale sauce for another time.)

5. Stir in the mascarpone, blending well, then scatter the cubes of butter over the sauce and cook until the butter melts, stirring constantly. Bring the sauce to a strong boil and remove from the heat. Season with more salt and pepper if needed. The vol-au-vents should be served immediately.

Serving Suggestion: To serve, spoon some of the crawfish and shrimp (without the sauce) into each puff-pastry shell and scatter more of the seafood directly on the plates. Fill the vol-au-vents with sauce and spoon additional sauce around them. Place the lids over the vol-au-vents and, if you are using the asparagus slices or parsley sprigs, garnish the plates with them. 🐚

Shrimp and Spinach "Cannelloni" with Champagne Butter Sauce

For 6 main-dish servings or 12 appetizer servings

You'll find two familiar cannelloni ingredients in this recipe—chopped spinach and ricotta cheese. Some of the other ingredients represent departures from tradition. The pasta is oven-ready ("no-boil") lasagna noodles rather than true, crêpe-like cannelloni sheets. And the spinach and ricotta are joined by chopped shrimp. Add a champagne butter sauce and you have an interesting, innovative and delicious dish.

FOR THE PASTA FILLING

2	tablespoons olive oil, divided
¾	pound small shrimp, peeled and chopped
1	teaspoon kosher salt, divided
1	teaspoon freshly ground black pepper, divided
1	pound baby spinach leaves with stems, washed and drained (drying not necessary)
1¼	pounds ricotta cheese, preferably made with whole milk
4	ounces finely grated Parmigiano-Reggiano cheese

1. In a heavy 10-inch skillet (preferably non-stick), heat 1 tablespoon olive oil over high heat until hot, about 45 seconds. Add the shrimp, ½ teaspoon kosher salt and ½ teaspoon pepper, and cook until the shrimp are just cooked through, about four minutes, stirring almost constantly.

2. Remove the skillet from heat. Transfer the shrimp to a colander or strainer to drain while cooking the spinach.

3. Wash and dry the 10-inch skillet, and in it heat 1 tablespoon olive oil over medium-high heat until hot, about one minute. Add one fourth of the spinach and cook just until it wilts enough to make room for more spinach, about one minute, tossing constantly with tongs. Add another batch of spinach (about the same size as the first) and repeat the procedure until all the spinach has been added and is just wilted, about one minute per addition of spinach.

4. Drain the spinach through a colander or strainer for 30 minutes, then wrap the spinach in a lint-free cloth napkin or dish towel (one that can be stained) and wring dry to extract all liquid possible. Coarsely chop the spinach and place in a large mixing bowl.

5. Add to the bowl the ricotta and Parmigiano-Reggiano cheeses. Mince the shrimp in a food processor and add to the bowl of spinach and cheese, mixing thoroughly with a wooden spoon or rubber spatula. Season with ½ teaspoon kosher salt and ½ teaspoon pepper, or to taste. Refrigerate in a covered container until ready to use.

NOTES

The cannelloni may be made up to the baking step a day in advance and kept tightly covered in the refrigerator.

The sauce should be prepared no more than one hour before serving.

ADVANCE STEPS

Prepare one of the following recipes:

- Crab stock on page 391
- Seafood stock on page 394
- Seafood-mushroom stock on page 395
- Chicken stock on page 390

Also, the recipe for:

- Champagne butter sauce on page 361 (Start the sauce recipe just before baking the cannelloni, and finish it just before the cannelloni comes out of the oven, as directed in Step 6 and 8 of the cannelloni section.)

SPECIAL EQUIPMENT

- A heavy 10-inch skillet, preferably non-stick
- A colander or a strainer
- A pair of tongs
- A lint-free cloth napkin or dish towel (one that can be stained)

12   oven-ready (no-boil) lasagna noodles, 3½ by 6¾ inches

¼   cup stock—either crab, seafood, seafood-mushroom or chicken

     non-stick vegetable spray or olive oil, to grease the baking pan

1   recipe champagne butter sauce

- A baking pan 9 inches square and 2¼ inches deep
- Heavy-duty aluminum foil

1. Gently separate the lasagna noodles and soak them in a large pan (such as one 13 by 9 inches) of hot tap water until soft and pliable, about 10 minutes. Meanwhile, use non-stick vegetable spray to grease a baking pan 9 inches square and 2¼ inches deep.

2. Once the noodles have soaked sufficiently, assemble the cannelloni as follows: Remove one noodle from the water and let it drip-dry briefly before placing it on a flat work surface. (Leave the remaining noodles in the water.)

3. Remove the filling from the refrigerator and mound ⅓ cup of it along one short side of the noodle to about 1 inch from the shorter end. Starting at the shorter end where the filling is, roll up the noodle until the filling is entirely covered by pasta plus about 1 inch of pasta overlap. Use a sharp knife to trim off the excess length (about 2 inches) of the noodle. The finished roll should be about 4 inches long and about 1¼ inches in diameter. Place the roll seam-side-down in the bottom of the prepared baking pan.

4. Repeat to assemble the remaining 11 rolls, adding them to the baking pan in a single layer as they are done. Slowly drizzle the stock over the cannelloni to moisten the exposed surface of each roll, spreading the stock with your fingertips. Seal the pan with heavy-duty aluminum foil. (If made ahead, refrigerate the cannelloni until time to bake for serving.)

5. Preheat the oven to 350°F.

6. Prepare the champagne butter sauce through Step 2 of the sauce recipe (in which the cream mixture is reduced). Remove from heat and set aside at room temperature.

7. Bake the cannelloni, still covered with foil, until the pasta is tender and filling is heated through, about 45 minutes. To test doneness, insert the tip of a knife blade into the center of one of the cannelloni. If the tip of the blade feels hot and the pasta was easy to pierce, they are ready.

8. About 10 minutes before the cannelloni are done, finish preparing the champagne butter sauce. Once the filled pasta tubes are baked and the sauce is finished, serve immediately.

Carefully remove the foil from the cannelloni so the steam doesn't burn you.

Serving Suggestion: For a main course, spoon ½ cup sauce in each of six heated individual pasta bowls. Cut two cannelloni in half diagonally and arrange the four halves in each pasta bowl in an X, with the cut ends pointing towards one another. For an appetizer, serve half the amounts indicated above. ❧

Shrimp Bolognese

For 6 main-dish servings

Bologna wasn't the birthplace of this particular pasta recipe, but we're confident that it would be received warmly in that Italian food capital, especially since the tomato sauce is enriched with cream and butter.

Shrimp and Italian sausage come together in the dish. Both are sautéed before they join the fettuccine pasta and robustly seasoned sauce.

1	leek, white part only
¾	cup peeled and cubed carrots (⅛-inch cubes)
1	pound dry fettuccine
2	tablespoons plus ½ cup olive oil, divided
5	ounces raw Italian sausage, casing removed and sausage broken into small bits
2	cups finely chopped onions
1	tablespoon minced fresh garlic
½	teaspoon kosher salt, divided, plus to taste
½	teaspoon freshly ground black pepper, divided, plus to taste
1½	pounds medium shrimp, peeled
3	tablespoons julienned basil leaves, ⅛ inch by 1½ to 2 inches
½	teaspoon crushed red pepper
3½	cups seafood marinara base sauce, at room temperature
2	tablespoons heavy cream
4	tablespoons unsalted butter, cut into 4 pats, at room temperature
6	small fresh basil tops, for garnish
	warm Italian bread, for the table

NOTE

Crawfish tails may be substituted for the shrimp.

ADVANCE STEP

Prepare the seafood-marinara base sauce recipe on page 375.

SPECIAL EQUIPMENT

• A very large mixing bowl
• A heavy, nonreactive* 12-to-14-inch sauté pan

*See Using Nonreactive Cookware, page 419.

1. Trim the root end from the leek and cut the stem in half lengthwise. Place the flat side on a cutting board and slice crosswise in ⅛-inch-thick pieces. You should have about 1 cup of slices. Wash them thoroughly to remove all the dirt between the leaves. Drain.

2. Blanch the carrot cubes in a 1-quart saucepan of boiling water until just tender, about three and a half minutes. Drain the cubes through a strainer and immediately rinse under cool tap water to stop them from cooking further. Drain again.

3. Heat 6 to 8 quarts of salted water and cook the fettuccine according to package directions to the al dente stage. Drain well in a colander and transfer to a very large mixing bowl. Toss with 2 tablespoons olive oil, mixing to coat all the strands with oil. Cover with a double thickness of damp paper towels and set aside at room temperature.

4. In a heavy, 12-to-14-inch sauté pan, heat ½ cup olive oil over high heat until hot, two to three minutes. Add the sausage bits, onions, leeks, carrots and garlic, stirring well. Add ¼ teaspoon kosher salt and ¼ teaspoon pepper. Sauté for two minutes, stirring fairly often and breaking up sausage into smaller pieces.

5. Add the shrimp and season with ¼ teaspoon kosher salt and ¼ teaspoon pepper. Sauté for one minute.

6. Stir in the basil and crushed red pepper, then the marinara sauce and cream. Bring to a boil. Reduce heat and simmer just until the shrimp are cooked through, about three minutes.

7. Scatter the pats of butter over the sauce, and cook and stir until all the butter is completely melted in, one to two minutes. Season with more kosher salt and pepper, if needed.

8. Add the cooked fettuccine, tossing to coat well with the sauce and reheat the fettuccine, about one minute. Remove from heat and serve immediately.

Serving Suggestions: Divide the dish among six heated individual pasta bowls, or serve family style in a large pasta bowl. Either way, use a large fork to twist the pasta in an attractive arrangement in the center of the bowl(s), leaving most of the shrimp and sauce surrounding the pasta. Arrange a few shrimp and spoon some of the sauce on top of the pasta. Add a basil top to each bowl, or if using one large bowl, decorate with the basil tops.

Serve with warm Italian bread.

Shrimp Clemenceau

For 4 to 6 servings

Chicken was the original main ingredient in this legendary and elegantly simple Creole creation, but over the years this version with shrimp has gained a following all its own.

Its namesake is presumed to be Georges "The Tiger" Clemenceau (1841-1929), the illustrious prime minister of France during the First World War and a hero to many New Orleans Creoles of that era.

However, it is also possible that the dish got its name from another Clemenceau—Pierre by name, and the grandson of The Tiger. The late Pierre Clemenceau—scholar, patriot and *bon vivant*—lived in New Orleans for many years before his death in the 1980s.

Fans of garlic and butter will find just the right balance of these two flavors in shrimp Clemenceau, along with a nice blend of richness and simplicity—all the more reason to serve crusty French bread with it to soak up the buttery juices.

1½	cups clarified butter, divided
1	large russet potato, peeled and cut into ½-inch cubes
4	large Portobello mushrooms, julienned into strips about 3 inches by ¼ inch
1½	pounds large shrimp, peeled and deveined with tails left on
2	tablespoons minced garlic
1½	cups green peas,* barely cooked
¼	cup minced Italian (flat-leaf) parsley leaves
1	teaspoon kosher salt
¼	teaspoon freshly ground black pepper

*Fresh peas are preferred, but frozen are acceptable.

ADVANCE STEP

Prepare the recipe for clarified butter on page 355.

SPECIAL EQUIPMENT

• A large cookie sheet
• A heavy 14-inch skillet

1. Line a large cookie sheet with several layers of paper towels and set it aside.

2. Over medium-high heat, preheat a dry, heavy 14-inch skillet for three minutes.

3. Pour ¾ cup of the clarified butter into the skillet and heat two to three minutes more, or just until the foam on the surface of the butter starts to brown.

4. Carefully slide the potatoes into the hot butter, and cook them they are until golden brown all over, about five minutes, turning them occasionally.

5. With a slotted spoon, transfer the browned potatoes to the cookie sheet lined with paper towels and set them aside.

6. With the heat remaining at the medium-high level, add the remaining ¾ cup of butter to the skillet, and heat for one minute.

7. Add the mushrooms and toss them until they are cooked through, two to three minutes.

8. Turn the heat under skillet to high and add the shrimp to the pan. Cook them until they begin to turn pink, about two to three minutes.

9. To the shrimp mixture add the garlic, peas, parsley and the reserved browned potatoes, stirring well. Continue cooking about two minutes more.

10. Season with the kosher salt and pepper and remove from the heat.

    Serving Suggestion: Serve immediately in heated shallow soup plates.

Shrimp Creole

For 4 to 6 servings

Thanks to the ancient Aztecs of Mexico and the Spanish colonizers of Louisiana, New Orleanians have been eating tomato dishes for many generations. The Aztecs received the tomato—which they called *tomatl*, or simply "plump fruit"—from the early cultures of South America, the birthplace of the plant. And the Spanish conquistadors eventually passed it on to the rest of the world, including New Orleans, which was a Spanish colony for some 40 years, beginning in 1762.

The presence of tomatoes, onions and sweet peppers in this shrimp dish makes it definitively Creole, since that is one of the typical combinations of ingredients used in traditional Creole cookery.

The appeal of shrimp Creole comes not only from its easy preparation and wonderful flavor, but also its light, healthful aspects. It is traditionally served with long-grain white rice, although pasta may be used as well.

A good accompaniment is crusty French bread. Those with a taste for peppery dishes may want to add a squirt or two of Louisiana pepper sauce.

4	tablespoons unsalted butter, divided
6	medium-to-large garlic cloves, minced
1	large white or yellow onion, chopped
2	medium-sized green sweet peppers, chopped
2	celery stalks, chopped
2	tablespoons tomato paste
7	perfectly ripe Creole* tomatoes, chopped
2	cups crab stock
	leaves from 3 sprigs of Italian (flat-leaf) parsley, minced
	leaves from 2 sprigs of thyme, minced
1¼	cups good-quality dry white wine, divided
2	teaspoons kosher salt, divided
¾	teaspoon freshly ground black pepper, divided
½	teaspoon ground cayenne, divided
32	raw large shrimp, peeled and deveined
1	teaspoon ground sweet paprika
3	green onions, green part only, sliced thin
	cooked long-grain white rice or pasta, for serving

*South Louisiana's Creole tomatoes are preferred for this recipe, although other good, peak-of-season regional varieties can be used.

NOTES

Using a crab stock instead of one with shrimp infuses this dish with a sweeter, richer flavor.

ADVANCE STEP

Prepare the recipe for crab stock on page 391.

SPECIAL EQUIPMENT

- A heavy, nonreactive,* 4-quart saucepan or Dutch oven
- A heavy 12-inch skillet

*See Using Nonreactive Cookware, page 419.

1. Over medium-high heat, melt 2 tablespoons of the butter in a heavy, nonreactive 4-quart saucepan.

2. Add the garlic and cook just until it starts to brown, about one minute. Add the white onions, sweet peppers and celery, and cook until the onions are clear, about 10 minutes, stirring frequently.

3. Add the tomato paste and cook and stir two minutes, scraping the pan bottom clean as you stir.

4. Add the tomatoes, stock, parsley, thyme, 1 cup of the wine, 1 teaspoon kosher salt, ½ teaspoon of black pepper and ¼ teaspoon of cayenne. Reduce the heat and simmer about 20 minutes.

5. Meanwhile, place the shrimp in a large mixing bowl and season with 1 teaspoon of salt, the paprika, ¼ teaspoon of black pepper and ¼ teaspoon of cayenne.

6. Over medium-high heat, melt the remaining 2 tablespoons of butter in a heavy 12-inch skillet.

7. Add the shrimp and sauté until they are about halfway cooked, about two minutes.

8. Add the remaining ¼ cup of wine, stirring thoroughly.

9. Once the tomato sauce has simmered 20 minutes, add the shrimp and liquid in the skillet to the sauce. Continue simmering just until the shrimp are cooked through, about two minutes more. Do not overcook the shrimp.

10. Stir in the green onions.

Serving Suggestion: Serve warm with cooked white rice or pasta.

Barbecue Shrimp

For 2 servings

Why this dish goes by the name of barbecue shrimp is anybody's guess, since it's not barbecued and it's not cooked or served with barbecue sauce.

The original version is said to have originated in New Orleans' Italian community a half-century or more ago, to be added to a very long list of the city's Italian-Creole classics. Improvisations on the original recipe are many, but no authentic barbecue shrimp dish could be described as dainty, considering the spices called for.

Since the shrimp themselves are cooked and served with heads and shells intact, they're usually eaten as one would eat whole boiled lobster—with a bib and a willingness to use your bare hands. While the head and tail are always removed before eating, many New Orleanians like to retain the shell covering the shrimp meat, as long as the covering is soft and thin enough to chew properly.

In this recipe, the emulsified sauce's richness is a result of combining butterfat with the shrimp's natural juices, black pepper and worcestershire sauce. The shrimp are cooked just to the point of being done, remaining succulent. And the sauce is a prime candidate for dipping into with crusty bread.

Finger lickin' is optional.

12	raw colossal shrimp,* unpeeled, with heads and tails left on
2	tablespoons worcestershire sauce
1½	tablespoons coarsely ground black pepper**
2	teaspoons Creole seasoning
1	teaspoon minced fresh garlic
1 to 3	tablespoons water, divided
	half of 1 lemon, seeded
¼	pound (1 stick) cold, unsalted butter, preferably Plugra or other European-style butter, cut into ½-inch cubes
	warm, crusty French bread, for serving

*If colossal shrimp are not available, use the largest you can find.
**To coarse-grind the peppercorns, use a blender or peppermill. The grind is important to the taste of the finished dish.

1. Place the unpeeled shrimp, worcestershire, coarsely ground pepper, Creole seasoning, garlic, and 1 tablespoon water in a heavy 10-inch, stainless-steel sauté pan. Squeeze the juice from the lemon half over the shrimp and add the rind and pulp to the pan.

2. Over high heat, cook the shrimp while gently stirring and occasionally turning the shrimp.

3. After about two minutes of cooking, the shrimp should start turning pink on both sides, indicating they are nearly half cooked.

NOTE

This dish is prepared only two servings at a time because increasing the number of shrimp beyond 12 would require increasing the dish's amount of sauce. Reducing the larger amount of sauce would require more cooking time, resulting in over-cooked shrimp.

ADVANCE STEP

- Prepare the recipe for Creole seasoning on page 385.

SPECIAL EQUIPMENT

- A heavy 10-inch stainless-steel sauté pan

4. If the shrimp are the colossal size, now add 2 tablespoons water to the pan. Otherwise, don't add water.

5. Reduce the heat to medium-high and continue cooking as you gradually add the cold pieces of butter to the pan. While turning the shrimp occasionally, swirl the butter pieces until they are incorporated into the pan juices, the sauce turns light brown and creamy as it simmers, and the shrimp are just cooked through. This will take about two minutes total if the shrimp are extra-large, and about three minutes total if they're colossal. Do not overcook the shrimp.

Serving Suggestion: Pour the shrimp and sauce into a heated pasta bowl with the lemon-half turned cut-side down, in the center. Serve the shrimp and sauce immediately, alongside slices of warm, crusty French bread for sopping up the sauce.

Rock Shrimp and Capellini
with Tomato & Arugula Butter Sauce

For 6 servings

Rock shrimp join a sauce of tomatoes and wilted arugula in this recipe, to ladle onto capellini pasta. Capellini is slightly thicker than *capelli d'angelo,* or "angel-hair" pasta.

The sauce is relatively light, and a tad of crushed red peppers add just a bit of heat to it. Standard olive oil is used to cook the dish, while extra-virgin olive oil gets drizzled on at the last moment for a finer flavor.

	plenty of salted water for cooking pasta
1	pound dry capellini
1	tablespoon plus ¼ cup olive oil (not extra-virgin), divided
18	ounces raw small rock shrimp,* peeled
¾	teaspoon kosher salt, divided, plus to taste
¾	teaspoon freshly ground black pepper, divided, plus to taste
3	tablespoons minced fresh garlic
1	teaspoon crushed red pepper
4	cups chopped Creole** tomatoes, drained
5	tablespoons finely chopped fresh Italian (flat-leaf) parsley leaves, divided
1½	cup good-quality dry white wine
¾	pound (3 sticks) cold unsalted butter, cut into 24 pats
6	ounces baby arugula, stems trimmed
6	teaspoons extra-virgin olive oil

*If this ingredient is difficult to find where you live, see Ingredient Sources on page 424.
**South Louisiana's Creole tomatoes are preferred for this recipe, although other good, peak-of-season regional varieties can be used also.

NOTES

For more information on rock shrimp, see page 38.

If rock shrimp are not available, other small shrimp may be substituted.

If using an electric stove top to prepare this recipe, please see recommendations on page 418.

SPECIAL EQUIPMENT

• A heavy, nonreactive* 14-inch sauté pan

*See Using Nonreactive Cookware, page 419.

1. Following package directions, heat the salted water and cook the capellini to the al dente stage (firm to the bite but cooked through). Do not overcook. Drain the pasta, rinse with cool tap water, and drain very well. Toss with 1 tablespoon olive oil. While bringing the pasta water to a boil and cooking the pasta, cook the shrimp and prepare the sauce.

2. Heat an empty heavy 14-inch sauté pan over high heat until hot, about four minutes. Add ¼ cup olive oil and the shrimp. Sprinkle ½ teaspoon kosher salt and ½ teaspoon black pepper over the shrimp. Sauté the shrimp until they are almost cooked through, about two minutes, stirring frequently so they cook evenly. Transfer them to a plate and set aside.

3. To the same sauté pan placed over high heat, add the garlic, crushed red pepper, tomatoes, 2 tablespoons parsley, ¼ teaspoon kosher salt and ¼ teaspoon pepper, stirring well. Sauté for one to two minutes, stirring almost constantly.

4. Add the wine and cook until the liquid in the pan reduces by half, about seven minutes, stirring occasionally.

5. Reduce the heat to medium and cook as you whisk in 2 pats of butter at a time, whisking constantly, until all the butter is added and incorporated into the sauce. Each addition of butter should be almost completely melted in before adding more. This will take roughly 10 minutes total.

6. Season with more kosher salt and black pepper if needed.

7. Add the reserved shrimp and cook to just reheat the shrimp, about one minute.

8. Add the cooked capellini and the arugula, tossing a few seconds to thoroughly mix all the ingredients and slightly wilt the arugula. Remove from heat and serve immediately.

Serving Suggestion: Divide the pasta and sauce evenly between six heated individual pasta bowls.

Drizzle each serving with 1 teaspoon extra-virgin olive oil and garnish with ½ tablespoon parsley.

For 6 main-course servings

Either garlic or lemon is a wonderful way to enhance the flavor of shrimp. This recipe includes both of them in a garlicky citrus vinaigrette that does double duty. It's used for cooking the shrimp as well as serving them.

Jumbo is the ideal size shrimp for the recipe, but somewhat smaller ones can be used in a pinch.

FOR THE CITRUS VINAIGRETTE

3	tablespoons freshly squeezed lemon juice
3	tablespoons key lime juice (fresh preferred)
½	cup chopped fresh Italian (flat-leaf) parsley leaves
2	tablespoons finely chopped fresh garlic
1¼	cups extra-virgin olive oil
¼	teaspoon kosher salt, or to taste
⅛	teaspoon freshly ground black pepper

1. In a large mixing bowl, combine the lemon and lime juice juices, parsley, and garlic, whisking until well mixed. Very gradually add the olive oil in a thin, steady stream, whisking constantly until all is incorporated and the mixture looks a bit creamy.

2. Whisk in ¼ teaspoon kosher salt and the pepper.

3. Before using the vinaigrette, refrigerate overnight in a covered container to let the flavors develop, then season with more salt if desired. Keep refrigerated and use within four days.

FOR FINISHING THE DISH

¼	cup olive oil, not extra-virgin
30	jumbo shrimp,* peeled and deveined, but with heads and tails left on
½	teaspoon kosher salt
½	teaspoon freshly ground black pepper
3	lemons, cut in half, for garnish
	warm French bread, for serving

*If jumbo shrimp are not available, use 2 to 2½ pounds of the largest shrimp (with heads and tails) you can find.

1. In a heavy, broad-based (about 12-inch-diameter) saucepan, heat the olive oil over high heat until it is just short of smoking, about two minutes.

NOTE

In this dish the shrimp keep their heads and tails to lend the dish more flavor.

SPECIAL EQUIPMENT

• A heavy, broad-based (about 12-inch-diameter) saucepan or Dutch oven, broad enough to hold all of the shrimp at once in no more than a double layer

2.   Add the shrimp in a single layer as much as possible, and include any heads that may have come detached. Sprinkle over the shrimp ½ teaspoon kosher salt and ½ teaspoon pepper and, without stirring, cook the shrimp for one minute.

3.   Reduce the heat to medium-high, and cook the shrimp until pink on both sides, about three minutes, turning each shrimp over at least once.

4.   Add 1½ cups of the citrus vinaigrette to the pan. Continue cooking until the vinaigrette just begins to bubble and the shrimp are barely done, about 45 seconds more, moving the shrimp around with a spoon so the vinaigrette flows evenly around all the shrimp.

5.   Remove from heat and let the shrimp sit in the pan for about 30 seconds, then pour the shrimp and sauce into a large shallow pasta bowl or onto a large serving platter.

6.   Drizzle the remaining vinaigrette over the shrimp and garnish with lemon halves.

Serving Suggestion: Serve family style while the shrimp are still piping hot, accompanied by warm French bread to sop up the sauce.

Crabmeat Lasagna with Crab-&-Chanterelle Butter Sauce

For 6 to 8 main-dish servings

Crab claw meat, which is somewhat sweeter in flavor than backfin crab lumps, is at the heart of this deliciously rich lasagna. Also, the claw meat pieces are relatively small, making the filling smoother.

A luxurious touch is added with fresh lump crabmeat and chanterelles in the butter sauce.

Serve simple accompaniments with the lasagna, such as a green salad and warm garlic bread. If fresh chanterelles are not available, it's much better to substitute a mix of other fresh mushrooms than to use dried ones.

FOR THE FILLING AND THE LASAGNA NOODLES

3½	tablespoons unsalted butter, divided, plus butter or non-stick vegetable spray for baking pan
2½	tablespoons all-purpose flour
2½	cups whole milk
4½	cups finely chopped onions
1½	teaspoons minced garlic
1	tablespoon olive oil
1½	pounds baby spinach leaves with stems, washed and drained (drying not necessary)
8	ounces ricotta cheese, preferably made with whole milk
8	ounces fresh crab claw meat, picked through
½	cup finely grated Parmigiano-Reggiano cheese
1	yolk from a large egg
1	teaspoon kosher salt, divided
½	teaspoon freshly ground black pepper, divided
	plenty of salted water for cooking lasagna noodles
16	dry lasagna noodles (not the no-boil type)
	butter or non-stick vegetable spray, for greasing the lasagna pan

1. For the béchamel sauce, which is a component of the filling, melt 2½ tablespoons butter in a heavy, 2-quart saucepan over medium-high heat. Stir in the flour until smooth. Cook about one minute, stirring constantly and scraping the pan bottom clean. Do not let the roux start to brown.

2. Stir in the milk and increase heat to high. Cook the béchamel, whisking or stirring constantly with a wooden spoon, until it thickens enough to leave a distinct trail on the back of the spoon when you draw a finger through it, about three minutes. Remove from heat.

NOTES

The lasagna may be assembled a day in advance and baked just before serving.

The sauce should be prepared within an hour of serving time or it might separate.

ADVANCE STEP

Prepare the seafood-mushroom stock recipe on page 395.

SPECIAL EQUIPMENT

- A heavy 2-quart saucepan
- A long-handled metal whisk or wooden spoon
- A heavy 12-inch skillet
- A heavy 5½-quart saucepan or Dutch oven
- A pair of tongs
- A lint-free cloth napkin or dish towel (one that can be stained)
- A baking pan 9 inches square and 2¼ inches deep
- Heavy duty aluminum foil

3. Let the béchamel cool to warm room temperature, about one hour, so its heat won't curdle the egg yolk when you finish the filling.

4. Meanwhile, melt 1 tablespoon butter in a heavy 12-inch skillet over medium heat. Add the onions and cook for 15 minutes. Stir in the garlic and continue cooking until the onions turn medium-brown, about five minutes more, stirring frequently. Set the onions aside at room temperature to cool before finishing the filling or, if prepared ahead, let cool and refrigerate in a covered container.

5. In a heavy 5½-quart saucepan, heat 1 tablespoon olive oil over high heat until hot, about one minute. Add half the spinach and cook just until it wilts enough to make room for the remaining spinach, about one minute, tossing constantly with tongs. Add the remaining spinach and continue cooking just until all the spinach in the pan is wilted, one to two minutes more.

6. Drain the spinach in a colander or strainer. Set aside the spinach until cool enough to handle, about 30 minutes at room temperature.

7. Wrap the cooled spinach in a lint-free cloth napkin or dish towel (one that you don't mind getting stained) and wring dry to extract all liquid possible. Coarsely chop the spinach. Refrigerate in a covered container if prepared ahead.

8. To finish the filling: In a large mixing bowl, combine the ricotta, crab claw meat, browned onions, cooked spinach, Parmigiano-Reggiano, egg yolk, ½ teaspoon kosher salt, ¼ teaspoon pepper, and 1 cup of the cooled béchamel. (Set aside the remaining béchamel to use as a coating on top of the lasagna.) Stir the filling fairly gently to mix thoroughly while keeping the crabmeat lumps intact as much as possible.

9. Refrigerate while cooking the lasagna noodles.

10. Bring to a boil the salted water for cooking the lasagna noodles. Add the noodles and cook to the al dente stage, about 12 minutes. Drain the noodles, rinse with cool tap water, and drain very well.

11. Cut the noodles into 9-inch lengths to fit a 9-inch square and 2¼-inch deep baking pan. Using butter or non-stick vegetable spray, generously butter or spray the bottom and sides of the pan.

12. To assemble the lasagna, arrange 4 cooked lasagna noodles on the pan bottom, and spread half of the filling evenly over the noodles. Add another layer of 4 noodles, then the remaining filling, and finish with a layer of 4 noodles.

13. Season the reserved béchamel sauce with ½ teaspoon kosher salt and ¼ teaspoon pepper, and pour the sauce over the lasagna, spreading it evenly with a rubber spatula. Seal the pan with heavy-duty aluminum foil and refrigerate if not baking immediately.

FOR THE CRAB-AND-CHANTERELLE BUTTER SAUCE AND BAKING THE LASAGNA

1	cup heavy cream
8	tablespoons cold unsalted butter, divided
3½	tablespoons all-purpose flour
4	cups cold or hot seafood-mushroom stock
1	teaspoon kosher salt, or to taste, divided
½	teaspoon freshly ground black pepper, or to taste, divided
1	tablespoon extra-virgin olive oil
2	tablespoons minced shallots
12	ounces fresh chanterelle mushrooms, brushed clean and left whole*
1	teaspoon fresh thyme leaves
1	pound fresh jumbo lump crabmeat, picked through

*If fresh chanterelles are not available, substitute a mix of fresh wild mushrooms, such as shiitake, oyster, cremini or trumpet mushrooms.

1. In a heavy 2-quart saucepan, bring the cream just to a boil over high heat, about two minutes. Reduce the heat to medium and continue cooking until the cream reduces to ½ cup, about six minutes. Remove from heat and set aside.

2. For the roux, in a heavy 3-quart saucepan melt 1 tablespoon butter over medium heat. Gradually add the flour to the butter, whisking constantly with a long-handled metal whisk until all the flour has been added and the mixture is smooth. Whisking constantly to prevent scorching, cook the roux for about two minutes. Do not let the roux start to brown.

3. Increase heat to high and gradually add the stock, whisking constantly until the roux is well blended with the stock. Cook until the sauce is noticeably thicker (it will still be relatively thin), about three minutes, whisking frequently. Reduce heat to maintain a simmer, and simmer for six minutes.

4. While the sauce is simmering, preheat the oven to 375°F for baking the lasagna.

5. Add the reserved reduced cream to the sauce, and season with ½ teaspoon kosher salt and ¼ teaspoon pepper, or to taste, whisking thoroughly. Continue cooking until the sauce is thick enough to leave a distinct track on the back of a spoon when you draw a finger through it, about six minutes. Remove this base sauce from heat and set aside at room temperature.

6. Now, bake the lasagna, covered, until heated through, about 45 minutes. Remove the foil and continue baking for 10 minutes more. Once the lasagna has been baking for about 35 minutes, begin finishing the sauce.

7. To finish the butter sauce: In a heavy 12-inch skillet combine 1 tablespoon butter and 1 tablespoon olive oil and place over high heat. Once the butter is almost melted, add the shallots and chanterelles. Cook until the mushrooms are soft but not mushy, about three minutes, stirring frequently.

SPECIAL EQUIPMENT

- A heavy 2-quart saucepan
- A heavy 3-quart saucepan
- A long-handled metal whisk
- A heavy 12-inch skillet

8. Meanwhile, cut 6 tablespoons butter in half-inch cubes and set aside momentarily. Reduce the heat to medium-low and cook as you add two of the reserved butter cubes at a time, whisking constantly, until all the butter is added and incorporated into the sauce. Each addition of butter should be almost completely melted in before adding more. This will take about five minutes total.

9. Increase the heat to medium and stir in the thyme, then add the reserved base sauce. Cook and stir for one minute.

10. Season the sauce with ½ teaspoon kosher salt and ¼ teaspoon pepper or to taste. If in doubt, slightly under-salt the sauce so its saltiness doesn't distract from the flavors of the lasagna.

11. Add the crabmeat and cook until just heated through, about two minutes, mixing gently so the lumps of crabmeat remain intact.

    Serving Suggestion: Once the lasagna has baked and the sauce is finished, serve immediately in heated individual pasta bowls with a portion of the sauce spooned over the top of each serving of lasagna.

Crabmeat and Eggplant "Cannelloni" with Roasted-Tomato Butter Sauce

For 6 main-dish servings or 12 appetizer servings

In this cannelloni recipe, rolled eggplant slices function as pasta tubes, enveloping a scrumptious stuffing with fresh crab. Color and more good flavor are added with the roasted-tomato butter sauce.

2   eggplants, each about 1½ pounds, 8 inches long and 4 inches in diameter
    about ½ cup plus 1 tablespoon extra-virgin olive oil, divided
1½ teaspoons kosher salt, divided
1½ teaspoons freshly ground black pepper, divided
1½ pounds baby spinach leaves with stems, washed and drained (drying is un-
    necessary)
½   pound ricotta cheese, preferably made with whole milk
1   pound claw crabmeat, picked through
1   yolk from a large egg
1   recipe roasted-tomato butter sauce
    warm, crusty bread, for serving

ADVANCE STEP

Just before baking the cannelloni, prepare the roasted-tomato butter sauce recipe on page 364.

SPECIAL EQUIPMENT

- A sharp-bladed mandoline or meat slicer (preferred) or a sharp knife
- 1 or more rimmed baking sheets for baking sliced eggplant
- Parchment paper
- A heavy 5½-quart Dutch oven
- A pair of metal tongs
- A lint-free cloth napkin or dishtowel (one that can be stained)

1. Preheat the oven to 350°F.

2. While the oven is preheating, trim the ends from the eggplants, but do not peel them. Using a sharp-bladed mandoline or meat slicer (preferred) or a sharp knife, slice the eggplants lengthwise into uniform ⅛-inch-thick pieces. (The eggplant slices need to be thin enough to roll up.) You will need 24 slices plus two or three extra slices in case you need to piece together the last few cannelloni to make all of them of uniform size.

3. Arrange the slices in a single layer on rimmed baking sheets that are lined with parchment paper, or prepare in batches using only one baking sheet. Brush the slices generously on both sides with extra-virgin olive oil, using a total of about ½ cup of oil.

4. Season the slices on the top side with kosher salt and pepper, using a total of 1 teaspoon salt and 1 teaspoon pepper distributed among all the slices.

5. Bake the slices, uncovered, until noticeably softer and pliable, but not very brown, about seven minutes. Remove the slices from the oven and set them aside.

6. In a heavy 5½-quart Dutch oven, heat 1 tablespoon olive oil over high heat until hot, about one minute. Add half the spinach and cook just until it wilts enough to make room for the remaining spinach, about one minute, tossing

constantly with tongs. Add the remaining spinach and continue cooking just until all the spinach in the pan is wilted, one to two minutes more.

7. Let the spinach drain in a colander until cool enough to handle, about 30 minutes at room temperature, then wrap the spinach in a lint-free cloth napkin or dish towel (that you don't mind getting stained) and wring dry to extract all liquid possible. Coarsely chop the spinach and place it in a large mixing bowl.

8. Add to the bowl the ricotta, crabmeat, egg yolk, ½ teaspoon kosher salt and ½ teaspoon pepper. Stir fairly gently with a spoon to blend thoroughly, while keeping the crabmeat lumps intact as much as possible.

9. Line a rimmed baking sheet with parchment paper. Set aside.

10. On a work surface, form 12 cannelloni as follows: Place one eggplant slice with the narrow (stem) end toward you. Leave enough space below this slice for a second one. Arrange a second eggplant slice below the first one, this time with the wide (bulb) end toward you and with the bottom slice overlapping the top one by ¼ inch.

11. Spread ⅓ cup of the filling toward the wide end of the slice closer to you. Starting at the wide end where the filling is, roll up the eggplant slices loosely into a log shape measuring roughly 1 inch in diameter and 6 inches in length.

12. Place each log seam-side down in a single layer on the prepared baking sheet as formed. You may have to piece the last two or three logs with shorter lengths of eggplant so all the cannelloni will be about the same length. Once all 12 cannelloni are formed, cover and refrigerate them while you're preparing the sauce.

13. Once the sauce is finished, remove the cannelloni from the refrigerator, uncover and bake in the 350° oven until the filling is just heated through, 10 to 15 minutes. To test for doneness, insert the tip of a knife blade into the center of one of the cannelloni. If the tip of the blade feels hot, the cannelloni are ready.

Serving Suggestion: For each main-course serving, use a spatula to transfer two cannelloni to each heated dinner plate. Stir the roasted-tomato butter sauce and spoon a portion (about ⅔ cup) over each serving of cannelloni. For each appetizer serving, use half these amounts.

Pass warm, crusty bread at the table.

Crabmeat and Lemon Cannelloni with Tomato and Basil Purée

For 6 main-dish servings or 12 appetizer servings

This is one of several recipes in this book that call for using both crab claw meat (for its sweetness) and jumbo lump crabmeat (for its succulence and impressive looks). In this dish, the cannelloni are rich and lemony and the fresh tomato is a perfect complement to the dish.

FOR THE CANNELLONI FILLING

1½	pounds cream cheese, very soft
⅓	cup very finely chopped white or yellow onions
¼	cup very finely sliced green onions, green parts only
3	tablespoons very finely chopped celery
2	tablespoons fresh lemon juice
1	tablespoon finely grated lemon zest
1	tablespoon minced fresh Italian (flat-leaf) parsley leaves
2	teaspoons kosher salt
½	teaspoon freshly ground black pepper
1	pound crab claw meat,* picked through

*If this ingredient is difficult to find where you live, see Ingredient Sources on page 424.

1. In a large mixing bowl, combine the cream cheese, white and green onions, celery, lemon juice and zest, parsley, and kosher salt and pepper. Mix thoroughly by hand, breaking up any lumps of cream cheese and incorporating them into the mixture.

2. Add the crab claw meat, mixing well. Refrigerate in a covered container until ready to use.

FOR THE TOMATO AND BASIL PURÉE

4	teaspoons vegetable oil
2	teaspoons olive oil
1	tablespoon minced fresh garlic
½	cup finely chopped onions
3	tablespoons finely chopped celery
4	cups good-quality dry white wine
3	cups chopped, perfectly ripe Creole* tomatoes
2	tablespoons finely sliced fresh basil leaves
1½	teaspoons kosher salt
¼	teaspoon freshly ground black pepper

NOTES

The cannelloni may be made up to the baking step a day in advance and kept well covered in the refrigerator.

The filling can also be used in ravioli.

SPECIAL EQUIPMENT

• A heavy, nonreactive* 4-quart saucepan

*See Using Nonreactive Cookware, page 419.

*South Louisiana's Creole tomatoes are preferred for this recipe, although other good, peak-of-season regional varieties can be used.

1. In a heavy, nonreactive 4-quart saucepan heat the vegetable oil and olive oil together over medium-high heat until hot, about one and a half minutes.

2. Add the garlic, stir well, and cook for 30 seconds. Add the onions and celery and, with a wooden spoon, scrape the pan bottom clean of any browned garlic. Cook for two minutes, stirring frequently.

3. Add the wine, mixing thoroughly. Stir in the tomatoes.

4. Bring the mixture to a boil. Reduce heat and simmer for 20 minutes, stirring occasionally.

5. Remove from heat and purée the mixture in a blender. Return the purée to the same saucepan. Add the basil, kosher salt and pepper and continue simmering for 10 minutes. Remove from heat and set aside at room temperature.

FOR FINISHING AND SERVING THE DISH

12	oven-ready (no-boil) lasagna noodles, each 3½ by 6¾ inches
	non-stick vegetable spray
1½	cups good-quality dry white wine, divided
3	tablespoons unsalted butter
1	pound jumbo lump crabmeat,* picked through
1	teaspoon kosher salt
¼	teaspoon freshly ground black pepper
1	tablespoon minced Italian (flat-leaf) parsley, for garnish
6	trimmed sprigs Italian (flat-leaf) parsley, for garnish

*If this ingredient is difficult to find where you live, see Ingredient Sources on page 424.

*If this ingredient is difficult to find where you live, see Ingredient Sources on page 424.

1. Gently separate the lasagna noodles and soak them in a large pan (such as a 9-by-13-inch pan) of hot tap water until soft and pliable, about 10 minutes. Meanwhile, use non-stick vegetable spray to grease a 9-inch square baking pan that is 2¼ inches deep.

2. Once the lasagna noodles have soaked sufficiently, assemble the cannelloni as follows: Remove one noodle from the water and let it drip-dry briefly before placing it flat on a work surface. (Leave the remaining noodles in the water.)

3. Remove the reserved filling from the refrigerator and mound a rounded ⅓ cup of it along one short side of the noodle to about 1 inch from the short edge. Starting at the shorter end where the filling is, roll up the noodle until the filling is entirely covered by pasta plus about 1 inch overlap of pasta. Use

SPECIAL EQUIPMENT

- A baking pan 9 inches square and 2¼ inches deep
- Heavy-duty aluminum foil
- A heavy, nonreactive* 9-inch skillet
- A heavy 12-inch skillet

*See Using Nonreactive Cookware, page 419.

*See Using Nonreactive Cookware, page 419.

a sharp knife to trim off the excess length (about 2 inches) of the noodle. The finished roll should be about 4 inches long and about 1¼ inch in diameter. Place the roll seam-side-down in the bottom of the prepared baking pan.

4.   Repeat to assemble the remaining 11 rolls, adding them to the baking pan in a single layer as they are done.

5.   Slowly pour 1 cup wine evenly over the 12 cannelloni to moisten the exposed surface of each roll. Seal the pan with heavy-duty aluminum foil. (If the cannelloni are made ahead, refrigerate them until time to bake for serving.)

6.   To finish the dish and serve, preheat the oven to 350°F.

7.   Bake the cannelloni, still covered with foil, until the pasta is tender and the filling is heated through, about 45 minutes. To test doneness, insert the tip of a knife blade into the center of one of the cannelloni. If the tip of the blade feels hot and the pasta was easy to pierce, the cannelloni are ready.

8.   About 10 minutes before the cannelloni are done, reheat the purée in a heavy, nonreactive 9-inch skillet over high heat.

9.   To sauté the jumbo lump crabmeat, heat an empty, heavy 12-inch skillet over medium-high heat for two minutes. Add ½ cup wine and the butter. Once the butter melts, add the crabmeat, and sprinkle over it the kosher salt and pepper. Cook until the crab is just heated through, about three minutes, stirring very gently and only once so the lumps stay intact. Once the cannelloni are baked and the purée and crabmeat are ready, carefully remove the foil so the steam doesn't burn you and serve immediately.

Serving Suggestions: If serving as a main course, spoon a generous ⅓ cup of the tomato and basil purée in the center of each of six heated dinner plates. Using a slotted spoon, carefully transfer two cannelloni, one at a time, to the center of each plate, crisscrossing the two. Sprinkle each portion with ½ cup of the crabmeat, then a light sprinkle of minced parsley, and garnish with a trimmed parsley sprig.

If serving as an appetizer, use one of the cannelloni per serving instead of two, and half of both the crabmeat and the sauce. ❦

Stuffed Crabs

For 10 to 12 stuffed crabs or 5 to 6 main-dish servings

These succulent stuffed crabs, which are jazzed up with a little lemon juice and zest, are a nice summer entrée or appetizer offering. They're also perfect as part of a selection of items on a seafood platter.

Among the traditional side dishes with stuffed crabs at New Orleans tables are potato salad, coleslaw and french fries.

⅜	pound (1½ sticks) plus 1 tablespoon unsalted butter, divided
1	cup finely chopped yellow onions
1½	teaspoons minced garlic
3	whites from large eggs, lightly beaten
¾	cup finely sliced green onions
1	tablespoon lemon zest
2	tablespoons fresh lemon juice
¼	teaspoon ground nutmeg, preferably freshly ground
8	ounces lump crabmeat, picked over
4	ounces crab claw meat, picked over
2	cups fresh soft breadcrumbs
¼	cup minced fresh (Italian) parsley leaves
½	teaspoon kosher salt
¼	teaspoon freshly ground black pepper
10 to 12	medium-to-large crab back-shells, scraped clean, washed thoroughly and drained well, or one of the other options listed in Notes, right

1. In a heavy 2-quart saucepan, heat 1 tablespoon of the butter over medium heat until it melts and starts to foam. Add the yellow onions and garlic to the pan and sauté until the onions are soft, three to four minutes, stirring frequently. Remove from heat and set aside to cool.

2. In a separate small saucepan, melt the remaining ⅜ pound butter and set it aside. In a large mixing bowl, combine the egg whites, green onions, lemon zest and juice, nutmeg, and both crabmeats. Fold the ingredients together with a rubber spatula to avoid breaking up the crabmeat.

3. In a medium-size mixing bowl, combine the breadcrumbs, parsley, kosher salt, pepper, and ½ cup of the reserved melted butter, mixing well. Add these to the crab mixture, folding together until well blended. Cover and refrigerate the stuffing overnight.

4. When ready to finish the dish for serving, preheat the oven to 400°F. Place 1 to 2 tablespoons of the stuffing in an oven-proof dish and bake five to 10 minutes until hot, then taste the stuffing to see if the rest of it needs more seasoning. Add more seasoning if desired.

NOTES

The stuffing should be made a day ahead to allow the flavors and seasonings to marry. Just before serving time, stuff the crab shells and bake them.

Containers for the stuffing: If you're using fresh crabs for this recipe, you can empty and clean 10 or 12 medium-to-large back shells for stuffing. Some retail stores and fish markets in New Orleans and Baltimore sell pressed-aluminum, crab-shaped shells that are about 5 inches long and 2½ inches wide. Your other options are to use ramekins, shell-shaped porcelain dishes or the natural, scallop-type baking shells sold in many kitchen stores. Do not use plastic containers of any kind.

ADVANCE STEP

Prepare the recipe for fresh soft breadcrumbs on page 382.

SPECIAL EQUIPMENT

• A heavy 2-quart saucepan
• A rimmed baking sheet

5. Leave the oven set at 400°. Fill the shells or other containers with the stuffing, mounding the tops.

6. Arrange the stuffed shells on an ungreased, rimmed baking sheet. Drizzle the remaining ¼ cup melted butter over the stuffing.

7. Bake the stuffing uncovered until it is crusty brown, about 20 minutes. Or, before baking, if the stuffing seems a little dry, add a small amount of water to the bottom of the baking sheet holding the stuffed crabs. Seal the sheet with aluminum foil and bake for 15 minutes, then uncover and continue baking five minutes more to crisp the stuffing.

Serve immediately.

Fried Soft-Shell Crabs with Hot-Pepper-Jelly Sauce

For 6 servings

Not only for the wonderful flavor of fresh soft-shell crabs, this recipe also is commendable for its instructions for dramatic presentation, with the crabs' claws pointing upward. Their taste is enhanced by the crisp fried crust and a hint of hot and sweet flavors from the hot-pepper-jelly sauce.

	canola oil, for deep frying
3	cups seasoned flour
2	cups whole milk
4	large eggs
½	teaspoon kosher salt
¼	teaspoon freshly ground black pepper
6	soft-shell crabs, about 7 ounces each
	either a bed of lettuce or 1 recipe of sweet potato hash, for serving
1	recipe hot-pepper-jelly sauce, for serving

1. Preheat the oven to 200°F.

2. Preheat the oil in a deep fryer to 350°. If not using a deep fryer, preheat 2½ inches of oil in a deep 5-quart Dutch oven to 350°.

3. Place the seasoned flour in a large mixing bowl.

4. For the egg wash, in a small mixing bowl whisk together the milk, eggs, kosher salt, and pepper until well blended.

5. Line a rimmed baking sheet with paper towels and set aside.

6. Pat the crabs dry with paper towels, and fry them one at a time as follows:

7. Just before frying, dredge the crab thoroughly in the seasoned flour and gently shake off the excess. Dip the crab in the egg wash, moistening it completely, then dredge it again in the flour, being sure all the legs are separated and coated with flour. Shake off the excess flour.

8. Using a pair of heat-proof tongs to hold the crab's body securely, position the crab immediately over and as close to the hot oil as safely as possible so that the legs are completely submerged in the oil.

9. Slowly count to five, then carefully turn the crab over so the legs face up, and gently ease the whole crab into the oil, releasing the body from the tongs. Without turning the crab, fry until golden brown, about three minutes.

NOTE

You may want to have your fishmonger clean the soft-shell crabs. If that is not practical, see the instructions for preparing the crabs for frying on page 30.

ADVANCE STEPS

Prepare the recipes for:

- Seasoned flour on page 384
- Hot-pepper-jelly sauce on page 371

If serving the crabs on a bed of sweet-potato hash, prepare the recipe for:

- The hash on page 347

SPECIAL EQUIPMENT

- Either an electric deep-fryer or a deep 5-to-6-quart Dutch oven
- A rimmed baking sheet
- Heat-proof tongs

10. Then, if the leg-side of the body is not yet golden brown, turn the crab over and let it fry a few seconds more.

11. Briefly drain the crab on the prepared baking sheet. It will be very hot at this point, so be careful not to burn yourself. After frying the first crab, transfer the baking sheet to the warm oven while frying the remaining crabs, adding them to the baking sheet as fried and drained.

12. Serve piping hot.

    Serving Suggestion: For the most dramatic presentation, serve the crabs legs up on individual heated serving plates, or serve them legs down on a large platter lined with a bed of lettuce or sweet-potato hash browns. At the last moment, drizzle each crab with 1 to 2 tablespoons of the hot-pepper-jelly sauce or to taste. 🐚

For 6 to 8 main-dish servings

Those who look for food that is spicy hot and very rich should relish this dish. If less peppery heat is desired, simply cut back on the crushed red pepper. Because the dish is so rich, the suggested servings are on the small side. This one begs to be served with warm French bread and a simple green salad.

	plenty of salted water for cooking linguine
1	pound dry linguine, or 1½ pounds fresh
4	tablespoons extra-virgin olive oil, divided
¾	pound pancetta, cut in ¼-inch cubes
1	pound peeled crawfish tails*
1	teaspoon kosher salt
1	teaspoon crushed red pepper
½	teaspoon freshly ground black pepper
3	cups heavy cream
3	yolks from large eggs
3	tablespoons freshly grated Parmigiano-Reggiano cheese
3	tablespoons freshly grated Romano cheese
3	ounces crawfish butter
	fresh Italian (flat-leaf) parsley leaves, thinly sliced, for garnish
6 to 8	whole boiled crawfish, for garnish, optional

*If this ingredient is difficult to find where you live, see Ingredient Sources on page 424.

ADVANCE STEP

Prepare the crawfish butter recipe on page 358.

SPECIAL EQUIPMENT

- Two mixing bowls, one large and one very large
- A heavy 12-inch sauté pan
- A pair of tongs

1. Heat the salted water and cook the linguine until it is almost al dente, roughly 10 minutes if dry, four minutes if fresh. Drain well and rinse with cool water.

2. Place the linguine in a very large mixing bowl and toss with 2 tablespoons olive oil, mixing to coat all the strands with oil. Cover the bowl with a double thickness of damp paper towels and refrigerate. (This may be done up to three hours ahead.)

3. In a heavy 12-inch sauté pan, combine 2 tablespoons olive oil and the pancetta. Cook over medium-low heat until the fat renders out of the meat but the meat itself is only slightly crispy, about 25 minutes, stirring occasionally.

4. Increase the heat to medium-high and add the crawfish tails to the pan. Stir in the kosher salt, crushed red pepper, and black pepper. Sauté for three minutes, stirring occasionally.

5. Stir in the cream and let the mixture reduce for two and a half minutes. Meanwhile, place the egg yolks in a large mixing bowl.

6. Once the crawfish mixture has cooked for two and a half minutes, reduce the heat to low. Remove 1½ cups of the cream from the crawfish mixture and very gradually add this cream to the egg yolks, whisking constantly so the yolks don't curdle.

7. Add the egg yolk mixture back to the crawfish mixture in the pan, and cook, stirring constantly, for about 30 seconds.

8. Add the cheeses, stirring until well blended, then add the crawfish butter and cook until the butter melts and blends into the dish, stirring constantly.

9. Add the cold linguine to the pan, tossing to coat well. Continue cooking until the linguine is heated through, about one and a half minutes more, tossing frequently with tongs. Serve immediately.

Serving Suggestions: Serve in a large heated pasta bowl or in six to eight individual bowls, twisting the pasta with tongs to mound it neatly in the center of the bowl(s).

If serving in a large pasta bowl, sprinkle about 2 teaspoons parsley over the pasta, and, if using, arrange the whole boiled crawfish around the edge of the bowl.

If serving the pasta in individual bowls, garnish each with ½ to 1 teaspoon parsley and 1 whole boiled crawfish.

Crawfish Étouffée with Green-Onion Rice

For 6 servings

Cajun folklore is filled with stories and legends, and many of them involve crawfish. One of the more inventive ones is this:

In the 1750s, when the Acadians first migrated from Nova Scotia to Louisiana, hundreds of North-Atlantic lobsters, sympathetic to the exiles, decided to follow them southward along the Atlantic Coast and through the Gulf of Mexico to the bayous. Along the way, as they swam, the lobsters somehow acquired progressively smaller shells. By the time they reached Louisiana, they had become what we now know as crawfish.

Since then, for generations of Southwest Louisiana's Cajuns, crawfish étouffée has been their quintessential dish.

The reason for the status and longevity of crawfish étouffée is easy to understand once you've tasted a really well made version of it, with its combination of deep earthy and seafood flavors.

The French verb *étouffer* means to smother, and in this case it refers to the cooking method of the traditional version of étouffée, cooked in a lidded pot with seasonings and crawfish "fat," which is actually the shellfish's liver.

Over the years, the dish has evolved to become one that's based with a roux and cooked uncovered. There have been many other variations on the étouffée theme. This one, for example, contains cream and tomatoes, and is served with rice flavored with green onion. Such improvisations are yet more evidence that Creole-Cajun cooking is not a catalog of static, unchangeable dishes, but a living, thriving part of South Louisiana's food culture.

4	ounces thick-cut bacon strips, applewood-smoked preferred, sliced crosswise into ¼-inch bits
2	tablespoons unsalted butter
1	tablespoon minced fresh garlic
1	cup finely chopped onions
1	cup finely chopped green sweet peppers
½	cup finely chopped celery
2	tablespoons Creole seasoning
¼	cup all-purpose flour
4	cups crawfish stock
1	cup chopped Creole* tomatoes
1	teaspoon kosher salt
1	teaspoon finely chopped fresh thyme leaves
1	teaspoon minced fresh Italian (flat-leaf) parsley leaves
1	teaspoon worcestershire sauce
½	cup heavy cream

ADVANCE STEP

Prepare the following recipes:

- Creole seasoning on page 385
- Crawfish stock on page 392

As close to serving time as possible:

- Green-onion rice on page 344

SPECIAL EQUIPMENT

- A heavy, nonreactive* 5-quart saucepan or heavy 5-quart Dutch oven
- A wooden spoon

*See Using Nonreactive Cookware, page 419.

2   pounds peeled fresh Louisiana crawfish tails**
1   recipe warm green-onion rice, for serving
1   tablespoon finely sliced green onions (green parts only), for garnish

*South Louisiana's Creole tomatoes are preferred for this recipe, although other good, peak-of-season regional varieties can be used.
**If this ingredient is difficult to find where you live, see Ingredient Sources on page 424.

1. Heat a heavy, nonreactive 5-quart saucepan over high heat until hot, about three minutes. Add the bacon, then the butter, stirring until the butter melts.

2. Reduce the heat to medium-high and cook the bacon until crisp, about three minutes, thoroughly scraping any browned bits off the bottom of the pan with a wooden spoon.

3. Reduce the heat to medium, and stir in the garlic, onions, sweet peppers and celery. Sauté for two minutes, stirring occasionally.

4. Stir in the Creole seasoning, and cook and stir about 30 seconds. Sprinkle the flour over the vegetables and stir thoroughly so the flour doesn't stick to the pan bottom as you let the mixture cook one minute.

5. Gradually add the stock, stirring constantly until well blended into the bacon mixture. Add the tomatoes, kosher salt, thyme, parsley and worcestershire.

6. Stir in the cream and bring to a simmer, then reduce heat to very low and simmer 10 minutes, stirring occasionally. Add the crawfish tails and continue cooking until the étouffée returns to a simmer. Remove from heat and serve immediately.

Serving Suggestion: Measure out 1 cup green-onion rice in a metal measuring cup, and invert the measuring cup in the center of a heated soup bowl, leaving the cup in place. Spoon around the measuring cup a portion (about 1 cup) of the étouffée, then lift away the cup. Repeat to prepare the remaining servings. Garnish each with a light sprinkle of green onions.

Crawfish Pizza with Pancetta & Roasted Garlic

For one 11-to-12-inch pizza or 2 servings

Cooks in South Louisiana never seem to run out of ways to cook crawfish, so the appearance of a crawfish pizza was probably inevitable.

The recommended crust for this pizza is found in the recipe for herbed dough on page 327. The recipe below is for one pizza, but the dough recipe is for three pizzas, each 11 to 12 inches wide. So you may want to use all of the herbed dough for three pizzas and treat your family or friends to a pizza party, serving up this crawfish pizza and two others of your choosing. Or you may triple the recipe below to serve three crawfish pizzas at once.

1	large (about ⅔ pound) red or yellow sweet pepper, or ½ cup of strips (¼ inch thick) store-bought roasted red or yellow sweet peppers
6	large, whole peeled garlic cloves
½	cup extra-virgin olive oil
	about 12⅔ ounces in weight herbed pizza dough, preferred, or an 11-to-12-inch ready-made thin pizza crust
¼	pound pancetta, cut into ¼-inch slices, and slices cut into ¼-inch cubes
	about 2 tablespoons cornmeal, for dusting the cookie sheet
	bread flour or all-purpose flour, for shaping dough
¼	teaspoon kosher salt
¼	teaspoon freshly ground black pepper
8	ounces drained fresh mozzarella cheese, cut into ¼-inch-thick rounds, strongly preferred, or 3 cups grated regular mozzarella cheese
¼	pound (¾ cup) peeled crawfish tails*
8	(3 ounces total) blanched artichoke hearts or frozen store-bought ones thawed, or canned marinated artichoke hearts, drained. (If large, halve or cut into bite-size bits.)
3	tablespoons finely sliced green onions, green parts only

*If this ingredient is difficult to find where you live, see Ingredient Sources on page 424.

1. If roasting the sweet pepper yourself, preheat the broiler.

2. Stem the sweet pepper and cut it in quarters lengthwise. Remove the core, seeds and membranes. Trim the curved ends to make the quarters lay as flat as possible.

3. Broil the sweet pepper quarters and trimmings, skin-side-up, about 5 inches from the heat source, until the flesh is tender but still plump and the skin blisters and turns very dark brown to black all over, about five minutes,

NOTES

Baking on a pizza stone will produce the crispest crust, but you will also get very good results baking the crust on a rimless cookie sheet or an inverted rimmed baking sheet.

Using fresh mozzarella rather than the standard type is highly recommended.

Four of the toppings may be prepared a day ahead. They are the sweet peppers, garlic, pancetta and artichoke hearts.

After straining the garlic oil (Step 7), save the remaining oil to use in vinaigrettes or marinades or to drizzle on bread.

ADVANCE STEPS

Prepare the pizza dough at least eight hours before assembling the pizza, preferably using the recipe for herbed dough on page 327. The dough should then be refrigerated.

If cooking the artichoke hearts yourself, prepare the blanched artichoke recipe on page 320.

Roasting and slicing the sweet pepper may be done a day ahead, as directed in Steps 1 through 5.

rotating the pieces occasionally with tongs. If in doubt, under-roast so the flesh is not overcooked.

4. Remove the sweet pepper pieces from the broiler and place them in a medium-size heat-proof bowl. Promptly cover the bowl with plastic wrap or a plate to let the sweet pepper steam for 15 minutes.

5. Peel the sweet pepper pieces and cut half of them into strips about ¼ inch wide and 2 inches long. Use the remaining pepper for another dish. If prepared ahead, cover and refrigerate until ready to use.

6. For the roasted garlic, in a deep, heavy 1-quart saucepan heat the garlic cloves in the olive oil, uncovered, for one hour over very low heat. If the cloves start darkening to more than medium-golden brown, remove the pan from heat and let the cloves steep in the hot oil for 30 minutes to one hour.

7. Drain the garlic cloves in a mesh strainer over a small heat-proof bowl to catch the oil. Set the cloves and garlic oil aside, separately, for up to an hour at room temperature. After one hour, cover and refrigerate until ready to use.

8. One hour before baking the pizza, remove the dough from the refrigerator to reach cool-room temperature. This will take about 20 minutes.

9. Meanwhile, cook the pancetta cubes in a heavy 8-inch skillet over medium-low heat until the fat is rendered out and the meat is somewhat crispy, about 15 minutes, stirring often toward the end of the cooking time. Drain the pancetta on paper towels. Set aside at room temperature, or refrigerate if prepared more than one hour ahead.

10. If using a pizza stone, place the stone on the lowest shelf of the oven and remove any other shelves in the oven to allow yourself plenty of space to safely maneuver when transferring the pizza to the pizza stone.

11. Whether using a pizza stone or not, preheat the oven to 500°F. If a pizza stone is used, preheat the oven for a solid 30 minutes to make sure the stone is very hot. Sprinkle 2 tablespoons cornmeal on a large rimless cookie sheet (more than 12 inches wide), inverted large rimmed baking pan, or a pizza peel, to keep the dough from sticking. Set aside.

12. Shaping the dough into a round: Once the dough reaches cool room temperature, place it on a lightly floured surface. With your fingertips, pat the dough from the center outward, gradually shaping it into a uniformly thick 11-to-12-inch round of dough. To keep the toppings in place while the pizza bakes, pinch the dough's edge to form a raised rim about ¾ inch high and about ½ inch thick.

For roasting the garlic in advance, see Steps 6 and 7 below.

SPECIAL EQUIPMENT
- A pair of heat-proof tongs
- A deep, heavy 1-quart saucepan
- A medium-size heat-proof bowl
- A small heat-proof bowl or glass measuring cup
- A heavy 8-inch skillet
- One of the following:
    A 14-inch-wide or larger pizza stone (preferred)
    A 12-inch-or-wider rimless cookie sheet or rimmed baking sheet
- A pizza peel
- A pastry brush
- A broad, large and sturdy spatula

13. As you work, lift the dough and turn it over several times. Handle it as gently as possible. If the dough becomes sticky, dust it with a little more flour.

14. Carefully transfer the dough to the cookie sheet, baking pan or pizza peel sprinkled with cornmeal. If any of the dough is sticking to the surface, carefully lift the dough to sprinkle more cornmeal beneath it.

15. Working quickly with a pastry brush, and using 1½ to 2 tablespoons of garlic oil, lightly brush the dough all over the surface, including the edge. Mash the garlic cloves, pull them apart with your fingers, and distribute the bits evenly over the dough up to (but not on) the thicker edge.

16. Evenly sprinkle the kosher salt and pepper over the dough.

17. Scatter the pancetta over the dough up to (but not on) the thicker edge, then arrange the mozzarella rounds up to the thicker edge.

18. Scatter as evenly as possible the red pepper strips, crawfish tails, artichoke hearts and green onions over the cheese. Drizzle 1 tablespoon garlic oil over all the toppings.

19. If not using a pizza stone: Place the cookie sheet or baking pan on the lowest shelf of the oven.

20. If using a pizza stone: You'll need to slide the dough onto the stone in the oven. Make sure the dough will move completely freely on the surface it was prepared on. If necessary, loosen the dough with a metal spatula. Next, line up the far edge of the cookie sheet or baking pan with the far edge of the hot pizza stone in the oven, being careful not to burn yourself. Slightly tilt and simultaneously jiggle again to make sure the pizza moves freely, then very gently slide the pizza onto the stone, being careful to keep any of the toppings from falling off.

21. Cook the pizza until the crust is crispy and dark golden brown, nine to 13 minutes.

    Serving Suggestion: Using a broad, large and sturdy spatula, transfer the pizza from the oven to a cutting board. Cut the pizza in wedges and serve while piping hot on heated plates.

Crawfish Won Ton "Ravioli" with Roasted-Tomato Butter Sauce

For 6 main-dish servings, allowing 4 or 5 won tons per serving plus several left over for freezing

At Ralph Brennan's Bacco restaurant, the crawfish mixture in this recipe fills pillows of ravioli pasta. Here, won tons are used instead. The sauce complements the won tons beautifully, adding a richness and a pleasant acidity.

FOR THE FILLING

¼	cup olive oil
1½	cups finely chopped onions
¾	cup finely chopped green sweet peppers
¾	cup finely chopped red sweet peppers
¾	cup finely chopped yellow sweet peppers
¾	cup finely sliced green onions, white and green parts
1	pound peeled crawfish tails,* coarsely chopped
2	tablespoons Creole seasoning
1	tablespoon Crystal pepper sauce or other relatively mild Louisiana pepper sauce
2	extra-large eggs, lightly beaten
½	cup very dry fine breadcrumbs

*If this ingredient is difficult to find where you live, see Ingredient Sources on page 424.

1. In a heavy 12-inch sauté pan, heat the olive oil over medium-high heat until just short of smoking, about two minutes.

2. Add the onions and sauté until they start becoming translucent, about three minutes, stirring occasionally.

3. Add the sweet peppers, green onions, crawfish, Creole seasoning, and pepper sauce, stirring well. Sauté until the peppers are crisp-tender, about four minutes, stirring occasionally.

4. Remove the filling from the heat and set it aside at room temperature until cool enough to handle, about 30 minutes, stirring occasionally.

5. Stir the eggs into the filling. Gradually add the breadcrumbs, mixing thoroughly. Refrigerate in a covered container until the breadcrumbs have absorbed the other flavors, at least two hours or overnight.

FOR PREPARING THE WON TONS

½	cup cornmeal, divided
1	egg, any size
96 to 100	won ton wrappers, 3 inches square

NOTES

The won ton filling may be made a day ahead.

Since the roasted-tomato butter sauce needs to be prepared as close to serving time as possible, form the won tons first and refrigerate them for up to four hours, then prepare the sauce as you're bringing the won tons cooking water to a boil.

The recipe for the roasted-tomato butter sauce is on page 364.

To create ravioli with rounded edges as pictured left, cut the ravioli into rounds just after filling them, using a 2½-inch cookie cutter.

ADVANCE STEP

Prepare the Creole seasoning recipe on page 385.

SPECIAL EQUIPMENT

• A heavy 12-inch sauté pan
• A rimmed baking sheet
• Parchment paper
• A pastry brush
• An 8-quart saucepan or Dutch oven

1. Line a rimmed baking sheet with parchment paper, then sprinkle the paper generously with cornmeal, using at least ⅓ cup.

2. In a small, shallow bowl, beat the egg with a fork until smooth. Lay a won ton wrapper on a work surface. Using a pastry brush, moisten the top of the wrapper all over with some of the egg.

3. Mound 1 level tablespoon of the filling in the center of the wrapper. Line up another wrapper over the top and gently press down around the filling and working outwards to remove air pockets. Repeat to prepare the remaining won tons. (You will have enough filling to make about 50 won tons.)

4. Place the finished won tons on the prepared baking sheet as formed. Once all the won tons are formed, sprinkle the tops lightly with cornmeal.

5. Refrigerate the won tons for up to four hours. If made further ahead, lay them out on a sheet pan between parchment paper and freeze until firm, then gently transfer them to a self-closing freezer bag, being careful not to break the fragile edges of the won tons. The won tons may be kept frozen for up to one month.

FOR COOKING AND SERVING THE WON TONS

	salted water, for cooking the won tons
1	recipe roasted-tomato butter sauce
3	tablespoons very finely sliced green onions, green parts only, for garnish
6 to 8	whole boiled crawfish, for garnish, optional

1. When ready to cook the won tons and make the sauce, put a generous amount of salted water on to boil in an 8-quart saucepan or Dutch oven.

2. Meanwhile, prepare the roasted-tomato butter sauce.

3. Ease small batches of the won tons (chilled or directly from the freezer) into the boiling salted water and cook uncovered until the won tons begin to float (indicating they are done), two to three minutes. Only cook the number of won tons you will actually be serving.

4. While the won tons are cooking, spoon roughly 2 tablespoons sauce in the bottom of each heated pasta bowl. As cooked, transfer four or five cooked won tons to each bowl with a slotted spoon.

   Serving Suggestion: Serve immediately with the remaining sauce spooned over the won tons. Garnish with the green onions and the whole boiled crawfish if you're using it. ❧

Fried-Oyster Poor Boy

For one 8-inch-long sandwich

Legend has it that the New Orleans poor boy sandwich was created in the 1920s, during a long strike by the city's streetcar conductors. Strikers were of course low on cash. So whenever one of them walked into a sandwich shop and grabbed a counter stool, the story goes, one of the servers would sometimes bellow, "Here comes another poor boy!" Then he'd be served the cheapest sandwich in the house.

Local purists contend that the authentic poor boy has to be made with New Orleans-style French bread, which features a thin but sturdy crust and a cottony texture. But the traditional sandwich fillings cover a wide range, from French fries to ham and cheese, and from hot roast beef with gravy to fried oysters, shrimp or even soft-shelled crabs.

Ask for a poor boy in the typical New Orleans shop and you'll be asked if you want it "dressed." Say yes and you'll usually find shredded iceberg lettuce, tomato slices, mayonnaise and possibly dill pickles inside the sandwich. But those garnishes are just the beginning of the options. Others are Louisiana pepper sauce, ketchup, Creole mustard, tartar sauce, horseradish and brushed-on melted butter. One way we like them is with the bread slathered with mayonnaise, Creole mustard and prepared horseradish, and then with torn Romaine lettuce leaves and thin slices of tomatoes and onions.

A good accompaniment is the classic potato salad (see recipe on page 338).

14 (about 8 ounces) fresh, small-to-medium raw oysters*
 1 cup seasoned flour
    vegetable oil for frying
 1 8-inch piece New Orleans-style French bread,** preferably poor boy bread
       with rounded ends
    dressings and garnishes of your choice

    *Louisiana oysters are ideal for this dish, but if you're near coastal waters
    with beds of fresh native oysters, by all means use them.
    **If New Orleans-style poor boy bread is not available, a possible substitute
    is a loaf (about 14 inches long and 3 to 4 inches in diameter) of sugarless,
    natural-yeast white bread with a low gluten content and a thin crust.

Prepare the recipe for seasoned
flour on page 384.

1. Drain the oysters for 15 minutes in a colander or coarse-mesh strainer. Place the seasoned flour in a large mixing bowl.

2. In a heavy, deep 12-inch skillet, heat ½ inch of oil over medium-high heat until it reaches 375°F, about three minutes.

3. Meanwhile, lightly toast the bread and cut it lengthwise without cutting one of the long sides all the way through (so it will open like a hotdog bun).

4. Once the oil is just short of reaching 375°, dredge the oysters in the seasoned flour, tossing them to coat all surfaces. Shake off any excess.

5. Carefully slide the oysters into the oil. (As the cold oysters come in contact with the hot oil, the oil may momentarily bubble up.)

6. Fry the oysters just until golden brown and crispy, about two minutes. Remove the oysters from the skillet with a slotted spoon, and drain briefly on paper towels.

7. Spread the bread with mayonnaise, brush with melted butter, or use your dressing(s) of choice. Arrange the oysters on the bread, and add whatever garnishes you like. Serve while piping hot.

NOTES

The size of the typical poor boy makes it adaptable to a large or small appetite. One sandwich could easily serve two people if offered with a salad or a cup of gumbo or soup.

Poor boys are easier to eat if the bread is not completely cut in two. That way, the uncut side helps to hold everything in place.

Just the fried-oyster part of the recipe can be used for making a delicious composed salad with fresh, crisp greens and a favorite salad dressing.

ADVANCE STEPS

Frying the oysters is a surprisingly quick process, so be sure to have all the poor boy ingredients and garnishes at hand before starting.

Prepare the recipe for seasoned flour on page 384.

SPECIAL EQUIPMENT

• A heavy, deep 12-inch skillet or sauté pan
• A large slotted spoon
• A frying thermometer
• Absorbent paper for draining the oysters

Oysters and Fettuccine and Alfredo Sauce with Smoked Tomatoes

For 6 servings

Pasta with seafood in a sauce has become a very familiar combination in New Orleans and the rest of South Louisiana. The pairing apparently came about with the realization that pasta could be substituted for rice, which has been the starch found more frequently in the region's seafood dishes.

The sauce in this recipe gets its smoky character from tomatoes. If you don't have a store-bought stove-top smoker, see Special Equipment below for a suggestion.

FOR THE SMOKED TOMATOES

1½ cups fine hickory-wood chips
    non-stick vegetable spray, if using a homemade smoker
2¾ pounds (4 or 5 large) perfectly ripe Creole or other vine-ripened tomatoes*
    heavy-duty aluminum foil, if using a homemade smoker

*Use the best tomatoes available, since they will provide the Alfredo sauce's predominant flavor.

1. Soak the hickory chips in water according to the directions in Advance Steps, right.

2. Place the smoker on the stove top. Scatter the wet wood chips evenly over the bottom of the space designed to hold the chips, but don't turn the burner on yet.

3. If using a homemade smoker, spray the perforated rack or cooling rack with non-stick vegetable spray.

4. Core the tomatoes and, if using a homemade smoker, transfer them to the perforated rack or cooling grid, core-side-up, in the smoker.

5. If using a store-bought smoker, follow the manufacturer's directions and smoke the tomatoes until smoked light to medium and the skins have split. (The cooking time will vary depending on the smoker.)

6. If using a homemade smoker, make sure the food is at the opposite end from the wood chips. Next, completely seal the tomatoes inside the roasting pan with heavy-duty aluminum foil and smoke the tomatoes over high heat until a good amount of smoke escapes when you open a small vent, about 10 minutes. Close the vent, then reduce heat to medium and continue smoking until the tomato skins are lightly colored from the smoke and have split, about 20 minutes more. Remove from heat.

NOTE

Some of the smoked tomatoes will be used in preparing the Alfredo sauce recipe. An additional amount will go into the sauce during the final steps of the recipe under "For the oysters and fettuccine." This is to give additional texture appeal to the finished dish.

ADVANCE STEPS

The tomatoes may be prepared up to two days in advance.

The ingredients list includes 1½ cups of hickory-wood chips. Before smoking the tomatoes, soak the chips in water for at least four hours or according to package directions. Drain them just before using, leaving them dripping wet.

SPECIAL EQUIPMENT

• A stove-top smoker,* either store-bought or a homemade, temporary one (preferred)

*If you don't have a commercial stove-top smoker, it's easy to make a temporary one at home with materials you probably already have on hand—namely, a roasting pan, heavy-duty aluminum foil and a perforated rack or metal cooling rack to fit in the roasting pan to

7. Very carefully (so you don't burn yourself from the steam) remove the lid or foil, and transfer the tomatoes to a platter to cool.

8. Once the tomatoes are cool, peel and chop the pulp. You should have 3 to 4 cups of chopped pulp and juice.

9. Measure out 1¾ cups of the tomatoes and juice and refrigerate them for adding to the Alfredo sauce. Measure out and refrigerate another ½ cup of the tomatoes and juice for finishing the oysters and fettuccine dish.

FOR THE ALFREDO SAUCE

2	yolks from large eggs
1¾	cups heavy cream
4½	ounces freshly grated Parmigiano-Reggiano cheese
1¾	cups peeled and chopped smoked tomatoes, from the recipe above
¼	teaspoon kosher salt, or to taste
¼	teaspoon freshly ground black pepper, or to taste

1. Place the egg yolks in a large heat-proof mixing bowl and lightly beat with a metal whisk. Set aside.

2. In a heavy, nonreactive 2½-quart saucepan heat together the cream and Parmigiano-Reggiano cheese over low heat for five minutes, whisking almost constantly. Increase the heat to high and continue cooking, whisking constantly, until the mixture is fairly smooth, about one minute. Remove from heat.

3. Very gradually add the hot cream and cheese mixture to the egg yolks, whisking constantly. Stir in the reserved 1¾ cups of smoked tomatoes.

4. Process this entire mixture in a blender to a smooth purée. If the sauce is thin (it should be the consistency of fairly thick heavy cream), return it to the saucepan and cook over medium heat just until it thickens, whisking constantly.

5. Remove the sauce from heat and season it with kosher salt and pepper to taste.

6. If the sauce was prepared ahead, let it cool and then refrigerate it in a covered, nonreactive container.

FOR THE OYSTERS AND FETTUCCINE

	about 3 tablespoons olive oil, divided
6	ounces pancetta, cut in ¼-inch slices, and slices cut in ¼-inch cubes
	plenty of salted water for cooking fettuccine
1	pound dry fettuccine
3	tablespoons minced fresh garlic

hold the food. One advantage of a homemade smoker is that it lends the tomatoes a little more color and taste from the wood smoke. Instructions for making the temporary smoker are on page 416.

Instructions for making the temporary smoker are on page 416.

NOTE

There should be some sauce left over. It may be put to other uses, such as being reheated gently in a double boiler over hot (not simmering) water, then tossed with cooked pasta and topped with grated Parmigiano-Reggiano cheese.

ADVANCE STEP

The sauce may be prepared one day in advance.

SPECIAL EQUIPMENT

- A large, heat-proof mixing bowl
- A metal whisk
- A heavy, nonreactive* 2½-quart saucepan
- A blender, preferred, or a food processor
- If preparing the sauce ahead, a double boiler

*See Using Nonreactive Cookware, page 419.

SPECIAL EQUIPMENT

- A heavy, nonreactive* 12-inch sauté pan
- A pair of tongs

*See Using Nonreactive Cookware, page 419.

¼ to ½	teaspoon crushed red pepper
½	cup peeled and chopped smoked tomatoes, drained
3	cups Alfredo sauce
½	teaspoon kosher salt, plus to taste
30	medium-to-large raw oysters, drained (about 1½ pounds)
6	teaspoons very finely sliced green onions (green parts only), for garnish

1. In a heavy, nonreactive 12-inch sauté pan, combine 1 tablespoon olive oil and the pancetta. Cook over medium-low heat until the fat renders out of the meat but the meat itself is only slightly crispy, 10 to 12 minutes, stirring occasionally. Remove from heat.

2. Meanwhile, heat the salted water and cook the fettuccine until it is almost al dente, according to package directions. Drain well and rinse with cool water. Drain again.

3. Place the fettuccine in a large mixing bowl and toss with 2 tablespoons olive oil, mixing to coat all the strands with oil. Cover the bowl with a double thickness of damp paper towels and set aside at room temperature.

4. Once the pancetta has been rendered, drain all except 2 tablespoons of the fat from the pan. If the rendering process did not produce 2 tablespoons of fat, add enough olive oil to the pan to make 2 tablespoons.

5. Place the pan over high heat. Add the garlic, crushed red pepper and reserved ½ cup of smoked tomatoes. Sauté for one minute, stirring constantly.

6. Reduce the heat to medium-low and add the 3 cups of Alfredo sauce and ½ teaspoon of kosher salt. Cook until the sauce is heated through, about two minutes, stirring frequently.

7. Add the oysters and cook just until they are plump and their edges curl, about two minutes.

8. Add the drained fettuccine to the pan, tossing with tongs to coat well with sauce. Continue cooking until the fettuccine is heated through, about one minute more, tossing almost constantly. Remove from heat and season with more kosher salt if needed. Serve immediately.

Serving Suggestion: Divide the oysters and fettuccine among six heated individual pasta bowls. Garnish each with 1 teaspoon green onions.

Alligator Sauce Piquante

For 6 servings

As the name indicates, sauce piquante has a peppery kick to it, although the pepper level can be raised or reduced to taste.

A rustic dish with a long Cajun heritage, sauce piquante is made with lots of extra seasonings and is traditionally served with rice. This recipe uses alligator tail meat, the cut sold by retailers. The sauce is versatile enough to be matched with any number of main ingredients—not only alligator but also turtle, pork, chicken, veal, conch, scallops and game.

Many sauce piquante fans keep a bottle of Tabasco handy when eating it.

1	tablespoon vegetable oil
1	cup plus 1 tablespoon all-purpose flour, divided
2	pounds alligator tail meat,* trimmed of all sinew, fat and silver skin
½	teaspoon coarse salt, preferably kosher salt, or to taste
½	teaspoon cayenne pepper
¼	teaspoon freshly ground black pepper, or to taste
5	tablespoons clarified butter, divided
6	cloves garlic, cut crosswise into very thin slices
1	cup chopped yellow onions
½	cup chopped celery
½	cup chopped green sweet peppers
2	cups chopped Creole tomatoes**
1½	tablespoons minced fresh jalapeño peppers***
3	tablespoons minced Italian (flat-leaf) parsley leaves, divided
2	tablespoons minced fresh thyme leaves
1	cup good-quality dry white wine
2½	cups chicken stock
	hot cooked white rice (preferably long-grain), stone-ground grits or couscous, for serving

*If this ingredient is difficult to find where you live, see Ingredient Sources on page 424.

**South Louisiana's Creole tomatoes are preferred for this recipe, although other good, peak-of-season regional varieties can be used.

***Jalapeños vary in heat level. The best way to reach the dish's desirable level is to begin with half of the amount the recipe calls for and adjust the amount of pepper to taste.

NOTES

The color of the roux in this recipe is keyed to the color chart on page 415.

This dish takes on added flavor when served the day after it is prepared.

ADVANCE STEPS

Prepare the recipes for:

- Clarified butter on page 355
- Chicken stock on page 390

SPECIAL EQUIPMENT

- A very small, heavy skillet or 6½-inch crepe pan
- A long-handled whisk or wooden spoon
- A kitchen mallet
- A heavy 12-inch sauté pan

1. For the roux, in a very small, heavy skillet, heat the oil over medium heat until hot, about one minute. Add 1 tablespoon of flour and cook, constantly whisking or stirring with a long-handled metal whisk or wooden spoon, until the flour turns a dark-chocolate brown, three to four minutes. Be careful not to scorch the roux. Promptly remove the roux from heat

and continue whisking thoroughly until it stops getting darker, two to three minutes. Set aside at room temperature.

2. Using a kitchen mallet, pound the pieces of alligator between two pieces of wax paper or parchment paper to tenderize the meat and make all pieces ¼-inch thick, then cut the meat into rough bite-sized pieces, cutting across the sinews whenever possible to further tenderize the meat. Season the meat with kosher salt, cayenne and black pepper. Place 1 cup of flour in a small mixing bowl and dredge half the alligator pieces in it, shaking off any excess.

3. Heat 2½ tablespoons of clarified butter in a heavy 12-inch sauté pan over medium-high heat until hot, one to two minutes. Add the dredged alligator meat in a single layer and cook until dark golden brown, five to seven minutes on each side. Transfer the pieces to a plate or bowl as they brown.

4. Wipe the pan clean with paper towels and heat another 2½ tablespoons clarified butter until hot. Dredge the remaining alligator in the flour, and brown them as you did the first batch. Return the first batch of meat to the pan with the second batch.

5. Reduce the heat to medium-low and stir in the garlic. Cook the garlic until it begins to brown, one to two minutes, stirring and turning over the meat pieces almost constantly. Add the onions, celery and sweet peppers. Cook until the onions are translucent, about five minutes, stirring frequently and continuing to turn the meat over so the vegetables will cook evenly.

6. Stir in the tomatoes and jalapeños and increase the heat to medium. Cook for about three minutes, then add 2 tablespoons of parsley and the thyme, wine and stock, stirring well. Scatter bits of the reserved roux over the mixture, and whisk or stir until the roux is blended in.

7. Bring the mixture to a boil, then reduce the heat and simmer the sauce until the alligator is tender, about 30 minutes, stirring occasionally. Adjust the salt and pepper seasoning toward the end of cooking if needed.

Serving Suggestion: Serve immediately, or make the dish a day ahead and reheat it at serving time.

Serve over rice, grits or couscous, garnishing each portion with some of the remaining 1 tablespoon of parsley. 🐚

Sautéed Frog Legs with Wilted Baby Spinach & Creamer Potatoes

For 4 main-dish servings

The taste for frog legs has long been considered distinctly French. And surely, many a Gallic gourmand has feasted on *cuisses de grenouille à la provençale*—frog "thighs" sautéed in butter with garlic and parsley. Legend has it that the illustrious Georges-Auguste Escoffier, when he headed the kitchen at London's posh Carlton Hotel, managed to get them on the Prince of Wales' table by calling them *cuisses de nymphes aurore*, or "thighs of the dawn nymphs."

The fact is frog legs, or thighs if you will, have long been looked on as a true delicacy in many parts of the world, among them southern Louisiana. Along the state's coastline, with its vast network of marshes, ponds and other waterways, frog legs have been a favorite food for generations, especially in the form of a peppery Cajun sauce piquante. According to the city fathers of Rayne, a town in the south-central part of the state, a resident named Donat Pucheu began selling frog legs to New Orleans restaurants in the 1880s.

The newcomer to frog legs will find their mild but pleasant flavor comparable to other white meats, including, of course, chicken. This recipe, which calls for no small amount of butter, produces a dish that's both hearty and elegant. With the possible addition of a salad or soup, it can easily function as a meal.

12	pairs (10 to 12 pairs per pound) fresh or frozen medium-size domestic frog legs*
3½	cups whole milk, approximately
2	medium-size (about 6 ounces each) ripe tomatoes
2	pounds unpeeled creamer or other young potatoes, scrubbed well, trimmed of blemishes and cut into quarters
3	quarts cool water, approximately
1	tablespoon plus 1½ teaspoons kosher salt, plus to taste, divided
1½	teaspoons freshly ground black pepper, plus to taste, divided
5	tablespoons clarified butter, divided
3	tablespoons olive oil, divided
1	cup all-purpose flour
6	ounces fresh baby spinach leaves with stems, washed and drained (drying not necessary)
2	large cloves garlic, sliced paper-thin
½	teaspoon finely grated lemon zest
2	tablespoons fresh lemon juice
4	tablespoons unsalted butter, not clarified
1	tablespoon minced fresh Italian (flat-leaf) parsley leaves

*If this ingredient is difficult to find where you live, see Ingredient Sources on page 424.

*If this ingredient is difficult to find where you live, see Ingredient Sources on page 424.

NOTES

Only the hind legs are used, and they come in pairs of different sizes, ranging from 14 to 18 pairs per pound to 10 to 12 pairs per pound. The best-quality legs are the domestic ones, most of which come from Florida.

Fresh frog legs can be found in the seafood section of some gourmet markets, but they're most frequently sold frozen. Frozen legs should be cooked as soon as they're thawed, since their "shelf life" is very short, a day or two at most.

Creamer potatoes are called for in this recipe, but other varieties may work as well. The rule of thumb in choosing potatoes is to look for the freshest-from-the-ground ones available.

1. Rinse the pairs of frog legs under cool running water, leaving the pairs connected.

2. Place the legs in a medium-size mixing bowl, and cover them with about 3 ½ cups milk. Let them soak for one hour at room temperature.

3. Peel the tomatoes, cut them in quarters and remove the seeds. Trim the quarters to be of even thickness, then cut each quarter in half lengthwise and in half crosswise to make four pieces, each about 1½ inches by 1¼ inches. Refrigerate the tomatoes until needed.

4. Preheat the oven to 200°F.

5. Place the potato quarters in a 5-quart saucepan or Dutch oven. Cover them with about 3 quarts water and add 1 tablespoon kosher salt. Bring the water to a boil, then reduce the heat and simmer until the quarters are fork tender, about 12 minutes.

6. Drain the potatoes well, return them to the pan and cover the potatoes to keep them warm.

7. Once the frog legs have soaked for one hour, drain them well, pat them dry with paper towels and arrange them in a single layer on a rimmed baking sheet. Season the frog legs on each side with a total of 1 teaspoon kosher salt and 1 teaspoon pepper.

8. In a heavy 12-inch sauté pan, heat 1 tablespoon of the clarified butter with 1 tablespoon of olive oil over medium-high heat until hot, about two minutes. While the butter and oil mixture is heating, place the flour in a large mixing bowl and dredge six pairs of frog legs in the flour, shaking off any excess.

9. Sauté the dredged frog legs in the hot butter and oil mixture just until golden brown, three to four minutes on each side. (Do not overcook them or the meat will become tough.) Arrange paper towels on another rimmed baking sheet, place the browned legs on the paper to drain and put the baking sheet in the 200° oven to keep the frog legs warm.

10. Wipe the sauté pan clean with paper towels and heat another 1 tablespoon clarified butter and 1 tablespoon olive oil for browning the remaining frog legs. Dredge the remaining legs in the flour and brown them as you did the first batch. Place the legs in the oven with the others to keep all warm while finishing the dish.

11. Wipe the pan clean again with paper towels and set it aside momentarily.

12. In a heavy 9-inch skillet, heat 2 tablespoons of clarified butter over medium-high heat until it sizzles, about one minute. Add the spinach leaves to the

ADVANCE STEP

Prepare the recipe for clarified butter on page 355.

SPECIAL EQUIPMENT

- 2 rimmed baking sheets
- A heavy 12-inch sauté pan or a heavy 12-inch skillet
- A heavy 9-inch skillet

skillet and turn them to coat all the leaves with the butter. Season with a little kosher salt and pepper and cook just until wilted, about one minute. Cover the spinach and set it aside.

13. In the clean 12-inch sauté pan, heat together 1 tablespoon of clarified butter and 1 tablespoon of olive oil over medium heat until the mixture is hot and starts to sizzle, about one and a half minutes.

14. Stir in the garlic and sauté just a few seconds until it starts to brown. Add the reserved tomato pieces and the lemon zest and sauté for two minutes, stirring almost constantly. Stir in the lemon juice, the 4 tablespoons regular (not clarified) unsalted butter, ½ teaspoon kosher salt and ½ teaspoon pepper. Swirl the pan to melt the butter evenly in the sauce.

15. Once the butter is melted, add the reserved potatoes and the parsley and continue cooking for 30 seconds more, tossing constantly.

16. Remove the potatoes and sauce from the heat and serve immediately.

Serving Suggestion: Place a small mound of wilted spinach in the center of each heated dinner plate. Arrange three pairs of frog legs on the plate, and spoon some of the potatoes and sauce from the pan over the legs. ✤

Creole Jambalaya

For 6 servings

This rice dish is one of the oldest in the traditional New Orleans Creole cook's repertoire. It shares characteristics with Spanish paëllas, but it has even stronger connections with traditional African rice cookery.

Some have speculated that "jambalaya" is a contraction of *jambon à la ya-ya*—marrying the French word *jambon*, for ham, with the old African Bantu word *ya-ya*, for rice.

Over the decades, jambalaya has taken on a multitude of identities in South Louisiana. The classic New Orleans dish with shrimp and ham is among the "red" jambalayas, thanks to the presence of tomatoes in it. In many of the Cajun communities to the west of the city, "brown" jambalayas, with oysters, giblets and lusty country sausages, are more familiar.

In present-day New Orleans homes, jambalaya's easy preparation makes it popular party fare, especially during such local celebrations as Mardi Gras and the New Orleans Jazz & Heritage Festival.

1	tablespoon unsalted butter (or 2 tablespoons if the pork and sausage are very lean)
4	ounces andouille sausage,* sliced into ¼-inch rounds
4	ounces pickled pork** or ham, cut into ¼-inch cubes
1	medium-size yellow onion, chopped
1	bunch of green onions, chopped, with white and green parts separated
1	medium-size green sweet pepper, chopped
2	cans (10 ounces each) crushed plum tomatoes
¼	cup canned tomato purée
2	cloves garlic, minced
1	whole bay leaf
1	teaspoon table salt
½	teaspoon ground black pepper
¼	teaspoon ground cayenne
¼	teaspoon dry thyme leaves
4	quarts chicken stock
1	tablespoon Louisiana pepper sauce
2	cups long-grain white rice, uncooked
1	pound raw medium shrimp, peeled

*Smoked or Polish sausage (kielbasa) may be substituted for the andouille.
**Pickled pork (or "pickled meat," as it is sometimes called) is a familiar seasoning meat in the traditional "pot cooking" of the American Deep South. It is often used to add flavor to greens, beans and other "pot food." In this jambalaya recipe, any good-quality ham may be used instead.

NOTE

This recipe can be prepared up to two days ahead by completing Steps 1 through 4, allowing the base sauce to cool a bit, then covering and storing it in the refrigerator. When it's time to finish the preparation, bring the base sauce to a boil and proceed from Step 5.

ADVANCE STEP

Prepare the recipe for chicken stock on page 390.

SPECIAL EQUIPMENT

• A heavy, nonreactive* 6-quart saucepan or Dutch oven
• A nonreactive lidded container for refrigerated storage

*See Using Nonreactive Cookware, page 419.

1. Over medium-high heat, melt the butter in a heavy, nonreactive 6-quart saucepan or Dutch oven.

2. Add the sausage and pickled pork or ham and cook until all of the fat is rendered out of the meats, about five minutes, stirring occasionally.

3. Add the yellow onions, the white part of the green onions and the sweet peppers. Cook the vegetables until they are clear, about five minutes, occasionally stirring and scraping the pan bottom clean.

4. Add the crushed tomatoes, tomato purée, garlic, bay leaf, table salt, black pepper, cayenne, and thyme. Cook and stir this base sauce about two minutes. (If the dish is being prepared ahead, allow the base sauce to cool, then place in a lidded nonreactive container and store it in the refrigerator for up to two days. For the final preparation, heat the base to a boil and proceed with the remainder of the recipe.)

5. Add the chicken stock and pepper sauce to the base and bring to a boil.

6. Reduce the heat to maintain a strong simmer, and simmer the liquid uncovered until it is reduced by one third, about one hour 15 minutes. Skim any foam or coagulates as they develop on the surface.

7. Return the liquid to a boil and stir in the rice.

8. Reduce the heat to medium, and cook uncovered until the rice is just short of being done (it should still be a little firm in the center), about 25 minutes, stirring occasionally.

9. Add the shrimp and cook until the rice is tender and the shrimp turn bright pink, about three minutes. Do not overcook.

10. Stir in the green part of the green onions.

    Serving Suggestion: Spoon the warm jambalaya onto a heated serving platter or into a wide, shallow serving bowl. ❧

Seafood-Stuffed Artichokes with Lemon Mayonnaise

For 6 to 8 servings

Artichokes, which are botanically related to thistles, are very tasty vegetables. The large artichokes known as "green globe" became especially popular in New Orleans after the arrival of thousands of Sicilian immigrants in the city between the late 19th and early 20th centuries.

The Sicilians brought with them the practice of stuffing a whole blanched artichoke by placing herbed breadcrumbs, other seasonings, olive oil and bits of shrimp or bacon between the leaves. Today, Sicilian-style, whole stuffed artichokes are sold ready to eat at many Italian-style delis and grocery stores in and around New Orleans.

That is the traditional dish that inspired this recipe, which uses shrimp, crab and crawfish.

2	tablespoons unsalted butter
1	cup small diced yellow onion
1	tablespoon minced garlic
8	ounces medium raw shrimp, peeled
8	ounces crab claw meat, picked through
8	ounces fresh crawfish tails, peeled*
½	teaspoon kosher salt
¼	teaspoon freshly ground black pepper
1	teaspoon Creole seasoning
1½	cups fresh soft breadcrumbs
¼	cup minced Italian (flat-leaf) parsley
¼	cup grated Parmigiano-Reggiano cheese
½	pound (2 sticks) melted unsalted butter, divided
6 to 8	whole green globe artichokes, blanched
1	recipe lemon mayonnaise, for serving

*If this ingredient is difficult to find where you live, see Ingredient Sources on page 424.

1. Preheat the oven to 400°F.

2. In a heavy, 12-inch sauté pan over medium-high heat place the 2 tablespoons of unsalted butter. When the butter melts and begins to foam add the diced onions and sauté until the onions are soft but not browned.

3. Add the garlic and shrimp and sauté for two minutes.

4. Add the crabmeat, crawfish, kosher salt, pepper and Creole seasoning and continue to sauté for one minute.

NOTES

This dish can be served as an entrée or as a shared appetizer.

The recipe makes enough stuffing for six to eight artichokes, depending on their size.

ADVANCE STEP

Prepare the following recipes:
- Creole seasoning on page 385
- Fresh soft breadcrumbs on page 382
- Blanched artichokes on page 320
- Lemon mayonnaise on page 369

SPECIAL EQUIPMENT

- A heavy 12-inch sauté pan
- A 9-by-13-inch glass baking dish

5. Remove the seafood mixture from the heat and set aside to cool.

6. In a medium-size bowl, place the breadcrumbs, parsley, Parmigiano-Reggiano cheese and ½ cup of the melted butter. Blend these ingredients well, using your hands.

7. Add the cooled seafood mixture to the breadcrumb mixture, including any liquid that may be in the sauté pan.

8. Fill the space in the center of the artichoke with a generous amount of the stuffing. Gently pull back some of the leaves and begin to push bits of stuffing between them.

9. Place the stuffed artichokes bottom-side down in a 9-by-13-inch glass baking dish.

10. Drizzle the remaining melted butter over the top of the stuffed artichokes.

11. Bake the artichokes uncovered in a 400° oven for about 20 minutes. The tops should be golden brown and the stuffing should be hot. Serve immediately.

Serving Suggestion: Pass the lemon mayonnaise at the table to use as a dipping sauce or serve it on the plates with the artichokes. ❀

Louisiana Seafood Boil (recipe opposite)

Louisiana Seafood Boil

For 8 to 10 servings

Generations of New Orleanians have feasted on crabs and shrimp in their shells boiled with lemon and spices. Some do it outdoors with a butane burner, consuming the shellfish at a table covered with newspapers and—if the table needs protection—lined with a plastic cover. Just as often, the festive event begins indoors on a stovetop, with everyone gathered at the kitchen table. Cold beer is the preferred beverage, but white wines—especially those with a bit of sweetness that can stand up to the spices—also pair well with the shellfish. Alsatian whites such as Gewürztraminer and Riesling are local favorites.

A dipping sauce is a popular accompaniment to a seafood boil. Two good ones are a seafood cocktail sauce (see the recipe on page 366), and a Creole rémoulade sauce (see the recipe on page 373).

12	quarts cool water
4	large onions, peeled and coarsely chopped
4	celery stalks, cut into 2-inch pieces
10	lemons, cut in half
5	bulbs of garlic, with tops cut off just enough to expose the flesh of the pods
2	cups kosher salt
½	cup Zatarain's brand liquid crab boil seasoning*
1	pouch Zatarain's brand dry-spice crab boil seasoning*
10	whole small bay leaves
⅓	cup whole black peppercorns
1	teaspoon ground cayenne pepper
2	pounds andouille sausage, cut into 2-inch-long pieces**
1	dozen live jumbo-size crabs
5	pounds whole (with heads and shells) large shrimp

*If this ingredient is difficult to find where you live, see Ingredient Sources on page 424.
**Smoked or Polish sausage (kielbasa) may be substituted for the andouille.

NOTES

Crabs and shrimp are called for in this recipe, but crawfish are eligible for inclusion, too.

For an added treat toss in raw medium whole potatoes, shucked corn on the cob, whole green-globe artichokes or even franks for the kids. These will absorb the spicy flavor of the liquid.

SPECIAL EQUIPMENT

- A 5-gallon or larger boiling pot
- A pair of large tongs
- A large strainer
- Tools for cracking crab shells and retrieving the meat, such as nutcrackers, lobster crackers, snail forks, cocktail forks and shellfish picks

1. Place all the ingredients except the crabs and shrimp in the boiling pot. Over high heat, bring the liquid to a boil.

2. Reduce the heat and simmer 10 minutes.

3. Add the crabs one at a time, holding them carefully with tongs to avoid being pinched. Let the liquid return to a simmer and cook for five minutes.

4. Add the shrimp and let the liquid once again return to a simmer.

5. When the final simmer point is reached, turn off the heat and let the shellfish steep, uncovered, for 10 minutes.

6. When the steeping is complete, promptly remove the shellfish and andouille from the pot with a large strainer and allow them to cool for a few minutes.

Serving Suggestion: Serve on platters or trays with cracking tools.

DESSERTS
&
DESSERT SAUCES

Almond Bark

Bread Pudding

Chocolate Bread Pudding

Praline Bread Pudding

Creole Cream Cheese Cheesecake

Chocolate Bourbon Pecan Pie

Dark Chocolate Cake

Crème Caramel

Mr. Ralph's Ice Cream Sandwiches

Lemon Icebox Pie

Peanut Butter Pie

Fluffy Sweet-Potato Pie

Creole Red Velvet Roulade

Chocolate Sauce

White-Chocolate Sauce

Caramel Sauce

Lightly Sweetened Whipped Cream

Whiskey Sauce

Almond Bark

For 2½ pounds of candy or 40 to 50 rough 2-inch pieces

This easy-to-make candy can be eaten as is or used as a garnish with such dishes as the chocolate bread pudding on page 280.

½ cup sliced almonds
4 cups (24 ounces) fine-quality bittersweet chocolate chips
3 cups (16½ ounces) fine-quality white chocolate chips

SPECIAL EQUIPMENT
- A rimmed baking sheet, about 17 by 12 inches by 1 inch
- Parchment paper
- A double boiler
- An icing spatula

1. Preheat the oven to 325°F.

2. Roast the almonds in a small baking pan until light golden, about five minutes, stirring once or twice. Watch them carefully so they don't over-brown.

3. Line a rimmed baking sheet, about 17 by 12 inches by 1 inch, with parchment paper. Set aside.

4. Melt the bittersweet chocolate chips in the top of a double boiler over hot (not simmering) water, stirring until smooth. Remove the top of the pan from over the hot water when the chips are about half-way melted to stir thoroughly.

5. Once the chocolate is smooth, remove it from heat and promptly pour it onto the baking sheet, spreading it in a thin, even layer with an icing spatula.

6. Refrigerate, uncovered, until firm, about 15 minutes.

7. While the dark chocolate is chilling, melt the white chocolate chips as you did the dark ones. Take extra care to heat the white chocolate over very low heat, since white chocolate scorches more easily than dark chocolate. Also, wash and dry the icing spatula.

8. Once the white chocolate is melted and the dark chocolate is firm, remove the dark chocolate from the refrigerator.

9. Immediately spread the white chocolate evenly over the dark chocolate with the icing spatula, working quickly so the warmth of the white chocolate barely has time to melt the dark chocolate. (Don't worry if it melts a little. It will give the white chocolate a pretty marbled look.)

10. Promptly sprinkle the almonds over the white chocolate, breaking them into coarse crumbs as you go, and gently pressing them into the chocolate to make sure they stick. Refrigerate the candy, uncovered, until just firm. After 30 to 40 minutes the candy should be firm enough to break into rough 2-inch pieces of "bark." Don't refrigerate until very firm before breaking into bark or the chocolate will be more difficult to break up.

Serving Suggestion: Use immediately or keep refrigerated, separated by sheets of wax paper, in airtight containers. The candy will keep at least one week. ❀

Bread Pudding with Whiskey Sauce

For 10 to 12 servings

For generations of Creole home cooks, bread gone stale has been a fine excuse to make a warm and custardy bread pudding. The city's traditional French bread is the usual ingredient, since it is ideally light and readily soaks up the liquid ingredients, in addition to having a very thin crust, which means the crust need not be removed before it goes into the custard mix.

10	large eggs
2¾	cups whole milk
2¾	cups heavy cream
1	cup sugar, divided
1½	teaspoons ground cinnamon, divided
½	teaspoon freshly ground nutmeg
1	piece day-old New Orleans-style French bread, about 23 inches long and weighing about 7½ to 8 ounces
¾	cup dark raisins
2½	tablespoons unsalted butter, cut into small bits
1	recipe whiskey sauce

NOTES

If New Orleans-style French bread is not available, you can get similar results using a sugarless, natural-yeast white bread with a low gluten content and a thin crust.

The pudding can also be made with brioche, challah, day-old croissants or other egg bread, as long as the crust is very thin.

ADVANCE STEPS

This recipe is prepared in two steps, requiring refrigerating the pudding for six or more hours before it is baked.

Prepare the recipe for whiskey sauce on page 317.

1. In a large mixing bowl, lightly beat the eggs with a metal whisk or an electric mixer. Add the milk, cream, ¾ cup of sugar, ¾ teaspoon of cinnamon and the nutmeg.

2. Continue beating until the custard mixture is smooth and the sugar has dissolved. Set aside.

3. Cut the bread loaf crosswise into 1-inch slices.

4. Line the bottom of a 9-by-13-inch glass baking dish with the slices, cut sides up, squeezing the slices in as necessary to form a single layer.

5. Pour the custard mixture over the bread and turn the slices over to assure they are saturated. Scatter the raisins evenly over the bread, pushing them into the bread with your fingertips.

6. Cover and refrigerate for six to eight hours, preferably overnight.

7. Three to four hours before serving time remove the pudding from the refrigerator and allow it to reach cool room temperature, about one and a half hours.

8. Meanwhile, mix together the remaining ¼ cup of sugar and ¾ teaspoon of cinnamon, blending them well. Evenly dot the top of the pudding with the bits of butter and sprinkle the cinnamon sugar over the top.

9. Once the pudding has almost reached cool room temperature, preheat the oven to 325°F.

10. Place the pudding dish in a larger pan and carefully pour enough boiling-hot water into the outer pan to come halfway up the sides of the pudding dish. Cover both the baking dish and the outer pan with a single sheet of heavy-duty aluminum foil and seal the edges.

11. Bake the pudding until it is almost firm in the center, about one hour, then remove the foil and continue baking until the pudding is firm in the center and nicely browned, about 45 minutes more.

12. Remove the pudding and its water bath from the oven. Take the pudding dish out of the larger pan of water and let the pudding sit for 15 minutes at room temperature.

Serving Suggestion: Serve on heated dessert plates with some of the whiskey sauce spooned on each serving. Refrigerate any leftover pudding and sauce. ✿

SPECIAL EQUIPMENT
- A metal whisk or an electric mixer
- A 9-by-13-inch glass baking dish
- A larger, shallow pan, such as a roasting pan, to use for a water bath for the baking dish
- Heavy-duty aluminum foil

Chocolate Bread Pudding
with Two Chocolate Sauces & Almond Bark

For 8 very generous servings or 12 standard-size servings

Bread puddings come in a multitude of variations. Here is a wonderfully rich and dense one specially designed for chocolate addicts. The sweetness of it comes, not from the pudding's custard, but from the two sauces and the garnish of almond-bark candy.

1	piece day-old New Orleans-style French bread,* about 23 inches long and weighing about 7½ to 8 ounces, cut into ½-inch cubes with crust on
3	cups heavy cream
½	cup whole milk
1¾	cups sugar, divided
1	2-inch-long piece of vanilla bean
1¼	pounds (3½ cups) semi-sweet chocolate chips
8	large eggs
1	recipe chocolate sauce, for serving
1	recipe white chocolate sauce, for serving
8 to 12	pieces almond bark, for garnish

    *If New Orleans-style French bread is not available, you can get similar results using a sugarless, natural-yeast white bread with a low gluten content and a thin crust.

NOTE

For the best results, refrigerate the uncooked bread pudding overnight before baking.

ADVANCE STEPS

Prepare the recipes for:

• Chocolate sauce on page 313
• White-chocolate sauce on page 314
• Almond bark on page 276

SPECIAL EQUIPMENT

• A 9-by-13-inch glass baking dish
• A heavy 3-quart saucepan
• Aluminum foil

1. Scatter the bread cubes in a 9-by-13-inch glass baking dish. Set aside.

2. In a heavy 3-quart saucepan, combine the cream, milk, and 1½ cups sugar. Cut the piece of vanilla bean in half lengthwise, and scrape the tiny beans into the cream mixture. (Discard the scraped bean pod or add it to granulated or powdered sugar to make vanilla sugar.)

3. Bring the cream mixture to a simmer over medium-high heat, whisking constantly until the sugar dissolves, then whisking occasionally.

4. Add the chocolate chips and continue cooking until the chocolate is melted, about two minutes more, whisking frequently and being sure to scrape the pan bottom clean as you whisk. Remove from heat.

5. In a large mixing bowl, lightly whisk the eggs until frothy. Very slowly add the chocolate mixture to the eggs, whisking constantly so the eggs don't curdle. Pour this custard mixture over the bread. Let the custard sit until cool enough for you to put your hands in it, about 10 minutes.

6. Once the custard is cool enough, toss the bread cubes with your hands, squeezing the cubes in the liquid to make sure all are well saturated. Cover and refrigerate overnight. About three hours before baking the pudding, remove the pan of pudding from the refrigerator, and evenly sprinkle the top with ¼ cup sugar. Let the pudding sit at room temperature for 45 minutes. Meanwhile, preheat the oven to 300°F.

7. Once the pudding has sat 45 minutes, seal the baking dish with aluminum foil. Bake the pudding until a toothpick inserted in the center comes out almost clean and the pudding looks solidified with no puddles of liquid on the surface, about two hours. Once done, it will also start developing a few small, shallow cracks on top and there will be an irresistible smell of chocolate emanating from the oven.

8. Remove the pudding from the oven and let it sit for 15 minutes at room temperature before serving.

Serving Suggestion: Cut the pudding into eight to 12 equal-size rectangles and place on heated dessert plates. Drizzle 2 to 3 tablespoons of the chocolate sauce on one half of each portion of pudding and the same amount of white chocolate sauce over the other half of the pudding. Position a piece of almond bark upright in the center of each serving for garnish.

Refrigerate any leftover pudding and sauces. ❧

Praline Bread Pudding with Praline Crème Anglaise & Caramel Sauce

For 12 to 15 servings

Bread puddings in many different variations are second nature to a New Orleans restaurant's dessert menu. This one brings a luscious praline flavor to the dessert. The pecan-and-brown-sugar crumble adds to its richness, so you may want to reduce the serving sizes a bit. While the pudding itself is served warm, the two sauces are chilled. For a non-alcoholic bread pudding, omit the praline liqueur.

FOR THE PRALINE CRÈME ANGLAISE

- 2 cups heavy cream
- 2 tablespoons praline liqueur, optional
- ½ cup granulated sugar, divided
- 1 4-inch piece vanilla bean
- 3 large eggs

1. In a heavy 2-quart saucepan, combine the cream, liqueur if using, and ¼ cup granulated sugar. Cut the piece of vanilla bean in half lengthwise, and scrape the tiny beans into the cream mixture.

2. Bring the cream mixture to a simmer over medium-high heat, whisking constantly until the sugar dissolves, then whisking occasionally. Remove from heat.

3. In a large, nonreactive mixing bowl, whisk together ¼ cup granulated sugar and the eggs until well blended. Very gradually add the cream mixture to the egg mixture, whisking constantly and vigorously so the eggs don't curdle.

   Once all the cream mixture has been added, let the crème anglaise cool briefly, then cover and refrigerate it for at least three hours or overnight before serving.

FOR THE BREAD PUDDING

- 1 piece day-old New Orleans-style French bread, 9 to 10 inches long and weighing about 3½ ounces
- 8 large eggs
- 1½ cups granulated sugar
- 3 cups heavy cream
- 1 4-inch piece vanilla bean
- ¼ cup praline liqueur, optional
- ½ cup dark raisins
- 1 recipe pecan-and-brown-sugar crumble (recipe follows on page 284)
- 1 recipe caramel sauce, for serving

SPECIAL EQUIPMENT

- A heavy 2-quart saucepan
- A large, nonreactive* mixing bowl

*See Using Nonreactive Cookware, page 419.

ADVANCE STEPS

The ingredients include day-old bread.

This recipe is prepared in two steps, requiring refrigerating both the pudding and the crème anglaise for at least three hours, preferably overnight, before the pudding is baked.

The recipe for caramel sauce on page 315 may be prepared up to three days in advance.

NOTES

If New Orleans-style French bread is not available, you can get similar results using a sugarless, natural-yeast white bread with a low gluten content and a thin crust.

The pudding can also be made with brioche, challah, day-old croissants or other egg bread, as long as the crust is very thin.

1. Remove the crust from the bread and cut the bread into ½-inch cubes. Set aside.

2. In a large, nonreactive mixing bowl, use a metal whisk to whisk together the eggs and granulated sugar until the sugar is fully incorporated into the eggs and the mixture is smooth. Whisk in the cream, blending well.

3. Cut the piece of vanilla bean in half lengthwise and scrape the tiny beans into the cream mixture, whisking until the beans are evenly distributed. Add the liqueur, if using, whisking to blend well. Add the reserved bread cubes and raisins, stirring thoroughly with a large mixing spoon until all the bread cubes are completely saturated. Cover and refrigerate at least three hours, preferably overnight.

4. About four hours before serving time remove the pudding from the refrigerator and let it reach cool room temperature, about one and one-half hours.

5. Once the pudding has almost reached cool room temperature, preheat the oven to 325°F.

6. Meanwhile, pour the bread pudding in a glass 9-by-13-inch baking dish, stirring to distribute all ingredients evenly in the dish. Seal the dish with heavy-duty aluminum foil.

7. Place the pudding dish in a larger pan and carefully pour enough boiling-hot water into the outer pan to come halfway up the sides of the pudding dish.

SPECIAL EQUIPMENT

- A large, nonreactive* mixing bowl
- A glass baking dish, 9 by 13 inches
- Heavy-duty aluminum foil
- A large, shallow pan, such as a roasting pan, to use for a water bath for the baking pan

*See Using Nonreactive Cookware, page 419.

8. Bake the pudding until it is firm in the center, about one hour and 15 minutes. Toward the end of the baking time, prepare the pecan and brown-sugar crumble (see below).

9. Once the pudding is firm in the center, remove the pudding and its water bath from the oven and immediately increase the oven setting to 350°F.

10. Remove the foil from the dish and evenly cover the top of the pudding with the crumble. Bake, uncovered and not in the water bath, at 350° until the top is lightly browned and looks crunchy, about 25 minutes.

11. Remove the pudding from the oven and let it sit for 20 minutes at room temperature before serving.

    Serving suggestion: Cut the pudding into 12 to 15 equal-sized rectangles and set aside momentarily. Spoon 3 tablespoons of the praline crème anglaise in the middle of each dessert plate with a lip. Spoon a portion of the bread pudding on top of the crème anglaise and drizzle about 1 tablespoon of chilled caramel sauce on the pudding.

    Refrigerate any leftover pudding and sauces.

FOR THE PECAN-AND-BROWN-SUGAR CRUMBLE

- 1¼ packed cups light brown sugar
- 1⅓ cups all-purpose flour
- ¼   pound (1 stick) unsalted butter, cut in ½-inch cubes and softened for 30 to 40 minutes
- 1   cup pecan pieces or chopped pecans
- 2½ tablespoons molasses

1. In a large mixing bowl, combine the brown sugar and flour with a large mixing spoon until well blended and any lumps are broken up.

2. Blend in the butter with your hands, leaving the mixture fairly lumpy with butter.

3. Add the pecans and molasses, mixing until well blended and all the ingredients are moistened.

    Serving Suggestion: Set aside at room temperature until called for in the bread pudding recipe. 🐚

Creole Cream Cheese Cheesecake with Caramel Sauce & Roasted Pecans

For one 9-inch cheesecake or 12 servings

While this cheesecake may appear to be a heavy dessert, it has a delectably light texture. The wonderfully subtle flavor comes from Creole cream cheese, which is surprisingly easy to make at home.

For an even more sinful touch, add a small ladling of caramel sauce for both color and flavor, and a good sprinkling of roasted pecans.

FOR THE CRUST

1¼	cup graham-cracker crumbs
2	teaspoons sugar
¼	teaspoon ground cinnamon
6	tablespoons unsalted butter, melted

1. In a medium-size mixing bowl, combine the graham-cracker crumbs with the sugar and the cinnamon, stirring them together until well blended.

2. Drizzle the butter over the mixture and thoroughly blend it in to moisten all of the crumbs.

3. Press the mixture evenly and firmly onto the bottom of a 9-inch spring-form pan. Set it aside.

FOR THE CHEESECAKE FILLING

2¼	pounds (or 4½ packages, 8 ounces each) Philadelphia-style cream cheese, softened
1½	cups Creole cream cheese, preferred, or well drained plain yogurt
2	tablespoons vanilla extract
2	cups sugar
6	large eggs
1	recipe caramel sauce, for serving, optional
¾	cup chopped pecans, lightly roasted, for serving, optional

1. Preheat the oven to 300°F.

2. In the large bowl of an electric mixer—preferably fitted with a paddle attachment—combine the two cream cheeses, vanilla and sugar. Beat the mixture on medium speed until it is well blended and creamy, about three minutes.

NOTES

Store-bought or homemade Creole cream cheese may be used. A recipe for it is found on page 331.

Well drained plain yogurt may be substituted for the Creole cream cheese.

The cheesecake is at its best when made a day ahead.

There may be up to a cup of filling left over. This can be baked, as a treat for the cook, in a ramekin or other heat-proof dish, at the same time the whole cheesecake is baked.

ADVANCE STEPS

If using a caramel sauce, prepare the recipe on page 315.

If using the pecan garnish, prepare the recipe for dry-roasted pecans on page 337.

SPECIAL EQUIPMENT

• A 9-inch spring-form pan
• An electric mixer, preferably fitted with a paddle attachment to minimize the amount of air beaten into the filling
• A rimmed baking sheet

3.   With the mixer still running, add the eggs one at a time, beating just until each is incorporated before adding the next. Do not overmix.

4.   Pour the filling into the prepared crust, leaving a ¼- to ½-inch space below the rim of the pan.

5.   Solidly tap the cake pan on the kitchen counter to expel any air bubbles from the cheesecake, and place the pan on a rimmed baking sheet in the preheated oven.

6.   Bake the cheesecake until it is puffed and firm and just starting to brown at the very edge, about two hours and five minutes.

7.   Testing for doneness: The cake is done when no batter sticks to your fingertips when you lightly press the cake in the center, but the cake will tremble slightly when the pan is very gently shaken.

8.   Remove the cheesecake from the oven, place it on a wire rack and let it cool for 15 minutes, then run a thin-bladed knife around the edge of the pan. This will help keep the top of the cheesecake from cracking as it continues to cool.

9.   Let the cake continue cooling on the rack to room temperature, about two hours. Do not refrigerate it to cool faster. This will cause it to crack.

10. Once the cheesecake is cooled, cover it loosely and refrigerate for serving the next day. Let it sit at room temperature for about an hour before serving.

Serving Suggestion: At the last minute, release the spring on the side of the pan and lift off the side. Place the cheesecake on a serving platter and, if using the caramel sauce and pecans, drizzle the cake with the sauce and sprinkle the top with the roasted pecans. ❀

Chocolate Bourbon Pecan Pie

For one 10-inch pie or 8 servings

When it comes to Southern-style desserts, pecan pie is the leader of the pack, thanks to its rich flavor. This recipe takes pecan pie to a new level of sumptuousness with the addition of bourbon whiskey and chocolate.

The dough recipe for this pie is unusual in several ways. It's prepared with slightly softened butter and cool water instead of cold butter and ice water. The dough is not chilled before it's rolled out. It contains a small amount of vinegar. And the pie pan is greased and floured. That said, we have tried out many pie crusts and—for this particular pie—this crust is the best.

3   large eggs, plus 1 egg of any size
½   cup sugar
1½ teaspoons kosher salt, divided
¼   cup Steen's cane syrup*
¾   cup plus 2 tablespoons dark corn syrup
2   tablespoons unsalted butter, melted and cooled
2   tablespoons good-quality bourbon whiskey, preferably Jim Beam (Sour-mash whiskey is not recommended.)
¼   pound (1 stick) unsalted butter, plus butter for greasing pie pan
1¾ cups all-purpose flour, plus flour to dust pie pan and roll out dough
1   teaspoon Steen's cane vinegar,* or distilled white or apple cider vinegar
⅓   cup cool water
3   tablespoons whole milk
2   cups pecan pieces or chopped pecans
1   cup good-quality semi-sweet dark-chocolate chips
    optional accompaniments and garnishes:
        about ½ cup caramel sauce
        vanilla ice cream
        lightly sweetened whipped cream
        mint leaves
        powdered sugar

*To order Steen's cane syrup or vinegar see Ingredient Sources on page 424.

NOTE

The pie's bourbon flavor diminishes considerably over time, so, if possible, serve it on the same day it's made.

ADVANCE STEPS

If using caramel sauce, prepare the recipe on page 315.

If using whipped cream, prepare the recipe on page 316.

SPECIAL EQUIPMENT

- Two large mixing bowls
- A 10-inch metal pie pan about 1¼ inches deep
- A pastry blender, or your fingertips
- A rolling pin
- A pastry brush
- A metal rack

1. In a large mixing bowl whisk together the 3 large eggs until frothy. Add the sugar and 1 teaspoon kosher salt, whisking vigorously until the sugar is thoroughly dissolved. Whisk in the cane syrup, corn syrup, melted butter and bourbon. Set this filling aside at room temperature.

2. Cut ¼ pound butter in ¼ inch cubes. Let the cubes soften at room temperature for 15 minutes. Meanwhile, generously butter a 10-inch metal pie pan about 1¼ inches, and dust with flour. Set aside.

3. Preheat the oven to 325°F.

4. In another large mixing bowl, thoroughly combine 1¾ cups flour with ½ teaspoon kosher salt. Add the slightly softened butter cubes and quickly work them into the flour with a pastry blender or your fingertips until the mixture looks like coarse meal with just a few pea-sized lumps of butter in it.

5. Add the vinegar to ⅓ cup cool water. Gradually add the vinegar water to the flour, tossing lightly with your hand or a fork until blended in. Gently gather the mixture together to form a ball. If it doesn't hold together, add another ½ tablespoon of water at a time until the mixture is sufficiently damp to hold together, using as little water as possible.

6. Shape the dough ball into a smooth 5-inch disk.

7. With a floured rolling pin, roll out the dough on a lightly floured surface into a circle about 14 inches in diameter and ⅜ inch thick. Very lightly flour the dough, fold it in half, and carefully transfer to the prepared pie pan. Unfold the dough and gently fit it into the pan.

8. With a small serrated knife, trim the excess dough flush with the outer rim of the pan, then pat the dough around the edge to neaten it. Chill the pie shell for three minutes to firm it slightly.

9. Remove the pie shell from the refrigerator and crimp the edge.

10. In a small mixing bowl whisk together the egg of any size and the milk, blending well. Brush a generous amount of this egg wash on the crimped edge with a pastry brush.

11. Evenly scatter the pecans and chocolate chips over the bottom of the shell. Thoroughly stir the reserved filling, then slowly pour it over the pecans and chocolate chips. Use a finger tip to gently stir the filling to coat all the pecan bits and chocolate chips with filling and evenly distribute them within the filling.

12. Bake the pie on the middle shelf of the oven until the center feels firm and bounces back when gently pressed with your fingertips, and the crust is golden brown, about one hour.

13. Transfer the pie to a metal rack to cool to warm room temperature, about one hour, before serving.

    Serving Suggestions: The pie may be served at room temperature or warm.

    If made ahead, let the pie cool thoroughly, then cover it loosely and refrigerate overnight. To re-warm, briefly heat in a 300° oven.

    If using caramel sauce, drizzle about 1 tablespoon of it around the edge of each dessert plate and position a wedge of pie on the plate.

    If desired, top the pie with vanilla ice cream or lightly sweetened whipped cream, and garnish with a mint leaf and a light sprinkle of powdered sugar on the pie and plate. ❦

Dark Chocolate Cake with Hot Fudge Sauce

For one 9-inch single-layer cake or 10 servings

Rare is the restaurant menu that doesn't contain a chocolate dessert. The world would certainly be a less enjoyable place without this virtually addictive flavoring.

The fudge sauce for this cake is an excellent all-purpose one to serve over other cakes or ice cream.

FOR THE CAKE

	non-stick vegetable spray for greasing the cake pan
2	cups sugar
1¾	cups all-purpose flour
¾	cup cocoa powder
1½	teaspoons baking powder
1½	teaspoons baking soda
1	teaspoon kosher salt*
2	large eggs
1	cup whole milk
2	teaspoons vanilla extract
½	teaspoon vegetable oil
1	cup hot strong coffee made with top-quality dark-roast beans (such as French roast)**
	lightly sweetened whipped cream, for serving
	brandied cherries*** for garnishing, optional

*Using kosher rather than regular salt will prevent the cake batter from boiling over as it's baking.
** The better the quality of the coffee beans, the better the cake will taste.
*** Cherries in kirsch or other spirits often can be found in specialty food stores.

1. Preheat the oven to 350°F.

2. Spray a 9-inch round cake pan with non-stick vegetable spray. Line the bottom of the pan with parchment paper cut to fit. Set the pan aside.

3. In the large bowl of an electric mixer (preferably fitted with a wire-whip attachment), on low speed blend together the sugar, flour, cocoa powder, baking powder, baking soda and salt, pushing the sides down with a rubber spatula. Make sure any lumps get broken up.

4. With the mixer still on low speed, beat in the eggs one at a time. Gradually add the milk, beating well to blend in.

NOTES

The cake is at its best on the day it is baked.

If you decide to bake it a day ahead, let it cool then wrap it snugly with plastic wrap and keep it refrigerated. Return the cake to room temperature for serving.

ADVANCE STEPS

Prepare the recipes for:
- Hot fudge sauce on page 293
- Lightly sweetened whipped cream on page 316, as close to serving time as possible

SPECIAL EQUIPMENT

- A 9-inch round cake pan
- Parchment paper
- An electric mixer, preferably fitted with a wire-whip attachment
- A rubber spatula

5. Beat in the vanilla and oil, then turn the speed to high and beat for two minutes, scraping the sides down with the spatula.

6. Reduce the speed again to low and gradually add the coffee, blending well. Increase the speed to medium and continue beating two minutes more.

7. Pour the batter into the prepared baking pan (the batter will be thin) and bake until the center of the cake bounces back when lightly pressed with your fingertips, 45 to 50 minutes.

8. Let the cake thoroughly cool in the pan placed on a wire rack, about two hours. Serve on the same day as made, or once the cake is cooled, remove it from the pan, peel away the parchment paper on the bottom, and wrap it snugly in plastic wrap. Keep the cake refrigerated until it is served. The whole cake or any leftovers will keep for five days if stored well wrapped in the refrigerator.

Serving Suggestions: When the cake is ready to serve, peel away the parchment paper on the bottom if it is still there. Cut the cake into wedges and place them on dessert plates.

If the cake is freshly made it may be too sticky to cut clean slices, in which case slice it with a knife that has been dipped in hot water and dried.

Drizzle each serving with hot fudge sauce to taste, then spoon a dollop of whipped cream either to one side of the cake or at its wider end.

If you are using the brandied cherries, decorate the whipped cream with three or four of them. Serve immediately.

FOR THE HOT FUDGE SAUCE

- 1 cup heavy cream
- ¼ pound (1 stick) plus 3 tablespoons unsalted butter
- 3 tablespoons hot strong coffee made with good-quality dark-roasted beans (such as French roast), plus a few tablespoons more if the sauce needs thinning
- ⅔ cup granulated sugar
- ⅔ cup, packed, dark brown sugar
- 1 cup cocoa powder
- 1 pinch salt (regular or kosher)

1. In a heavy 2-quart saucepan over medium heat, heat together the cream, butter and coffee until the mixture reaches a boil, whisking frequently.

2. Whisk in the granulated sugar, then add the dark-brown sugar, breaking up any lumps as you whisk constantly. Cook, still whisking constantly, until the sugars are completely dissolved, one to two minutes.

NOTES

If the sauce is prepared ahead and becomes too thick, it may be thinned with dark coffee.

SPECIAL EQUIPMENT

- A heavy 2-quart saucepan
- You may also need a hand-held immersible blender to make sure the just-cooked hot fudge sauce turns out smooth.

3. Reduce the heat to medium-low and whisk in the cocoa powder and salt. Continue cooking until the sauce is smooth, about two minutes, whisking constantly. If after about two minutes of cooking the sauce isn't smooth, remove the pan from heat and use a hand-held immersible blender to beat out any lumps remaining in the sauce.

Serving Suggestions: Serve the sauce while it's still warm, or once it's cool, store it in the refrigerator in an airtight container until ready to reheat for serving. It will keep for at least one week covered and refrigerated. Reheat for serving in the top of a double boiler over hot (not simmering) water, whisking constantly to keep it from scorching. If needed, thin with a little more strong-brewed dark-roast coffee. ❧

Crème Caramel

For 4 servings

Custards have been a familiar dish in many countries for many years. The Spanish have their *crema catalana* and the Mexicans their *flan*. The Italians forgo the egg for their otherwise custardy *panna cotta*. And what would English cooking be without its custardy trifle?

French Creoles gave New Orleans *crème brûlée* and *crème renversée*, the latter so called because the baked custard is turned upside down onto the serving plate. However, modern-day New Orleanians know crème renversée as crème caramel, drawing attention to the light sauce of caramelized sugar that lines the cooking vessel and adds flavor to the custard.

The recipe below produces a silky-smooth, gently sweetened and rich dessert. The flavor is also invigorated with a bit of spicy-sweet gewürztraminer wine.

FOR THE CUSTARD

5	yolks from large eggs
13	tablespoons sugar, divided
2	cups heavy cream
1	4-inch piece vanilla bean
7	tablespoons gewürztraminer wine

1. Preheat the oven to 300°F. Simultaneously in the same oven, preheat a water bath for the custards, using a 9-by-13-inch baking pan (or a similar pan large enough to hold the ramekins with a little space left over) into which you have poured ¾ inch water.

2. In a medium-size mixing bowl, combine the egg yolks and 3 tablespoons sugar, whisking with a metal whisk until well blended. Set the mixture aside.

3. In a 2-quart saucepan, combine the cream with 3 tablespoons sugar. Slit the vanilla bean in half lengthwise, and scrape the tiny seeds into the pan. Add the bean halves to the pan and stir until the sugar dissolves. Heat the mixture over medium heat just until it starts to boil, being careful not to let it boil over.

4. Remove the scalded cream from heat and very gradually add it to the egg yolks, whisking constantly so the yolks don't curdle.

5. Strain this custard mixture through a fine-mesh strainer into a clean mixing bowl. Set it aside to cool while making the caramel syrup. (NOTE: Once the vanilla bean has been rinsed well and air-dried, it can be added to granulated or powdered sugar to make vanilla sugar.)

NOTES

Cooking the caramel syrup to coat the ramekins requires close attention so the syrup does not overcook, becoming bitter in taste and too dark in color.

The syrup is never stirred, but gently swirled in the saucepan, to keep the sauce from becoming grainy.

The recipe calls for 8-ounce ramekins. If smaller ones are used, the baking time may have to be reduced slightly.

SPECIAL EQUIPMENT

- A 9-by-13-inch baking dish
- A metal whisk
- A fine-mesh strainer (the finer the mesh the better)
- Four 8-ounce individual ramekins or gratin dishes
- A heat-proof tablespoon
- A heavy 1-quart saucepan
- Four rimmed dessert plates

1. Before starting to make the syrup, have the four ramekins and a heat-proof tablespoon at hand.

2. For the syrup, in a heavy 1-quart saucepan combine the gewürztraminer with 7 tablespoons sugar. Do NOT stir. Cover the pan and bring the mixture to a simmer over high heat, about one minute.

3. Remove the pan from the heat, remove the cover and gently swirl the liquid (do not stir or slosh the liquid up the side of the pan) to make sure the sugar is dissolved.

4. Leaving the pan uncovered, place it over medium heat and let the liquid boil (at this point do not swirl the pan and, remember, no stirring) until the bubbles are thick and relatively large, 1½ to two minutes.

5. Continue boiling while gently swirling the pan just until the darker syrup at the bottom of the pan (underneath the foamier liquid on the surface) turns a medium caramel brown, six to seven minutes. Promptly remove from heat.

6. Working quickly and within one ramekin at a time, use the tablespoon to spoon 3 tablespoons of the foamy syrup over the bottom of a ramekin, promptly swirling the syrup and pushing it with the spoon to thinly coat the bottom of the dish. If necessary, very briefly reheat the syrup still in the sauce-pan to re-liquefy it as you coat the remaining ramekins.

7. Once all the ramekins have been coated, pour equal portions of the custard on top. Arrange the dishes in the preheated water bath so they don't touch each other. Bake uncovered until the centers of the custard are firm, 45 to 55 minutes.

8. To test for doneness, carefully remove a ramekin from the water bath and very gently shake it. If it is done, the center will tremble slightly but will no longer be watery.

9. Remove the finished custards from the hot water and let them cool at room temperature for 45 minutes, then cover and chill at least three hours before serving.

10. Unmold the chilled custards just before serving. To unmold, carefully run a sharp, thin-bladed knife between the custard and the edge of each ramekin and place a rimmed dessert plate over the top. Reverse the ramekin and dessert plate, so the custard can slowly slip out onto the plate and the last bit of syrup can drip out.

    Serving Suggestion: This dessert may be refrigerated for a short time, but ideally it should be served on the day it is made. Extended refrigeration tends to stiffen the custard.

Mr. Ralph's Ice Cream Sandwiches

For 6 very generous-sized sandwiches

These large and impressive-looking dessert sandwiches contain about an inch of ice cream between two slices of cake. Not only are they surprisingly simple to make, but, because they can be prepared up to four days ahead, they're also easy on the cook.

	non-stick vegetable spray
1	cup all-purpose flour
½	cup plus 2 tablespoons cocoa powder
1	teaspoon baking powder
½	teaspoon baking soda
½	teaspoon table salt
⅓	cup vegetable oil
1¼	cups sugar
2	large eggs
½	cup warm water
2	pints chocolate-malt ice cream or ice cream flavor of choice
	caramel sauce, optional
	hot fudge sauce, optional

1. Preheat the oven to 375°F.

2. While the oven preheats use non-stick vegetable spray to spray the bottom and sides of a standard jelly-roll pan with outside measurements of about 11 inches by 17 inches by ¾ inch. Line the bottom of the pan with a piece of parchment paper cut to fit, and spray the top of the paper with more vegetable spray. Set aside.

3. In a medium-size mixing bowl thoroughly combine the flour, cocoa powder, baking powder, baking soda and table salt, being sure to break up all lumps.

3. In a large mixing bowl, whisk together the oil and sugar until the mixture looks like wet sand. Add the eggs, one at a time, incorporating the first egg into the mixture before adding the second one.

4. Add one third of the dry ingredients to the egg mixture, whisking thoroughly. Next, whisk in half the warm water, then one third more of the dry ingredients. Whisk in the remaining warm water, then the last third of the dry ingredients.

5. Pour the batter into the prepared jelly-roll pan, and spread it in an even layer with an icing spatula or a rubber spatula. (The batter will be fairly thin.) Tap the pan soundly on a counter top about three times to expel air bubbles.

NOTES

The original recipe calls for chocolate-malt ice cream, but any flavor can be used.

The sandwiches may be cut smaller for informal meals or snacks and served without the sauces. But if they're served for dessert after a special meal, the sauces are a luscious must-have.

ADVANCE STEPS

If using sauces, prepare either or both of the following recipes:

- Caramel sauce on page 315
- Hot fudge sauce on page 293

SPECIAL EQUIPMENT

- A standard jelly-roll pan measuring about 11 inches by 17 inches by ¾ inch
- Parchment paper
- An icing spatula or rubber spatula
- A metal rack
- A large cutting board or the bottom of a baking sheet
- A small cookie sheet

6. Bake the cake until it bounces back when lightly pressed with your finger tips, 14 to 16 minutes. Remove the cake from the oven and set it on a metal rack to let it completely cool in the pan, about 25 minutes.

7. Loosen the edges of the cake with a paring knife, and cover the cake with a second piece of parchment paper cut to the size of the cake. Place a large cutting board or the bottom of a baking sheet on top of the paper-covered cake, and invert the whole assembly. Tap the underside of the baking pan to make sure the cake releases, and lift the jelly-roll pan off the cake. Peel the parchment paper from the bottom of the cake.

8. Using a paring knife, trim a thin strip from all sides of the cake and square the corners to make it look neat and to get rid of any dry edges. Cut the cake crosswise into two equal-size rectangles. Line a small cookie sheet with parchment paper. The cookie sheet should be only slightly larger than the cake rectangle. Carefully transfer one of the cake rectangles to the cookie sheet.

9. Let the ice cream stand at room temperature for 15 minutes to soften slightly. Evenly spread the ice cream over the cake rectangle already on the cookie sheet and cover with the second cake rectangle. Place the rectangular ice-cream loaf, uncovered, in the freezer to let the ice cream harden, at least three hours or overnight.

10. If prepared a day or more ahead, once the ice cream has hardened, cover the loaf loosely with aluminum foil and keep it frozen until it's time to cut for serving. You also may cut it into sandwiches as described below, wrapping each sandwich in plastic wrap and freezing it in a self-sealing plastic freezer bag.

    Serving Suggestion: To serve, slice the loaf into six rectangular portions by cutting the loaf in half lengthwise, then cutting each half crosswise into thirds. If using both the caramel and hot fudge sauces, spoon 1 to 2 tablespoons of the caramel sauce on each chilled dessert plate, and position the ice cream sandwich on top, then drizzle 1 tablespoon or more of the hot fudge sauce over the sandwich. 🐚

Lemon Icebox Pie

For one 9-inch pie or 8 servings

The pluses of this pie—aside from its luscious flavor—are the simplicity of it and the little time it takes to prepare. It's especially good served with a few fresh berries, such as strawberries or blueberries that have been left unsweetened.

FOR THE CRUST

1¼	cups graham-cracker crumbs
2	tablespoons light or dark brown sugar, packed
6	tablespoons unsalted butter, melted

1. Preheat the oven to 300°F.

2. Combine the graham-cracker crumbs, brown sugar and butter in a medium-size mixing bowl, stirring them together until well blended.

3. Press the mixture evenly and firmly onto the bottom of a 9-inch pie pan, shaping it into a crust with your fingers and pressing the crumbs down.

4. Place another 9-inch pie pan or use the bottom of a rounded mixing bowl on top of the crust and press down to tighten the crumbs and firm up the crust.

5. Bake for five minutes.

6. Set the crust aside at room temperature, with the oven temperature remaining at 300°.

FOR THE FILLING

5	yolks from large eggs
2	cups sweetened condensed milk, from two 14-ounce cans
½	cup plus 1 tablespoon freshly-squeezed lemon juice
1½	tablespoons very finely grated lemon zest
½	teaspoon vanilla extract

1. In a large mixing bowl, lightly beat together the egg yolks and condensed milk with a metal whisk, blending until smooth.

2. Whisk in the lemon juice, lemon zest and vanilla.

3. Pour the filling into the prepared graham-cracker crust and bake the pie in the 300° oven for 20 to 25 minutes, or until the center of the filling is set. The pie is done when only a little of the filling sticks to your fingertip when you lightly touch the pie in the center, but the surface where touched looks noticeably dryer than the filling underneath. You can also very gently shake the pie to tell if it is set.

NOTES

Key lime juice can be substituted for the lemon juice.

The flavor of Meyer lemons is too subtle for this pie filling.

Refrigerating the pie overnight improves both the flavors and textures.

You may want to top the pie slices with dollops of lightly sweetened whipped cream (see the recipe on page 316).

SPECIAL EQUIPMENT

- Two 9-inch pie pans, or 1 pie pan and the bottom of a rounded mixing bowl
- A metal whisk
- A wire rack

4. Remove the pie from the oven and place it on a wire rack to let it cool at room temperature. After it has cooled, refrigerate it for at least four hours, preferably overnight, until it is very cold. While the pie is chilling it should be well covered so it doesn't absorb any refrigerator odors.

    Serving Suggestion: Wrapped leftovers will keep well in the refrigerator for up to one week. 🐚

For one 12-inch pie or 16 servings

Peanut butter and chocolate are a lip-smacking combination, especially when the proportions of the chocolate and peanut flavors are just right. This pie, a best-seller at the Red Fish Grill, has a nice balance of crunchiness (in the very flaky crust) and smoothness (in the rich and silky filling). The richness also is moderated with a judicious amount of sweetness.

FOR THE CRUST

5	ounces (1¾ cups crushed) salted pretzels, crushed
¼	cup plus 2 teaspoons granulated sugar
¼	cup plus 2 tablespoons semi-sweet chocolate chips
⅜	pound (1½ sticks) unsalted butter, melted

1. Preheat the oven to 325°F.

2. Combine all the crust ingredients in a medium-size mixing bowl and mix them until they are thoroughly blended and all ingredients are moistened.

3. Press the mixture evenly and firmly onto the bottom of a 12-inch spring-form pan.

4. Bake the crust for 15 minutes, then remove it from the oven.

5. Let the crust cool at room temperature for 15 minutes, then refrigerate it for at least 15 minutes, or cover the crust and keep it refrigerated until the pie is ready to be assembled.

FOR THE GANACHE

14	ounces semi-sweet chocolate, chopped into small bits
3	tablespoons unsalted butter
1½	cups heavy cream
3	tablespoons plus ½ teaspoon granulated sugar

1. Slowly melt the chocolate and butter together in the top of a double boiler over hot (not simmering) water, stirring occasionally.

2. Remove the top of the double boiler from over the hot water when the chocolate is about half melted to stir thoroughly. Be careful not to let any water splash into the pan containing the chocolate.

3. Stir the chocolate and butter mixture occasionally as it melts. Periodically lift the top of the double boiler off the pan so it's bottom does not get too hot,

NOTES

The pie is made at least one day ahead so it can firm up in the refrigerator or freezer. It may be made up to two weeks ahead if it is kept well covered in the freezer, or up to three days ahead if it is covered and refrigerated.

Fresh homemade peanut butter is preferred for this pie. Purchased peanut butter made only with peanuts and salt also works well. To make your own peanut butter, purée 1 pound unsalted peanuts together with 1 teaspoon coarse kosher salt in a food processor, pulsing until creamy. Depending on the size of your food processor, you may need to do this in batches.

ADVANCE STEPS

The butter, peanut butter and cream cheese for the filling should be set out at room temperature at least two hours before making the filling so all will be very soft by the time they are called for.

If using optional garnishes, prepare the recipe(s) for either or both of the following:

- Chocolate sauce on page 313
- Lightly sweetened whipped cream on page 316

which could scorch the chocolate. Be careful not to let any water splash into the pan of chocolate and butter as they melt.

4. Meanwhile, combine the cream and granulated sugar in a 1-quart saucepan and bring the mixture to a simmer over medium heat, stirring until the sugar is dissolved. Keep the cream warm over very low heat. Once the chocolate and butter are melted, stir thoroughly until they are blended and smooth.

5. Very slowly pour the hot cream into the chocolate, constantly stirring with a rubber spatula or a metal whisk so the chocolate doesn't get lumpy.

   Keep the ganache warm in the top of the double boiler (placed either off the heat, covered, or over very low heat, uncovered) while preparing the filling and assembling the pie.

FOR THE FILLING AND PEANUT TOPPING

1 pound unsalted butter, left at room temperature until very soft but not melted
1 pound creamy peanut butter, left at room temperature until very soft
1 8-ounce package Philadelphia-style cream cheese, left at room temperature until very soft
1 one-pound box confectioner's sugar
1 teaspoon vanilla extract
1 cup unsalted peanuts
1 recipe chocolate sauce and/or 1 recipe lightly sweetened whipped cream as optional garnishes

1. Using a very large mixing spoon or an electric mixer on low speed, blend the butter, peanut butter, cream cheese, confectioner's sugar and vanilla. When the ingredients are thoroughly blended, set the bowl aside.

2. Lightly roast the peanuts in a large dry skillet over low heat, stirring almost constantly, just until they start to brown. (You also can also roast them in a 325° oven on a small rimmed baking sheet, checking them often so they don't burn.)

3. Let the peanuts cool to room temperature, then crush them in a self-sealing plastic bag with a kitchen mallet until they are broken into small to medium bits. Set the peanuts aside.

TO ASSEMBLE THE PIE

1. Using a rubber spatula or an icing spatula, evenly spread half (1½ cups) of the chocolate ganache on top of the pie crust.

2. Place the pan in the freezer—at a level position—for about 30 minutes, or in the refrigerator for about one hour until the ganache is very firm.

SPECIAL EQUIPMENT
- A 12-inch spring-form pan
- A double boiler
- A rubber spatula or a metal whisk
- A very large mixing spoon or an electric mixer
- A rubber or icing spatula
- A kitchen mallet

3. Place half of the filling on top of the firm ganache, spreading the filling evenly with the spatula. Then spread the remaining 1½ cups of ganache evenly over the filling.

4. Return the pie to the freezer for about 45 minutes, or to the refrigerator for about 1½ hours, until the ganache is once again very firm. Spread the remaining filling evenly over the firm ganache, then sprinkle the crushed peanuts over the filling. Cover the pie well and freeze or refrigerate it overnight.

    Serving Suggestions: The pie should still be cold when it is served. If it is frozen, thaw it before serving, either in the refrigerator for four to six hours, or at room temperature for about two hours.

    At serving time run a thin-bladed knife around the sides of the spring-form pan and remove the sides. Place the pie (still on the bottom part of the spring-form pan) on a very large serving platter for a pretty presentation, or cut the pie into wedges and serve them on dessert plates.

    If the chocolate sauce and/or whipped cream garnishes are used, pass the chocolate sauce in a bowl at the table and pass the whipped cream in a second bowl. The whipped cream also may be piped on each serving or a dollop of it may be spooned atop each wedge.

    Any leftovers should be kept frozen or refrigerated.

Fluffy Sweet-Potato Pie

For one 9-inch pie or 8 servings

The words *sweet potato* and *yam* are used interchangeably in many parts of the country, although they are in fact distant relatives. The yam, which is much larger and more fibrous, is common in Africa and some parts of Latin America. But the sweet potato has been a staple of Southern pantries for generations.

Sweet-potato pie can be a very satisfying dessert, without being super-rich in flavor or calories. It may be served simply as is, or with a sprinkle of dry-roasted pecans or a dollop of lightly sweetened whipped cream, or both. Traditionally, this pie is especially favored at Thanksgiving and Christmas, but it is a delicious comfort food throughout the year.

FOR THE PIE CRUST

1½	cups all-purpose flour, plus flour to roll out dough
2	tablespoons granulated sugar
½	teaspoon kosher salt
4	tablespoons very cold unsalted butter, cut into ¼-inch cubes
4	tablespoons chilled solid vegetable shortening, cut into small bits
3 to 5	tablespoons ice water

1. Into a large mixing bowl, sift 1½ cups flour with the sugar and kosher salt. Add the butter and shortening, and quickly work them into the flour with a pastry blender or your fingertips until the mixture looks like coarse meal with just a few pea-size lumps of butter in it.

2. Gradually add the ice water to the dough, 1 tablespoon at a time, until you've added 3 tablespoons water, tossing lightly with your hand or a fork until blended in. Gently gather the mixture together to form a ball. If it doesn't hold together, add another ½ tablespoon of water at a time until the mixture is sufficiently damp to hold together, using as little water as possible.

3. Shape the dough ball into a smooth 5-inch disk. Wrap the disk snugly with a double layer of plastic wrap.

4. Refrigerate for at least one hour or overnight before rolling out.

FOR THE PIE FILLING AND FINISHING THE PIE

¼	pound (1 stick) unsalted butter, softened, plus butter for aluminum foil
¼	cup, packed, light brown sugar
¼	cup granulated sugar
¼	teaspoon kosher salt
3	large eggs
2¾	cups cooked sweet potato pulp (from about 2½ pounds sweet potatoes, about 3 medium-to-large sweet potatoes)

NOTE

If you are using optional ingredients, see the following recipes:

- Dry-roasted pecans on page 337
- Lightly sweetened whipped cream on page 316

ADVANCE STEP

The pie dough and filling may be made a day in advance.

Cook the sweet potatoes until very tender, about two hours at 400°F. Remove and discard any fibrous parts of the cooked sweet potato pulp before measuring out the 2¾ cups pulp in the ingredients list, left.

SPECIAL EQUIPMENT

- A pastry blender (or you may use your fingertips).

        ¼   cup fresh orange juice

       1½   tablespoons very finely grated or minced orange zest

        1   teaspoon ground cinnamon

        ½   teaspoon ground nutmeg, preferably freshly ground

        ½   teaspoon pure vanilla extract

        2   tablespoons good-quality brandy, optional

        1   egg white from any size egg

        ¼   cup dry-roasted pecans and lightly-sweetened whipped cream, optional

- An electric mixer, preferably fitted with a whip attachment
- A rubber spatula
- A rolling pin
- A 9-inch glass pie pan
- Light-weight aluminum foil
- Pie weights (or 1 pound dried beans or 2 pounds raw rice)
- A pastry brush
- A pie shield (or a 2-inch-wide ring of aluminum foil) to protect the edge of the pie from burning
- A metal rack

1. In the large bowl of a mixer (preferably fitted with a whip attachment), beat together the butter, sugars and kosher salt on medium speed until fluffy, one to two minutes. Beat in the eggs, one at a time, beating until each egg is completely blended in before adding another, and pushing the sides down with a rubber spatula.

2. Add the sweet potato pulp to the bowl and beat until the filling is very smooth and noticeably fluffier, about five minutes. Add the orange juice, orange zest, cinnamon, nutmeg, vanilla and, if using, the brandy, blending well. (If made ahead, cover and refrigerate.)

3. Preheat the oven to 375°F.

4. If the pie dough was refrigerated for more than an hour, let it sit at room temperature 15 to 20 minutes until flexible enough to roll out.

5. With a floured rolling pin, roll out the dough on a lightly floured surface into a circle about 12½ inches in diameter and ⅛ inch thick. Very lightly flour the dough, fold it in half, and carefully transfer to a 9-inch glass pie pan. Unfold the dough and gently fit it into the pan.

6. With a small serrated knife, trim the excess dough flush with the outer rim of the pan, then pat the dough around the edge to neaten it. Chill the pie shell three minutes to firm the dough slightly.

7. Remove the pie shell from the refrigerator and crimp the shell's edge.

8. Lightly butter the shiny side of a 12-by-14-inch piece of light-weight aluminum foil and, with the buttered side down, gently press the foil fairly snugly against the side and bottom of the shell, letting the excess hang over the side of the pan. Fill the foil with pie weights.

9. Bake the pie shell on the middle shelf of the oven just until the surface of the dough under the foil is set (noticeably dry). The dough will still look raw and will not be at all browned at this point, about 17 minutes. Test for doneness after 15 minutes, and if needed bake a bit longer.

10. Once the surface of the pie shell is set, remove the pan from the oven, leaving oven set at 375°. Lift away the foil containing the pie weights. If part of the shell is puffed up, pierce that part with a fork. Use a pastry brush to brush a generous amount of the egg white over the bottom and up the sides of the shell but not on the crimped edge. You will have egg white left over.

11. Return the shell to the oven and bake until light golden on the bottom and edge, 10 to 12 minutes. Remove from oven, again leaving oven set at 375°.

12. Spoon the filling into the shell and smooth the top. Cover the crimped edge with a pie shield or use a 2-inch-wide ring of aluminum foil to prevent the edge from burning. Bake for 30 minutes, then remove the foil and continue baking 10 to 15 minutes more until the filling has finished cooking and the crust is golden brown on the edge and bottom. (Lift the pie up to examine the crust bottom through the glass.)

13. Transfer the pie to a metal rack to cool at least 15 minutes before serving.

    Serving Suggestions: The pie may be served at room temperature or warm. It may be kept at room temperature for 24 hours, then cover and refrigerate. To reheat, place in a 250°F oven briefly.

    If using the accompaniments, just before cutting the pie scatter the roasted pecans over the top, then cut the pie in wedges and top each portion with a dollop of whipped cream. ❧

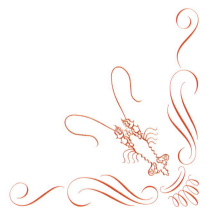

Creole Red Velvet Roulade
with Café-Brûlot Crème Anglaise

For one roulade or 8 generous servings

Red velvet cake, a favorite in the South, gets a new lease on life in this recipe. A sponge cake is lathered with a mousse of white chocolate and rolled into a spiral. Then it is sliced before getting a dousing of crème anglaise that's been blessed with the ingredients of café brûlot.

Café brûlot is a spicy flambéed coffee served tableside from special large silver bowls in New Orleans' old-line Creole restaurants. It is made by steeping sticks of cinnamon, whole cloves and zests of lemon and orange in strong and very hot New Orleans-style coffee. Brandy is added before the liquid is ignited, to create dancing tongues of blue fire. The flames are doused and the spicy, pungent coffee is then ladled into special cups.

The little ceremony is every bit as romantic as it sounds.

(A recipe for café brûlot appears on page 408.)

FOR THE SPONGE CAKE

	non-stick vegetable spray
9	yolks from large eggs, chilled
7	whites from large eggs, at room temperature
1½	cups granulated sugar
½	cup cocoa powder, sifted
1	tablespoon red food coloring

1. Preheat the oven to 375°F.

2. While the oven preheats, spray a rimmed baking sheet, about 12 by 17 inches and 1 inch deep, with non-stick vegetable spray. Line the bottom of the pan with parchment paper and spray again. Set aside.

3. In the large bowl of an electric mixer, beat the egg yolks on high speed for about five minutes until pale yellow and until, when you can lift the beater(s), the yolks drip onto the surface of the beaten yolks and make a "ribbon" pattern for a brief moment before sinking in.

4. Transfer the egg yolks to a medium-size mixing bowl. Wash and dry the electric mixer bowl and beater(s).

5. Beat the egg whites in the cleaned electric mixer bowl on high speed until frothy, one to two minutes. Add the sugar and continue beating until soft peaks form, about one minute more.

6. Gradually add the egg yolks to the egg-white mixture, folding them together with a rubber spatula.

7. Fold in the cocoa powder and food coloring, blending thoroughly.

8. Spoon the batter into the prepared baking sheet, spreading evenly. Tap the baking sheet solidly on a counter three or four times to expel air bubbles.

9. Bake the cake, uncovered, until a toothpick inserted comes out almost clean and the cake is just starting to pull away from the sides of the pan, about 17 minutes. Do not overcook or the cake will crack when rolled up.

10. Remove the baking sheet from the oven and place it on a metal rack to let it thoroughly cool in the pan, about 45 minutes.

11. Snugly wrap the cooled cake, still in the pan, with plastic wrap and refrigerate until well chilled, at least one hour.

NOTE

The sponge cake, the filling and the crème anglaise need to be made well ahead, so they have time to chill before and after the roulade is assembled.

The cake may be prepared up to eight hours ahead.

SPECIAL EQUIPMENT

- A rimmed baking sheet about 12 by 17 inches with a 1-inch rim
- Parchment paper
- An electric mixer
- A rubber spatula
- A metal rack

FOR THE WHITE-CHOCOLATE MOUSSE

   2   cups (11 ounces) fine-quality white chocolate chips
   ¾   cup heavy cream
 9½   ounces cream cheese, at room temperature
   ½   cup powdered sugar
   ¾   teaspoon vanilla extract

1. Refrigerate or freeze the large bowl of an electric mixer and the beater(s) until cold, about 15 minutes.

2. Meanwhile, melt the white chocolate chips in the top of a double boiler over hot (not simmering) water, stirring with a rubber spatula until smooth; remove the top of the pan from over the hot water when the chips are about half way melted to stir thoroughly.

3. Remove the double boiler from heat, leaving the bowl of melted white chocolate over the hot water.

4. In the chilled large bowl of an electric mixer, beat the cream on medium speed just until stiff peaks form. Do not over-beat.

5. Transfer the whipped cream to a bowl, cover, and refrigerate until called for in the recipe.

6. Clean the bowl and beater(s) of the electric mixer. In the cleaned bowl, combine the cream cheese, powdered sugar and vanilla. Beat on low speed until well blended, about two minutes, stopping the mixer as needed to push the sides down with the rubber spatula. Do not over-beat or the mousse will be too fluffy.

7. Add the melted white chocolate to the mixture, mixing well with the rubber spatula until smooth. Fold in the chilled whipped cream.

8. With the rubber spatula, evenly spread this mousse mixture over the bottom of a 9-by-13-inch glass baking dish.

9. Cover the dish with plastic wrap and refrigerate until well chilled and fairly stiff, at least one hour.

FOR ASSEMBLING THE ROULADE

   2   teaspoons granulated sugar, divided

1. Loosen the edges of the cake with a paring knife. Sprinkle 1 teaspoon granulated sugar evenly over the top of the cake and cover it with parchment paper cut to the size of the cake. Place a large cutting board (or the bottom of a

NOTE

The mousse may be prepared up to eight hours ahead.

SPECIAL EQUIPMENT

- An electric mixer
- A double boiler
- A rubber spatula
- A glass baking dish, 9 by 13 inches or a similar size

NOTE

The roulade may be assembled up to eight hours ahead.

SPECIAL EQUIPMENT

- A paring knife

baking sheet the same size as the cake or larger) on top of the parchment-covered cake, and invert the whole assembly.

2. Tap the underside of the baking sheet to make sure the cake releases, and lift the baking sheet off the cake. Peel the parchment paper from the cake and sprinkle 1 teaspoon granulated sugar over it.

3. Cover the cake with a piece of parchment paper that is slightly larger than the cake. Place the cutting board (or the bottom of a baking sheet the same size as the cake or larger) on the cake. Invert again, so the cake is sitting on the parchment paper.

4. Using a paring knife, carefully trim a thin strip about ¼ inch wide from all sides of the cake and square the corners to make the cake look neat and to get rid of any dry edges.

5. Remove the chilled mousse from the refrigerator and evenly scatter spoonfuls of it onto the cake. Let the mousse soften about five minutes, then spread the mousse evenly over the top with an icing spatula.

6. Fold one of the long sides of the cake over part of the mousse and roll the cake and mousse into a log. Use the parchment paper to help do the rolling, but do not wrap up the parchment inside the log.

7. Next, wrap the parchment paper around the roulade and refrigerate it, still on the cutting board or baking sheet, until it is fairly firm, at least an hour and a half or up to eight hours.

8. While the roulade is chilling, make the crème anglaise.

FOR THE CRÈME ANGLAISE AND TO SERVE

	enough ice to fill a large mixing bowl
½	cup granulated sugar, divided
4	yolks from large eggs
½	cup whole milk
½	cup heavy cream
1½	teaspoons finely grated lemon zest
1½	teaspoons finely grated orange zest
½	teaspoon (rounded) ground cinnamon
1½	teaspoons good-quality brandy
1½	teaspoons brewed espresso
2	whole cloves
2	cups cool water

1. Prepare a large mixing bowl of ice. Rest a medium-size mixing bowl on the ice. Set aside.

- Parchment paper
- A large cutting board, or the bottom of a baking sheet at least as large as the one that the cake was baked in
- An icing spatula

NOTE

The sauce may be prepared up to six hours ahead.

ADVANCE STEP

Brew a small cup of espresso or other strong, dark-roast coffee.

2. In another large mixing bowl, combine ¼ cup sugar with the egg yolks, whisking until well blended. Set aside.

3. In a heavy 2-quart saucepan, combine ¼ cup sugar with the milk and cream. Bring to a boil over high heat, stirring until the sugar dissolves.

4. Remove the scalded milk mixture from the heat and slowly add it to the egg yolks, whisking constantly and blending well.

5. Return the egg yolk mixture to the saucepan. Add the lemon zest, orange zest, cinnamon, brandy, espresso and cloves.

6. Cook the sauce over medium-high heat, being careful not to let it reach a boil, until slightly thickened, about two minutes, stirring constantly with a wooden spoon and being sure to scrape the pan bottom well as you stir.

7. Immediately remove the sauce from the heat and strain through a fine-mesh strainer into the reserved mixing bowl positioned on top of the ice. Add 2 cups water to the ice. Stir the sauce often as it sits on the ice a few minutes so it will cool as quickly as possible.

8. Once the sauce is cool, cover and refrigerate it for at least an hour and a half before serving.

Serving Suggestions: Just before serving, remove the roulade from the refrigerator and peel off the parchment paper. Cut a thin (about ¼ inch thick) slice on the diagonal from both ends of the log to make the end servings look neat. Cut the cake, again on the diagonal, into eight equal slices, and place each slice on a chilled dessert plate. Drizzle each serving with 2 tablespoons of the crème anglaise. If any sauce is left over, divide it among the portions of roulade.

Besides being served as a dessert for eight, the roulade may be cut into 16 or more slices (and each slice halved if you like), and dabbed with sauce for arranging on a large buffet-table platter. ◓

SPECIAL EQUIPMENT
• A heavy 2-quart saucepan
• A wooden spoon
• A fine mesh strainer (the finer the better)

Chocolate Sauce

For 1¾ cups

This chocolate sauce can perform many roles at dessert time, as a sumptuous addition to everything from cakes to ice cream and beyond.

- 1 cup heavy cream
- ½ cup sugar
- ¾ cup semi-sweet chocolate chips
- 1 tablespoon unsalted butter

SPECIAL EQUIPMENT

- A heavy 1-quart saucepan

1. In a heavy 1-quart saucepan, combine the cream and sugar. Bring the mixture to a simmer over medium-high heat, whisking until the sugar is dissolved.
2. Reduce the heat to low and gradually add the chocolate chips, whisking until each addition is completely melted into the cream before adding more.
3. Add the butter and continue cooking, whisking constantly, until the butter is incorporated into the sauce. Remove from the heat.

Serving Suggestion: Serve the sauce while it's still warm, or, once it's cool, store in the refrigerator in an airtight container until ready to reheat for serving. It will keep for up to one week covered and refrigerated. Reheat for serving in the top of a double boiler over hot (not simmering) water, whisking constantly to keep the sauce from scorching.

White-Chocolate Sauce

For 2 cups

White chocolate came to the United States in the early 1980s. The name has always been something of a misnomer, since, unlike true chocolate, it contains neither chocolate liquor nor cocoa solids. It does contain sugar, cocoa butter and milk solids.

10	ounces (2½ cups) white chocolate chips
1½	cups heavy cream
3	tablespoons unsalted butter
1	tablespoon sugar

1. Place the white-chocolate chips in a medium-size mixing bowl and set aside.

2. In a heavy 2-quart saucepan, combine the cream, butter and sugar. Bring the mixture to a boil over medium-high heat, whisking constantly.

3. Remove from heat and pour the cream mixture over the reserved chips, whisking until the mixture is smooth.

    Serving Suggestion: Serve the sauce while it's still warm, or once it's cool store it in the refrigerator in an airtight container until ready to reheat for serving. It will keep for at least one week covered and refrigerated.

    Reheat for serving in the top of a double boiler over hot (not simmering) water, whisking constantly to keep it from scorching.

NOTE

When reheating, take care to melt the sauce very slowly so it doesn't scorch.

SPECIAL EQUIPMENT

• A heavy 2-quart saucepan

Caramel Sauce

For a generous 1½ cups

Caramel sauce is always a welcome addition to puddings, ice cream and other desserts.

1   cup heavy cream
½   cup lightly packed dark brown sugar
½   cup granulated sugar
1   2-inch piece vanilla bean

SPECIAL EQUIPMENT

• A heavy 1-quart saucepan

1. In a heavy 1-quart saucepan, bring the cream to a boil over high heat. Add the brown sugar, whisking thoroughly. Whisk in the granulated sugar and continue cooking and whisking about 30 seconds more. Remove from heat.

2. Cut the piece of vanilla bean in half lengthwise, scrape the tiny beans into the sauce, and whisk to blend.

    Serving Suggestion: Serve the sauce while it's still warm, or once it's cool store it in the refrigerator in an airtight container until ready to reheat for serving. It will keep for at least one week covered and refrigerated. Reheat for serving in the top of a double boiler over hot (not simmering) water, whisking constantly to keep it from scorching.

Lightly Sweetened Whipped Cream

For 3¼ cups

When a dessert can be improved with a bit of added moistness and richness, this easy-to-make whipped cream comes in handy.

1½ cups very cold heavy cream
1 2-inch piece vanilla bean
1 tablespoon confectioner's sugar

1. Place the very cold heavy cream in a chilled, large stainless-steel mixing bowl. If the temperature in your kitchen is above 80°F, set the mixing bowl in another bowl containing ice.

2. Cut the piece of vanilla bean in half lengthwise, and scrape the tiny beans into the cream. Whisk the cream vigorously until it is noticeably thicker.

3. Add the confectioner's sugar and continue whisking just until soft peaks form (if serving with cake), or until stiff enough to form dollops (if using with other desserts). Do not over-whip or the cream will quickly turn to butter. Serve immediately.

NOTES

Prepare the whipped cream at the last possible moment before serving.

If using to garnish cake, beat the cream to a slightly softer consistency than you would if it were served with other desserts.

ADVANCE STEP

Place the mixing bowl and metal whisk (or electric-mixer beaters) in the refrigerator or freezer until very cold.

SPECIAL EQUIPMENT

- A large stainless-steel mixing bowl
- A metal whisk with thin wires or an electric mixer

Whiskey Sauce

For a scant 2 cups

This recipe produces a sauce with a distinctive whiskey flavor. Served warm, it's perhaps the favorite embellishment for a Creole-style bread pudding. It also pairs well with ice cream or cake.

When chilled, it is delicious with fresh berries.

6 yolks from large eggs
½ cup sugar
1 cup heavy cream
1 teaspoon vanilla extract
¼ cup Irish whiskey

NOTES

Reheating is not recommended, since this usually produces a texture similar to scrambled eggs.

SPECIAL EQUIPMENT

• A heavy 1-quart saucepan
• A double boiler

1. In a large mixing bowl vigorously whisk together the egg yolks and sugar until light textured and a pale lemon color, about three minutes.

2. In a heavy 1-quart saucepan, bring the cream to a boil over medium-high heat, whisking constantly. Remove from heat and very gradually pour the cream into the egg mixture, whisking vigorously all the while.

3. Transfer the mixture to the top of a double boiler and place it over slow-simmering water.

4. Cook the sauce, whisking constantly, until it is noticeably thicker and coats the back of a wooden spoon, about eight minutes. Be careful not to overheat the sauce or let it boil. If lumps begin forming in it, remove it from the heat immediately and whisk it until smooth before proceeding to finish cooking.

5. Remove from the heat and add the vanilla and whiskey.

    Serving Suggestion: The sauce may be served immediately or kept in a warm spot until ready to serve.

    Refrigerate leftovers to serve cold over fresh berries or the dessert of your choice. 🐚

ACCOMPANIMENTS,
ETC.

Blanched Artichokes

Three-Pepper Coleslaw

Firecracker Cornbread

Crawfish Beignets

Herbed Dough

Crawfish Bread

Creole Cream Cheese

Pan-Fried Eggplant Rounds

Maque-Choux

Mirliton Slaw

Dry-Roasted Pecans

Classic Potato Salad

Brabant Potatoes

Potatoes Pontalba

Dirty Rice

Green-Onion Rice

Seafood-Vegetable Rice

Sweet-Potato Hash Browns

Slow-Roasted Roma Tomatoes with Fresh Tarragon

Stewed Creole Tomatoes

Blanched Artichokes

For 6 servings

The first step in any recipe using green globe artichokes is to blanch them. This softens the vegetable's flesh—the inside bits at the bases of the leaves, as well as the small, thick disk called the artichoke bottom or the heart, located where the leaves meet the stem.

The flesh at the base of blanched artichoke leaves can be eaten, although, since the leaves are prickly and very fibrous, care must be taken not to chew or swallow them whole. Many artichoke lovers dip the tender leaf bottoms into clarified butter, mayonnaise or other sauces. They scrape off the fleshy bit by placing the leaf firmly between the teeth and pulling. The remaining part of the leaf is discarded.

As for the bottoms, they are used whole or chopped. The whole bottoms, which are like tiny saucers, can be "stuffed" as you would mushroom caps. In the traditional New Orleans brunch dish called eggs Sardou, a tender artichoke bottom is topped with creamed spinach, a poached egg and hollandaise sauce.

6	large green globe artichokes, rinsed well
2	teaspoons whole black peppercorns
4	lemons, halved
1	tablespoon kosher salt
6	quarts water, or enough to cover the artichokes in the pot by 2 inches

1. In a 10-quart soup or stockpot, combine the artichokes, peppercorns, lemon halves and kosher salt. Add cool water to cover the artichokes by about 2 inches.

2. Weight down the artichokes with a heavy pot lid that is somewhat smaller than the simmering pot or some other object to keep the artichokes submerged during cooking. This will help to cook all of them evenly.

3. Turn on the heat and bring the water to a simmer. Continue simmering the artichokes, turning them over once or twice while they cook. After simmering for about 25 minutes, the artichoke leaves should detach easily when they are gently pulled.

4. Once the leaves come off easily, drain the artichokes and set them aside to cool.

   If you will be using the artichokes whole, they are now ready for serving or refrigeration.

   If you will be using the separated bottoms and leaves, continue to Step 5.

5. Once the artichokes have cooled, pull all of the leaves from the stems, as well as those surrounding the disk-like bottom. Discard the small purple-tipped leaves and the leaves attached to the hearts. (Save the large leaves if you'll be using them for dipping into clarified butter or mayonnaise-based dipping sauces.)

6. Remove and discard the round fuzzy "choke" from the tops of the artichoke hearts. Slice off the hearts at the point where they join the stems. The hearts are now ready to use whole.

7. If you are preparing this recipe for the oyster and artichoke bisque on page 134, you will also be using the artichoke's tender inner stems. With a paring knife or vegetable peeler, shave off the fibrous outer layers of the stems. Finely chop the shaved stems and the bottoms. This chopped mixture is now ready to use in other recipes.

*If you are blanching the artichokes as an advance step for the oyster and artichoke bisque recipe on page 134, you may want to reserve some of the cooking liquid to add to the bisque.

Three-Pepper Coleslaw

For 6 servings

Coleslaw has been a favorite side dish with seafood for generations. This one's sweet and acidic flavors make it an especially good accompaniment to fish and shellfish dishes.

1	firm head green cabbage, about 1¼ pound
1	recipe hot-pepper-jelly sauce
½	cup apple-cider vinegar
2	tablespoons sugar
2	tablespoons minced fresh Italian (flat-leaf) parsley leaves
1	tablespoon kosher salt
¼	teaspoon freshly ground black pepper
1½	cups peeled and julienned carrots (1½ inches by ⅛ inch)
1	cup julienned onions (1½ inches by ⅛ inch)
1	cup finely sliced green onions, green parts only

NOTE

Be sure to serve the coleslaw on the same day it's prepared since it tends to lose crispness after a few hours.

ADVANCE STEP

Prepare the recipe for hot-pepper-jelly sauce on page 371.

1. Remove the outer leaves from the cabbage head. Wash the head, core it, and cut it into ⅛-inch-thick slices. Place in a large mixing bowl.

2. In a small mixing bowl, thoroughly combine the hot-pepper-jelly sauce with the vinegar, sugar, parsley, kosher salt and pepper. Add the mixture to the bowl of cabbage, along with the carrots, onions and green onions, mixing well.

   Serving Suggestion: Cover and refrigerate at least one hour before serving. 🐚

Firecracker Cornbread

For one 9-inch round loaf or 6 to 8 servings

A New Year's Day feast in New Orleans often centers around blackeyed peas, eaten to bring luck during the coming 12 months. This well seasoned, spicy hot and colorful cornbread would be a great accompaniment to the peas, as well as many other Southern-style dishes. The flavor is deliciously enhanced by the addition of fresh corn to the batter.

2 ears sweet corn in the husk, each 8 to 9 inches long

¼ pound (1 stick) unsalted butter, softened and cut in ¼-inch cubes, plus butter or bacon fat to grease the baking pan

1¼ cups yellow cornmeal

¼ cup plus 2 tablespoons all-purpose flour

1 tablespoon sugar

1½ teaspoons kosher salt

1 teaspoon baking powder

1 cup finely sliced green onions, green parts only

2 tablespoons minced fresh jalapeños with seeds, or more to taste*

2 yolks from large eggs

1 cup whole milk

NOTE

The cornbread may be prepared up to three hours ahead and kept uncovered at room temperature.

SPECIAL EQUIPMENT
• A 9-inch glass or metal pie pan

* If your jalapeños are fairly mild, use 3 tablespoons minced, being sure to include the seeds, which contain much of the heat of the peppers.

1. Preheat oven to 350°F.

2. Soak the ears of corn in the husk in a pan of water for 30 minutes. Drain and bake uncovered on a baking sheet until corn is just cooked, about 35 minutes. Let the corn cool, then strip off the husks and silk, and cut the kernels from the ears. You should have about 1¼ cups.

3. Increase the oven setting to 400°F.

4. Generously butter or grease a 9-inch glass or metal pie pan and set it aside.

5. In a large mixing bowl thoroughly combine the cornmeal, flour, sugar, kosher salt and baking powder. Add the reserved corn kernels, and the green onions and jalapeños, mixing well.

6. Add the butter cubes and egg yolks, mixing well with your hands until all the dry ingredients are moistened. Add the milk, mixing just until large lumps are broken up and the milk is blended in. Do not over-mix.

7. Spoon the batter into the prepared pie pan and smooth the top with the back of the spoon. Tap the pan solidly on a counter three or four times to expel air bubbles.

8. Bake the cornbread until it is golden brown and a toothpick inserted into the thickest part comes out clean, 20 to 30 minutes, depending on whether your pan is glass or metal. Remove from oven and let sit 30 minutes before cutting into wedges for serving.

Serving Suggestion: If prepared in advance, reheat in a microwave oven or covered in a conventional oven.

For about 50 appetizer-size beignets (8 or 9 servings) or 25 main-dish-size beignets (4 servings)

Beignets were never unique to New Orleans, but the city has become more closely identified with these sweetish puffs of deep-fried dough than any other place in the world.

The beignet (pronounced as ben-YAY) is a relative of the American fritter or cruller. It was first brought to New Orleans from France more than two centuries ago. Pillow-shaped and dusted with confectioner's sugar, beignets remain a favorite accompaniment to a steaming cup of café au lait (coffee with milk).

Sweet beignets are much more common, but savory ones—especially with seafood fillings—are appearing on many New Orleans restaurant menus. This version is filled with crawfish and aromatic vegetables—sweet pepper, onions and corn—accompanied by a tartar sauce whose flavor is boosted with tarragon and roasted tomatoes.

The recipe gives you a choice of two beignet sizes. The smaller ones can function as either the first course of a meal or as hors d'oeuvres at parties. The larger ones are the right size for main courses, or for a side dish in place of hush puppies.

Both the beignets and the tartar sauce are adaptable to other roles. The crawfish can be replaced with shrimp, lobster, or a mixture of crab and smoked flaked redfish. If you have leftover beignet batter, it can be kept refrigerated and fried the next day. (If the batter is stored longer, a bit more baking powder will be needed.)

The tartar sauce is also good with virtually any fried seafood, and would perform as a dressing for a Niçoise-type salad or a chicken salad, or for grilled vegetables.

FOR THE TOMATO-TARRAGON TARTAR SAUCE

2	medium-size (about 1 pound) Creole* tomatoes
	non-stick vegetable spray
⅓	cup (scant) finely chopped shallots
½	cup rice-wine vinegar
2	tablespoons tomato paste**
1	tablespoon dry mustard
⅓	cup (scant) chopped fresh tarragon leaves, preferably French tarragon variety
2	yolks from large eggs
1½	cups vegetable oil
½	cup olive oil

*South Louisiana's Creole tomatoes are preferred for this recipe, although other good, peak-of-season regional varieties can be used.
**If the tomatoes are at their peak of goodness, use only 1 tablespoon tomato paste.

ADVANCE STEPS

Prepare the recipe for Creole seasoning on page 385.

Prepare the tartar sauce a day before serving and refrigerate it, covered, to let the flavors develop.

Also, the tomatoes may be baked a day ahead, if they are then kept covered in the refrigerator. (See Steps 1 and 2 opposite.)

1. Preheat the oven to 350°F.

2. Core the tomatoes and cut in half. Score an X through the skin of each half and place cut side down in a small baking pan. Spray the skin with non-stick vegetable spray. Bake uncovered until the skin blisters and is lightly browned, about 15 minutes. Remove the tomatoes from the oven and let them cool to room temperature. (The tomatoes may be prepared to this point a day ahead, if they are then kept covered in the refrigerator.)

3. In a heavy, nonreactive 2-quart saucepan, combine the shallots, vinegar, tomato paste and dry mustard, stirring to blend well. Heat the mixture over low heat to bring to a simmer and cook for a total of 17 minutes.

4. Once the tomatoes are cool, peel and squeeze most of the seeds out of each half and discard. Then squeeze the tomatoes into bits as you add them to the simmering shallot mixture.

5. Bring to a boil over high heat. Reduce heat to medium and cook until the tomato mixture becomes a thick sauce, about 10 minutes, stirring as often as needed to keep it from scorching. Remove from heat and stir in the tarragon.

6. Spread the tomato sauce on a heat-proof plate and refrigerate, uncovered, until cool, about 30 minutes.

7. In the bowl of a food processor, combine the egg yolks with the cooled tomato sauce. Turn on the processor and very slowly add the vegetable and olive oils. Once all the oil is added, continue processing a few seconds more if needed until creamy.

8. Refrigerate the tartar sauce overnight in a covered, nonreactive container before using.

SPECIAL EQUIPMENT
- A heavy, nonreactive* 2-quart saucepan
- An electric food processor

*See Using Nonreactive Cookware, page 419.

FOR THE CRAWFISH BEIGNETS

- ⅓ cup finely chopped red onions
- ⅓ cup finely chopped red sweet peppers
- ⅓ cup finely chopped green sweet peppers
- ⅓ cup freshly shucked corn kernels
- 2 tablespoons Creole seasoning
- 1 tablespoon baking powder
- 1 teaspoon kosher salt
- 2 cups all-purpose flour
- 2 large eggs
- 8 ounces shelled crawfish tails*
- ½ cup (5 ounces weight) plus 1½ tablespoons light lager beer**
  vegetable oil, for deep frying
  mixed salad greens***

SPECIAL EQUIPMENT
- A deep-fat fryer or a deep 12-inch skillet or sauté pan
- An electric food processor
- A frying thermometer
- A slotted spoon

*If this ingredient is difficult to find where you live, see Ingredient Sources on page 424.

**Such as Abita Amber beer, produced in Louisiana, if it's available.

***If the beignets are for a main course, allow 1½ ounces (2 cups lightly packed) of salad greens per person. If for an appetizer, allow ½ ounce (a rounded ⅓ cup) per person.

1. In a large mixing bowl, combine the red onions, red and green sweet peppers, corn, Creole seasoning, baking powder, and kosher salt, mixing well. Mix in the flour, then the eggs, then the crawfish and beer, blending the batter thoroughly. Set aside momentarily.

2. Heat the oil in a deep-fat fryer or heat ½ inch of oil in a deep 12-inch skillet or sauté pan over medium-high heat until it reaches 350°.

3. If the beignets will be served as an appetizer or side dish, use 1 level tablespoon (½ ounce) batter for each beignet. If as a main-dish, use 2 level tablespoons (1 ounce) for each beignet.

4. Either way, fry the beignets in small batches, using a tablespoon to scoop out the batter from the measuring spoon and gently ease it into the hot oil. Fry until golden brown on both sides and cooked through, about three minutes for an appetizer size, and about five minutes for a main-dish size, frequently turning them.

5. Remove the beignets from the fryer with a slotted spoon and drain briefly on paper towels. Serve while piping hot.

Serving Suggestions: If this is an appetizer, mound a rounded ⅓ cup of lightly packed mixed salad greens on each salad plate. Arrange five or six small beignets around the greens and drizzle 2 tablespoons of tartar sauce on the greens.

If this is a main course, mound a rounded 2 cups (1½ ounces) of lightly packed greens on each dinner plate. Arrange six to eight larger beignets around the greens and drizzle ½ cup of tartar sauce on the greens. 🐚

Herbed Dough

For 2 pounds 6 ounces of dough

This dough would work well as a crust for any pizza with savory toppings.

½ cup hot water (105° to 115°F)
1 package (1¼ ounces) of active dry yeast
5 cups bread flour, divided
1½ cups whole milk
⅓ cup extra-virgin olive oil
2½ teaspoons kosher salt
½ teaspoon dried basil leaves
½ teaspoon dried oregano leaves
½ teaspoon dried thyme leaves
 non-stick vegetable spray

SPECIAL EQUIPMENT
• An electric mixer with a dough hook attachment
• A metal whisk

1. In the large bowl of an electric mixer, use a metal whisk to blend together the hot water, yeast, and ¼ cup bread flour. Set aside, uncovered, in a warm place until foamy, about 10 minutes.

2. To the foamy yeast mixture, add 4¾ cups bread flour, the milk, olive oil, kosher salt, basil, oregano and thyme. With the mixer fitted with the dough hook attachment, mix on the lowest speed until all the ingredients are blended, one to two minutes.

3. Increase the speed on the mixer by one setting and knead for five minutes. Remove the bowl from the mixer stand and spray the top of the dough with non-stick vegetable spray. Cover the bowl with plastic wrap.

4. Let the dough rise in a warm place until doubled in size, two to two and a half hours.

5. Gently punch down the dough and transfer it from to the bowl to a work surface.

6. Divide the dough into three equal portions. Wrap each portion snugly in plastic wrap and refrigerate for at least eight hours or up to three days, or place the wrapped portions in a self-sealing freezer bag and freeze for up to one month. Thaw frozen dough several hours in the refrigerator.

7. Now the dough is ready to shape into circles, following the directions on the pizza recipe used, or to shape into rectangles, following the directions in the crawfish bread recipe on the following page. 🐚

Crawfish Bread

For 3 loaves or about 18 half-inch slices

Stuffed breads are a fairly new development on the culinary scene in New Orleans and South Louisiana. The breads are especially suitable for party food or snacking. This one is filled with a well seasoned, but not spicy-hot, crawfish stuffing. It's delectable served straight from the oven.

FOR THE STUFFING

1	pound peeled crawfish tails*
4	tablespoons unsalted butter
1¼	cups finely chopped yellow onions
½	cup finely chopped green sweet peppers
2½	teaspoons Creole seasoning, divided
½	teaspoon kosher salt, plus to taste
¼	teaspoon ground cayenne, plus to taste
1	teaspoon minced fresh garlic
2	cups finely sliced green onions, green parts only
8	ounces grated Fontina or provolone cheese
	freshly ground black pepper, to taste

*If this ingredient is difficult to find where you live, see Ingredient Sources on page 424.

ADVANCE STEPS

Prepare the recipes for:

• Creole seasoning on page 385

• Herbed dough on page 327, allowing eight hours for the dough to chill before assembling the bread loaves for baking

SPECIAL EQUIPMENT

• A large colander

• A heavy 10-inch skillet or sauté pan

• A heavy 1-quart saucepan

1. Separate the crawfish tails if stuck together and drain them for 30 minutes in a large colander placed over a large bowl to catch the crawfish juice. Set the drained juice and crawfish tails aside momentarily. (There should be approximately 2 tablespoons of drained juices from the crawfish at this point. Once the stuffing is sautéed, it too will be drained over the same bowl. The two combined liquids will later be reduced and added back to the stuffing, giving it additional richness.)

2. In a heavy 10-inch skillet, melt the butter over medium-high heat. Add the yellow onions, sweet peppers, 1 teaspoon Creole seasoning, ½ teaspoon kosher salt, ¼ teaspoon cayenne and the garlic, stirring well. Sauté the mixture until the vegetables are soft but not yet starting to brown, about five minutes, stirring occasionally.

3. Add the reserved crawfish tails and sprinkle 1½ teaspoons Creole seasoning over them. Thoroughly stir the mixture, then continue cooking and stirring one minute more. Remove from heat. Clean the colander used for draining the crawfish and place it over the bowl of drained crawfish juice.

4.   Transfer the hot crawfish stuffing to the colander and let drain 20 minutes, stirring the crawfish occasionally and using the back of a sturdy mixing spoon to lightly press as much liquid as possible through the holes in the colander. You will end with about ½ cup drained liquid. Set aside momentarily.

5.   Spread the drained stuffing into a thin layer on a heat-proof platter (or in a cake or pie pan) and refrigerate, uncovered, until well chilled, about one hour.

6.   Meanwhile, transfer the reserved drained crawfish liquid to a heavy 1-quart saucepan. Cook over medium-high heat until the liquid reduces to 1 to 2 table-spoons, about 10 minutes. Remove from heat and evenly drizzle the liquid over the crawfish stuffing in the refrigerator.

7.   Once the stuffing is completely chilled, transfer it to a large mixing bowl and add the green onions and cheese, mixing well. Taste for level of salt, cayenne and black pepper and add if needed.

FOR FINISHING THE BREAD

SPECIAL EQUIPMENT
- A pastry brush
- A rimmed baking sheet

1   cup whole milk
1   egg, any size
1   recipe for herbed dough, thawed if frozen
    flour, for shaping dough
¼   teaspoon kosher salt, about

1.   Preheat oven to 350°F.

2.   Meanwhile, in a small mixing bowl, make an egg wash by lightly whisking together the milk and egg.

3.   Remove the herbed dough from the refrigerator. Separate the dough into thirds. Use each portion of dough to prepare a log-shaped loaf as follows:

4.   On a floured surface and with floured hands, shape one third of the dough into a rectangle 11 by 6 inches, and as close to ½ inch thick as possible.

5.   Spread one-third of the filling on the dough rectangle, leaving a ½-inch-wide border along each side.

6.   With a pastry brush, spread some of the egg wash on three borders of the rectangle—both of the short sides and one long side, leaving one border without egg wash.

7.   The dough is now ready to be rolled into a log-shaped loaf. Starting at the long side with no egg wash on its border, carefully roll up the dough into a log shape and transfer it to an ungreased, rimmed baking sheet.

8.   Once all three log-shaped loaves are on the baking sheet, brush some of the egg wash on top of each. (You should have egg wash left over.) Sprinkle the loaves very lightly with a total of about ¼ teaspoon of kosher salt.

9.   Bake the loaves on the middle shelf of the oven until the dough is cooked through, about 40 minutes.

Serving Suggestion: Cut into half-inch slices and serve while piping hot.

Creole Cream Cheese

For about 4 cups

Once a breakfast favorite throughout South Louisiana, Creole cream cheese has faded from the consciousness of most descendants of the Creoles and Acadians of yore.

At one time several New Orleans dairies delivered their cream cheeses to local food stores and homes, to be enjoyed as part of a morning meal. The soft, white, unaged cheese is similar in some ways to ricotta or farmer's cheese. Traditionally, the curd was eaten either sweet (sugared and studded with fresh strawberries) or salted and peppered. Another frequent addition was half-and-half or fresh, heavy cream.

Some local purists claim that the true flavor of Creole cream cheese cannot be duplicated outside South Louisiana because certain unidentified bacteria—in the air or the milk—are necessary to produce the real thing.

In any event, the tart and silky-textured cheese is making a bit of a comeback on its home turf. It is now for sale in several food stores and farmers' markets in the New Orleans area.

This recipe is based on the one used by the now-defunct Gold Seal Creamery, which operated in New Orleans from 1920 until 1986. With the right utensils it is surprisingly simple to make, and only four ingredients are required.

2	quarts skim milk
½	cup buttermilk
	a small pinch of salt
3 to 4	drops liquid vegetable rennet*

*Be sure to purchase liquid vegetable rennet with a current date of freshness or the cheese may come out stringy. If this ingredient is difficult to find where you live, see Ingredient Sources on page 424.

1. Combine all the ingredients in a large mixing bowl, preferably stainless steel, stirring thoroughly.

2. Without stirring again, let the mixture stand undisturbed at cool room temperature and out of drafts until it separates into firm curds and liquid whey, 24 to 36 hours. If covering the bowl is necessary, use one or two layers of cheesecloth to allow fresh air to get to the mixture.

3. Once the curds and whey have separated, place a rack over a shallow pan. Arrange the cheese molds, or a large colander lined with several thicknesses of cheesecloth, on top of the rack. Gently ladle the curds into the mold(s), keeping the curds in as large chunks as possible, and filling the mold(s) to the top, since the curds will shrink substantially as they drain. Refrigerate the

NOTES

Be sure to use immaculate utensils and an extra-clean workspace for preparing the cheese.

If the liquid is allowed to drain from the solids long enough, the cheese becomes the consistency of standard American-style cream cheese, which makes a very pleasant-tasting spread.

For traditional New Orleans breakfast food and for use in the recipe for Creole cream cheese cheesecake on page 285, the cheese should be drained for a shorter time so it comes out soft and creamy, about the consistency of very thick yogurt.

This recipe can be doubled.

mold(s)—still on the rack over the shallow pan—until the cheese no longer drips and is the consistency of very thick yogurt. If using homemade molds, make sure the holes are large enough for the whey to drip through.

Serving Suggestion: Use the cheese immediately or place it in one or more closed containers and refrigerate for up to one week.

SPECIAL EQUIPMENT

• A large mixing bowl (preferably stainless steel)

• A ladle or large mixing spoon

• A rack on which the molds or colander can sit

• A shallow pan to go under the rack to catch the whey as it drips. (Make sure the rack and pan will fit in your refrigerator.)

• Either cheese molds (see Special Note on cheese molds, below) or a large wire colander with a flat bottom (the easiest method)

• Several thicknesses of cheesecloth for draining about 2 quarts of curds (the solids) and whey (the liquid)

SPECIAL NOTE ON CHEESE MOLDS

Using store-bought cheese molds is one option to separate the curds from the whey. However, the easiest method to separate the curds from the whey is to use a large wire colander with a flat bottom in place of the molds.

Strainers made specifically for making yogurt cheese also work well, as do homemade molds fashioned from plastic food containers, which should be pricked to pierce several small holes in the bottoms and sides, allowing the liquid to drain.

For information on retail sources of cheese molds, see Ingredient Sources on page 424.

Pan-Fried Eggplant Rounds with Avery Island Aioli

For 18 slices or 6 side-dish servings

New Orleans cooks know eggplant as an excellent ingredient to use in eggplant parmigiana or with crab and shrimp as a stuffing. And they know that this tasty vegetable also can perform very well on its own—in this instance sporting a coating of egg wash and breadcrumbs, to be pan-fried in clarified butter.

A bracing Louisiana-style aioli is suggested as an accompaniment.

(To create a simple version of eggplant parmigiana, layer the rounds in a pan and bake them covered with marinara sauce and freshly grated Parmigiano-Reggiano cheese.)

2	cups fresh soft breadcrumbs
2	rounded tablespoons minced fresh Italian (flat-leaf) parsley leaves
2½	teaspoons kosher salt, divided
⅛	teaspoon plus ¼ teaspoon freshly ground black pepper, divided
1½	cups seasoned flour
1	cup whole milk
2	large eggs
1	eggplant (about 1 pound, 6 ounces)
1	cup (about) clarified butter, divided
1	recipe Avery Island aioli

ADVANCE STEPS

Prepare the recipes for:

- Fresh soft breadcrumbs on page 382
- Seasoned flour on page 384
- Clarified butter on page 355
- Avery Island aioli on page 353

SPECIAL EQUIPMENT

- A heavy 12-inch sauté pan

1. In a pie plate or large shallow bowl, thoroughly combine the breadcrumbs with the parsley, ½ teaspoon kosher salt, and ⅛ teaspoon pepper.

2. Place the seasoned flour in another pie pan or large shallow bowl.

3. In a medium-size mixing bowl, lightly whisk together the milk and eggs for the egg wash.

4. Trim the ends from the eggplant. Peel the eggplant and slice it crosswise into ¼-inch-thick slices until you have cut 18 slices.

5. Spread the eggplant slices on a work surface and season both sides with kosher salt and pepper, using a total of 2 teaspoons salt and ¼ teaspoon pepper distributed among all the slices.

6. In a heavy 12-inch sauté pan, heat ¼ inch (about ½ cup) of clarified butter over medium heat until hot but not smoking, about three minutes.

7. While the butter is heating, bread the eggplant slices one at a time, as follows: moisten the eggplant slice with the egg wash, and dredge in the seasoned flour, shaking off any excess. Moisten again with the egg wash and dredge in the breadcrumbs and parsley mixture, again shaking off any excess.

8. Once the butter is hot, carefully slide six of the eggplant slices into the butter. Reduce the heat to medium and pan-fry the rounds until dark golden brown on both sides, about two minutes on each side. Drain on paper towels.

9. Add ¼ cup more clarified butter to the pan, and pan-fry another batch of six eggplant slices. Drain on paper towels.

10. Add another ¼ cup clarified butter to the pan and fry the last six eggplant slices. Drain on paper towels.

Serving Suggestions: As soon as all the eggplant slices are fried and drained, serve them promptly with the Avery Island aioli as a dipping sauce. Or arrange the eggplant slices in a single layer on a rimmed baking sheet lined with a few layers of paper towels and warm them, uncovered, in a 200°F oven for up to 20 minutes before serving. 🐚

Maque-Choux

For 6 servings

Maque-choux may be the oldest dish in the entirety of Louisiana-Creole cookery. The word itself is believed to have originated with the local Indians, who in the early 1700s introduced the newly arrived French colonists to their indigenous vegetables, game and seafood.

The French settlers soon developed a taste for sweet corn, in such Native-American dishes as *sagamité*, a kind of hominy or corn porridge to which fish or meat was often added.

Another Indian contribution was maque-choux, which, according to at least one source, was originally a stew of corn and onions. Over the decades Creole cooks of New Orleans occasionally improvised with additions such as chopped sweet pepper, tomato or celery, and other seasonings and spices.

As a side dish, maque-choux can be a delightful substitute for plain corn.

2	tablespoons unsalted butter
3	medium-sized garlic cloves garlic, sliced thin
1	cup finely chopped yellow onions
½	cup finely chopped green sweet peppers
½	cup finely chopped celery
1	medium-size Creole* tomato, chopped
4	cups fresh sweet corn, preferably yellow, cut from about 5 large cobs
½	cup chicken stock or vegetable stock
4	sprigs fresh thyme, finely chopped
1½	teaspoons kosher salt
½	teaspoon freshly ground black pepper

*South Louisiana's Creole tomatoes are preferred for this recipe, although other good, peak-of-season regional varieties can be used.

1. Over medium-high heat, melt the butter in a heavy 3-quart, nonreactive saucepan. Add the garlic and cook until it turns just golden, 20 to 30 seconds.

2. Add the onions, sweet peppers and celery and cook for five minutes, stirring occasionally.

3. Add the tomatoes and corn, mixing thoroughly, and cook for five minutes.

4. Stir in the stock, thyme, kosher salt and pepper. Bring to a boil, then reduce the heat and simmer for 15 minutes.

Serving Suggestion: Serve warm or, if made ahead, let cool, then cover and refrigerate until time to reheat for serving. 🐚

NOTE

The recipe may be prepared a day in advance.

ADVANCE STEP

Prepare the recipe for either of the following:

- Chicken stock on page 390
- Vegetable stock on page 397

SPECIAL EQUIPMENT

- A heavy 3-quart, nonreactive* saucepan

 *See Using Nonreactive Cookware on page 419.

Mirliton Slaw

For 2½ cups or 6 servings

Many a New Orleans home garden contains a vine laden with mirlitons, the pale-green, pear-shaped squash that was grown and eaten by the ancient Aztecs and Mayans of Mexico.

Mexicans know the mirliton as the chayote, and in the United States it's often called a vegetable pear.

One reason mirliton vines are common in New Orleans is their adaptability to the city's semi-tropical climate. Another is their subtle flavor, which is similar to that of zucchini and makes them compatible with shrimp, green seasonings and a host of other ingredients.

As a side dish, this mirliton slaw is as versatile as the ever-popular coleslaw, but with an added zip provided by bits of sweet pepper.

2 cups "shoestring" strips of peeled mirlitons
¼ cup finely chopped sweet peppers
¼ cup finely chopped red onions
2 tablespoons plus 2 teaspoons fresh lemon juice
2 teaspoons minced fresh Italian (flat-leaf) parsley leaves
½ teaspoon olive oil
½ teaspoon kosher salt
⅛ teaspoon freshly ground black pepper

Combine all ingredients and let chill 15 minutes, then serve as soon as possible, ideally within 15 minutes for the crispest slaw.

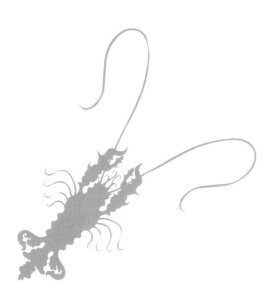

Dry-Roasted Pecans

Pecans are more fragrant and flavorful when they are dry roasted. Take your choice of two methods for dry roasting shelled pecans, either on top of the stove or in the oven.

IN A SKILLET

1. Place shelled pecan pieces or halves in a dry heavy skillet large enough to hold them in a single layer.

2. Cook them, uncovered, over medium heat until fragrant and lightly browned or until medium-dark, about five to seven minutes, stirring almost constantly.

3. Remove the pecans from heat and promptly transfer them to a heat-proof plate to cool.

IN THE OVEN

1. Preheat the oven to 350°F.

2. Bake shelled pecan pieces or halves on an ungreased rimmed cookie sheet until fragrant and lightly browned, or until medium-dark, about eight to 10 minutes, stirring frequently.

3. Remove the pecans from the oven and promptly transfer them to a heat-proof plate to cool.

   Serving Suggestion: Store the cooled pecans in a covered container in the refrigerator for up to one week.

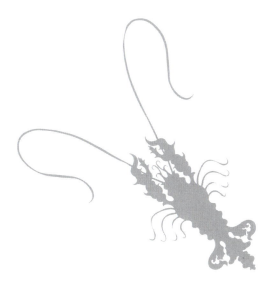

Classic Potato Salad

For 5 generous cups or 8 to 10 side-dish servings

In South Louisiana, mustard is frequently added to potato salads, lending a bit of tang to their taste. They're a favorite side dish with gumbos and barbecue, and a staple at picnics. This recipe produces a good, basic one that's nice and creamy. It can be prepared a day ahead and kept covered in the refrigerator.

2	pounds small new red potatoes, rinsed well
	water for cooking potatoes
1	tablespoon plus 1¼ teaspoons kosher salt, plus to taste, divided
2	hard-boiled eggs, peeled and finely chopped
¼	cup finely chopped yellow or white onions
¼	cup finely chopped green onions, white and green parts
2	tablespoons finely chopped celery
2	teaspoons minced fresh Italian (flat-leaf) parsley leaves
¾	cup mayonnaise, plus to taste
¼	cup prepared mustard
2	tablespoons apple-cider vinegar
½	teaspoon freshly ground black pepper, plus to taste

ADVANCE STEP

If making your own mayonnaise, try the basic mayonnaise on page 369.

SPECIAL EQUIPMENT

• A 4-quart saucepan or 4-quart pot

1. Place the potatoes in a 4-quart saucepan and cover with water. Add 1 tablespoon kosher salt and bring to a boil over medium-high heat. Cook until fork tender, 20 to 25 minutes. Drain and refrigerate until cool, about 30 minutes.

2. Remove the potatoes from the refrigerator and cut away any blemishes but leave the skins on. Chop the potatoes in rough ¼- to ½-inch pieces.

3. In a large mixing bowl, combine the potatoes with the hard-boiled eggs, yellow or white onions, green onions, celery and parsley. Add the mayonnaise, mustard, vinegar, 1¼ teaspoons of kosher salt and the pepper. Thoroughly mix the ingredients while mashing some of the potatoes so the finished salad will be lumpy but creamy. Add more mayonnaise, salt and pepper if desired. Cover and refrigerate.

Serving Suggestion: Serve chilled. 🐚

Brabant Potatoes

For 8 servings as a side dish

Brabant potatoes are named for a province in Belgium, which probably means this is where the dish originated.

A recipe for the potatoes appeared in the 1918 edition of Fannie Farmer's Cookbook, which called for parboiling the potatoes before roasting them with melted butter.

The more traditional New Orleans-Creole method is to toss the potato cubes in butter before baking them and then pan-frying them in fat. Also, some New Orleans cooks parboil and then fry them in clarified butter. For the frying agent, this recipe calls for pork lard or duck or chicken fat. This should dry the potatoes as they cook, retaining the fluffy texture inside while making the outside dry and crisp.

4	large (4½ to 5 pounds) russet potatoes, peeled and cut into ½-inch cubes
1	tablespoon unsalted butter, melted
¾	teaspoon coarse kosher salt, plus to taste
½	teaspoon freshly ground black pepper, plus to taste
2	tablespoons duck fat, pork lard or rendered chicken fat

NOTE

It should not be necessary to drain the potatoes on paper towels after frying or serve them with a slotted spoon because there should be virtually no excess fat left in the pan.

SPECIAL EQUIPMENT

• A very large stainless-steel mixing bowl
• Two rimmed baking sheets that will fit side by side in the oven
• A heavy 12-inch sauté pan

1. Preheat the oven to 300°F.

2. Place the potato cubes in a very large stainless-steel mixing bowl and add the butter, kosher salt and pepper, tossing until all the cubes are coated evenly.

3. Spread the cubes in a single layer on two rimmed baking sheets that will fit side by side in your oven. Bake them uncovered until they are golden and almost tender but still slightly crisp, 40 to 45 minutes, turning the potatoes over at 10-minute intervals to brown evenly. Remove from the oven. (At this point, the potatoes may be set aside, uncovered and at room temperature, for up to about 20 minutes before finishing the dish.)

4. Heat the duck fat, pork fat or rendered chicken fat in a heavy 12-inch sauté pan over high heat until hot and just short of smoking. Add the potato cubes to the pan, tossing to coat the cubes on all sides with fat. Cook just until the potatoes are tender and heated through, three to five minutes, tossing almost constantly. Season them with more salt and pepper if needed and remove the pan from heat.

Serving Suggestion: Serve the potatoes piping hot.

For 4 servings

French cooks tip their toques to their country's nobility in their famous potato dish *pommes de terre duchesse*.

New Orleanians, not to be outdone, do the same when they make Pontalba potatoes, named for an illustrious Creole grande dame who became a baroness on her marriage to a French nobleman.

She was Micaela Almonester y Pontalba, and she left a monumental imprint on the New Orleans cityscape in the form of the gorgeous Pontalba Apartments, a pair of buildings constructed in the mid-1800s on two sides of Jackson Square, perpendicular to St. Louis Cathedral.

3	medium-sized (about 2 pounds) Idaho potatoes, peeled and cut into ½-inch cubes
1	teaspoon kosher salt, plus to taste
1	quart cool water
¼	cup clarified butter
2	teaspoons minced garlic
1	cup finely chopped yellow onions
⅓	cup English peas
⅓	cup finely chopped tasso*
2	teaspoons finely chopped fresh thyme leaves
1½	tablespoons unsalted butter
	freshly ground black pepper to taste

ADVANCE STEP

Prepare the recipe for clarified butter on page 355.

SPECIAL EQUIPMENT

- A 3-quart saucepan
- A colander
- A 12-inch sauté pan or a deep 12-inch skillet

*Tasso is a spicy, dry-cured ham from traditional Cajun cooking (for ordering information see page 424). In this recipe, the same amount of fried and finely crumbled bacon may be substituted for the tasso.

1. Combine the potatoes and kosher salt in a 3-quart saucepan, and cover with the cool water.

2. Bring the water to a boil over high heat.

3. Reduce the heat and simmer the potatoes until they are almost cooked but still a little crunchy, about three minutes.

4. Remove the potatoes from heat, drain them in a colander, and rinse them under cool tap water a minute or two to help stop the cooking process. Drain them well again.

5. Place the colander on a plate or pan with a rim and refrigerate the potato cubes until they are thoroughly cooled, about 45 minutes.

6. About 20 minutes before serving time, heat the clarified butter in a 12-inch sauté pan over medium-high heat for about two minutes, or until it is hot. Add the chilled potatoes, and cook them for about seven minutes, or until they start to turn golden brown, stirring them occasionally.

7. Stir in the garlic and cook it for about two minutes, or until it starts to brown.

8. Add the onions, peas, tasso and thyme, and cook everything for about five minutes, or until the onions are translucent.

9. Add the whole butter to the pan. Cook and stir in the butter for a few seconds, or until it melts.

10. Taste the potatoes and season to taste with salt and pepper. Remove them from the heat and serve immediately.

SPECIAL TIPS

Two little tricks help to make the potatoes in this dish come out delightfully crispy with a tender but not mushy inside:

First, don't overcrowd the sauté pan. The cubes of potatoes should be little more than a single layer deep in the pan bottom. Second, after the potato cubes are parboiled, it is important to chill them so their insides don't overcook during the final browning process.

This recipe also uses two different butters. The potatoes are first browned in clarified butter to infuse them with a distinctively good flavor and richness and also because clarified butter can withstand higher temperatures without burning. The dish is finished with regular butter because it does the best job of rounding out the various flavors of the dish.

Dirty Rice

For 6 to 8 side-dish servings

Louisiana's Acadians have occasionally used a bit of whimsy when naming a dish. Hence, this "dirty rice," so named for the bits of chopped or ground meat mixed in with the rice kernels. Like gumbos and étouffées, dirty rice comes in almost limitless variations, depending on the cook's favorite ingredients. Chopped chicken giblets, pork or sausage meat are the ones most frequently favored.

Dirty rice is often prepared on the stove top, but this recipe calls for baking, which makes it especially moist and fluffy.

It can function as a main course or as a side dish with such Creole-Acadian specialties as red beans and étouffées.

4	tablespoons unsalted butter
1	tablespoon plus 1 teaspoon minced fresh garlic
1	cup finely chopped yellow onions
½	cup finely chopped celery
½	cup chopped green sweet peppers
1	tablespoon Creole seasoning
⅛	teaspoon ground cayenne
5	ounces chicken livers, chopped
4	ounces ground pork
½	teaspoon kosher salt, plus to taste
1	cup raw, white long-grain rice, rinsed
2½	tablespoons minced Italian (flat-leaf) parsley leaves
2	tablespoons minced fresh thyme leaves
2	cups chicken stock
2	tablespoons worcestershire sauce
½	cup finely sliced green onions, green and white parts

ADVANCE STEPS

Prepare the recipes for:

- Creole seasoning on page 385
- Chicken stock on page 390

SPECIAL EQUIPMENT

- A heavy, oven-proof 2-quart saucepan*

*If an oven-proof saucepan is not available, you may use one that is not oven-proof up to the baking step, then bake the rice in a 2-quart casserole.

1. Preheat the oven to 350°F.

2. In a heavy, oven-proof 2-quart saucepan melt the butter over medium-high heat. Stir in the garlic and cook just until it starts to brown, about 45 seconds, stirring almost constantly.

3. Stir in the yellow onions, celery, sweet peppers, Creole seasoning and cayenne, mixing well. Cook until the onions become translucent, about three minutes, stirring occasionally.

4. Add the chicken livers, pork, ½ teaspoon kosher salt and the rice, stirring thoroughly and breaking up clumps of pork. Cook until the meat is no longer pink, about two minutes, stirring constantly to prevent the mixture from burning.

5. Add the parsley, thyme, stock, worcestershire and green onions, blending well. Bring the liquid to a simmer, then cover the saucepan. (If your saucepan isn't oven-proof, transfer the mixture to an ungreased 2-quart casserole and cover.)

6. Bake until the rice is tender, about 25 minutes. Remove it from the oven and fluff it. Taste the rice and add more salt if needed.

Serving Suggestion: Serve the rice immediately or make it a day ahead. If it is made ahead, let the rice cool down before it is refrigerated, then reheat it for serving. ☙

Green-Onion Rice

For about 9 cups

This rice can be served with any gumbo in this cookbook. Its oniony flavor makes it an especially good accompaniment to an almost limitless number of other dishes in place of regular cooked rice.

2	tablespoons unsalted butter
½	cup finely chopped white or yellow onions
¼	cup finely chopped celery
2¼	generous cups raw long-grain white rice
1	cup finely sliced green onions, mostly green parts
1	tablespoon minced fresh Italian (flat-leaf) parsley leaves
4½	cups water
2	teaspoons kosher salt, plus to taste
¼	teaspoon freshly ground black pepper

SPECIAL EQUIPMENT

• A heavy 3-quart saucepan

1. In a heavy 3-quart saucepan, melt the butter over medium-high heat. Add the onions and celery, and stir well. Cook until the onions are translucent, about one minute.

2. Stir in the rice and cook and stir about one minute.

3. Stir in the green onions, parsley and water. Add 2 teaspoons kosher salt and the pepper.

4. Bring the liquid to a strong simmer, then cover, reduce heat to very low, and cook until the rice is tender, about 20 minutes. Remove from heat and season with more salt if needed.

Serving Suggestion: Fluff the rice and serve warm.

Seafood-Vegetable Rice

For 4 to 6 side-dish servings

This rice, dotted with bits of shrimp and crabmeat and boldly seasoned, has a pleasant texture and would be delicious beside just about any fish or seafood dish.

½	cup raw basmati rice
3	cups water, divided
1	teaspoon kosher salt, divided, plus to taste
2½	tablespoons peeled and cubed (⅛-inch cubes) butternut squash*
4	tablespoons (2 ounces) crab butter
5	medium-size shrimp, peeled and chopped fine
2	ounces lump crabmeat, picked through
¼	cup plus 2 tablespoons minced fennel bulb
¼	cup plus 2 tablespoons minced red onions
¼	cup plus 2 tablespoons minced red sweet peppers
¼	cup plus 2 tablespoons minced green sweet peppers
1½	teaspoons minced fresh garlic
¼	teaspoon freshly ground black pepper, plus to taste
1	medium-size Creole** tomato, peeled, seeded and chopped
1	tablespoon very finely sliced chives
1½	teaspoons very finely chopped fresh Italian (flat-leaf) parsley leaves

*If you are serving this rice with the baked flounder and salmon-roe butter sauce, blanch 5 tablespoons of butternut squash cubes. The extra 2½ tablespoons will go into the sauce.

**South Louisiana's Creole tomatoes are preferred for this recipe, although other good, peak-of-season regional varieties can be used.

NOTES

Prepare the rice as close to serving time as possible, and no more than 30 minutes ahead.

If you are serving the rice with the baked flounder and salmon-roe butter sauce on page 166, please see the first footnote to the ingredients list to the left.

ADVANCE STEP

Prepare the crab butter recipe on page 356.

SPECIAL EQUIPMENT

- A heavy 1-quart saucepan
- A heavy 10-inch skillet, preferably non-stick

1. In a heavy 1-quart saucepan, combine the rice with 2 cups water and ½ teaspoon kosher salt. Partially cover the pan and bring the liquid to a boil over high heat.

2. Reduce the heat to medium-low and simmer, still partially covered, until the rice is tender and all the liquid is absorbed, about 10 minutes. Cover and set aside to keep warm.

3. In another small saucepan over high heat, bring to a boil 1 cup water and ¼ teaspoon kosher salt. Add the butternut squash and blanch for one minute. Drain, rinse with cold tap water to shock and drain again. Set aside at room temperature.

4. In a heavy 10-inch skillet, preferably non-stick, melt the crab butter over medium-high heat. Add the shrimp, crabmeat, fennel, red onions, red and green

sweet peppers, garlic, ¼ teaspoon kosher salt and ¼ teaspoon pepper. Cook the vegetables until soft, about three minutes, stirring almost constantly.

5.   Stir in the tomatoes and cook for 30 seconds, then add the reserved rice, stirring thoroughly. Cook until the rice is just heated through, about one minute, stirring frequently.

6.   Stir in 2½ tablespoons of the blanched butternut-squash cubes and cook for one minute. If you are making extra squash to use in the salmon-roe butter sauce, set aside the extra 2½ tablespoons until called for in the sauce recipe.

7.   Stir in the chives and parsley, and remove from heat.

Serving Suggestions: Let the rice sit for five minutes, then season with more kosher salt and pepper if needed. Serve immediately.

If you are serving the rice with the crispy baked flounder and salmon-roe butter sauce, set aside the rice in a warm place while preparing the flounder and its sauce. Serve the rice within 30 minutes.

Sweet-Potato Hash Browns

For about 7½ cups or 6 to 8 side-dish servings

Sweet potatoes are most familiar as a "candied" vegetable, but they make for other tasty side dishes as well. In this version, they share company with red onion, olive oil, spices and pancetta, the Italian bacon that is not smoked, but cured in seasonings. The result is a confluence of sweet, savory and spicy flavors.

This serves as a good side dish for simply prepared seafood or meats, such as sautéed fish or roasted chicken.

1½	tablespoons extra-virgin olive oil
¾	pound pancetta, cut into ¼-inch slices and slices cut in ¼-inch cubes
1	medium-sized red onion (about 12 ounces), peeled, quartered and cut cross-wise into ¼-inch slices
1	teaspoon kosher salt
1	teaspoon ground ginger
½	teaspoon freshly grated nutmeg
½	teaspoon freshly ground black pepper
¼	teaspoon ground cayenne pepper
8	cups (about 3½ pounds) chopped raw sweet potatoes (½-inch pieces)
4	tablespoons unsalted butter

SPECIAL EQUIPMENT
- A heavy 12-inch sauté pan, preferably non-stick

1. In a heavy 12-inch sauté pan, preferably non-stick, heat the olive oil over medium-high heat for one minute. Add the pancetta and sauté until it just begins to brown, about six minutes, stirring fairly often.

2. Add the red onions and sauté, stirring occasionally, until they just begin to soften, two to three minutes, stirring occasionally. Meanwhile, in a small bowl combine the kosher salt, ginger, nutmeg, and the black and cayenne peppers.

3. Add the sweet potatoes to the pan, stirring well. Sprinkle the salt mixture over the potatoes and cook for 10 minutes, stirring occasionally and scraping the pan bottom clean as you stir. If not using a non-stick pan, at this point you may need to add a little more oil if the mixture is sticking excessively.

4. Reduce the heat to medium and cook until the sweet potatoes are tender but still firm to the bite, about 10 more minutes, stirring occasionally.

5. Add the butter and continue cooking until the butter is fully melted and blended into the hash browns, one to two minutes more, stirring constantly. Remove from heat.

Serving Suggestion: The sweet-potato hash browns may be served immediately or prepared up to one hour in advance and set aside at room temperature. For serving, reheat on the stove top over medium heat. ✽

Slow-Roasted Roma Tomatoes with Fresh Tarragon

For 16 tomato halves

In addition to being an ingredient in the recipe for pompano en papillotes on page 176, these aromatically scented tomatoes come in handy for other dishes, especially salads. They also would be good sautéed with some garlic and extra-virgin olive oil, then tossed with pasta.

By roasting the tomatoes only to the point of being cooked—but not totally dry—their essential flavor is intensified. You can cut back or increase the recipe as needed.

8	ripe Roma tomatoes
2	teaspoons extra-virgin olive oil
16	fresh tarragon leaves
4	teaspoons unsalted butter, each teaspoon cut in fourths
	kosher salt, to taste
	freshly ground black pepper, to taste

SPECIAL EQUIPMENT
- A rimmed cookie sheet
- Parchment paper
- A pastry brush

1. Preheat oven to 225°F.

2. Line a rimmed cookie sheet with parchment paper. Cut the tomatoes in half lengthwise and arrange them cut side up and at least ½ inch apart on the parchment paper.

3. Use a pastry brush to brush the cut sides with olive oil.

4. Place 1 tarragon leaf on the top of each tomato half, then place ¼ teaspoon butter on top. Season lightly with kosher salt and pepper.

5. Bake uncovered until about half of the moisture has cooked away, about 45 minutes. Remove tomatoes from the oven and let them cool to room temperature, then use a small spoon to scoop out the seeds from the tomatoes.

   Serving Suggestion: If not using the tomatoes immediately, drizzle them with a little extra-virgin olive oil and refrigerate them in a covered container. They will keep up to three days refrigerated.

Stewed Creole Tomatoes

For 6 servings

The marvelous flavor of fresh tomatoes make them a delicious accompaniment to a wide range of dishes. This recipe, which calls for succulently ripe, locally grown tomatoes, while not being too acidic, has a pleasant herbal aftertaste.

It's an excellent side dish with just about any fish, regardless of the preparation, as well as with chicken or pork.

2	tablespoons extra-virgin olive oil
1	cup finely chopped onions
1	cup finely chopped celery
4	pounds (8 large) Creole tomatoes,* peeled and quartered
1½	teaspoons kosher salt
½	teaspoon freshly ground black pepper
2	tablespoons finely sliced fresh basil leaves
2	tablespoons finely chopped fresh Italian (flat-leaf) parsley leaves
1	tablespoon minced fresh thyme leaves

*South Louisiana's Creole tomatoes are preferred for this recipe, although other good, peak-of-season regional varieties can be used also.

SPECIAL EQUIPMENT

• A heavy stainless-steel (or other nonreactive*) 5½ quart saucepan or Dutch oven

• A slotted spoon

*See Using Nonreactive Cookware, page 419.

1. In a heavy stainless-steel 5½-quart saucepan, heat the olive oil over medium heat until hot, about three minutes. Add the onions and celery and sauté for three minutes, stirring occasionally.

2. Stir in the tomatoes, kosher salt, and pepper. Cook for 20 minutes, stirring as often as needed to keep the bottom from scorching.

3. Add the basil, parsley and thyme, and continue cooking five minutes more. Remove from heat.

Serving Suggestions: Serve the tomatoes warm, dishing them out with a slotted spoon. The dish may be prepared a day ahead. If serving the tomatoes fairly promptly, cover and set aside until serving time. If prepared further in advance, cool, then cover and refrigerate until ready to reheat for serving. 🐚

SAUCES,
BUTTERS
&
DRESSINGS

Basic Aioli and Variations

Blue-Cheese Dipping Sauce or Salad Dressing

Clarified Butter

Crab Butter

Crawfish Butter

Maître d'Hôtel Butter

Champagne Butter Sauce

Crab Butter Sauce

Lemon Butter Sauce

Roasted-Tomato Butter Sauce

Seafood Cocktail Sauce

Hollandaise Sauce

Basic Mayonnaise & Lemon Mayonnaise

Meunière Sauce

Hot-Pepper-Jelly Sauce

Ravigote Sauce

Rémoulade Sauce

Seafood-Marinara Base Sauce

Lemon-Thyme Tartar Sauce

Spicy Vinaigrette

Basic Aioli and Variations

For a scant 1½ cups

Garlic is a defining ingredient in aioli, the bracing mayonnaise from the south of France.

This basic aioli can be used on its own as a mayonnaise or dip, or with a variety of seafood and meat dishes. Included with the basic recipe below are three variations—one with Creole mustard, another with extra pepper and a third with a pleasantly tart lemon flavor.

1	large egg
2	teaspoons minced fresh garlic
2	teaspoons fresh lemon juice
½	teaspoon Dijon mustard
1	cup canola oil
½	teaspoon kosher salt, plus to taste
⅛	teaspoon freshly ground black pepper, plus to taste

SPECIAL EQUIPMENT

- An electric blender
- A nonreactive* container

See Using Nonreactive Cookware, page 419.

1. In a blender, combine the egg, garlic, lemon juice and mustard. Pulse about three times to blend well.

2. With the blender's motor still running, very gradually add half of the oil in a thin, steady stream, blending just until all is incorporated and the mixture is the consistency of mayonnaise. Turn off the blender and push the sides down with a rubber spatula.

3. Turn on the blender again and very gradually add the remaining oil, blending just until all is incorporated. Do not over-mix or the oil will separate and rise to the surface. Season with ½ teaspoon kosher salt and ⅛ teaspoon pepper.

4. Before using, refrigerate overnight in a covered, nonreactive container to let the flavors develop, then season with more salt and pepper if desired. Keep refrigerated and use within four days.

VARIATIONS ON BASIC AIOLI

Each yields 1½ cups

Creole-mustard aioli: To a fresh batch of basic aioli add 1½ tablespoons of Creole mustard,* blending just a few seconds until they are well incorporated.

*If this ingredient is difficult to find where you live, see Ingredient Sources on page 424.

Avery Island aioli: When you carry out Step 1 of the basic aioli recipe, also add 2½ tablespoons Crystal pepper sauce (or other mild-flavored Louisiana pepper sauce), 5 quick splashes of Tabasco sauce and a small pinch of ground cayenne.

Lemon aioli: To a fresh batch of basic aioli, mix in 1 firmly-packed tablespoon very finely grated lemon zest and ¼ teaspoon freshly ground black pepper.

Blue Cheese Dipping Sauce
or Salad Dressing

For 1½ cups

This dipping sauce can be used to dress a fried-oyster poor boy sandwich or as a dressing for mixed green salads or sliced, salted and peppered tomatoes. It is also an excellent dip for vegetables or baked snacks.

4	ounces Stilton or other good-quality blue cheese, crumbled
¾	cup mayonnaise, preferably homemade
2	tablespoons buttermilk
2	tablespoons sour cream
1	tablespoon distilled white vinegar
1½	tablespoons vegetable oil
1	tablespoon minced flat-leaf (Italian) parsley leaves
⅛	teaspoon kosher salt
⅛	teaspoon freshly ground black pepper

ADVANCE STEP

If you choose to use a home-made mayonnaise, a recipe for it appears on page 369.

Combine all the ingredients in a medium-size mixing bowl, blending well with a whisk.

Serving Suggestion: Before using the dipping sauce, refrigerate it in a covered container at least four hours or overnight to let the flavors develop, then season with more kosher salt and pepper if desired. Keep refrigerated and use within four days. 🐚

Clarified Butter

For about 1½ cups

Whole butter is a blend of fat, milk solids and water. Clarified butter, also called drawn butter, is simply the butterfat obtained by separating it from the solids and water. This clear golden liquid often performs as a sinfully delicious dip for cooked artichoke leaves, lobster and other shellfish.

Cooks prefer clarified to whole butter for sautéing or pan-frying because it has a higher smoke point, meaning that, at higher temperatures, it doesn't burn as quickly as whole butter does.

Occasionally, both whole and clarified butters are used in the same recipe. Similarly, clarified butter and another fat, such as olive oil, are sometimes used together in a dish.

This recipe can be multiplied or divided.

1 pound unsalted butter

SPECIAL EQUIPMENT
• A heavy-bottomed 2-quart saucepan

1. Heat the butter in a heavy-bottomed 2-quart saucepan over medium-high heat just until melted.

2. Reduce the heat to low and continue cooking about two minutes until a layer of clear golden liquid (which is the clarified butter or butterfat) has developed between the foam on top and the milk solids and milky water that have separated from the butter and sunken to the bottom of the pan.

3. Remove the pan from the heat, and skim and discard the foam on top.

4. Ladle the clarified butter into a clean pan or large glass measuring cup, being careful not to include any of the milk solids and water as you work.

5. Discard the milk solids and water.

Serving Suggestion: Use the clarified butter immediately or let it cool briefly, then store it in an airtight container in the refrigerator for later use. It will last up to one month. 🐚

Crab Butter

For two logs of butter, each a generous 8 ounces

This lemony-colored compound butter is infused with the flavors of crabmeat by slowly steeping fresh "gumbo crabs" in the butter. Crab butter can enhance or enrich the flavor of seafood bisques, soups and sauces, as well as cooked fish.

1¼	pounds fresh (not frozen) raw gumbo crabs*
½	teaspoon sea salt, preferably Hawaiian Alaea Sea Salt**
¼	teaspoon freshly ground white pepper
¼	teaspoon ground turmeric
1½	pounds cold unsalted butter, preferably Plugra or other European-style butter, divided

*Hard-shell crabs that are too scrawny to yield good lump crabmeat and are used to provide crab flavor to gumbos and other preparations.

**If this ingredient is difficult to find where you live, see Ingredient Sources on page 424.

1. Using your hands, break the crabs in pieces as much as possible and transfer the pieces to a heavy 5-quart saucepan. Use a heavy-duty kitchen mallet or heavy-duty potato masher (or other sturdy utensil) to crack all the body and pincer shells as thoroughly as possible on both sides of the crabs.

2. Add to the pan the sea salt, white pepper and turmeric. Cut 1¼ pounds of the butter into rough 1½-inch cubes and scatter the butter cubes over the crabs. Cut the remaining ¼ pound butter in ½-inch cubes, cover and refrigerate until called for in the recipe.

3. Cook the crab-and-butter mixture over the lowest heat possible until the butter reaches 120°F on a candy thermometer and all the crab shells are reddish-orange (indicating that the crabs are cooked through), 25 to 30 minutes. During this cooking time the butter will very slowly melt and steep the crabs as it melts. (This extremely slow process gives the finished butter more crab flavor than if you boil the crab shells in melted butter.)

4. While the crab shells are steeping, stir the mixture every five minutes and occasionally push the shells against the side and bottom of the pan with the back of a sturdy spoon to extract as much fat and flavor from the shells as possible.

5. The butter may separate a little as the crabs steep, which is okay, but don't let the butter completely clarify. If it appears to be clarifying, remove the pan from the heat periodically to let the mixture cool, then return it to the heat so the steeping process can continue. Once the steeping process is completed,

NOTES

Plugra or other European-style unsalted butter makes the best-tasting crab butter. Unlike standard American butter, the European product does not give off water during the steeping stage of this recipe's preparation.

When wrapping the butter for refrigeration, do not use plastic wrap in place of waxed or parchment paper. Plastic wrap produces folds and creases in the soft butter.

SPECIAL EQUIPMENT

- A heavy 5-quart saucepan or Dutch oven
- A heavy-duty kitchen mallet or heavy-duty potato masher (or other sturdy utensil)
- A candy thermometer
- A fine-mesh strainer
- 2 large mixing bowls
- A very-fine mesh strainer (the finer the better) or several thicknesses of cheesecloth
- Waxed or parchment paper

strain the mixture through a fine-mesh strainer placed over a large mixing bowl, pushing the liquid through the strainer with the back of a sturdy spoon.

6. Into another large mixing bowl strain the butter again through a very-fine mesh strainer (the finer the better), or through several layers of cheesecloth, to remove all traces of crab shell from the butter. Cover the crab butter and refrigerate it until stiff but not completely hard, about 4½ hours.

7. If pressed for time, prepare a shallow ice bath in your kitchen sink by dumping two trays of ice cubes into the stoppered sink and run enough cool tap water into it to come halfway up the sides of the bowl of strained butter. Place the bowl into the ice bath and stir the butter constantly until it is solid enough to beat with an electric mixer, about five minutes, being careful to not get water into the bowl. Refrigerate the strained butter while the ¼ pound of cubed butter is softening (see Step 8).

8. To finish the crab butter, let the remaining ¼ pound of cubed butter sit at room temperature for 10 minutes to slightly soften. Then, remove the crab butter from the refrigerator and place it in the large bowl of an electric mixer, discarding any water that may have accumulated underneath the butter.

9. Gradually add the ¼ pound butter cubes to the crab butter, 1 or 2 cubes at a time, beating on low speed just until all the butter cubes are almost blended in (there may still be small bits of cubed butter in the mixture), about one to two minutes total. Do not over-beat or, once the butter is re-chilled, it won't solidify properly for making sauces.

10. Cut off two pieces of waxed or parchment paper, each about 9 inches wide and 12½ inches long. Place half the crab butter on each piece of paper about 2 inches from one of the 12½-inch edges. Form each portion of butter into a log about 9 inches long using the paper to help you shape the log. Snugly roll up the logs in the paper and twist the ends of the paper to seal the butter inside.

Serving Suggestion: Place the logs in a self-sealing plastic bag and refrigerate overnight before using. The butter will keep refrigerated for up to five days or frozen for up to three months. 🐚

For two logs of butter, each 7 to 8 ounces

This compound butter is infused with the flavors of crawfish by slowly steeping fresh crawfish in the butter. It is richly flavorful and can be used to enhance many dishes.

1½   pounds live crawfish* (select active crawfish that are the largest and fattiest possible)

3   quarts water

1½   teaspoons kosher salt

1¼   pounds cold unsalted butter (preferably Plugra or other European-style butter), divided

*Select active crawfish that are the largest and fattiest possible. If this ingredient is difficult to find where you live, see Ingredient Sources on page 424.

1. Place the crawfish in a large colander and thoroughly rinse under cool running water to remove all traces of mud or dirt. Drain crawfish and clean the colander.

2. Combine the water and kosher salt in a 6-quart saucepan. Bring the water to a boil over high heat, then add the live crawfish and cook uncovered for two minutes without stirring. Remove the pan from heat and drain the crawfish in the colander.

3. Place the drained crawfish in a heavy 5-quart saucepan. Use a heavy-duty kitchen mallet or heavy-duty potato masher (or other sturdy utensil) to crack all the body and pincer shells as thoroughly as possible on both sides of the crawfish.

4. Cut 1 pound of the cold butter into rough 1-inch cubes and scatter the butter cubes over the crawfish. Cut the remaining ¼ pound butter in half-inch cubes, cover and refrigerate until called for in the recipe.

5. Cook the crawfish-and-butter mixture over the lowest heat possible until all the butter melts, stirring every five minutes. This will take roughly 15 minutes. During this cooking time the butter will very slowly melt and steep the crawfish as it melts. (This extremely slow process gives the finished butter more crawfish flavor than if you boil the crawfish shells in melted butter.)

6. Once all the butter is melted, set heat to low and continue cooking until the butter reaches 120°F on a candy thermometer and all the crawfish shells are reddish-orange (indicating that the crawfish are cooked through), about 30 minutes. While the crawfish shells are steeping, continue to stir the mixture every five minutes and occasionally push the shells against the side and

NOTES

Plugra or other European-style unsalted butter makes the best-tasting crawfish butter. Unlike standard American butter, the European product does not give off water during the steeping stage of this recipe's preparation.

When wrapping the butter for refrigeration, do not use plastic wrap in place of waxed or parchment paper because it produces folds and creases in the soft butter.

SPECIAL EQUIPMENT

- A large colander
- A 6-quart or similar-size saucepan
- A heavy 5-quart saucepan or Dutch oven
- A heavy-duty kitchen mallet or heavy-duty potato masher (or a similar sturdy utensil)
- A candy thermometer
- A fine mesh strainer
- Two large mixing bowls
- Either a very fine mesh strainer (the finer the better) or several layers of cheesecloth
- Waxed or parchment paper

bottom of the pan with the back of a sturdy spoon to extract as much fat and flavor from the shells as possible.

7. The butter may separate a little as the crawfish steep, which is okay, but don't let the butter completely clarify. If it appears to be clarifying, remove the pan from the heat periodically to let the mixture cool, then return it to the heat so the steeping process can continue. Once the steeping process is completed, strain the mixture through a fine-mesh strainer placed over a large mixing bowl, pushing the liquid through the strainer with the back of a sturdy spoon.

8. Now into another large mixing bowl strain the butter again through a very-fine-mesh strainer or through several layers of cheesecloth, to remove all traces of crawfish shell from the butter. Cover the crawfish butter and refrigerate it until stiff but not completely hard, about 4½ hours.

9. If pressed for time, prepare a shallow ice bath in your kitchen sink by dumping two trays of ice cubes into the stoppered sink and run enough cool tap water into it to come halfway up the sides of the bowl of strained butter. Place the bowl into the ice bath and stir the butter constantly until it is solid enough to beat with an electric mixer, about five minutes, being careful to not get water into the bowl. Refrigerate the strained butter while the ¼ pound of cubed butter is softening (see Step 10).

10. To finish the crawfish butter, let the remaining ¼ pound of cubed butter sit at room temperature for 10 minutes to slightly soften. Then, remove the butter from the refrigerator and place it in the large bowl of an electric mixer, discarding any water that may have accumulated underneath it.

11. Gradually add the ¼-pound butter cubes to the crawfish butter, one or two cubes at a time, beating on low speed just until all the butter cubes are almost blended in (there may still be small bits of cubed butter in the mixture), about one to two minutes total. Do not over-beat or, once the butter is re-chilled, it won't solidify properly for making sauces.

12. Cut off two pieces of waxed or parchment paper, each about 9 inches wide by 12½ inches long. Place half the crawfish butter on each piece of paper about 2 inches from one of the 12½-inch edges. Form each portion of butter into a log about 8 inches long using the paper to help you shape the log. Snugly roll up the logs in the paper and twist the ends of the paper to seal the butter inside.

Serving Suggestion: Place the logs in a self-sealing plastic bag and refrigerate overnight before using. The butter will keep refrigerated for up to five days or frozen for up to three months. ❧

Maître d'Hôtel Butter

For about 9 tablespoons

In its classic French version, *beurre maître d'hôtel* contains simply butter, chopped parsley and lemon juice. But many New Orleans cooks like to add a few personal touches, such as garlic, thyme, shallots and even Herbsaint, the anisette liqueur that originated in the city.

Compound butters can provide a delightful finishing touch to an almost limitless number of dishes, especially grilled fish and poultry, and meats cooked in various ways. They also come in handy for finishing simple sauces and whenever you want to add a little extra flair to vegetables and starches.

Maître d'hôtel butter, like all compound butters, can be shaped into a log and rolled in parchment paper and plastic for storage in the refrigerator or freezer. When needed, it is sliced as you would slice a log of cookie dough.

¼	pound unsalted butter, left at room temperature until very soft
2	tablespoons minced fresh thyme leaves
2	tablespoons minced Italian (flat-leaf) parsley leaves
1	tablespoon freshly squeezed lemon juice
1½	teaspoons minced shallots
1	teaspoon minced garlic
¼	teaspoon kosher salt
⅛	teaspoon freshly ground black pepper

Combine all ingredients together in a medium-size mixing bowl, whisking until well blended.

Serving Suggestion: Use immediately, or roll in waxed or parchment paper into a log that is about 5 inches long and 1¼ inches in diameter, then wrap the log snugly in plastic wrap. The butter will keep in the refrigerator for up to two weeks, or frozen for up to two months. ✦

Champagne Butter Sauce

For about 3¼ cups

This sauce would be a wonderful match for many a seafood dish. Try it with steamed asparagus or other simply prepared vegetables, as well.

½	cup plus 1 tablespoon good-quality champagne
3	tablespoons rice vinegar
3	tablespoons minced shallots
3	tablespoons heavy cream
1½	pounds cold unsalted butter, cut into about 36 pats, at room temperature

1. In a heavy, nonreactive 2-quart saucepan, combine the champagne, vinegar, and shallots. Cook over medium-high heat until the liquid in the mixture reduces to 1 to 2 tablespoons, about six minutes.

2. Add the cream and cook until the liquid in the pan reduces to 1 to 2 tablespoons, about two minutes. (The sauce may be prepared to this point up to 45 minutes ahead and left at room temperature. Reheat the cream mixture briefly over medium heat, whisking constantly, before proceeding to Step 3.)

3. Reduce the heat to medium-low and cook as you add 2 pats of butter at a time, whisking constantly, until all the butter is added and incorporated into the sauce; each addition of butter should be almost completely melted in before adding more. This will take roughly 10 to 15 minutes total. Remove from heat.

4. If serving the sauce immediately, strain it through a fine-mesh strainer into a medium-size saucepan. If not serving promptly, strain the sauce into the top of a double boiler and serve as soon as possible and definitely within one hour, keeping the sauce warm, uncovered, over hot (not simmering) water. ❧

NOTE

If using an electric stove top to prepare this recipe, please see recommendations on page 418.

SPECIAL EQUIPMENT

- A heavy, nonreactive* 2-quart saucepan
- A fine-mesh strainer
- A double boiler, if preparing ahead

*See Using Nonreactive Cookware, page 419.

Crab Butter Sauce

For 1⅔ cups

This versatile sauce, created for pompano en papillote, is also wonderful with virtually all other fish preparations—baked, sautéed, fried or grilled.

¼   cup good-quality dry white wine
¼   cup heavy cream
6   ounces cold crab butter, cut into 6 pats
3   ounces cold unsalted butter, preferably Plugra or other European-style butter, cut into 6 pats
½   teaspoon salt, kosher salt preferred
⅛   teaspoon freshly ground black pepper
3   to 4 ounces jumbo lump crabmeat, picked through, optional

NOTES

If using an electric stove top to prepare this recipe, please see recommendations on page 418.

If using this sauce for the pompano en papillotes recipe on page 176, do include the lump crabmeat in the sauce if at all possible.

ADVANCE STEP

Prepare the crab butter recipe on page 356.

SPECIAL EQUIPMENT

• A heavy, nonreactive* 2-quart saucepan
• If preparing the recipe ahead, a double boiler

*See Using Nonreactive Cookware, page 419.

1. Place the wine in a heavy, nonreactive 2-quart saucepan and cook over medium-high heat until the wine reduces to 2 tablespoons, about three minutes. Whisk in the cream and bring to a boil, then let the mixture boil for one minute. (The sauce may be prepared to this point up to 45 minutes ahead and left at room temperature. Reheat the cream mixture briefly over medium heat, whisking constantly, before proceeding to Step 2.)

2. Reduce the heat to medium-low and cook as you add 1 pat of each type of butter at a time, whisking constantly, until all the butter is added and incorporated into the sauce; each addition of butter should be almost completely melted in before adding more. This will take roughly 10 to 15 minutes total.

3. Add the kosher salt and pepper and continue cooking until the sauce is emulsified, about one minute more, whisking constantly. Remove from heat.

Serving Suggestions: The sauce is at its best when it's served immediately. If this is not practical, transfer it to a double boiler and keep it warm, uncovered, over hot (not simmering) water for no longer than an hour before serving.

If you are using the optional crabmeat, add it to the sauce just before serving, or garnish the sauce with the crabmeat once the sauce has been spooned onto the serving plates. ❀

Lemon Butter Sauce

For about 1¾ cups

This lemon butter sauce is excellent as a simple sauce spooned onto simply prepared fish and shellfish.

1½	cups good-quality dry white wine
½	cup fresh lemon juice
½	teaspoon minced or very finely grated lemon zest
1	teaspoon apple-cider vinegar
1	teaspoon minced shallots
1	teaspoon minced garlic
1	teaspoon, packed, minced fresh thyme leaves
2	tablespoons heavy cream
⅞	pound (3½ sticks) cold unsalted butter, cut into about 20 pats
1	teaspoon kosher salt, or to taste
¼	teaspoon freshly ground black pepper, or to taste

NOTES

If using an electric stove top to prepare this recipe, please see recommendations on page 418.

SPECIAL EQUIPMENT

- A heavy, nonreactive* 3-quart saucepan
- A fine-mesh strainer
- A double boiler, if preparing ahead

*See Using Nonreactive Cookware, page 419.

1. In a heavy, nonreactive 3-quart saucepan, combine the wine, lemon juice and zest, vinegar, shallots, garlic, and thyme. Cook over medium-high heat until the liquid in the mixture reduces to 1 to 2 tablespoons, about five minutes.

2. Add the cream and cook until the liquid in the pan reduces to 1 to 2 tablespoons, about four minutes. (The sauce may be prepared to this point up to 45 minutes ahead and left at room temperature. Reheat the cream mixture briefly over medium heat, whisking constantly, before proceeding to Step 3.)

3. Reduce the heat to medium-low and cook as you add 2 pats of butter at a time, whisking constantly, until all the butter is added and incorporated into the sauce; each addition of butter should be almost completely melted in before adding more. This will take roughly 10 to 15 minutes total. Remove from heat.

4. Whisk in the kosher salt and pepper.

5. If serving the sauce immediately, strain through a fine-mesh strainer into a small saucepan. If not serving promptly, strain the sauce into the top of a double boiler and serve as soon as possible and definitely within one hour, keeping the sauce warm, uncovered, over hot (not simmering) water. 🐚

Roasted-Tomato Butter Sauce

For 4 cups

Roasting the tomatoes deliciously enhances the flavor of this butter sauce, which is excellent with mussels and other seafood, and all types of pasta.

TO PREPARE THE TOMATOES

2   pounds (about 6 medium-size), very ripe Creole* tomatoes

*South Louisiana's Creole tomatoes are preferred for this recipe, although other good, peak-of-season regional varieties can be used also.

1.   Preheat the oven to 350°F.

2.   Rinse the tomatoes and roast them in the oven on a rimmed baking sheet, core side down, until the skin starts to separate from the tomato pulp but hasn't yet burst open, 20 to 25 minutes.

3.   Remove the tomatoes from the oven and set aside until cool enough to handle.

4.   Peel and core the tomatoes, holding them over a bowl to catch the juice. Chop the pulp and add it to the juice. If prepared ahead, refrigerate in a covered container.

NOTE

The tomatoes may be roasted and chopped a day ahead, but the sauce should be prepared no more than two hours ahead or it may separate.

TO PREPARE THE BUTTER SAUCE

1   tablespoon olive oil
3   tablespoons minced shallots
¼   cup good-quality sweet vermouth
1   tablespoon rice vinegar
2   tablespoons heavy cream
1   pound cold unsalted butter, cut into about 16 pats, at room temperature
1   teaspoon kosher salt, or to taste
½   teaspoon freshly ground black pepper, or to taste

1.   In a heavy, nonreactive 5½-quart saucepan, heat the olive oil over high heat until hot, about two minutes. Add the shallots and cook until soft, about three minutes, stirring occasionally.

2.   Add the vermouth and vinegar and cook until the liquid in the mixture reduces by half, one to two minutes.

3.   Add the cream, then drain the tomatoes and add them to the pan, mixing well.

NOTE

If using an electric stove top to prepare this recipe, please see recommendations on page 418.

SPECIAL EQUIPMENT

• A heavy, nonreactive* 5½-quart saucepan
• A double boiler, if preparing the sauce ahead

*See Using Nonreactive Cookware, page 419.

4. Reduce the heat to maintain a simmer and cook until the mixture reduces by about half and is fairly thick, eight to 10 minutes, stirring occasionally. (The time will vary according to how juicy the tomatoes are.)

5. Add the butter cubes one at a time, constantly whisking until all of the butter is incorporated into the sauce. Each addition of butter should be almost completely melted in before adding more. This will take 10 to 15 minutes total. Remove from heat and whisk in the kosher salt and pepper.

    Serving Suggestion: If not serving the sauce immediately, transfer it to the top of a double boiler, and serve as soon as possible (definitely within two hours), keeping the sauce warm, uncovered, over hot (not simmering) water. 🐚

Seafood Cocktail Sauce

For a generous 1 cup

A cold, ketchup-based cocktail sauce is probably the all-time favorite dip for cold seafood—especially boiled shrimp or crawfish and raw oysters or clams. A bit of Louisiana-made pepper sauce gives this one some extra Creole zip.

1 tablespoon prepared horseradish, plus a little for garnish
1 cup ketchup
1 tablespoon fresh lemon juice
1 teaspoon mild Louisiana pepper sauce, such as Crystal brand
½ teaspoon worcestershire sauce
   pinch of kosher salt
   pinch of freshly ground black pepper

1. In a nonreactive, medium-size mixing bowl, thoroughly blend together 1 tablespoon of the horseradish with all the other sauce ingredients.

2. The sauce may be served immediately, but it reaches its peak of flavor after being chilled in an airtight, nonreactive container for one or two days before it is used. It will last several days in the refrigerator.

Serving Suggestion: Just before serving the sauce, adjust the seasonings to your taste and garnish the center of the serving bowl with a little prepared horseradish.

NOTE

This sauce is especially good a day or so after it is made, when the flavors have married.

SPECIAL EQUIPMENT

- A nonreactive,* medium-size mixing bowl
- A nonreactive container for refrigerator storage

*See Using Nonreactive Cookware, page 419.

For 1½ cups

In classical French cookery, hollandaise is considered one of the "mother sauces." That is, it serves as the base for such other sauces as béarnaise, flavored with tarragon, shallots and wine; choron, with tomatoes added, and Nantua, flavored with crawfish essence. All of these are also found in the catalog of New Orleans' classical Creole cuisine.

Hollandaise is best known as a component of eggs Benedict. But its buttery, eggy character makes hollandaise compatible with not only fish and eggs, but also meat and even vegetables, especially asparagus and broccoli.

The sauce is difficult to make on the first try, since it requires a delicate fusion of egg yolks, butter and lemon juice. But every ounce of effort is worth the rich and delicious taste.

1½	cups clarified butter
½	cup good-quality chardonnay (preferred) or other relatively dry white wine
3	tablespoons fresh lemon juice, divided
1	tablespoon apple-cider vinegar
1	teaspoon minced shallots
⅛	teaspoon (rounded) freshly ground black pepper
4	yolks from large eggs
1	tablespoon plus 1½ teaspoons hot tap water, divided, if needed to thin sauce
¼	teaspoon Tabasco sauce
½	teaspoon kosher salt, or to taste

NOTE

The sauce should be prepared at the last moment and served as quickly as possible.

ADVANCE STEP

Prepare the clarified butter recipe on page 355.

SPECIAL EQUIPMENT

- A heavy 2-quart saucepan
- A deep-fry thermometer
- A heavy 4-quart saucepan
- A medium-size stainless-steel mixing bowl

1. In a heavy 2-quart saucepan, heat the clarified butter over low heat until it reaches 140°F on a deep-fry thermometer, about two minutes. Heating to 140° will make it less likely that the finished sauce will separate. Set aside.

2. In a heavy 4-quart saucepan, combine the wine, 1 tablespoon lemon juice, vinegar, shallots, and pepper. Cook over medium-high heat until the mixture reduces by half, five to seven minutes. Remove from heat.

3. In a medium-sized stainless steel mixing bowl placed over a pan of barely simmering (not boiling) water, heat the egg yolks for 15 seconds, whisking vigorously all the while and making sure the bowl never touches the simmering water.

4. Add the wine reduction to the yolks. Cook, whisking vigorously and constantly, until the sauce is pale yellow and the consistency of thick cream, four to six minutes. Every few seconds remove the bowl from over the pan to let the steam escape so the yolks don't start to curdle. Remove from heat.

5. Recheck the temperature of the clarified butter to make sure it is 140°. If necessary, reheat it a few seconds to return it to 140°.

6. Off the heat, very gradually add the butter to the yolk mixture, drop by drop at first, while you energetically whisk the mixture. Make sure each addition of butter is completely incorporated before adding more; if the sauce starts thickening to a pudding consistency before all the butter has been added, immediately stop adding butter and whisk in 2 tablespoons lemon juice, then if the sauce is still not thin enough, whisk in 1 teaspoon hot tap water before resuming slowly adding the remaining butter.

7. Once all the butter is incorporated into the sauce, whisk in the 2 tablespoons lemon juice (if not already added to thin the sauce), the Tabasco, and ½ teaspoon kosher salt or to taste. If the sauce still needs thinning, whisk in up to 1 tablespoon plus ½ teaspoon additional hot tap water.

Serving Suggestion: Serve immediately or within about 30 minutes, keeping the sauce off of direct heat, uncovered, on a warm stovetop with a folded dish towel between the bowl and the stove.

RESCUING A "CURDLED" HOLLANDAISE

Hollandaise tends to separate or "curdle" if overheated. Preventing this requires low heat, close attention and constant stirring.

If butter is added too quickly or is too hot, the albumen in the egg will harden, shrink and separate from the liquid. If the hollandaise sauce looks like scrambled eggs, it cannot be saved. However, if the sauce has just separated, or "curdled," pour it from the double boiler into a clean-as-possible mixing bowl. Drop a teaspoon of boiling water into the bowl and gradually whisk little dribbles of curdled sauce into the hot water, letting each addition blend and thicken before adding more.

A precaution: Do not try to store hollandaise sauce, since it is an ideal medium for bacterial growth. Also, refrigeration causes the butter to solidify and separate.

Basic Mayonnaise & Lemon Mayonnaise

For 2 cups

This basic mayonnaise recipe can be used as the foundation for any number of dipping sauces or dressings with the addition of herbs, spices, purées and citrus juices. By simply adding lemon zest to the recipe it is transformed into a deliciously tart lemon mayonnaise, which pairs especially well with seafood, cold meats and boiled or stuffed artichokes, or can be the basis for tartar sauce, such as the lemon-thyme tartar sauce on page 377.

FOR BASIC MAYONNAISE

2   yolks from large eggs
1   tablespoon distilled white vinegar
1   teaspoon dry mustard
2   cups vegetable oil
1   teaspoon fresh lemon juice
¼   teaspoon kosher salt plus to taste
¼   teaspoon freshly ground white pepper

SPECIAL EQUIPMENT

- A large, nonreactive* mixing bowl
- A nonreactive* container for refrigerator storage

*See Using Nonreactive Cookware, page 419.

1.   In a large, nonreactive mixing bowl, combine the egg yolks, vinegar, and dry mustard, whisking about 30 seconds until the mixture becomes slightly foamy and the mustard is thoroughly blended in.

2.   Very gradually add the oil in a thin, steady stream, whisking constantly until all is incorporated and the mayonnaise is thick.

3.   Whisk in the lemon juice, ¼ teaspoon salt and the pepper.

4.   Before using, refrigerate overnight in a covered, nonreactive container to let the flavors develop, then season with more salt if desired. Keep refrigerated and use within four days.

FOR LEMON MAYONNAISE

2   tablespoons minced or very finely grated lemon zest, from about 2 lemons
1   tablespoon cool water

Into a freshly prepared batch of the basic mayonnaise blend the lemon zest and cool water.

Serving Suggestion: Refrigerate overnight before using. 🐚

Meunière Sauce

For ⅔ cup or 6 servings

In some New Orleans restaurants trout meunière is served after the fish is sautéed, or sometimes fried, and this brown sauce is spooned onto it. As given here, the sauce may be used with other fish species, as well as scallops, frog legs and such delicate meats as veal.

⅜   pound (1½ sticks) unsalted butter
1   teaspoon kosher salt
1   teaspoon worcestershire sauce
1   teaspoon red wine vinegar
2   teaspoons fresh lemon juice
1   tablespoon finely chopped Italian (flat-leaf) parsley leaves

1. Over low heat, melt together the butter and kosher salt in a heavy 2½-quart saucepan.

2. Meanwhile, with a metal whisk, combine the worcestershire, vinegar and lemon juice. Set this mixture aside.

3. When the butter is completely melted, increase the heat to medium, and, whisking continuously, cook the butter about five minutes, or until it turns the color of medium-dark chocolate.

4. Promptly reduce the heat to low and very gradually add the worcestershire-vinegar-lemon-juice mixture, whisking constantly, until all ingredients are incorporated and the foaming has almost stopped (this will take about one minute). Remove the saucepan from the heat and whisk about 30 seconds more. Set the sauce aside at room temperature while cooking the fish.

5. Just before serving, warm the sauce over medium-low heat, adding the parsley at the last moment. Be sure to restir the warmed sauce well—so that equal amounts of the browned particles are in each portion—immediately before spooning it onto whatever dish you're serving. ❧

NOTES

By very slowly adding the worcestershire, vinegar and lemon juice to the melted butter you'll be able to taste the essence of these three ingredients in the finished sauce.

The sauce may be served immediately after cooking or refrigerated one day ahead and reheated just before serving.

SPECIAL EQUIPMENT

• A heavy, 2½-quart saucepan is ideal for preparing this sauce.
• A metal whisk

Hot-Pepper-Jelly Sauce

For 1 cup

This tangy sauce is quite versatile. It performs very nicely as a garnish with fried seafoods, and also can be a flavorful component of coleslaw.

½ cup apple juice
½ cup sugar
½ cup apple cider vinegar
½ cup plus 2 tablespoons minced red sweet peppers
¼ cup plus 2 tablespoons minced yellow sweet peppers
1 tablespoon minced fresh jalapeño peppers, or to taste
2 teaspoons cornstarch
2 teaspoons cool water

NOTE

The sauce may be made up to three days ahead.

SPECIAL EQUIPMENT

• A heavy, 1-quart nonreactive* saucepan

*See Using Nonreactive Cookware, page 419.

1. In a heavy, 1-quart nonreactive saucepan combine the apple juice, sugar and vinegar. Cook over medium heat until the sugar is dissolved, about two minutes, stirring constantly.

2. Add the sweet and jalapeño peppers and bring to a boil over high heat. Reduce the heat and simmer for 10 minutes, stirring occasionally and skimming any foam that develops on the surface.

3. Once the mixture has simmered just short of 10 minutes, stir together the cornstarch and cool water to make a thin paste and use a metal whisk to whisk the paste into the sauce. Continue simmering until the sauce is noticeably thicker, about five minutes more, skimming if more foam develops.

Serving Suggestions: Remove the sauce from the heat and let it sit at room temperature for 30 minutes before serving. (The sauce will thicken more as it cools but will still be thin enough to pour.) Or, if made ahead, let the sauce cool then refrigerate in a covered container. Let it sit again at room temperature for about 30 minutes before serving. 🐚

For 1½ cups, or 2⅓ cups with optional crabmeat

The variations on vinaigrettes and mayonnaises are virtually endless, but few cold dressings can match a well composed ravigote sauce.

The tartness of the ravigote sauces in classical French cuisine came from such ingredients as shallots, onion, capers, gherkins and tarragon. Their bases have included white wine, cream and veloutés.

In composition and flavor, New Orleans' French-Creole ravigote sauce lies somewhere between France's rémoulade and our familiar American-style tartar sauce. Traditionally it has been used with cold seafood, particularly crab and shrimp, and sometimes with fried fish or shellfish.

This ravigote recipe gets its vigor from such ingredients as peppers, lemon and horseradish, and its richness from mayonnaise and hard-boiled egg.

1	teaspoon dry mustard
1	tablespoon fresh lemon juice
1	cup mayonnaise
¼	cup red sweet peppers, minced
¼	cup green sweet peppers or Anaheim peppers, minced
1½	tablespoons small capers, drained and chopped
1	tablespoon minced Italian (flat-leaf) parsley leaves
1	tablespoon Dijon mustard
1	teaspoon prepared horseradish
½	teaspoon freshly ground black pepper
½	teaspoon dried tarragon leaves, or 1 teaspoon minced fresh tarragon leaves
1	teaspoon Louisiana pepper sauce
1	large egg, hard-boiled and finely chopped
½	cup lump crabmeat, picked through, optional

NOTES

If the ravigote is to be used with the crab cakes recipe on page 56 or the recipe for fried green tomatoes on page 63, the sauce's ingredients should include the lump crabmeat.

The ravigote sauce will keep for up to two days refrigerated in an airtight container.

ADVANCE STEP

If a homemade mayonnaise is preferred, see the recipe on page 369.

SPECIAL EQUIPMENT

• A medium-size, nonreactive* mixing bowl

• A nonreactive* covered container, if made ahead

*See Using Nonreactive Cookware, page 419.

1. In a medium-size, nonreactive mixing bowl, dissolve the dry mustard in the lemon juice. Stir in the mayonnaise.

2. Gently fold in the red and green sweet peppers, capers, parsley, mustard, horseradish, black pepper, tarragon, pepper sauce and egg.

    Serving Suggestions: Cover the sauce and refrigerate it—at least one hour or up to four hours—until it is ready to serve, then taste and adjust the seasonings to your liking.

    If you are using crabmeat in the sauce, gently blend it in just before serving, being careful to keep the crab lumps from breaking up too much. ❧

For about 2¼ cups

This versatile cold sauce is a Creole variation on the traditional French rémoulade. The two share a few similarities—especially in the mustard content of the Creole one, which also gets an extra piquancy from cayenne and black pepper.

The rémoulade recipe below also diverts a bit from tradition by calling for Anaheim and sweet peppers, which add a flavor dimension without violating the spirit of Creole tradition.

Rémoulade's most popular companion is boiled shrimp, but the sauce's invigorating tartness makes it a tasty addition to crab and other seafood dishes, cold meats, raw or cooked vegetables, stuffed eggs and salads.

2	tablespoons olive oil
1	medium-to-large red sweet pepper
1	medium-size fresh Anaheim pepper
½	cup minced white or yellow onions
½	cup finely chopped green onions, white and green parts
¼	cup finely chopped celery
¼	cup fresh lemon juice
3	tablespoons finely chopped Italian (flat-leaf) parsley leaves
3	tablespoons Creole mustard*
3	tablespoons tomato ketchup
2	tablespoons prepared horseradish
2	teaspoons minced fresh garlic
1	teaspoon kosher salt
¼	teaspoon ground cayenne
⅛	teaspoon freshly ground black pepper
¾	cup vegetable oil

*Any good-quality, whole-grain mustard may be substituted for the Creole mustard. For retail sources of Creole mustard, see Ingredient Sources on page 424.

1. Preheat the oven to 475°F.

2. Lightly grease a small rimmed cookie sheet with some of the olive oil.

3. Coat the whole sweet pepper and Anaheim pepper with the rest of the olive oil.

4. Place the peppers on the cookie sheet. Roast them uncovered in the oven until the skins start to blister and blacken, about 15 minutes, turning them at least once. Remove the peppers from the oven and place them in a small heat-proof bowl. Promptly cover the bowl with plastic wrap and let sit 10 minutes. (This step will help to separate the skins from the peppers so they'll be easier to peel.)

NOTES

The sauce can be made up to two days ahead. If you make it on the day it's to be served, you also can get a head start by roasting and peeling the Anaheim and sweet peppers in advance, following steps 1 through 6.

While the peppers are roasted with olive oil, the base of the sauce is vegetable oil, a milder-flavored oil that allows the tastes of the seasonings to come through.

SPECIAL EQUIPMENT

• A food processor
• A nonreactive* container, if prepared ahead

*See Using Nonreactive Cookware, page 419.

5.   Peel the peppers, remove the veins and seeds, and chop coarse.

6.   Place the chopped peppers and all the other ingredients except the vegetable oil in a food processor and purée for 30 seconds.

7.   With the food processor still running, slowly drizzle the vegetable oil into the sauce.

8.   Taste and adjust the seasonings.

Serving Suggestion: Serve the sauce immediately, or refrigerate it in an airtight nonreactive container for up to two days.

Seafood-Marinara Base Sauce

For about 4½ cups

The shrimp bolognese recipe on page 216 uses 3½ cups of this seafood-marinara base sauce. If you're using all or a portion of this base sauce in a dish other than shrimp bolognese, simply "finish" it by adding salt and pepper to taste. The finished sauce can be used to enhance the flavor of an assortment of other seafood or vegetable dishes, e.g., by pouring it over fish fillets before baking them, using it in an eggplant parmesan-type dish, or spooning it over your favorite pasta.

1 pound lobster* heads, tails and shells from raw lobsters, rinsed
8 ounces shrimp heads (if available) and shells from raw shrimp, rinsed
1 dozen raw mussels in their shells, rinsed
1 large onion, peeled and coarsely chopped
3 celery stalks, sliced into ½-inch pieces
1 carrot, peeled and sliced into ½-inch rounds
3 whole garlic cloves, peeled
1 teaspoon dried oregano leaves
2 cups good-quality, relatively dry white wine, preferably chardonnay
2 cans (28 ounces each) whole plum tomatoes, with liquid
3 tablespoons cornstarch
3 tablespoons water
   kosher salt and freshly ground black pepper to taste (only if you are using the sauce for a dish other than shrimp bolognese)

*If lobster in any form is not available, use a total of 12 ounces shrimp shells and 16 mussels.

NOTES

If possible, the base sauce should be made a day or two ahead so the flavors have time to develop richness.

When choosing mussels, look for those with closed shells to make sure they are alive.

SPECIAL EQUIPMENT

• A heavy, nonreactive* 10-quart soup or stockpot
• A large wooden spoon
• A large strainer (the finer the mesh the better) or a strainer lined with several layers of cheesecloth
• A heavy, nonreactive* 2-quart saucepan
• A nonreactive* container

*See Using Nonreactive Cookware, page 419.

1. In a heavy, nonreactive 10-quart soup or stockpot, combine the lobster heads, tails and shells, the shrimp heads and shells, and the mussels. Add the onions, celery, carrots, garlic, oregano and wine. Bring the liquid to a boil over medium-high heat, while using a large wooden spoon to lightly crush all the shells. This will take about four minutes.

2. Reduce the heat and simmer until the liquid reduces by half, about eight minutes, stirring occasionally.

3. Add the tomatoes and their liquid, stirring thoroughly with the wooden spoon and crushing the tomatoes and other ingredients in the pan as much as possible.

4. Bring the liquid to a boil over medium-high heat. Reduce the heat and gently simmer for 45 minutes, stirring occasionally. Remove from heat.

5. Strain the sauce through a large, fine-mesh strainer or several layers of cheese-cloth placed in the strainer, into a large mixing bowl, using the bottom of a sturdy spoon to force as much liquid through as possible.

6. Transfer the strained sauce to a heavy, nonreactive 2-quart saucepan and bring to a simmer over high heat, stirring occasionally. Meanwhile, stir together the cornstarch and the 3 tablespoons water until the mixture is a smooth, thin paste.

7. Gradually add the cornstarch paste to the simmering sauce, whisking constantly.

8. Return the sauce to a simmer and continue simmering until the sauce coats the back of the wooden spoon, about 10 minutes.

9. Strain the sauce again as you did in Step 5 above, and let it cool.

   Serving Suggestion: Refrigerate in a covered, nonreactive container for one to two days before using.

Lemon-Thyme Tartar Sauce

For about 2¼ cups

This slightly pungent tartar sauce is a fine accompaniment to fried seafood.

1½ cups freshly prepared lemon mayonnaise
½ cup very finely chopped dill pickles
¼ cup finely sliced green onions, mostly green parts
2 tablespoons fresh lemon juice
1½ teaspoons very finely grated fresh lemon zest
1 tablespoon plus 1 teaspoon minced fresh thyme leaves
1 tablespoon minced fresh Italian (flat-leaf) parsley leaves
1 tablespoon capers, rinsed and chopped very fine
¼ teaspoon kosher salt, plus to taste
¼ teaspoon Tabasco sauce, or other relatively hot Louisiana pepper sauce
⅛ teaspoon freshly ground black pepper, plus to taste

ADVANCE STEP

Prepare the recipe for lemon mayonnaise on page 369.

SPECIAL EQUIPMENT

• A medium-size, nonreactive* mixing bowl

• A nonreactive* container

*See Using Nonreactive Cookware, page 419.

1. Thoroughly combine all the tartar sauce ingredients in a medium-size, nonreactive mixing bowl.

2. Before using, refrigerate overnight in a covered, nonreactive container to allow time for the flavors to bloom, then season with more kosher salt and pepper if needed. The sauce will keep refrigerated for up to four days.

Spicy Vinaigrette

For 2 cups

The versatility of vinaigrette goes far beyond its compatibility with green salads. This one can serve as a marinade for fresh crab claws, boiled shrimp and for fish or other seafood that are to be grilled. It would also be a bracing dressing for potato salad or a cold pasta salad.

¼ cup minced red onions
¼ cup very finely chopped red sweet peppers
¼ cup very finely chopped green sweet peppers
2 tablespoons minced fresh garlic
2 teaspoons kosher salt
2 teaspoons freshly ground black pepper
1½ teaspoons crushed red peppers
1 teaspoon dried basil leaves
1 teaspoon dried oregano leaves
1 teaspoon dried thyme leaves
1 cup extra-virgin olive oil
¼ cup red-wine vinegar
2 teaspoons mild-flavored honey, such as clover honey

NOTES

Prepare the vinaigrette at least one day before using to allow the flavors to develop. It may be prepared up to three days in advance.

SPECIAL EQUIPMENT

• A medium-size nonreactive* mixing bowl
• A metal whisk

*See Using Nonreactive Cookware, page 419.

1. In a medium-size, nonreactive mixing bowl, combine all the ingredients, whisking until well blended. Cover and refrigerate overnight.

2. If the oil congeals, return the vinaigrette to room temperature and whisk vigorously immediately before using. ☙

SEASONINGS,
FLOURS
&
BREADCRUMBS

Fresh Soft Breadcrumbs

Pecan Flour

Seasoned Flour

Creole Seasoning

Fresh Soft Breadcrumbs

For about 3 cups

This recipe produces soft and moderately fine breadcrumbs that work well for many of the dishes in this book that require a coating, stuffing or topping.

3 to 3¼ ounces New Orleans-style French bread pieces, slightly dried out but not stale

1. Tear or cut the bread, including the crust, into pieces about a half-inch thick to produce 3 to 3¼ ounces in weight.

2. With the motor of the blender or food processor running, drop the bread pieces in small batches into the feeder for a few seconds, or until the bread is processed into moderately fine crumbs.

3. Empty the container after finishing each batch to avoid packing the crumbs together.

Serving Suggestion: Use at once or store in an airtight container for up to four hours for maximum freshness. 🐚

NOTES

New Orleans-style French bread is best for this recipe. The next-best is a sugarless, natural-yeast white bread with a low gluten content.

The bread should be sufficiently free of moisture to prevent gumminess in the crumbs.

SPECIAL EQUIPMENT

• An electric blender or food processor

Pecan Flour

For 2 cups

This pecan flour gives extra flavor and texture to any sautéed fish or seafood dish that calls for dredging in flour.

1   cup pecan pieces
⅔   cup seasoned flour

1. In a food processor fitted with a steel blade combine the pecan pieces with 3 tablespoons of the seasoned flour. Pulse mixture about 15 seconds until the pecans start to break into smaller bits.

2. Stop the machine, add the remaining flour and pulse about 30 seconds until the mixture is the consistency of coarse meal. Do not over-mix or the pecans will turn into pecan butter.

Serving Suggestion: Use immediately or store in an airtight container at cool room temperature or in the refrigerator for up to one month. 🐚

ADVANCE STEP

Prepare the seasoned flour recipe on page 384.

SPECIAL EQUIPMENT

• An electric food processor

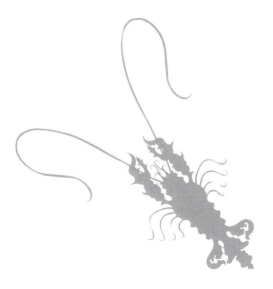

Seasoned Flour

For 1 cup

Seasoned flour is a basic staple in a New Orleans pantry. It is always on hand to coat seafood and meats for frying or sautéing, or boosting the flavor of some savory dish that calls for all-purpose flour.

½ cup all-purpose flour
¼ cup corn flour
1 tablespoon cornstarch
1 tablespoon kosher salt
1 tablespoon sweet paprika
1 teaspoon onion powder
1 teaspoon freshly ground black pepper
½ teaspoon garlic powder
¼ teaspoon ground cayenne pepper

Thoroughly combine all the ingredients in a small mixing bowl.

Serving Suggestion: The seasoned flour can be stored in an airtight container in a refrigerator or other cool, dark place for up to three months.

Creole Seasoning

For a scant 1 cup

This Creole seasoning mix comes in handy when preparing many popular New Orleans-style dishes. The dried herbs and spices composing the blend were chosen for their flavor compatibility with many main ingredients. Many New Orleans home cooks like to sprinkle the seasoning mix on fish, shellfish, meats and even vegetables before cooking, or to add the mix when "sweating" or browning onions and other aromatic vegetables in oil or fat.

½ cup sweet paprika
¼ cup kosher salt
1 tablespoon freshly ground black pepper
1 teaspoon onion powder
1 teaspoon garlic powder
1 teaspoon ground cayenne pepper
1 teaspoon dried thyme leaves
1 teaspoon dried oregano leaves

NOTE

The seasoning mix keeps well if stored in an airtight container in a cool, dark place. You may want to make a batch periodically to always have some on hand.

Thoroughly combine all the ingredients in a small mixing bowl and place the mixture in an airtight container in a cool, dark place for up to three months.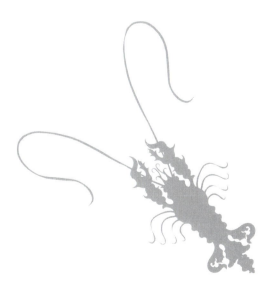

STOCKS

Fish Fumet

Beef Stock

Chicken Stock

Crab Stock

Crawfish Stock

Seafood Stock

Seafood-Mushroom Stock

Shrimp Stock

Vegetable Stock

Fish Fumet

For 4 to 6 quarts

In classical French cooking, this type of light fish stock is called a *fumet de poisson*, or simply a fumet. The French also occasionally use the word *fond* to designate a meat stock, especially if it is a *fond de veau*, made with veal.

<table>
<tr><td>3</td><td>pounds fish bones and/or heads with gills and blood lines removed</td></tr>
<tr><td>8</td><td>quarts cool water, divided</td></tr>
<tr><td>2</td><td>large onions, peeled and coarsely chopped</td></tr>
<tr><td>5</td><td>celery stalks, cut into ½-inch pieces</td></tr>
<tr><td>2</td><td>cups good-quality dry white wine</td></tr>
<tr><td>10</td><td>sprigs Italian (flat-leaf) parsley</td></tr>
<tr><td>5</td><td>whole bay leaves</td></tr>
<tr><td>1</td><td>teaspoon black peppercorns</td></tr>
</table>

1. Place the fish bones and/or heads in an 8-quart stockpot and cover with water. Bring the liquid to a boil.

2. After it reaches a boil remove the liquid from the heat and strain it through a fine-mesh strainer.

3. Discard the liquid. This will rid the fish of impurities and produce a clearer fumet.

4. Wash out the stockpot and return the fish bones to the pot. Add the onions, celery, wine, parsley, bay leaves and peppercorns and cover with 4 quarts of water.

5. Increase the heat level to bring the liquid to a boil. When it begins boiling, lower the heat to a gentle simmer and cook, uncovered, for 30 minutes.

6. A layer of foam and coagulants eventually will appear on top of the liquid. These impurities should be removed with a ladle or large spoon.

7. When the simmer is complete, strain the stock through a fine-mesh strainer.

Serving Suggestion: Use the stock immediately or allow it to cool and store in the refrigerator overnight or in the freezer for up to one month. 🐚

NOTES

When using fish bones or shrimp shells for a stock or fumet, it is imperative that they be absolutely fresh.

Avoid using oily fish, or the bones from large fish.

If the heads are to be used, the gills must be removed and all blood washed away.

SPECIAL EQUIPMENT

- An 8-quart stockpot or Dutch oven
- A large strainer (the finer the mesh the better)

Beef Stock

For 3 quarts

Roasting the beef bones and then browning the vegetables in the fat and drippings produces a rich brown stock, full of intense flavors, that will raise the bar on taste in a variety of soup dishes.

3   pounds beef bones with marrow, such as leg bones or knuckles
2   large onions, peeled and coarsely chopped
2   carrots, coarsely chopped
4   celery stalks, coarsely chopped
2   tablespoons tomato paste
2   cups good-quality dry red wine
10 sprigs Italian (flat-leaf) parsley
5   whole bay leaves
8   quarts cool water, divided

NOTE

Cooking time is approximately six hours.

SPECIAL EQUIPMENT

• An 8-quart stockpot
• A large strainer (the finer the mesh the better)

1.   Preheat the oven to 350°F.

2.   Place the beef bones in a roasting pan in a single layer and roast them until golden brown on all sides, about two hours, turning at least once. Remove them from the oven.

3.   Set the bones aside, reserving the fat and pan drippings, which will be used in the stock.

4.   Transfer the fat and drippings from the roasting pan to an 8-quart stockpot. Place the pot over high heat and add the onions, carrots and celery. Cook the vegetables until they turn golden brown, about 10 minutes, stirring occasionally.

5.   Reduce the heat to medium and stir in the tomato paste. Cook the mixture until the tomato paste turns a dark, rich red, about four minutes, stirring almost constantly.

6.   Stir in the wine and simmer five minutes, stirring and scraping the bottom of the pot until it is clean.

7.   Add the roasted bones, parsley sprigs and bay leaves, and cover with water. Bring the liquid to a boil, then reduce the heat and simmer, uncovered, for six hours. During this time, skim any foam or coagulants from the surface as they develop, and replenish the water as the liquid evaporates.

8.   When the simmer is complete, strain the stock through a fine-mesh strainer.

Serving Suggestion: Use the stock immediately or allow it to cool, and store in the refrigerator overnight or in the freezer for up to one month.

Chicken Stock

For about 3½ quarts

When a recipe calls for a chicken stock, this one should fill the bill. If the recipe produces more stock than you can use immediately, be sure to freeze the excess for future use.

2   tablespoons canola oil
2   onions, peeled and chopped coarse
2   carrots, peeled and cut in ½-inch rounds
4   celery stalks, cut in ½-inch slices
4   pounds chicken backs, wings and/or necks
3   thyme sprigs
5   whole bay leaves
2   cups good-quality dry white wine
    about 3 quarts cool water

1. Heat the oil in an 8-quart stockpot over high heat. Add the onions, carrots and celery and cook until the vegetables turn golden brown, about 10 minutes, stirring occasionally.

2. Add the chicken, thyme and bay leaves. Add the wine and 3 quarts cool water or more if needed to cover the other ingredients.

3. Bring the liquid to a boil, then immediately reduce the heat—do not boil—and slowly simmer, uncovered, for four hours. During this time, skim any foam or coagulants from the surface as they develop, and replenish the water as the liquid evaporates.

4. When the simmer is complete, strain the stock through a fine-mesh strainer.

    Serving Suggestion: Use immediately or let the stock cool down and store it in a covered container in the refrigerator overnight or in the freezer for up to one month. 🐚

Crab Stock

For 3 to 4 quarts

A mild seafood stock with just a touch of tomato paste, this crab stock can be used in a range of recipes.

3   pounds gumbo crabs*
2   tablespoons unsalted butter
2   large onions, peeled and coarsely chopped
3   celery stalks, coarsely chopped
2   carrots, cut into half-inch rounds
2   tablespoons tomato paste
2   cups good-quality dry white wine
4   quarts cool water
5   small whole bay leaves

*Hard-shell crabs that are too scrawny to yield good lump crabmeat and are used to provide crab flavor to gumbos and other preparations.

NOTE

Roasting the crab shells and crushing or breaking them up adds richness to the stock.

SPECIAL EQUIPMENT
- One of the following:
  A metal meat tenderizer
  A kitchen mallet
  A large sturdy mixing spoon
- A heavy, nonreactive* 8-quart stockpot or Dutch oven
- A large strainer (the finer the mesh the better)

*See Using Nonreactive Cookware, page 419.

1. Preheat the oven to 350°F.

2. Place the crab shells in a single layer in a roasting pan, and roast them just until the shells turn bright red, about 30 minutes.

3. After the shells have been allowed to cool slightly, leave them in the pan and, with a meat tenderizer, kitchen mallet or edge of a large sturdy mixing spoon, crush the shells or break them into pieces as much as possible. Set the pan aside with the shell pieces and any pan juices.

4. Melt the butter in a heavy, nonreactive 8-quart stockpot over medium-high heat. Add the onions, celery and carrots and cook until the vegetables turn golden, about 12 minutes, stirring occasionally.

5. Reduce the heat to medium and stir in the tomato paste. Cook the mixture about three minutes, stirring almost constantly. Stir in the wine. Add the crab shells, any pan juices, the cool water and the bay leaves.

6. Bring the liquid to a boil, then reduce the heat and simmer, uncovered, for 45 minutes. During this time, skim any foam or coagulants from the surface as they develop, and replenish the water as the liquid evaporates.

7. When the simmer is complete, strain the stock through a fine-mesh strainer.

Serving Suggestion: Use the stock immediately or allow it to cool down and store it in the refrigerator overnight or in the freezer for up to one month.

Crawfish Stock

For about 9 cups

This recipe begins with a crab stock. Fresh live crawfish are purged and crushed to be added, along with seasonings, to the crab stock. The final product is a full-flavored stock that may be used in virtually any crawfish recipe that includes a stock.

5	tablespoons clarified butter
4	pounds live, purged crawfish (see Advance Steps, right)
10	cups crab stock, divided
1	cup finely chopped onions
1	cup finely chopped green sweet peppers
½	cup finely chopped celery
1	cup chopped Creole* tomatoes
1	tablespoon tomato paste

*South Louisiana's Creole tomatoes are preferred for this recipe, although other good, peak-of-season regional varieties can be used.

ADVANCE STEPS

Prepare the recipes for:

• Clarified butter on page 355
• Crab stock on page 391

Just before preparing the crawfish stock, purge the 4 pounds of live crawfish according to the instructions on page 35.

SPECIAL EQUIPMENT

• A heavy 8-quart saucepan or 8-quart Dutch oven with a lid
• A heavy-duty kitchen mallet or sturdy mixing spoon
• A coarse-mesh strainer or colander
• A sturdy ladle
• A fine-mesh strainer*

*If a fine or very fine strainer is not available, do the last straining through several layers of cheesecloth.

1. In a heavy 8-quart saucepan with a lid, heat the clarified butter over very high heat until very hot, two to three minutes. Slip the purged crawfish carefully into the saucepan, and quickly cover the pan. Reduce heat to high and cook three minutes, then uncover pan.

2. Add 2 cups of the crab stock and cook for about 15 minutes. During this cooking time, and using a heavy-duty kitchen mallet or sturdy mixing spoon, firmly press the utensil down on each crawfish to crush its shell into the smallest bits you can. This will take roughly eight minutes to do and should produce a good, earthy crawfish aroma and a liquid that has a pleasant crawfish flavor, which is essential to ending up with a stock that tastes of crawfish essence. As you are crushing the crawfish, be careful not to slosh the hot liquid in the pan on you.

3. If the liquid in the pan reduces to about ½ cup before the 15 minutes cooking time has elapsed, and if you have crushed the crawfish shells sufficiently, proceed to Step 4. If not, add 1 cup of the remaining 8 cups crab stock to the pan and cook a little longer while crushing the shells more thoroughly.

4. Now add the onions, sweet peppers, celery and tomatoes, stirring thoroughly. Stir in the tomato paste and cook for one minute.

5. Add the remaining 7 or 8 cups crab stock and bring mixture to a boil. Reduce the heat and simmer, uncovered, for 40 minutes.

6. Remove from heat and let the mixture cool about five minutes.

7. Next, strain the stock in batches through a coarse-mesh strainer (or colander) placed over a pan or heat-proof mixing bowl, pressing on the shells and vegetables firmly with the back of a sturdy ladle to extract all liquid possible. Discard the shells and vegetables in the strainer after straining each batch.

8. Next, strain the stock through a fine-mesh strainer (the finer the better) or through several layers of cheesecloth. If needed, strain the stock again to make sure it is completely free of tiny shell particles.

Serving Suggestion: Use the stock immediately or allow it to cool down and store it in the refrigerator overnight or in the freezer for up to one month. 🐚

Seafood Stock

For 6 quarts

This stock is adaptable to virtually any seafood recipe that calls for a stock.

<table>
<tr><td>1½</td><td>pounds fish bones (no heads or tails) from raw flounder, drum or other non-oily, white-fleshed fish</td></tr>
<tr><td>2</td><td>pounds gumbo crabs*</td></tr>
<tr><td>1</td><td>pound raw shrimp shells and cleaned-out heads</td></tr>
<tr><td>2</td><td>medium-size onions, coarsely chopped</td></tr>
<tr><td>4</td><td>celery stalks, coarsely chopped</td></tr>
<tr><td>1</td><td>carrot, peeled and coarsely chopped</td></tr>
<tr><td>6</td><td>Roma tomatoes, coarsely chopped</td></tr>
<tr><td>3</td><td>garlic cloves, minced</td></tr>
<tr><td>12</td><td>sprigs Italian (flat-leaf) parsley</td></tr>
<tr><td>12</td><td>whole black peppercorns</td></tr>
<tr><td>4</td><td>whole bay leaves</td></tr>
<tr><td>1</td><td>tablespoon salt, preferably coarse sea salt</td></tr>
<tr><td>1</td><td>tablespoon dried thyme leaves</td></tr>
<tr><td>8</td><td>quarts cool water</td></tr>
</table>

SPECIAL EQUIPMENT
- A 12-quart stockpot
- A kitchen mallet or a large, sturdy mixing spoon
- A large strainer (the finer the mesh the better)

*Hard-shell crabs that are too scrawny to yield good lump crabmeat and are used to provide crab flavor to gumbos and other preparations.

1. With a coarse vegetable brush under cool running water, scrub the fish bones clean, scrub away the blood lines and place the bones in a 12-quart stockpot.

2. Rinse the crabs under cool running water. Break them in half and use a kitchen mallet or the edge of a large sturdy mixing spoon to break up or crush the shells as much as possible.

3. Add the crab shells, the shrimp shells and the shrimp heads to the pot with the fish bones. Then add the onions, celery, carrots, tomatoes, garlic, parsley, peppercorns, bay leaves, sea salt and thyme.

4. Pour the water into the pot, covering all the ingredients with the water. Over high heat, bring the liquid to a boil. Lower the heat to maintain a gentle simmer and cook, uncovered, for 40 minutes, skimming any foam or coagulants from the surface as they develop, replenishing the water as the liquid evaporates.

5. When the simmer is complete, strain the stock through a fine-mesh strainer.

6. You should end up with about 6 quarts of strained stock. If you have less, make up the difference with water.

Serving Suggestion: Use the stock immediately or allow it to cool down and store in the refrigerator overnight or in the freezer for up to one month. ✿

Seafood-Mushroom Stock

For about 3 quarts

The mushrooms add some mellowness to the flavor of this stock, which functions well in seafood soups, gumbos and bisques.

1½ pounds of shells (and cleaned-out heads if possible) from two or more of the following: raw lobsters, shrimp, "gumbo crabs" and raw cleaned top shells from hard-shelled crabs*

½ pound closed mussels, scrubbed and beards (the hair-like growths on shells) pulled off

½ pound portobello or white button mushrooms with stems, cleaned**

1 large onion, peeled and coarsely chopped

3 celery stalks, leaves discarded, coarsely chopped

1 fennel bulb, quartered, optional

1 tablespoon whole black peppercorns

4 quarts cool water

*Be sure to use at least two kinds of shellfish to make this stock, preferably all three—lobster, shrimp and crabs. "Gumbo crabs" are hard-shell crabs that are too scrawny to yield good lump crabmeat and are used to provide crab flavor to gumbos and other preparations.

** If using portobello mushrooms, scrape away the gills and coarsely chop the mushrooms.

SPECIAL EQUIPMENT
- An 8-quart stockpot or Dutch oven
- A large fine-mesh strainer (the finer the mesh the better)

1. Place all the ingredients for the stock in an 8-quart stockpot. If the shells are not submerged in water, add more water. Bring the liquid to a boil over high heat. Reduce heat and simmer, uncovered, for one hour, skimming any foam or coagulants from the surface as they develop.

2. Remove the stock from heat and let it sit at room temperature, uncovered, an additional one hour to steep.

3. Strain the stock through a fine-mesh strainer.

Serving Suggestion: Use the stock immediately or allow it to cool down and store it in the refrigerator overnight or in the freezer for up to one month. 🐚

Shrimp Stock

For about 1½ quarts

This shrimp stock is another that is versatile enough to use in any seafood recipe that calls for a stock.

½ pound shrimp heads and tails
1 medium-sized onion, peeled and chopped
1 stalk celery, chopped
4 sprigs Italian (flat-leaf) parsley
4 sprigs thyme
4 small whole bay leaves
2½ quarts cool water

SPECIAL EQUIPMENT

- A heavy 5½-quart stockpot or Dutch oven
- A large strainer (the finer the mesh the better)

1. In a heavy 5½-quart stockpot or Dutch oven, combine all the stock ingredients.

2. Bring the liquid to a boil, then reduce the heat and slowly simmer, uncovered, for 90 minutes. During this time, skim any foam or coagulants from the surface as they develop and replenish the water as the liquid evaporates.

3. When the simmer is complete, strain the stock through a very fine mesh strainer.

Serving Suggestion: Use the stock immediately or allow it to cool down and store it in the refrigerator overnight or in the freezer for up to one month. 🐚

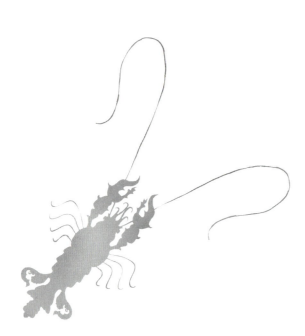

Vegetable Stock

For about 3 quarts

A good vegetable stock is quick and easy to make, and its mild and pleasant flavor makes it a good base for many soups.

This stock also can come in handy when seafood stocks are not available for finfish or shellfish recipes. But a seafood-based stock should always be the first choice when making seafood bisques, soups, gumbos and stews.

4	onions, peeled and coarsely chopped
1	bunch celery, including leaves, coarsely chopped
3	carrots, peeled and coarsely chopped
2	turnips, peeled and chopped
1	cup mushroom stems, cleaned, optional
4	French-type shallots, peeled and chopped
1	cup whole garlic cloves, peeled
3	whole bay leaves
3½	quarts cool water

SPECIAL EQUIPMENT
- An 8-quart stockpot
- A large strainer (the finer the mesh the better)

1. Place all ingredients in an 8-quart stockpot.

2. Over high heat, bring the liquid to a boil, then reduce the heat and simmer, uncovered, for 45 minutes.

3. When the simmer is complete, strain the stock through a fine-mesh strainer.

    Serving Suggestion: Use the stock immediately or allow it to cool down and store it in the refrigerator overnight or in the freezer for up to one month. 🐚

SPIRITS

Sazerac

Ojen Cocktail

Ramos Gin Fizz

Pimm's Cup

Hurricane

Planter's Punch

Milk Punch

Bloody Mary

Brandy Alexander

Mint Julep

Kir Royale

Red Fish Grill Iced Tea

Red Fish Grill Lemonade

Jazz Kitchen Coffee

Irish Coffee

Ralph's Coffee

Café Brûlot Diabolique

Spirits

It should be a given that New Orleans has a very old acquaintance with liquor, in light of its having been the country's favorite party town as long as anybody can remember.

The city's reputation in this regard is underlined by those who contend that the first actual cocktails were created in New Orleans, although their original function may have been more medicinal than recreational. The very word "cocktail" is believed by some to be a derivative of the French word for egg cup, *coquetier* (pronounced as cawk-uh-TYAY). According to these adherents, imbibers in New Orleans during the early 19th century sipped their picker-uppers from coquetiers. (As yet, no one has provided a rationale for anyone choosing to drink from an egg cup rather than a glass.)

What is certain is that New Orleans has produced more than its share of famous cocktails over the last century and a half, the gin fizz, the Sazerac and the hurricane among them. In this chapter you'll find recipes for those and other drinks that enjoy wide popularity in the Crescent City.

New Orleans' proximity to Central America and the Caribbean also made it a place where coffee roasting was a major industry—and drinking coffee a major pastime—beginning in the late 18th century. At the end of this chapter is a recipe for café brûlot *diabolique*, a legendary coffee flamed with brandy and liqueur, brought over from France and drunk by generations of New Orleanians.

Cheers!

Note: Some of these recipes call for **simple syrup**, which is made by dissolving one part superfine white granulated sugar in one part water. One method is to heat the water and sugar. Another is to place the sugar and water in a tightly covered jar or bottle and vigorously shake it for about a minute. The liquid will be cloudy for several minutes. Once the syrup is clear, shake it again for a few seconds.

Sazerac

The Sazerac cocktail was first served in 1859, in a bar and coffee house operated in the French Quarter by one John B. Schiller. The establishment, known as the Sazerac Coffee House, was so named because its owner's sideline was selling a cognac made by a French distiller, Sazerac-de-Forge et Fils.

The first Sazerac cocktail contained two ingredients: brandy and the bitters produced at Antoine Peychaud's apothecary on Royal Street, three blocks from Schiller's bar.

In 1870 one of Schiller's bartenders, Thomas Handy, opened his own establishment in the Quarter and served a variation of the original drink. This new Sazerac was made with bitters, rye whiskey rather than brandy, and the legendary (and notorious) spirit known as absinthe, which was then very much in vogue. Once absinthe became unlawful, it was replaced in the Sazerac by Herbsaint, a locally made anisette liqueur that has survived into the 21st century.

1	teaspoon simple syrup		2	ounces rye whiskey, Old Overholt preferred
3	dashes Angostura bitters		¼	teaspoon Herbsaint* anisette liqueur
6	drops Peychaud's* bitters			a small piece of lemon rind

*If this ingredient is difficult to find where you live, see Ingredient Sources on page 424.

Fill an old fashioned glass with ice and allow to chill. Combine simple syrup, bitters and rye whiskey over ice but do not shake. Dump ice from old fashioned glass and add anisette. Coat the inside of the glass and pour out the excess. Strain in the other ingredients. Twist lemon rind into the glass and then rub rind around the lip of the glass to transfer oils. Do not put the rind into the drink. ❀

Ojen Cocktail

Ojen is a Spanish anisette liqueur that has had a long New Orleans connection. The Ojen cocktail is essentially a frappé that has historically been served at many Carnival balls held during the weeks before Mardi Gras. At one time it was purported to have contained absinthe. The spirit gets its name from the town of Ojen in the Andalusia region of Spain.

1½	ounces Ojen* anisette liqueur		splash of soda, optional
2	dashes Peychaud's* bitters		

*If this ingredient is difficult to find where you live, see Ingredient Sources on page 424.

Pour the ingredients into an old fashioned glass packed with ice. Stir well and serve. ❀

Ramos Gin Fizz

New Orleans bar owner Henry C. Ramos kept the recipe for his gin fizz cocktail a secret from the time he created it in 1888 until the 1920s, when he made the formula public as a protest against Prohibition.

The popularity of the drink reached a peak between 1910 and 1920. During the Mardi Gras seasons of that era, Ramos had as many as 35 employees at The Stag, his bar on Carondelet Street, agitating shakers filled with the cocktail's ingredients.

The ideal gin fizz is silky smooth, with a very delicate floral, spicy flavor.

1	egg white
1½	ounces dry gin
1¼	ounces simple syrup
½	ounce fresh lemon juice
½	ounce cream
2	drops orange flower water*

Combine all ingredients over ice and shake very vigorously for at least one minute. Strain into a highball glass with no ice.

*If this ingredient is difficult to find where you live, see "Cocktail ingredients" in Ingredient Sources on page 424. 🐚

Pimm's Cup

We have James Pimm, owner of a London oyster bar, to thank for the Pimm's Cup. He first concocted it in 1823 with gin, quinine and a number of herbs as an aid to digestion. Until the 1960s there were six different Pimm's Cups, each based with a different spirit. Now, only Pimm's No. 1 Cup, with a gin base, is available year-round.

While the drink is most popular in southern England, New Orleanians adopted it many, many years ago. Served with the traditional cucumber slice, it's the perfect quaff on a hot summer's day.

2	ounces Pimm's No. 1 Cup
1	ounce sour mix
4	ounces ginger ale
	cucumber slice, for garnish

Combine all ingredients with ice, shake vigorously, strain into a highball glass. Fill to top with ginger ale and garnish with a cucumber slice. 🐚

Hurricane

The hurricane is a drink closely identified with New Orleans' fabled Bourbon Street. Its tropical character makes it an excellent cooler.

1½ ounces light rum
1½ ounces dark rum
 2 ounces orange juice
 2 ounces pineapple juice
 ½ ounce fresh lime juice
 ½ ounce grenadine syrup
 1 ounce simple syrup
    maraschino cherry
 ½ orange slice

Combine all ingredients with ice, shake vigorously, and strain into a hurricane glass filled with ice. Garnish with a maraschino cherry and half an orange slice or other fresh fruit.

Planter's Punch

1½ ounces light rum
1½ ounces dark Jamaican rum
 1 ounce fresh-squeezed lime juice
 4 ounces fresh orange juice
 1 teaspoon grenadine syrup
    maraschino cherry
 ½ orange slice

Combine ingredients over ice and shake vigorously. Strain into a tall glass over ice and garnish with a maraschino cherry and half an orange slice or other fresh fruit.

Milk Punch

There must be places where sipping a cocktail at ten in the morning may be a no-no, but New Orleans is not one of them. It is a city where having an "eye opener" just a few hours after sunrise is looked on as a way, on the right occasion, to put oneself in the proper mood for the day.

The more traditional eye openers include Bloody Marys and mimosas. This frothy, nutmeg-topped drink has its own claims to tradition, having been popular among generations of New Orleanians.

In some circles, bourbon is the functioning pick-me-up. Others say brandy, especially a cognac, tempers the drink's sweetness somewhat.

2 ounces milk
2 ounces cream
1½ ounces bourbon whiskey or brandy
1 teaspoon simple syrup
1 teaspoon vanilla
    freshly grated nutmeg, for garnish

Combine all ingredients over ice, shake vigorously. Strain into a wine glass with no ice. Garnish with the nutmeg.

Bloody Mary

For a 1-gallon pitcher of Bloody Mary mix

2 (48-ounce) cans tomato juice
12 ounces Worcestershire sauce
1 teaspoon black pepper
3 teaspoons prepared horseradish
1 teaspoon celery salt
    Tabasco pepper sauce to taste
1 (10-ounce) can beef broth
4 ounces fresh lime juice
    celery sticks, spiced green beans or spiced okra, for garnish, optional

Blend all ingredients and chill until ready to serve. When serving, combine 1½ ounces vodka to 4 ounces Bloody Mary mix in an old-fashioned glass over ice. Stir well and garnish with celery, spiced green beans or spiced okra.

Brandy Alexander

2½ ounces brandy
1½ ounces dark crème de cacao coffee liqueur
1½ ounces half-and-half
    freshly grated nutmeg, for garnish

Combine all ingredients over ice, shake vigorously. Strain into a wine glass with no ice. Garnish with the nutmeg.

A variation on the recipe is to place in a blender 1 scoop of vanilla ice cream and about 1 cup of small ice cubes, along with the ingredients above, and blend until smooth. 🐚

Mint Julep

8 leaves fresh mint
2 ounces simple syrup
    crushed ice
2 ounces Kentucky bourbon whiskey
    mint sprig

In a silver julep cup or highball glass combine 8 leaves fresh mint and 2 ounces simple syrup. Muddle (lightly crush and stir) the leaves and simple syrup, then fill the glass with crushed ice. Add the bourbon and stir the drink until the outside of the glass becomes frosted. Garnish with a sprig of fresh mint. 🐚

Kir Royale

1 ounce crème de cassis liqueur, French brands* preferred
champagne
small piece of lemon rind

*If a French brand is not available, use Chambord black-raspberry liqueur.

Pour the crème de cassis into a champagne flute. Fill the glass with champagne.

Twist the lemon rind and rub the oils over the lip of the glass. Do not put the rind in the glass.

Red Fish Grill Iced Tea

1½ ounces Absolut Raspberry vodka
1 ounce fresh lemon juice
Coca-Cola

Combine vodka and lemon juice in a highball glass filled with ice. Top off with Coca-Cola and stir.

Red Fish Grill Lemonade

1½ ounces citrus rum, Cruzan preferred
¾ ounce Chambord
2 ounces fresh lemon juice
soda
a slice of fresh lemon

Combine ingredients over ice and shake vigorously. Strain into a highball glass over ice. Garnish with a fresh lemon slice and finish with a splash of soda.

Jazz Kitchen Coffee

½ ounce brandy
½ ounce praline liqueur
   freshly brewed coffee
   whipped cream

Combine the brandy and praline liqueur in a thick 10-ounce glass or an Irish coffee mug. Fill to ⅔ with fresh coffee. Spoon in whipped cream.

Irish Coffee

1 ounce Irish whiskey
2 sugar cubes
   freshly brewed coffee
   whipped cream
1 dash green crème de menthe

Place the sugar cubes in a thick 10-ounce glass or Irish coffee mug and pour in the Irish whiskey. Fill to ⅔ with fresh coffee. Spoon in whipped cream and drizzle the cream with crème de menthe for color.

Ralph's Coffee

½ ounce Nocello liqueur
½ ounce Frangelico liqueur
   freshly brewed coffee
   whipped cream

Combine Nocello and Frangelico in a thick 10-ounce glass or an Irish coffee mug. Fill to ⅔ with fresh coffee. Spoon in whipped cream.

Café Brûlot Diabolique

For 10 to 12 servings

If New Orleans' food culture is in a class by itself, it is partly because of the quaint and colorful aspects of the city's gastronomic traditions, some of which go back more than a century.

There is no better example of this than *café brûlot,* a flaming dessert coffee introduced to the city by one or more of the restaurant waiters and cooks who arrived from France during the 1800s in substantial numbers.

Café brûlot (from the French verb *brûler,* "to burn") has a mystique all its own. In a restaurant, preparing it calls for an impressive little ceremony. A waiter stands before a special, large silver bowl that holds coffee, cognac, orange liqueur, clove and cinnamon. With a silver ladle he lifts a bit of the hot alcoholic liquid from the bowl and ignites it, along with long spirals of orange and citrus peel, creating a dazzling dance of blue and red flames. Thus the name *diabolique* ("devilish").

In New Orleans' old-line Creole restaurants, café brûlot diabolique is made with a specially designed bowl and sieved ladle, and is served with unique tall, porcelain pedestal cups.

This recipe can be made with a stainless-steel saucepan on your stove top, and served in demitasses or double espresso cups. If you have a large kitchen, your guests can gather 'round to enjoy seeing you recreate the loveliest of all Creole dining rituals.

1	large lemon, rinsed well and blotted dry
1	medium-size orange, rinsed well and blotted dry
25 to 40	whole cloves
5	ounces by volume (½ cup plus 2 tablespoons) good-quality orange-flavored liqueur, preferably Triple Sec
5	ounces by volume (½ cup plus 2 tablespoons) good-quality brandy, such as cognac or Armagnac
4	cinnamon sticks
2½	cups hot, strong, dark-roast coffee, freshly brewed

1. Using a sharp paring knife, begin by cutting the rind from the lemon in one long spiral about 1 inch wide. Start the cut at the lemon's stem end, first forming a round "hook" at the beginning of the spiral. (Later, you'll hang the lemon rind by the "hook" onto the handle of a metal ladle while the rind is being flamed.)

2. Cut the rind from the orange in the same way, again forming a "hook" at the beginning of the spiral.

3. Now press the pointed ends of the cloves into the outer side of the lemon and orange spirals, spacing the cloves about 1 inch apart. Set the spirals aside.

NOTE

If you have never flamed a dish, you should practice doing it at least once before preparing this recipe.

Before igniting the alcohol, be sure there is nothing on or near the stove that can catch fire.

To prevent being burned, do not ignite the liqueur and brandy that is in the saucepan. Do so only when the liquid is in the ladle, as directed in the recipe.

When igniting the alcohol, keep your face away from the saucepan.

Because the flames from the burning alcohol typically rise at least 2 to 3 feet, this recipe should not be prepared on a stove with a low hood, nor in a kitchen with a ceiling lower than 8 feet from the floor.

4. Combine the liqueur, brandy, and cinnamon sticks in a heavy 2-quart saucepan with high sides. Before continuing with the recipe, check to make sure there is nothing near the alcohol that could catch fire during the flaming process. Keep in mind that the flame may rise 2 feet or more.

5. Bring the mixture to a boil over high heat. This should take about three minutes.

6. Once the mixture has reached a boil, dip the long-handled metal ladle into the brandy and liqueur, filling the ladle about halfway. Lift the ladle out of the saucepan, holding it about 8 inches above the alcohol. Keep your face away from the saucepan and the ladle as you use a long kitchen match or butane gas lighter with a long neck to carefully ignite the alcohol in the ladle. (Do not ignite the liquid in the saucepan.)

7. Immediately pour the flaming liquid from the ladle into the saucepan. The flame should spread atop the liquid.

8. Promptly take the spirals of citrus rind by their "hook" ends and attach them to the lower end of the ladle handle. Within one hand, lift the saucepan an inch or two above the heat source. You'll hold the saucepan there until the flame dies out, which will take roughly three minutes. During this time, use your other hand to continually lift the ladle and spirals out of the flaming liquid and then lower them back into it.

9. Once the flames have died out, reduce the heat to low and release the spirals of rind from the ladle into the pan. Slowly add the coffee to the pan. When the coffee is hot, serve immediately while the pan is still over low heat.

   Serving Suggestion: Ladle the coffee into café brûlot cups or demi-tasse cups, leaving the citrus rinds, cloves and cinnamon sticks behind. Each cup may be sweetened to taste. 🦪

ADVANCE STEP

Have all the ingredients measured out and the special equipment at hand.

SPECIAL EQUIPMENT

- A stainless-steel or other nonreactive,* heavy 2-quart saucepan about 6½ inches in diameter and 4½ inches deep
- A long-handled metal ladle
- A long kitchen match or a butane gas lighter with a long neck
- 10 to 12 café brûlot cups or demitasse cups with a ¼-cup capacity

*See Using Nonreactive Cookware on page 419.

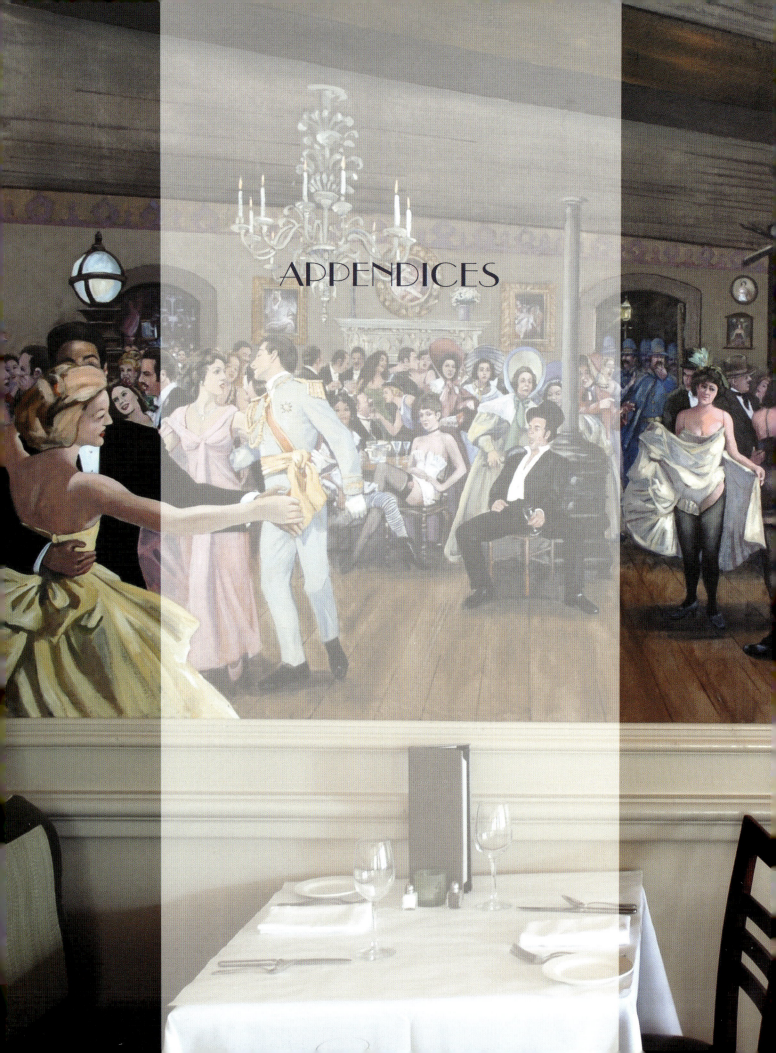

APPENDICES

Tips and Special Instructions

TIPS ON MAKING ROUX

Numerous recipes in this book contain roux, and the instructions for making a specific roux for a specific dish are given in the method sections of those recipes.

Roux is nothing more than a paste made by browning flour in oil or fat. It is used not only to thicken soups, gumbos, stews, sauces and many other savory dishes, but also to enrich and deepen their flavor.

In restaurant kitchens roux is often made over high heat because cooks become expert at making it quickly. Home cooks usually cook it much more slowly, sometimes for an hour or longer, over very low heat. In this book, we've taken the middle ground, recommending that the roux be cooked over moderate heat so the process takes only a few minutes, but gives you time to correct the heat level before the roux has a chance to burn.

You'll find that with just a little practice roux-making is simple. Here are some basics to keep in mind.

1. Remain alert. During and immediately after cooking, roux can be extremely hot. Be careful not to let it splash onto your skin, since it can cause serious burns.

2. The pan and utensils used should be completely dry.

3. The pan should be large enough for vigorous stirring or whisking without causing spills or splashes.

4. Use a long-handled metal whisk or spoon to keep your hands away from the hot roux. Creole and Cajun cooks often prefer a wooden spoon over a metal one.

5. To help avoid burning the roux and to maintain its consistency, use a pan with a heavy base with a bottom and side that curve.

6. No matter what heat level a roux recipe calls for, always feel free to use a lower level from the start or reduce the heat as you're cooking it, especially if you feel like you might be on the verge of burning it. You can also remove the pan completely from the heat and stir it constantly until you feel you have control of it again.

7. If you have little or no experience in making roux you can always make it in advance. Once it comes to cool room temperature, store it in the refrigerator in a closed glass jar. Often some of the oil separates from a roux as it sits. This oil is normally poured off, but it can also be used to sauté vegetables that go into the dish you're preparing.

8. If you see small black particles in the roux, this means it is burnt. It must be discarded and you must start anew. This is why roux must be stirred constantly and why the heat level must be at a low level if you think it may be starting to burn. 🐚

Roux colors referenced in this book, counterclockwise from the bottom:
Blond, Golden, Peanut Butter, Dark Chocolate

MAKING A STOVE-TOP SMOKER

Two recipes in this cookbook are for smoked food, one for scallops and the other for the tomatoes accompanying a dish of oysters and fettuccine. The equipment needed for both recipes is a stove-top smoker.

If you don't have a stove-top smoker, numerous models are available from retailers. Another option is to create a temporary stove-top smoker that can easily be made for the home kitchen with heavy-duty aluminum foil and the right equipment. The process involves placing pieces of food on a rack, elevated above (but not directly over) wood chips, into a sealed roasting pan on the burners of your stove.

You'll need a roasting pan that is 16 inches long, 11 inches wide and about 5 inches deep. You'll also need a rack to hold the food above the smoldering wood chips. The rack can be either the one designed to set into the roasting pan (these racks are often perforated) or a smaller one, such as a cooling rack, that will fit easily into the roasting pan. The instructions are provided below and on the following page.

Three cautionary notes:

- Do not ignite the wood chips at any point. With the stove burner set on high, the chips should eventually begin smoldering on their own.

- Once the smoking process begins, the food on the elevated rack should never be directly above the wood chips but rather to the side of them.

- Very carefully (to avoid burns from the steam) remove the lid or foil and transfer the food to a platter to cool.

1. Before smoking the food, soak 1½ cups of wood chips in water for at least four hours or according to the wood chips' package directions. Drain the chips just before using, leaving them dripping wet. Line the roasting pan's bottom and sides with heavy-duty foil.

2. Cut three more pieces of the foil into rectangles measuring 18 by 22 inches. With your hands gently twist or squeeze each piece of foil into a "rope" about 1 to 2 inches thick and about 18 inches long.

3. Position one of the foil ropes flush against one of the short sides of the roasting pan, bending any excess rope to place it flush against the long side of the pan.

4. Place the second foil rope parallel to the first one and about 4 inches from it, again positioning any excess flush against the long side of the pan. The open space between these two ropes will hold the wood chips.

5. Position the third foil rope flush against the opposite short side of the roasting pan, again bending any excess rope to place it flush against the long sides of the pan.

6. If necessary, adjust the second and third foil ropes so they can elevate and support the rack.

7. Place the wet wood chips in the space between the first two ropes.

8. Place the rack for holding the food atop the second and third foil ropes.

9. If you're using the smoker with a recipe in this cookbook, place the food to be smoked on the food rack on the opposite end from the wood chips and smoke the food as directed in the recipe. The rack may extend above the wood chips, but the food itself should not be placed directly above the wood chips.

10. Completely seal the roasting pan with heavy-duty aluminum foil and smoke the food over high heat. The length of smoking time will depend on the size and density of the food pieces and how intense you want the smoke flavor to be. About five minutes after the chips begin to smoke, taste a piece of the food. This should give you an idea of how much time will be needed to reach the level of smoke flavor you want. 🐚

PREPARING BUTTER SAUCES ON AN ELECTRIC STOVE TOP

When using an electric stove top in preparing butter sauces, the following method is recommended.

1. Prepare the recipe up to the last step before butter is to be added.

2. Remove the saucepan from the burner.

3. At this point, before adding the butter, the electric burner's temperature must be reduced to medium-low. Otherwise, it will be too intense for the sauce to emulsify.

4. Once the electric burner reaches medium-low, return the sauce to the stove and continue cooking as you add 2 pats of butter at a time. Whisk the sauce constantly, until all the butter is incorporated. Each pat of butter should be melted and whisked in before more is added.

5. Once all of the butter has been blended in, remove the sauce from heat and continue as directed in the sauce recipe.

SEASONING A CAST-IRON SKILLET

Cast-iron cookware probably has been around for centuries, and cast-iron skillets are basic equipment in some home kitchens, especially in the southern United States. Fans of cast iron point to its pluses: It's an excellent heat conductor, it heats evenly and consistently, it's inexpensive and, with proper care, it will last a lifetime. It also can be used both on the stove top and in the oven.

When well seasoned, a cast-iron pot or pan will be stick-resistant and require no additional oil. Seasoning is a fairly simple process.

1. First be sure the skillet is clean and completely dry.

2. Dip a folded paper towel in 1 tablespoon of clarified butter and rub the butter into the bottom and sides thoroughly.

3. Add $\frac{1}{3}$ cup of salt, preferably kosher, to the skillet and, with a thick cotton towel, scrub the bottom and sides with the salt.

4. Place the skillet over medium-high heat until it is very hot.

5. Remove the pan from the heat, and let it cool slightly. With the same cotton towel, very carefully wipe the skillet clean, being careful not to burn yourself. Discard the salt.

The skillet is now ready to use.

USING NONREACTIVE COOKWARE

When a recipe contains acidic ingredients, care should be taken to use the right cookware, utensils and storage containers.

Examples of acidic ingredients are tomatoes, vinegar, fruit (especially citrus and grapes) and fermented products such as yogurt. When any of these ingredients are used in a recipe, they should not come in contact with reactive metals.

Reactive metals include aluminum, copper, iron and zinc. They all react chemically with acidic foods, producing a metallic taste and discoloration.

Nonreactive cookware, utensils and storage containers—those which do not affect the taste and color of ingredients—are made of stainless steel, glass, enamel, ceramics, clay and heat-proof plastic. 🐚

A Glossary of Creole and Acadian Food Terms

The following are general definitions of traditional Creole and Acadian (or "Cajun") culinary terms. Some recipes in this cookbook are variations on the more traditional preparations.

Amandine. Loosely translated from the French, the term essentially means "with almonds." In trout amandine the fish is first cooked *à la meunière* (see "Meunière, à la") and then sprinkled with slivers of toasted almonds.

Andouille. A mildly spiced and smoked Acadian sausage of lean pork, it often flavors gumbos, red beans and rice, and jambalayas.

Barbecue shrimp. The shrimp are not barbecued but cooked in their shells. The classic version contains a blend of olive oil, butter or margarine and is usually seasoned with bay leaf, garlic, and other herbs and spices.

Béarnaise. This French sauce of egg yolk and butter with tarragon, shallots, wine, vinegar and seasonings is used on fish and meats.

Beignet. In its most familiar form, a beignet is a rectangular puff of fried dough sprinkled with powdered sugar. The term can also refer to savory fritters or crullers containing seafood or chopped meat.

Bisque. A thick, heartily seasoned soup, bisque is most often made with crawfish, crab or shrimp. Cream appears in the French versions.

Bouillabaisse. A Creole bouillabaisse is a stew of various fish and shellfish in a broth seasoned with saffron and often more assertive spices.

Bread pudding. In the traditional version, stale French bread is soaked in a custard, sometimes combined with raisins, and baked. A frequent addition is a warm, sugary sauce flavored with whiskey or rum.

Cayenne. A bright-red, moderately "hot" pepper that has been used to season a variety of New Orleans-Creole dishes since the 18th century. Cayenne gets its name from a town in French Guiana, on the northern coast of South America.

Court-bouillon *(koo-bee-yawn)*. In Creole parlance, the word designates a classic preparation of fish (especially redfish) baked with tomatoes, peppers and onions. Others know it as an intensely flavored stew of fish and shellfish in a dark, rich and much-reduced broth.

Creole cream cheese. The variety of cream cheese traditionally prepared in South Louisiana. Made from clabbered milk, it has a very soft curd, and by tradition is usually eaten at breakfast with fresh fruit.

Creole mustard. A traditional brown whole-grain mustard that also may contain such other ingredients as horseradish and vinegar.

Dirty rice. This side dish is a cousin of jambalaya (see opposite). The name comes from the tiny bits of meat, especially giblets or sausage, that are cooked with seasonings in white rice.

Dressed. A "dressed" poor boy sandwich usually contains lettuce, tomato and mayonnaise or mustard.

Etouffée. Literally, "smothered," the term is used most often to designate a thick stew of crawfish tails cooked with crawfish liver (better known as "fat"), onions, celery and sweet pepper.

Filé. The Creole word for ground sassafras. The local Indians introduced New Orleans' early settlers to this laurel-like herb. It has since been used as a handy thickener for gumbos as well as a condiment lending a gentle earthiness to a gumbo's flavor.

Gumbo. From *quingombo*, an African word for okra, it can refer to any number of stew-like soups made with seafood or meat and flavored with okra or ground sassafras (filé) and myriad other seasonings. Frequent main ingredients are various combinations of shrimp, oysters, crab, chicken, andouille, duck, turkey and game. A definitive gumbo is served with boiled white rice.

Herbsaint. The brand name of an anise-flavored liqueur that originated in New Orleans. The name (pronounced as "AIRB-sant") was derived from "absinthe," although Herbsaint never contained wormwood, an essential ingredient in true absinthe.

Jambalaya. Rice is the indispensable ingredient in jambalaya. The rice is cooked with meat (especially sausage), and seafood in tomato and other seasonings. Shrimp and ham make frequent appearances in it, as do sausage, sweet pepper and celery.

Maque-choux. The local Indians introduced a version of this side dish to the early settlers of Louisiana. In it, corn kernels are cooked with combinations of onion, sweet peppers and tomatoes, and sometimes bits of salt pork.

Meunière, à la. This French method of preparing fish (and, in Louisiana, soft-shell crabs as well) entails dusting the food with seasoned flour, sautéing it in brown butter, and using the butter with lemon juice as a type of sauce. In some New Orleans versions, a brown sauce is added.

Mirliton. A pale-green member of the squash family, the mirliton is known in Mexico as the *chayote*. In the United States it is often identified as a vegetable pear. The most popular mirliton preparation in New Orleans is to fill hollowed-out halves with the vegetable's pulp, shrimp and seasoned breadcrumbs, and bake them.

Okra. These fuzzy, pale-green pods are use to thicken and flavor gumbos. They are also fried or pickled, or cooked down as a seasoned vegetable with such other additions as tomatoes.

Oysters en brochette. Literally translated from the French, it means oysters "on a skewer." In New Orleans it means whole oysters and bits of bacon dusted with seasoned flour, skewered, and deep-fried. Traditionally, they're served on toast with lemon and brown butter.

Oysters Rockefeller. Baked oysters on the half-shell in a sauce of puréed aromatic greens laced with anise liqueur. Spinach is used in many recipes.

Panéed. A French term meaning coated with breadcrumbs, as "panéed veal," made by dredging veal cutlets in breadcrumbs before they are pan-fried.

Poor boy. A hefty sandwich, the poor boy is made with New Orleans-style French bread and any number of fillings. Roast beef, fried shrimp, oysters, ham and meatballs in tomato sauce are common. A poor boy "dressed" typically is garnished with lettuce, tomato, and mayonnaise or mustard.

Ravigote. In Creole usage, this piquant French mayonnaise usually contains capers and other pungent additions, and in New Orleans is used as a dressing for cold lumps of crabmeat and other shellfish.

Rémoulade. The classic Creole rémoulade is a variation of the French version. It is a brick-red whipped mixture of olive oil with mustard, scallions, cayenne, lemon, paprika and parsley, and is most often served atop cold boiled shrimp or lumps of crabmeat.

Roux. Flour browned in lard or oil to form a thickener, most often for stews, gravies and gumbos. The color can be anything from slightly tan to dark-chocolate. The roux is often flavored with combinations of onions, scallions, celery, parsley, garlic and sweet pepper.

Sauce piquante. The literal translation is "peppery sauce." A hefty dose of cayenne gives the sauce its reddish hue and its peppery kick. Turtle, rabbit and in recent times, alligator, are the most frequent main ingredients.

Sweet potato. A sweet root vegetable with a potato-like skin and a pinkish pulp that becomes a bright orange when baked or fried. It is sometimes mistakenly identified as a yam.

Tasso. Acadian settlers in Louisiana developed the recipe for this lean, intensely seasoned ham. It is used sparingly to flavor sauces and gumbos. 🐚

Seafood and Wine

Recent decades have seen an ever-burgeoning number of wine-savvy Americans. Likewise, the number of different wines available to them is constantly increasing, as wine makers continually come up with new ideas for every step of wine production, and vineyards take root in parts of the world that were previously devoid of viniculture.

For those reasons and others, many of the old rules in the world of wine are constantly being updated. One such is that white wines are drunk with seafood and white meat, while reds are called for when red meat is on the table. There is some logic in that long-held principle: Seafoods are normally lighter than red meat, so they call for lighter wines, and lighter wines tend to be white rather than red. But the choices among light reds have increased dramatically over the years, increasing the chances of their compatibility with chicken and fish.

In the end, who can dictate what constitutes a good seafood-and-wine pairing? If it works for you, it works.

Those looking to tradition for some guidance in choosing the right wine might consider the popular choices in the restaurants of New Orleans from the 1850s to the 1950s, when France and Germany were by far the world's foremost producers. To serve with their elegant French-Creole fish and shellfish dishes, restaurateurs stocked white wines with a certain complexity, and low levels of oak and tannins (the astringent qualities produced by grape skins and seeds). A tinge of sweetness was expected, along with a consistent balance of fruit and acidity.

Also favored were wines big and assertive enough to stand up to robust Creole seasonings, yet not too overpowering in relation to the food's flavors. Then as now, fish and shellfish dishes were paired with wines that have the acidity seafood often needs, which is why a squirt of lemon juice goes so well with many seafoods. (Among the obvious exceptions here would be a dish sauced with an ingredient high in acid, such as tomatoes.)

Long before the wines of California and other regions appeared on the scene, these were the wines often paired with seafood in New Orleans:

- Alsatian Rieslings, the spicier Gewürztraminers and, to a lesser extent, Pinot Blancs
- White burgundies such as Mâconnais, Chablis and Pouilly-Fuissé
- the Bordeaux region's Sauvignon Blancs
- the Loire Valley's Muscadets, Sancerres and Pouilly-Fumés
- the Rieslings and other Kabinetts of the Rhine
- Champagne or other sparkling wines

Today's imbibers are presented with much wider choices. Among the whites widely considered compatible with fish or shellfish are:

- California's and Oregon's Sauvignon Blancs, Chenin Blancs, Pinot Gris, Gewürtztraminers, Sémillons and Chardonnays (many of which are especially suited for buttery sauces)
- France's Marsannes, Viogniers, Muscats and Roussanes
- Austria's Grüner Veltliners

Among red wines, those often recommended for seafood pairings are the light- to medium-bodied ones, such as:

- Pinot Noirs (a favorite red with salmon)
- Gamay Beaujolais (a good choice with simpler shellfish dishes)
- Merlots (the lighter-bodied ones are considered especially good with tuna)
- Zinfandels and Australian Shiraz (especially for spicier seafood preparations)

A note on beer: Your favorite beer—especially if it's one of the lighter ones—should not be ruled out as an accompaniment to the spicier New Orleans-style seafood dishes, especially boiled crawfish, shrimp or crabs, and fried shrimp, soft-shell crab or fish. Once your flavor buds have been hit with hot spices, they require simply flavored brews with low levels of malt and hops. Examples are golden or blond ale, American wheat ale and lightly hopped lagers. 🐚

Ingredient Sources

Note: Telephone numbers beginning with 800, 888, 877 or 866 are toll-free. All others are local.

ANDOUILLE AND TASSO

Chef John Folse and Company. www.jfolse.com. Telephone: (800) 256-2433. (225) 644-6000. 2517 S. Philippe Ave., Gonzales, LA 70737. *Andouille, tasso.*

Chef Paul Prudhomme. www.chefpaul.com. Telephone: (504) 731-3590. *Andouille, tasso.*

Comeaux's. www.comeaux.com. Telephone: (800) 323-2492. 709 Park Way Dr., Breaux Bridge, LA 70517. *Andouille, tasso.*

Creole Country Sausage Factory. Telephone (504) 488-1263. 512 David St., New Orleans, LA 70119. *Andouille, tasso and other South-Louisiana charcuterie.*

Jacob's World Famous Andouille. www.cajunsausage.com. Telephone: (877) 215-7589. (985) 652-9080. 505 West Airline Hwy., LaPlace, LA 70068. *Andouille, tasso.*

Poche's Market. www.pochesmarket.com. Telephone: (800) 376-2437. (337) 332-2108. 3015-A Main Hwy., Breaux Bridge, LA 70517. *Andouille, tasso* (10-pound minimum for either or both).

CANE SYRUP AND CANE VINEGAR

Cajun Grocer. www.cajungrocer.com. Telephone: (888) 272-9347. *Cane syrup.*

Frugé's Cajun Crawfish. www.cajuncrawfish.com. Telephone: (888) 254-8626. Fax (337) 334-8477. P.O. Box 393 Branch, LA 70516. *Cane syrup.*

Steen's Cane Syrup. www.steensyrup.com. Telephone: (800) 725-1654. P.O. Box 339, 119 N. Main St., Abbeville, LA 70510. E-mail: steens@steensyrup.com. *Cane syrup, cane vinegar.* (Other orders taken by telephone. Available online in gift box.)

CHEESE MOLDS

Cheesesupply.com. www.cheesesupply.com. Telephone: (866) 205-6376. CheeseSupply, P.O. Box 31125, Bellingham, WA 98228.

Dairy Connection Inc. www.dairyconnection.com/hobbyiest.html. Telephone: (608) 242-9030, Fax (608) 242-9036. 501 Tasman St., Suite B, Madison, WI 53714. E-mail: getculture@ameritech.net.

COCKTAIL INGREDIENTS

HERBSAINT ANISETTE LIQUEUR

In the New Orleans area, most major wine and spirits retailers sell Herbsaint.

Beverages and More. www.bevmo.com. Also in many California cities.

Internet Wines & Spirits. www.internetwines.com. Telephone: (618) 394-9800. 10800 Lincoln Trail, Fairview Heights, IL 62208.

OJEN ANISETTE LIQUEUR

OJEN ANISETTE LIQUEUR

Martin Wine Cellar. www.martinwine.com. Telephone: (888) 407-7496. (504) 896-7300. 714 Elmeer Ave., Metairie, LA. 70005-2731. The only source of Ojen anisette liqueur in the United States.

ORANGE FLOWER WATER

In the New Orleans area, most major wine and spirits retailers sell orange flower water.

Amazon.com. www.amazon.com. Search "Gourmet Food" section of the Web site for "orange flower water."

The Spice House. www.thespicehouse.com/spices/orange-flower-water. Telephone: (312) 274-0378.

PEYCHAUD'S BITTERS

Amazon.com. www.amazon.com. Search "Gourmet Food" section of the Web site for "Peychauds cocktail bitters."

Sazerac.com. www.sazerac.com/bitters.html Telephone: (504) 831-9450. P.O. Box 52821 New Orleans, LA 70121.

WHITE-PEACH PURÉE

The Perfect Purée of Napa Valley, LLC. www.perfectpuree.com. Telephone: (800) 556-3707. (707) 261-5100. Fax (707) 261-5111. 2700 Napa Valley Corporate Dr., Suite L, Napa, CA 94558. E-mail: info@perfectpuree.com. Processing takes an additional 3 to 4 days. Shipping minimum is three 30-ounce jars.

DURUM FLOUR

The Great Valley Mills. www.greatvalleymills.com. Telephone: (800) 688-6455.

King Arthur Flour Baker's Catalogue. www.kingarthurflour.com. (800) 827-6836. (802) 649-3361. 135 Route 5 S., Norwich, VT 05055.

RENNET

Rennet is available in many cities at specialty food stores, such as Whole Foods Market.

Amazon.com. www.amazon.com. Search "Gourmet Food" section for "rennet."

New England Cheesemaking Supply Co. www.cheesemaking.com. Telephone: (413) 628-3808. Fax (413) 628-4061. P.O. Box 85, Ashfield, MA 01330.

SEAFOOD

Burger's Smokehouse. www.smokehouse.com. Telephone: (800) 345-5185. 32819. Hwy. 87, California, MO 65018. *Frog legs.*

Cajun Grocer. www.cajungrocer.com. Telephone: (888) 272-9347. *Redfish, shrimp, live crabs, lump crabmeat, crab claw meat, live crawfish, frog legs.*

Chef John Folse and Company. www.jfolse.com. Telephone: (800) 256-2433. (225) 644-6000. 2517 S. Philippe Ave., Gonzales, LA 70737. *Oysters, crawfish tails, lump crabmeat, crab claw meat.*

The Crawfish Depot. http://thecrawfishdepot.com. 14854 Hayne Blvd., New Orleans, LA 70128. E-mail: unclebucks@cox.net. *Crawfish tails, live crawfish.*

Exotic Meats USA. www.exoticmeats.com. Texas store: 1003 NE Loop 410, San Antonio, TX 78209. Telephone: (800) 680-4375. (210) 828-6328. Fax (210) 828-6327. Washington State store: 2245 148th Ave NE, Bellevue, WA 98007. Telephone: (800) 680-4375. (425) 641-1069. *Crawfish tails, alligator tail meat, alligator sausage.*

Frugé's Cajun Crawfish. www.cajuncrawfish.com. Telephone: (888) 254-8626. Fax (337) 334-8477. P.O. Box 393, Branch, LA 70516. *Live crawfish, crawfish tails, shrimp.*

Linton's Seafood Inc. www.lintonsseafood.com. Telephone: (877) 546-8667. Fax (410) 968-0199. 4500 Crisfield Hwy., Crisfield, MD 21817. E-mail: marylandseafood@aol.com. *Soft-shell crabs, lump crabmeat, crawfish tails, shrimp, alligator tail meat, frog legs.*

Louisiana Crawfish Co. www.lacrawfish.com. Telephone: (888) 522-7292. (318) 379-0539. 140 Russell Cemetery Rd, Natchitoches, LA 71457. E-mail: jd@lacrawfish.com. *Live crawfish, crawfish tails, shrimp.*

New Orleans Over Night Inc. www.nuawlins.com. Telephone: (800) 682-9546. (504) 243-9500. 14854 Hayne Blvd. New Orleans, LA 70128. *Live crabs, soft-shell crabs, gumbo crabs, crabmeat, live crawfish, crawfish tails, shrimp, oysters, alligator tail meat, turtle meat.*

Quality Seafood Market. www.qualityseafoodmarket.com. Telephone: (512) 454-5828. 5621 Airport Blvd., Austin, TX 78751. *Alligator sausage.*

Tony's Seafood Market. www.tonyseafood.com. Telephone: (800) 356-290. (225) 357-9669. 5215 Plank Rd., Baton Rouge, LA 70805. *Finfish, live crabs, gumbo crabs, soft-shell crabs, crabmeat, oysters, live crawfish, crawfish tails, oysters, shrimp, alligator tail meat, turtle meat.*

Wild Ocean Seafood Market. www.wildoceanmarket.com. Telephone: (866) 945-3623. *Frozen rock shrimp, tail meat or split and cleaned only, no whole rock shrimp.*

Note: In Los Angeles, *The New Orleans Fish Market* offers fresh, seasonal Louisiana seafood, including crawfish and blue crabs. No ordering service is offered. Telephone: (323) 296-3817. 2212 W. Vernon Ave. (corner of Arlington), Los Angeles, CA 90008.

SPICES, CONDIMENTS AND SEASONINGS

Cajun Grocer. www.cajungrocer.com. Telephone: (888) 272-9347. *Filé powder, seafood-boil seasoning, Creole mustard, cayenne pepper, pepper sauces.*

Chef John Folse and Company. www.jfolse.com. Telephone: (800) 256-2433. (225) 644-6000. 2517 S. Philippe Ave., Gonzales, LA 70737. *Filé powder, pepper sauces.*

Chef Paul Prudhomme. www.chefpaul.com. Telephone: (504) 731-3590. *Filé powder, Creole mustard, pepper sauces, dried peppers.*

Frugé's Cajun Crawfish. www.cajuncrawfish.com. Telephone: (888) 254-8626. Fax (337) 334-8477. P.O. Box 393 Branch, LA 70516. *Filé powder, Creole mustard.*

Hawaii Specialty Salt Co. www.hawaiisalt.com. Telephone: (808) 965-8076. Fax: (808) 965-0230. P.O. Box 5768, Hilo, HI, 96720. E-mail: info@hi-salt.com. *Alaea Brand sea salt.*

Louisiana Crawfish Co. www.lacrawfish.com. Telephone: (888) 522-7292. (318) 379-0539. 140 Russell Cemetery Rd., Natchitoches, LA 71457. E-mail: jd@lacrawfish.com. *Crawfish-boil seasoning.*

Louisiana Fish Fry Products. www.louisianafishfry.com. Telephone: (800) 356-2905. (225) 356-2905. 5267 Plank Road, Baton Rouge, LA 70805. *Filé powder, cayenne pepper, crab-boil seasoning, pepper sauces.*

New Orleans Over Night Inc. www.nuawlins.com. Telephone: (800) 682-9546. (504) 243-9500. 14854 Hayne Blvd., New Orleans, LA 70128. *Creole mustard.*

The New Orleans School of Cooking and Louisiana General Store. www.nosoc.com. Telephone: (800) 237-4841. (504) 525-2665. An extensive line of *Louisiana spices, condiments, seasonings and pepper sauces.*

Zatarain's. www.zatarains.com. Zatarain's Brand products: *Creole mustard, cayenne, crab-boil seasoning, filé powder, liquid boil seasoning.*

Index

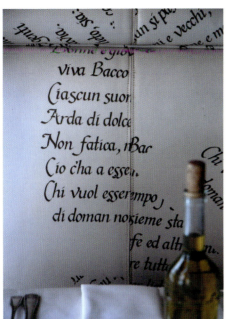